Adaptive Health Management Information Systems

Concepts, Cases, and Practical Applications

Third Edition

Edited by

Joseph Tan, PhD

Professor
Business Department
Wayne State University
School of Business Administration
Detroit, Michigan

with

Fay Cobb Payton, PhD

Associate Professor
Information Systems/Technology
North Carolina State University
College of Management
Raleigh, North Carolina

JONES AND BARTLETT PUBLISHERS

Sudbury, Massachusetts

BOSTON   TORONTO   LONDON   SINGAPORE

World Headquarters
Jones and Bartlett Publishers
40 Tall Pine Drive
Sudbury, MA 01776
978-443-5000
info@jbpub.com
www.jbpub.com

Jones and Bartlett Publishers
Canada
6339 Ormindale Way
Mississauga, Ontario L5V 1J2
Canada

Jones and Bartlett Publishers
International
Barb House, Barb Mews
London W6 7PA
United Kingdom

Jones and Bartlett's books and products are available through most bookstores and online booksellers. To contact Jones and Bartlett Publishers directly, call 800-832-0034, fax 978-443-8000, or visit our website www.jbpub.com.

Substantial discounts on bulk quantities of Jones and Bartlett's publications are available to corporations, professional associations, and other qualified organizations. For details and specific discount information, contact the special sales department at Jones and Bartlett via the above contact information or send an email to specialsales@jbpub.com.

This publication is designed to provide accurate and authoritative information in regard to the Subject Matter covered. It is sold with the understanding that the publisher is not engaged in rendering legal, accounting, or other professional service. If legal advice or other expert assistance is required, the service of a competent professional person should be sought.

Production Credits
Publisher: Michael Brown
Production Director: Amy Rose
Associate Editor: Katey Birtcher
Editorial Assistant: Catie Heverling
Senior Production Editor: Tracey Chapman
Senior Marketing Manager: Sophie Fleck
Manufacturing and Inventory Control Supervisor: Amy Bacus
Composition: Cape Cod Compositors, Inc.
Cover Design: Kristin E. Parker
Cover Image: © John Teate/ShutterStock, Inc.; © silvano audisio/ShutterStock, Inc.
Printing and Binding: Malloy, Inc.
Cover Printing: Malloy, Inc.

Library of Congress Cataloging-in-Publication Data
Tan, Joseph K. H.
  Adaptive health management information systems : concepts, cases, & practical applications / Joseph Tan with Fay Cobb Payton.—3rd ed.
    p. ; cm.
  Rev. ed. of: Health management information systems. 2nd ed. Gaithersburg, Md. : Aspen Publishers, 2001.
  Includes bibliographical references and index.
  ISBN-13: 978-0-7637-5691-8 (pbk.)
  ISBN-10: 0-7637-5691-1 (pbk.)
  1. Information storage and retrieval systems—Health services administration.   2. Management information systems.   I. Payton, Fay Cobb.   II. Tan, Joseph K. H. Health management information systems.   III. Title.
  [DNLM: 1. Management Information Systems.   2. Health Services Administration. W 26.5 T1608a 2009]
  RA971.6.T36   2009
  362.1068'4—dc22

                                                                                    2008054201

6048

Printed in the United States of America
13 12 11 10 09   10 9 8 7 6 5 4 3 2 1

New to This Edition

Adaptive Health Management Information Systems, Third Edition, is for instructors who want to keep pace with rapid changes in the field of healthcare management information systems (HMIS) and health informatics (HI). This new edition is not simply an update of the second edition—it is a completely reorganized, expanded, and rewritten text containing all new contributions, special sections, and streamlined discussions of more established as well as hot current topics. These are spiced with motivating scenarios; real-world examples; mini-cases; stimulating chapter questions; illustrative graphics, tables, and exhibits; and additional readings. Significant updates and complete revisions have been integrated throughout the text—so much so that readers familiar with the previous edition would not recognize this work as a derivative of the other.

Specific updates

- *Content.* Rich, comprehensive topics covered range from HMIS history; chief executive officer/chief information officer roles and responsibilities; health IT and Internet use; HMIS enterprise software; virtual communities and networks; patient-centric management systems; HMIS interoperability; HMIS strategic planning; HMIS developments; HMIS project management; HMIS standards, governance, and international perspectives; and HMIS innovation.
- *Scenarios.* Realistic and real-world scenarios set the stage for topic discussion and to motivate the student readers; a short reflection is also given at the end of each scenario.
- *Technology Briefs.* Concise briefs cover specific HMIS knowledge domains such as the Internet and associated technologies; hardware, software, and user interfaces; network technologies; database concepts; and data mining and data warehousing.
- *Research Brief.* Brief extends reading and provides supplementary research data.
- *Policy Brief.* Brief covers key policy issues relating to the Health Insurance Portability and Accountability Act (HIPAA), privacy, confidentiality, and security issues.
- *Mini-Cases.* Short cases illustrate concepts, and related mini-case questions promote class discussions among students.
- *Chapter Questions.* Long- and short-answered questions stimulate classroom discussions and promote learning of various topics and examples discussed in the text.

- *Editor's Notes.* Appended to chapters contributed by various authors, these notes bridge the chapter contents with the other chapters and parts of the text, thereby providing readers with an overview of the intended organization of the text.
- *Major Cases.* Part V provides a selection of major cases to enhance understanding of teaching materials and promote further interactions between students and instructors.

Dedication

To the memory of my parents, who brought me into this world;
to my students and colleagues, who have enjoyed my work and benefited
from my 20-year career of teaching and research in the fields of healthcare services
and administration, business information systems, and healthcare informatics;
and to my immediate family members, who have helped in every way
to mature my academic publishing and writing career.

—Joseph Tan

Acknowledgments

Above and beyond those to whom I am indebted while putting together the earlier editions of this text, I would like to thank those newly added academic and professional contributors, including those who were brought on board by co-editor, Dr. Fay Cobb Payton. Dr. Payton has personally shared in parts of the writing of this revised edition and Mr. Joshia Tan helped make this revised edition not only a completely different kind of text, but one much more appealing and valuable for instructors and students alike. Aside from contributing his very own case as a closure to the text and spearheading the writing of several briefs and chapters, Mr. Tan has contributed to the repackaging of the materials in this text in such a way as to help student readers better digest those more complex and highly technical parts of the previous editions by rearranging and rewriting key portions of previously published materials for lighter and easier reading.

There are two other individuals whom I must especially thank: Dr. Kai Zheng, a professor at the University of Michigan School of Public Health and School of Information, and Mr. Jonathan Dunford, a graduate student studying in the joint MBA–Masters in Health Services and Administration program at the University of Michigan. Dr. Zheng has kindly—and meticulously—reviewed some of the more critical chapters of this revised edition, especially Chapter 1, while Mr. Dunford has generously assisted in summarizing several of the motivating scenarios appearing at the beginning of the chapters. I am also indebted to numerous Wayne State University students, whose names would fill countless pages if I were to list them one by one; I will choose to keep this simple for fear of missing anyone important. To date, these students have contributed to many repeated discussions, year after year, about where they felt changes would have made previous editions of this text more valuable in classroom teaching and during online discussion sessions. A good number of these students have enjoyed and greatly benefited from my teaching and have also encouraged me to elaborate on new and emerging topics, most of which, unfortunately, I can only incorporate briefly and sparingly due to space limitation; otherwise, we would have ended up with a four-volume introductory text if all of the research gathered by myself, my assistants, and my students were to be incorporated, in one way or another, as different chapters, briefs, and cases. Indeed, I have also taken this opportunity, with the help of Mr. Joshia Tan, to substantially reduce the volume of words to convey the same key messages contained in the previous editions through the innovative use of *Technology*, *Research*, and *Policy Briefs*. In so doing, we have eliminated most of the dated materials.

I am grateful to all who have contributed, especially for their collaborative spirit and willingness for me to revise and edit freely their submitted pieces throughout the lengthy duration of this project. Their willingness for me to redirect their contributions to a common theme, to conform to a set format or a particular layout, to confine and revise the writing to a particular topic or area of research, to eliminate much of the overlapping information in earlier drafts, and to make substantive changes when necessary—without the need to consult with them over and over again—is highly admired because it has helped merge the different contributed pieces into a unified whole. More importantly, a special acknowledgment is due to the generosity of the publisher to extend the deadline for me to complete all of the revisions I wanted to see going into this latest edition at a time when I was swamped with the parallel production of several other major works. I would also like to take this opportunity to thank the three anonymous reviewers engaged by the publisher for going over the submitted drafts, pointing out any errors, and providing various suggestions to improve the appeal of the different chapter layouts and contents. Without the patience shown to me by key personnel at Jones & Bartlett Publishers, I know the end product of this revised edition would have been vastly limited. I am also indebted to Dean Homer Schmitz of St. Louis University, who kindly agreed to pen the Foreword for this latest edition swiftly on a very tight time constraint. His mentorship and advice for advancing my academic career has always been one that I truly admire and enjoy.

All in all, I greatly appreciate and thankfully acknowledge all of the assistance, encouragement, and understanding from each and every person who participated in any way, shape, or form, in the various stages and processes involved in the production of this work, from beginning to end. Once again, I am particularly grateful to my son, Joshia Tan, who took precious time out of his extremely busy summer 2008 work schedule to help me prepare this third edition for publication. And I must certainly acknowledge the unceasing support, encouragement, and understanding of my wife, Leonie Tan, throughout the duration of this project.

To all of these individuals and to my family members, friends, students, and relatives, I offer my many thanks for the support provided to me. Much of the value of this work is due to their contributions and assistance.

—Joseph Tan

Contents

About the Editors

Primary author and editor **Joseph Tan**, PhD, is a professor of business information systems/information technologies (IS/IT) and healthcare informatics. He is the editor-in-chief of *International Journal of Healthcare Information Systems & Informatics* (IJHISI). He has served as acting director for the master's of health administration program at the Faculty of Medicine, University of British Columbia; as chair of the Information Systems and Manufacturing Department of Wayne State University's School of Business Administration; as consultant to the Ontario Council of Graduate Studies; as well as a research fellow and advisor to various professional research institutes and nonprofit and for-profit organizations. His professional background spans a broad spectrum of disciplinary expertise and research interests, with a demonstrated ability to serve in both academia and industry. He is the lead investigator in re-defining the frontiers of interdisciplinary and translational business and health IT knowledge development and expansion, including active involvement in collaborative research and multi-disciplinary joint-grant submissions. He has achieved recognized scholarship in teaching and learning with students' nominations for teaching excellence awards, and he networks widely with key decision and policy makers as well as academic scholars and practitioners at local, provincial/state, national, and international levels, including private, public, and nongovernmental organizations and universities.

Dr. Tan has been asked to provide keynote speeches at doctoral seminars and conferences and has been invited to conduct research seminars and/or make appearances at numerous major universities around the world. His work is widely cited, and he has more than 100 academic publications, including a four-volume encyclopedia and numerous research monographs and teaching textbooks. He has taken leadership roles in team-based research, curriculum and program development and accreditation, peer-reviewed journal publications and book reviews, online education and programming, planning and organization of symposiums and conferences, development of book series, special issue journals, and federal grant proposals. His past 20-year academic experience includes full-time employment in academia, private and nonprofit sector organizations, as well as consulting and engaging in executive program development activities catering to executives and foreign delegation. His overall career focus is on reshaping the landscape of IS/IT applications and promotion in e-healthcare informatics through cross-disciplinary thinking/project partnering with diverse practitioners, clinicians, researchers, and a variety of user communities.

Co-editor **Fay Cobb Payton**, PhD, is an associate professor of IS/IT at North Carolina State University (NCSU), where she serves as the IS area coordinator. She is the vice chair of the AIS SIG-Health International group and is an active member of the Institute of Electrical and Electronics Engineers (IEEE) medical technology policy group. She is currently serving as a member of the NCSU Advisory Board for the Women in Science and Engineering Program. She has worked on consulting and/or research projects with Ernst & Young/CAP Gemini Health Care IT Practice, IBM, Blue Cross Blue Shield of Ohio and North Carolina, Duke Medical Center, the North Carolina Medical Society, Quintiles Transnational, and Time-Warner. Her research interests include healthcare informatics (AIDS/HIV among African American and sub-Saharan African populations; health disparities), data management (data analytics and quality), and social exclusion (including the digital divide/equity and STEM [Science, Technology, Engineering, and Mathematics] pathways). She has published in many peer-reviewed publications, including *Journal of the AIS*; *The Information Society*; *Journal of Organizational Computing and EC*; *IEEE Transactions*; *Communications of the ACM*; *Health Care Management Review*; *Computer Personnel, Information and Management*; *Decision Sciences Journal on Innovative Education*; *Computers and Society*; and *International Journal of Technology Management*.

Dr. Payton served on the editorial board of *ITProfessional*—an IEEE computer society journal—for four years and is the co-editor of the Health Care section for the National Science Foundation (NSF)-sponsored *African Journal of Information Systems*. She is also the co-editor of a *Journal of the AIS* special issue—"Healthcare: People and Processes." She is part of a research team that received an NSF ADVANCE grant. She has actively served in an advisory role for The PhD Project and the project's IS Doctoral Student Association.

Editorial assistant **Joshia Tan** is a sophomore (and on the Dean's List) at the Olin Business School, Washington University, in St. Louis, Missouri. Even at an early age, Mr. Tan displayed an affection for and interest in a vast range of pursuits, so it comes as no surprise that, years later, he is involved in an incredible variety of activities. He serves as a college council representative, writes and distributes for *Eleven Music Magazine*, and works at the WashU Law School. A National Merit Scholar and Washington University in St. Louis Book Award recipient, Mr. Tan has also received numerous other awards, including graduating cum laude, the AP Scholar with Distinction award, Cranbrook Prize Papers, Michigan Math Prize Competition Finalist, and Brook Film Festival's 3rd place award as lead actor and co-director of *The Broken Silence*. In addition, one of Mr. Tan's most recognized film productions, *Tao Te Cranbrook*, has been presented at a number of classes and seminars in the Business Department, School of Business Administration, Wayne State University, Michigan. He has also brought his activities to new levels by sharing them with others; for example, he volunteered for two years as a snowboarding counselor for Bloomfield Hills Ski & Snowboard club in Michigan. He also played violin with various schools' orchestras and served as assembly pianist for one his schools.

The literary world plays a large role in Mr. Tan's life, as he has co-authored "The Oliver Home Case" (with J. Tan/G. Demiris) and "CyberAngel: The Robin Hood Case" (with J. Tan), both appearing in J. Tan (Ed.) *E-Health Care Information Systems: An Introduction for Students & Professionals* (San Francisco: Jossey-Bass, 2005): 52–55 and 290–294, respectively. In 2008, Mr. Tan self-published *The Apprentice Bistro: A Feast for Amateur Writers*, an adaptation of his 2007 Davidson Fellows entry—for which he received an honorable mention. More recently, he has completed another major work, *Concord in Calamity: Taming the Awakening Armageddon*. Mr. Tan is also an avid traveler with numerous countries under his belt; he keeps a steadfast hold on his life dream of seeing the world—and changing it for the better. True to this vision, he has studied various languages, including English, French, and two different dialects of Chinese. Moreover, to better appreciate the Chinese language and culture, he spent an entire semester fulfilling the challenge of his dream by accepting an invitation to work as an intern in Shanghai, China. Furthermore, he incorporates this dream into his hobbies, such as drawing from international influences for his dabbles in the musical and culinary arts. Ultimately, it is this vision that continues to drive him; it is this dream that he works toward; and it is this dream that may, years later, very well become reality.

Contributors

Amal Al-Madouj
Clinical Research Assistant, Epidemiology Research Unit
Biostatistics, Epidemiology, and Scientific Computing
King Faisal Specialist Hospital and Research Centre
Riyadh, Kingdom of Saudi Arabia

Amal Al-Madouj is a clinical research assistant at the Biostatistics, Epidemiology, and Scientific Computing Department, King Faisal Specialist Hospital and Research Centre, Riyadh, Kingdom of Saudi Arabia (KSA). She graduated from the Health Sciences College and has been awarded an associate degree in the field of health record administration.

In 2001, she joined the Epidemiology Research Unit (ERU) at King Faisal Hospital and Research Centre, Riyadh, KSA. She has been involved in various projects as co-principal investigator and co-investigator.

Nuri Basoglu, PhD
Associate Professor
Department of Management Information Systems
Bogazici University
Istanbul, Turkey

Dr. Nuri Basoglu is an associate professor in the Department of Management Information Systems, Bogazici University, Istanbul, Turkey. His research interests are sociotechnical aspects of information systems, customer-focused product development, information technology adaptation and wireless service design, intelligent adaptive human computer interfaces, and information systems strategies. He has published articles in journals such as *Technology Forecasting and Social Change, Journal of High Technology Management and Technology in Society*, and *International Journal of Services Sciences*.

Dr. Basoglu received his BS in industrial engineering from Bogazici University in Turkey, and his MS and PhD in business administration from Istanbul University.

Bryan Bennett
President and Founder
Insight Data Group LLC
Riverwood, Illinois

Bryan Bennett is the founder and chief executive officer of Insight Data Group (IDG) and is an internationally renowned data-driven business strategy professional with more than 15 years of data and database marketing experience serving clients in the banking, credit card, investment, telecommunications, pharmaceutical, and insurance industries. His work has led to the identification of new customer insights and business opportunities, resulting in improved operations and efficiencies.

Mr. Bennett is also a proven thought leader with articles and whitepapers requested by and published in several national and international journals and magazines. In addition to a whitepaper published in the *Journal of Financial Transformation,* he is a frequent contributor to national publications and is the primary contributor to IDG's *Biz Insights* newsletter. He has been invited to speak at several conferences and has developed and delivered training sessions for several organizations. Mr. Bennett teaches the graduate-level course "Audience Insight" for West Virginia University's (online) Integrated Marketing Communications Program. He is a member of the Chief Marketing Officer Council, Reuters Insight Community of Experts, Gerson Lehrman Group Consulting Council, and the IT Senior Management Forum. Mr. Bennett has an MBA in marketing, finance, management policy, and management information systems from the Kellogg Graduate School of Management at Northwestern University and a BS in accounting from Butler University. He is also a certified public accountant.

Jon Blue, PhD
Assistant Professor
Department of Accounting and Management Information Systems
University of Delaware
Newark, Delaware

Dr. Jon Blue is an assistant professor in the Department of Accounting and Management Information Systems at the University of Delaware. He received a PhD in business with a concentration in information systems from Virginia Commonwealth University. His primary research interests are healthcare informatics, decision support systems, information technology adoption and implementation, and information systems project management. He is on the editorial board of the *International Journal of Healthcare Delivery Reform Initiatives.*

Prior to his academic career, Dr. Blue worked for more than 20 years in large companies—specifically IBM, Hewlett-Packard, and 3Com. In these companies, he worked in and managed domestic, as well as worldwide, organizations in various fields, including software and Internet development and testing, technical consulting, operations, sales, marketing, and engineering. His last corporate position was as the worldwide senior director of e-business professional services. In this position, he led a worldwide solutions management e-business professional services (consulting) organization and was responsible for the entire division's profit and loss.

Tugrul U. Daim, PhD
Associate Professor
Department of Engineering and Technology Management
Portland State University
Portland, Oregon

Dr. Tugrul U. Daim is an associate professor of engineering and technology management at Portland State University. He is published in many journals, including *Technology in Society, Technology Forecasting and Social Change, International Journal of Innovation and Technology Management, Technology Analysis and Strategic Management, International Journal of Healthcare Information Systems & Informatics*, and *Technovation*.

Dr. Daim received his BS in mechanical engineering from Bogazici University in Turkey, MS in mechanical engineering from Lehigh University in Pennsylvania, another MS in engineering management from Portland State University, and a PhD in systems science–engineering management from Portland State University.

Jayfus T. Doswell, PhD
Founder, President, and CEO
Juxtopia, LLC
Distinguished Professor of Biotechnology
School of Math, Science, and Technology
Elizabeth City State University
Elizabeth City, North Carolina

Dr. Jayfus T. Doswell is the founder, president, and chief executive officer of Juxtopia LLC, a biomedical and information technology company with a mission to improve human performance. Dr. Doswell is also the chairperson of The Juxtopia Group Inc., a nonprofit 501c3 organization with a mission to improve human learning performance with science and technology research that adapts to individual learning needs. Additionally, Dr. Doswell is a distinguished professor of biotechnology at Elizabeth City State University (ECSU), located in North Carolina, where he is responsible for instructing the next generation of leaders fund-raising, entrepreneurship, and outreach. Dr. Doswell sits on several not-for-profit boards and is an active member of the American Public Health Association (APHA) Health Informatics and Information Technology (HIIT) special interest group, American Telemedicine Association (ATA), Association of Computing Machinery (ACM), Institute of Electrical and Electronics Engineering (IEEE), and the National Society of Black Engineers (NSBE). Prior to starting Juxtopia in 2001, Dr. Doswell led several commercial software engineering teams, ranging from Lockheed Martin and SAIC to BearingPoint.

Dr. Doswell and Juxtopia currently lead research and product development combining artificial intelligence, telemedicine/tele-health, bioinformatics, computational biology, and biosensors.

Kelley M. Duncanson, PhD

Assistant Professor of Management and Accounting
School of Business
College of The Bahamas
Nassau, Bahamas

Dr. Kelley M. Duncanson is an assistant professor of management and accounting in the School of Business at the College of The Bahamas. Her primary research interests include decision support systems, simulated learning, student budgeting and personal finance, organizational citizenship behavior, and student learning techniques. She consults with businesses regarding management and accounting systems issues. She has published in the *Business Research Yearbook* and *Global Business Perspectives* and has presented papers at the International Academy of Business and Economics and INFORMS conferences. She received her PhD in management from Jackson State University, Jackson, Mississippi.

Naser Elkum, PhD

Professor and Research Methodologist
Biostatistics
King Faisal Specialist Hospital and Research Centre
Riyadh, Kingdom of Saudi Arabia

Dr. Naser Elkum is a professor and research methodologist of biostatistics at King Faisal Specialist Hospital and Research Centre. In 1997, he earned his PhD in statistics from Queen's University, Canada. Subsequently, he worked as a manager of the biostatistics and data management department at Pharma Medica Research Inc. (PMRI), Mississauga, Canada. Currently, he is scientist and head of biostatistics unit at King Faisal Specialist Hospital and Research Centre, Riyadh, KSA.

Dr. Elkum has more than 15 years of health science work experience in internationally recognized institutions, including National Cancer Institute of Canada Clinical Trials Group, Queen's University, Canada; Health Canada; Laboratory Center of Disease Control, Ottawa, Canada; Pharma Medica Research Inc., Mississauga, Canada; and King Faisal Specialist Hospital and Research Centre, Riyadh, KSA. He provides statistical leadership in studies in various areas of population health research, clinical research, and health services and outcomes research.

SherRhonda Gibbs, PhD candidate

Department of Management and Marketing
Jackson State University
Jackson, Mississippi

SherRhonda Gibbs is a PhD candidate in management at Jackson State University; her program status is ABD (all but dissertation). She received her BS degree in computer science from Grambling State University in Louisiana. She also holds a Master's of Business Administration degree from Winona State University in Minnesota. Her research concentration is in technology entrepreneurship, entrepreneurial opportunity recognition, careers, information technology, and small business. Ms. Gibbs has made numerous academic presentations on diverse topics both nationally and internationally. She has published in, among others, the *International Journal of Globalization and Small Business* and *E-Business Review*. As a Cal State–San Bernardino ITTN fellowship recipient, she has been certified in technology entrepreneurship, transfer, and commercialization. Last year, she received the AOM Careers Division, Best Doctoral Student Paper Award. Ms. Gibbs has also received entrepreneurial leadership awards and service recognition for her work with entrepreneurship students at Jackson State.

William Greer, PhD
Senior Clinical Planner
Health Statistics
Sidra Medical and Research Center
Weill Cornell Medical College
Doha, Qatar

Dr. William Greer is currently a senior clinical planner in health statistics at Sidra Medical and Research Center in Qatar. Originally a physicist, he obtained his PhD in bioengineering in 1978 from Strathclyde University in Scotland, where he developed an integrated mathematical model of the neural and chemical control of breathing in humans. His postdoctoral research was divided between an epidemiological study of musculoskeletal injuries in Mt. Isa Mines, Australia, and the application of control systems techniques to the analysis of totally closed breathing circuits at Manchester University, England. In 1980, he joined the National Institute for Medical Research in London, where he initially commissioned its new mainframe computer system prior to spending several years collaborating with biologists in computational and mathematical aspects of developmental biology and neurobiology, including the development of the first computerized mapping system for biological electron microscopy. While at the National Institute, he also developed one of the first bioinformatics software packages (MGS), which was later adopted by a number of U.K. research institutions and universities. In 1986, he moved to the King Faisal Specialist Hospital and Research Centre in Riyadh, Kingdom of Saudi Arabia, where he carried out biocomputing, epidemiological, biostatistical, and bioinformatics research for the next 10 years.

In 1995, Dr. Greer relocated to Edinburgh as an independent research consultant in biostatistics and pharmacogenomics. During this period, he became responsible for the data management and analysis of one of the largest collections of normative bone mineral density measurements in women, at the Bone Densitometry Unit in the Nuffield Hospital, Oxford. In 1998, he returned to King Faisal Specialist Hospital and Research Centre to develop a new Scientific Computing Research Unit, focusing on clinical image analysis, biological simulation, geographical information systems (GIS), and bioinformatics. In 2005, he assumed a faculty position in public health at the Weill Cornell Medical School in Qatar, where—in addition to developing research on diabetes in Qatar—he was responsible for teaching biostatistics, epidemiology, and evidence-based medicine. His current research interests include diagnostic aspects of postmenopausal osteoporosis, epidemiological applications of GIS, biological and physiological modeling, and the computational analysis of promoter regions of DNA.

Henry J. Groot, MS
Director
Information Resources
Holy Cross Health System Corporation
South Bend, Indiana

Henry J. Groot is the director of information resources at the corporate offices of Holy Cross Health System Corporation. His accomplishments include positioning the decision support function to support the decision makers in multiple business units and clinical settings and to support their information needs by increasing use, understanding, and application of information for analysis and reporting. The deployment of decision support has spanned across disciplines such as finance, corporate development, utilization and quality assurance, and operations. Mr. Groot received his MS in management information systems from Purdue University, West Lafayette, Indiana. His work has been published in *Healthcare Informatics* and *Topics in Healthcare Information Management*.

Sandhya Keeroo
C-DAC School of Advanced Computing
University of Mauritius
Quatre Bornes, Mauritius

Sandhya Keeroo is an information technology (IT) graduate and is presently working on an MBA at the University of Mauritius. Her research on healthcare IT, a multidisciplinary field of paramount necessity, presents unrivaled challenges to enhance ostensibly unyielding problems across the medical field. She is honored to bring forward a handy and an informative resource that would catalyze further research as well as contribute to the win–win paradigm shift pertinent to wellness and treating illness. She is thrilled to claim that this chapter will help identify elusive broken links that still exist and eradicate problems of heterogeneity in clinical knowledge.

William Klepack, MD
Primary Care Physician
Dryden Family Medicine
Medical Director
Tompkins County Health Department
Dryden, New York

Dr. William Klepack is board certified in family practice and received his MD from Johns Hopkins University Medical School in Baltimore, Maryland, after obtaining his undergraduate degree in physics and science from the Massachusetts Institute of Technology. His three years of family practice residency training were at the University of Rochester, Family Medicine Program. Following residency he practiced in Nome, Alaska, with the U.S. Public Health Service for two years. Returning to the "lower 48" he joined a group practice in Bath, New York, where he stayed for eight years before moving to Tompkins County, New York, in July 1989.

Dr. Klepack is medical director of the Tompkins County Health Department. His particular interests include patient education, public health, preventive care, electronic health records, disease management, and orthopedic medicine.

Rajiv Kohli, PhD
Associate Professor
Management Information Systems
College of William & Mary
Williamsburg, Virginia

Dr. Rajiv Kohli is an associate professor of management information systems (MIS) at the College of William & Mary. He received his PhD from the University of Maryland, Baltimore County. Dr. Kohli serves as an associate editor for *MIS Quarterly* and is a member of editorial boards of several international journals.

For more than 15 years, Dr. Kohli has worked or consulted with IBM Global Services, SAS Corporation, United Parcel Service, AM General, MCI Telecommunications, Westinghouse Electronics, Wipro Corporation, and Godrej Industries (India), in addition to several healthcare organizations. Prior to joining full-time academia in 2001, he was a project leader in decision support services at Trinity Health. Dr. Kohli has held positions at the City University of Hong Kong, China; University of Canterbury, New Zealand; Sloan School of Management, Massachusetts Institute of Technology, Cambridge, Massachusetts; and the University of Cambridge, United Kingdom.

Academic studies have ranked Dr. Kohli among the top 20 MIS researchers worldwide. Dr. Kohli's research is published in *MIS Quarterly, Management Science, Information Systems Research, Journal of Management Information Systems,* and *Communications of the ACM,* among other journals. He is a co-author of *IT Payoff: Measuring Business Value of Information Technology Investment,* published by Financial Times Prentice-Hall. Dr. Kohli has been a recipient of several grants in information systems research.

Victor W. A. Mbarika, PhD
Director
ICITD
Editor-in-Chief
The African Journal of Information Systems (AJIS)
Southern University and A&M College
Baton Rouge, Louisiana

Dr. Victor W. A. Mbarika has been in the forefront of academic research into information communications and technologies (ICT) implementation in Africa. Dr. Mbarika is serving at Southern University and A&M College at Baton Rouge, Louisiana, and has received several National Science Foundation and state grants.

Professor Mbarika has more than 90 published works, including three books; five book chapters; 31 peer-reviewed journal papers in premier outlets such as *IEEE Transactions, CACM, JAIS, ISJ, The Information Society,* and *Journal of the American Society for Information Sciences;* and more than 45 papers at premier conferences such as IFIP, ICIS, DSI, AMCIS, and HICSS. He has chaired several mini-tracks/workshops at DSI and AMCIS, where he introduced the first mini-track on ICT in developing countries. His publication outlets clearly reflect the impact he is having on the information systems, computer science, information science, and engineering communities.

Philip F. Musa, BSEE, MSEE, MBA, PhD, PE
Associate Professor
Department of Management and Information Systems
The University of Alabama at Birmingham
Birmingham, Alabama

Dr. Philip F. Musa is an associate professor of management and information systems in the School of Business at the University of Alabama at Birmingham. He teaches various courses such as project management, supply chain management, quality management, strategic information systems, electrical engineering, and operations management. He holds a BSEE, an MSEE, an MBA, and a PhD, all from Texas Tech University. He has published research in various prestigious journals, including *Communications of the ACM, Information Systems Journal, Communications of AIS, European Journal of Information Systems, Journal of Global Information Technology Management, Journal of Global Information Management*, and *Journal of Information Systems Education.*

Dr. Musa has served on special assignments related to PhD programs to other universities around the world. In addition to serving on the editorial boards of several academic and practitioner journals, Dr. Musa has presented at and published in dozens of proceedings of national and international information systems conferences such as America's Conference on Information Systems, the International Federation for Information Processing, Information Resource Management Association, Global Information Technology Management, and Decision Sciences Institute, among others. He has also served as chair or on program committees of many of the professional conferences and dissertation committees. Dr. Musa is an academic professional member of APICS, senior member of the Institute of Electrical and Electronics Engineers (IEEE), member of the Association of Information Systems (AIS), and a lifetime member of Phi Kappa Phi. He is a licensed professional engineer (PE) with backgrounds in electrical engineering and the semiconductor industry. He is also a certified supply chain professional (CSCP).

Liam O'Neill, MS, PhD
Associate Professor
Department of Health Management and Policy
School of Public Health
University of North Texas, Fort Worth
Fort Worth, Texas

Dr. Liam O'Neill is an associate professor in the School of Public Health at the University of North Texas Health Science Center in Fort Worth, Texas. He earned an MS in operations research from the University of North Carolina and a PhD in operations management from Pennsylvania State University. Prior to his present position, he was on the faculty at Cornell University and the University of Iowa.

Dr. O'Neill's primary research interests are in healthcare operations and information systems, including hospital efficiency analysis, hospital marketing, technology diffusion, and managerial benchmarking using data envelopment analysis. He has published more than 20 articles and book chapters in scholarly journals, such as *Health Care Management Science*, *Management Science*, *Medical Care Research and Review*, *Neurology*, *Anesthesia and Analgesia*, *Naval Research Logistics*, and *Socio-Economic Planning Sciences*. In addition, his research has received awards from the Production and Management Society and the Western Decision Sciences Institute. He is on the editorial board of *Health Care Management Science* and *International Journal of Healthcare Information Systems and Informatics* and is past-president of the Health Care Applications Section of Institute for Operations Research and Management Science (INFORMS).

Anantachai Panjamapirom, MS, MBA, PhD Candidate
School of Health Professions
University of Alabama at Birmingham
Birmingham, Alabama

Anantachai Panjamapirom is from Bangkok, Thailand. He is currently a doctoral student in administration health services in the School of Health Professions at the University of Alabama at Birmingham (UAB). He earned an MS in information and communication sciences from Ball State University, Muncie, Indiana, and an MBA from UAB. He holds a B.Eng. in civil engineering from Mahidol University, Bangkok, Thailand. While he worked as a web designer in the Division of Continuing Medical Education (CME), School of Medicine at UAB for three years, he was involved in conceptualizing, designing, producing, and maintaining more than 20 educational Web sites for different grant-funded research studies. The majority of these studies employ Web-based interventions as a strategic tool to conduct research on the decision-making patterns and behavioral predictors of healthcare providers.

Mr. Panjamapirom has collaborated with multiple research organizations such as the Alabama Quality Assurance Foundation (AQAF), the UAB Center for Education and Research on Therapeutics of Musculoskeletal Disorders (CERTs), the UAB Center for Outcomes and Effectiveness Research and Education (COERE), and the UAB Center for Emergency Care and Disaster Preparedness. He is a member of various professional organizations such as American Medical Informatics Association (AMIA), Academy of Management (AOM), American Public Health Association (APHA), and Association of University Programs in Health Administration (AUPHA). He has presented at the annual conferences of AOM, APHA, and Academy Health. He is also a member of Beta Gamma Sigma.

Nupur Prakash, PhD
Professor and Dean
School of Information Technology
Guru Gobind Singh Indraprastha University
Delhi, India

Dr. Nupur Prakash is a professor and the dean at the School of Information Technology, Guru Gobind Singh Indraprastha University (GGSIPU), Delhi, India. She holds a PhD in engineering and technology and has worked as a scientist at the Central Scientific Instruments Organisation (CSIO), Chandigarh, India, on microprocessor-based cross-correlation flow meters. She has also worked at Punjab Engineering College, Chandigarh, India, and was the head of the computer science and engineering department.

Dean Prakash has been the principal of Indira Gandhi Institute of Technology at GGSIPU, Delhi. Her research interests include wireless communications, mobile computing, network security, and cryptography. She has authored and/or presented 40 research papers in various national and international journals and conferences.

Homer Schmitz, PhD
Professor and Interim Dean
School of Public Health
St. Louis University
St. Louis, Missouri

For more than 40 years Dr. Schmitz has accumulated extensive executive experience in managing the operations, information systems, planning, and finances of various sectors of the healthcare market, including a 450-member multi-specialty physician practice, a managed care organization with more than 250,000 enrollees, an EMS organization with more than 100 vehicles, and a 500-bed acute care teaching hospital. He is a nationally recognized author and lecturer in healthcare management. During his career, he has authored or co-authored five books and more than 80 articles in peer-reviewed technical and professional journals.

Dean Schmitz has lectured at more than 90 national and international meetings and seminars. Numerous national and international healthcare consulting assignments have been carried out, including domestic engagements with the Center for Health Services Research of the University of Southern California, the Lutheran Hospital Society of Southern California, and Arthur D. Little. International engagements have been completed in Syria, the United Arab Emirates, Qatar, and South Africa. Professional memberships held included those in the American Hospital Association, the Healthcare Financial Management Association, and the Medical Group Management Association. In addition, he is a life member of the Healthcare Information Management Systems Society (where he has held national committee appointments) and holds Fellow status. Dr. Schmitz is also on the editorial boards of two healthcare journals. His research interests include information systems, ambulatory services management, and health services financing.

Sanjay Prakash Sood, MTech
C-DAC School of Advanced Computing
University of Mauritius
Quatre Bornes, Mauritius

Sanjay Prakash Sood, MTech, specializes in healthcare technologies. He has pioneered telemedicine projects in India, Benin, and Mauritius. He has been a telemedicine consultant to the World Health Organization and a consultant on healthcare technologies for a World Bank Project in Punjab, India. He is also associated with the United Nations (UN Office for Outer Space Affairs, Vienna) for telemedicine. He has been the principal resource person (medical informatics) for a premier Indian government organization (C-DAC: Centre for Development of Advanced Computing) and was the co-investigator/project manager for the National Telemedicine Project (Development of Telemedicine Technology) in India. He has authored more than 50 publications, including five chapters on cutting-edge applications of information technology in health care. Mr. Sood has been a member of the executive council of the International Society for Telemedicine and eHealth. He is a recipient of international scholarships and travel grants. He is the director and founder of C-DAC Operations in Mauritius and is currently researching (PhD) diffusion and adoption of e-health technologies in hospitals. He may be contacted via www.spsood.com.

Jing Kai Zhang, PhD

Dr. J. K. Zhang was awarded his PhD degree by the University of Surrey, and his research funding came from the School of Biomedical Engineering, University of Surrey, and from the Henry Lester Trust, United Kingdom. His research interest is in data mining, distributed system architecture, healthcare management information systems, and system interoperability. He has published in several journals, including *Journal of Computer Science* and *Science Publications*, and he has presented at The International MultiConference of Engineers and Computer Scientists; the International Conference on IEEE Biomedical and Pharmaceutical Engineering, Singapore; and in the International Conference on IEEE E-he@lth in Common Europe, Krakow, Poland.

Kai Zheng, PhD
Assistant Professor
Health Management and Policy
School of Public Health
Assistant Professor, Information
School of Information
University of Michigan
Ann Arbor, Michigan

Dr. Kai Zheng is an assistant professor of health management and policy in the School of Public Health and an assistant professor of information in the School of Information at the University of Michigan. He is also affiliated with the Medical School Center for Computational

Medicine and Biology and the Michigan Institute for Clinical and Health Research. Dr. Zheng's research and teaching are in the area of information systems, particularly focusing on health informatics, which studies the use of information, communication, and decision technologies in healthcare delivery and management. He holds a PhD in information systems and health informatics from Carnegie Mellon University, where his dissertation, entitled "Design, Implementation, User Acceptance, and Evaluation of a Clinical Decision Support System for Evidence-Based Medicine Practice," received the 2007 William W. Cooper Doctoral Dissertation Award in Management or Management Sciences.

Foreword

When I joined the health information world many years ago disc drives storing 5 to 10 megabytes of information and costing upward of $200,000 were the standard; central processing units with memories of 512K to 1024K and costing many thousands of dollars were the rule; elaborate climate-controlled environments costing tens of thousands of dollars were mandatory; elaborately trained operators were required to be present at all times that the technology was being used; and an online, real-time order entry system was rare and very expensive. At that time there were less than a dozen such systems in the United States that were actually working as true real-time order entry and data collection systems. Their computing power was probably less than what we carry around on our belts today. We talked about how healthcare organizations had more data than they knew what to do with but that very few had more information than they could use.

The distinction between data and information is subtle but important. The technology has changed enormously with regard to price and performance but the problem has not changed. We still wrestle with the question of how we can better provide the information that a decision-maker needs in a timely, accurate, and cost-effective manner. In addition to the enormous changes in technology, the explosive increase in information availability seriously complicates the problems of information management. In today's world of the Internet and Web services, there is the additional problem of discriminating between reliable and accurate information and unreliable information while at the same time protecting the privacy and confidentiality of healthcare consumers who are seeking help in understanding their specific situation.

Against this backdrop of complicating factors and profound change Joseph Tan with Fay Cobb Payton and colleagues deliver a richly informative and well-organized text that addresses many of the issues facing health information users seeking answers in this more complex and rapidly changing world. They examine the dynamics of merging healthcare organizations with health information systems. They scrutinize the tools and methodologies that are available to the information seeker from traditional sources to the Internet and related technologies. They investigate new social groupings for health information dissemination such as community net-working and building virtual communities. All of this is accomplished while also providing an excellent coverage and insight into current management and technology issues related to build-ing effective information systems in healthcare organizations. The task of building and manag-ing these enormously complex systems in an environment that is changing so rapidly is daunting. Joseph Tan with Fay Cobb Payton and colleagues have done an excellent job of de-scribing not only the technology and information needs of this dynamic time but also have done an extraordinary job of investigating those influential forces or critical success factors that have an impact on current and future-oriented health information management systems and their use to support a growing network of multi-provider healthcare delivery services in an age of globalization, continuing knowledge explosion, and technological innovation diffusion.

I would be remiss if I did not acknowledge the many insightful contributions that Joseph Tan has made to the field of health information systems over the years. These contributions have been pragmatic as well as scholarly and have impacted enormously the way health infor-mation systems are viewed and used. This book will only add to that legacy.

—Homer H. Schmitz, PhD
Interim Dean and Professor
School of Public Health
Saint Louis University
Saint Louis, Missouri

Preface

Adaptive Health Management Information Systems, Third Edition, is a gift especially designed for the professional readers and instructors who want their students to keep pace with rapid changes in the evolving field and knowledge domains of healthcare management information systems (HMIS) and health informatics (HI). This new edition is not simply an update of the second edition—it is, in fact, a completely reorganized, expanded, and thoroughly revised manuscript containing new and logically ordered contributions partitioned into five major themes connecting the 14-chapter series. It is supplemented with *Research, Technology*, and *Policy Briefs*, plus five major cases. Simply stated, significant updates and complete revisions to every part of the previous edition have been meticulously generated throughout the text—so much so that readers who may be familiar with the previous edition would not have recognized this work as a derivative of the other. It is analogous to producing a new hybrid vehicle but doing away with most of the parts empowering the old model design that is purely gasoline-based.

As we moved across and beyond the 21st century, the active cross-pollination of ideas and fresh knowledge from multiple disciplines—including advances in information science and pervasive technology, management theories and information systems practices, the marriage of the health sciences with ubiquitous computing technologies, and the ever-increasing volumes of healthcare informatics and telematics publications—are beginning to influence the growth and knowledge explosion of the HMIS field. To this end, this newly minted HMIS text contains streamlined discussions of more established, state-of-the-art as well as hot emerging topics ordered under each of the five major themes discussed later, spiced with motivating scenarios; real-world examples; mini-cases; stimulating chapter questions; illustrative graphics, tables, and exhibits; and notes and supplementary and additional readings.

One advantage, as evidenced both on the book cover and throughout the different parts of the book, is the wide spectrum of topics covered in a variety of forms by the different contributing authors as shown in the Table of Contents. In this new edition, the five-part clusters used in previous editions have been completely reconstituted along the following themes:

Part I, which encompasses Chapters 1 through 3, lays the foundation for HMIS conceptualization. Part II, covering Chapters 4 through 7, concentrates on HMIS technology and applications, whereas Part III, including Chapters 8 through 11, shifts focus to HMIS planning and management. Part IV, comprising Chapters 12 through 14, addresses HMIS standards, governance, policy, globalization, and future. Finally, five major cases highlighting HMIS practices and implementation lessons are presented in Part V. Each of these major themes progressively flows into one another to unveil different aspects of the hidden HMIS gem.

More particularly, Part I offers the readers an overview of HMIS foundational concepts and attempts to showcase the significance of having an education in the discipline. Chapter 1 starts off with the historical development of the HMIS field, traces a roadmap to guide readers in navigating through the different parts and chapters of the text, details the basic HMIS components and functions, and reflects upon HMIS cultures. Chapter 2 focuses on key roles and responsibilities of senior executives in healthcare services organizations vis-à-vis taking the HMIS leadership through a process comprising vision, strategy, and intelligent execution. To succeed, these executives must show characteristics of being trustworthy, inspirational, and ready to motivate others, as well as learning to be effective communicators. An accompanying *Research Brief* offers insight into how HMIS devices as simple as a PDA can be used to cut down on wait time in an emergency department. Chapter 3 redirects the attention of the readers to online health information seeking behaviors among Internet versus non-Internet users and touches on access and digital equity considerations. An interesting question raised here is: can the Internet and associated technologies be used to provide emotional support and empowerment to online health information seekers? *Technology Brief I*, which presents a refresher course on the fundamentals of Internet and associated technologies for healthcare services organizations, complements the chapter reading. Altogether, the significance of HMIS influence can be seen throughout history (Chapter 1); on individuals, groups, and organizations (Chapter 2); as well as on society at large (Chapter 3). The key message conveyed in Part I is that of the increasing significance of HMIS proliferating through every aspect of both our personal and organizational life and addresses, in large part, the "whys" of educating health informatics, management, and professional students in the HMIS discipline.

Part II challenges the readers to examine the HMIS technology and applications theme. Isolated legacy systems such as hospital information systems; financial, budgeting, and payroll systems; nurse scheduling systems; admission-discharge-transfer systems; purchasing and inventory control systems; facility planning systems; and basic clinical workflow systems used for decades in healthcare facilities will soon give way to emerging enterprisewide systems—namely, supply chain management (SCM), customer relationship management (CRM), and enterprise resource planning (ERP). Chapter 4, therefore, begins a discussion on these three systems, SCM, CRM, and ERP—enterprisewide systems believed to be emerging as the next-generation HMIS administrative applications that will significantly affect the future quality of healthcare services delivery. *Technology Brief II* features hardware, software, and computer-user interface design and supplements the chapter reading. Chapter 5 continues this same line of thought by highlighting network-based HMIS technology and applications, specifically, community health information networks (CHIN) and regional health information organizations (RHIO). *Technology Brief III* summarizes health organization merger arrangements vis-à-vis the telecommunications and network infrastructures that are appropriate for these arrangements and is offered as supplementary reading. The central message here is the wide-ranging applications of HMIS technologies for bringing community organizations together as partners for healthcare services delivery.

Representing a natural expansion of concepts discussed in HMIS administrative applications and technologies (Chapter 4) as well as CHIN and RHIO (Chapter 5) is the concept of patient-centric management systems and integrated HMIS systems discussed in Chapters 6 and 7, respectively. Among the most popular HMIS applications and technologies employed in today's healthcare services organizations are electronic health records (EHR), computerized physician order entry (CPOE), and clinical decision support systems (CDSS), which are the subjects of Chapter 6. As noted in the chapter title, these applications represent a movement toward patient-centric management systems because the technology is ultimately designed to elevate patient care by providing the caregivers with relevant, current, accurate, reliable, available, and accessible health information. Therefore, the significance of these systems for benchmarking both administrative and clinical performance across healthcare services organizations cannot be overly emphasized. *Technology Brief IV*, focusing on database, data-mining, and data-warehousing concepts for healthcare services organizations, has been appended to this chapter to augment the readers' understanding not only of the internal structure, content, and functionalities of these systems, but also to provide insights into the enabling and empowering nature of these systems for the end-users. Finally, the benefits and challenges of these patient-centric management systems are also discussed in the context of electronic health records, which is the HMIS cornerstone of both the U.S. and Canadian healthcare services delivery systems.

Finally, Chapter 7, which focuses on the topic of HMIS integration, concludes the Part II discussion of HMIS technology and applications. Apparently, maintaining legacy systems in healthcare services organizations can be both costly and increasingly cumbersome due to the lack of interoperability among disparate applications. Indeed, these isolated systems will eventually result in unsatisfactory delays to patient care and will continue to take a toll on both clinicians' and employees' time and productivity. The application of Web services as a way to transform healthcare organizational HMIS into seamless integrated systems is certainly a major step that promises to benefit the healthcare services organizations in the longer term, not just temporarily. Therefore, the technology discussed in Chapter 7 is extremely innovative. Not only would this technology help ready readers to move away from islands of legacy systems in light of the rapid advances in HMIS technology and applications, but the message conveyed could also help the readers adopt new HMIS thinking as well as assist them to take the next steps toward achieving a higher and wider HMIS perspective. Altogether, the knowledge acquired in Part II offers the readers a wide-ranging survey of the "whats" of HMIS technology and applications.

This brings us to Part III, which focuses on HMIS planning and management. Chapter 8 concentrates on HMIS strategic planning and information requirements because these are two of the early, but critical, steps in the administration of HMIS planning and management for healthcare services organizations. This chapter therefore lays the groundwork for the "hows" of realizing HMIS initiatives in practice (Part III), not just the "whys" (Part I) and "whats" (Part II). Beyond instructing students, practitioners, and administrators on how to align HMIS goals and objectives with corporate goals and objectives and how to go about deciding on the best alternative means of developing the system that would fit well with organizational information requirements and culture (Chapter 8), the next steps will have to include a thorough familiarity with HMIS analysis and development methodologies (Chapter 9); followed by practical advice on HMIS design, implementation, and evaluation through a focus on data stewardship (Chapter 10); and the proper managing of pre-implementation preparation, implementation processes, and post-implementation upkeep, as well as ongoing IT service management (Chapter 11). Part III, therefore, bridges HMIS technology and applications (Part II) on the one hand and HMIS standards, governance, policy, and international perspectives (Part IV) on the other. This then takes us to Part IV.

Part IV acquaints the readers with HMIS standards, governance, policy, globalization, and future. It begins with Chapter 12, featuring a comprehensive review of HMIS standards—a topic of increasing significance for HMIS students, practitioners, and researchers. Major standards relating to data coding (vocabulary), data schema (structure and content), data exchange (messaging), and Web standards are formulated by groups of enthusiastic standards developers through standards development organizations to evolve a common language for sharing health information electronically among care providers. This chapter also links the readers back to the earlier parts of the text regarding HMIS foundational conceptualization and the use of data for managerial decision making and online health data searches (Part I). Again, the concepts of standards link the readers back also to the significance of sharing information among community health networks and the challenge of overcoming interoperability among disparate systems by integrating HMIS technology and applications via Web services (Part II). A *Policy Brief* on the Health Insurance Portability and Accountability Act (HIPAA), privacy, and security issues complements the reading for Chapter 12.

Beyond HMIS standards, Chapter 13 attempts to widen the readers' perspectives on HMIS by moving into the topic of HMIS globalization and e-health. Apparently, the application of e-health conceptualization demonstrates to whom the concepts of information and communication technologies (ICT) in health care, as well as HMIS in healthcare services organizations, relate to most in everyday life: humankind. Accordingly, HMIS used in the context of Chapters 1 through 12 of this text are now expanded to an e-health perspective used specifically in the globalization context of Chapter 13. In this sense, both e-health and HMIS may be conceived as umbrella terms encompassing all ICT and related e-technologies applied in a global healthcare services context. Hence, there is a true parallelism in terms of the need for ICT governance, policies, and sharing of ICT innovations among developed, developing, and underdeveloped countries for both HMIS and e-health. In light of this, the term *HMIS* has been inserted throughout Part IV, where appropriate, to sound the underlying message of the similar challenges facing designers and administrators of healthcare systems—whether it is to be deployed as an isolated system for healthcare providers (health informatics), an integrated system for healthcare services organizations (HMIS), or an Internet-based system for entire populations (e-health).

Up to this point, the readers should not be surprised by the inclusion of a chapter on innovation diffusion, Chapter 14, constitutes the final chapter of this *adaptive* HMIS text and brings closure to Part IV—or to the entire text. It does this by highlighting the barriers to HMIS implementation and innovation diffusion and by providing key theoretical concepts for HMIS innovation management. Evidently, the benefits of HMIS should extend beyond just individuals, even beyond healthcare provider groups and healthcare services organizations. HMIS must be *adaptive* to change, to innovations, and to everyone's business. Before HMIS can diffuse so as to raise the quality of healthcare services, not only in the United States and Canada, but also all over the world, HMIS developers must learn to *integrate*, *adapt*, and *innovate* the technology. As with the management of any innovation, HMIS innovation diffusion management is definitely not going to be an easy, static process. Instead, it is a very *dynamic* and *adaptive* one, depending on how the healthcare services delivery system changes vis-à-vis the organizational changes affected by movements in the larger political, technological, social, and cultural environments in which any HMIS innovation is to be deployed. Put together, Part IV has to do with addressing the "whos" of HMIS effects.

Finally, the five major case studies in Part V cluster largely around the notion of HMIS implementations in diverse organizational environments, whether these be in the past (Cases 1 and 4), the present (Cases 2 and 3), or in the future (Case 5). These cases combine the elements of the HMIS conceptualization (Part I); the HMIS technology and applications (Part II); the HMIS planning and management (Part III); and the HMIS standards, governance, policy, and future (Part IV).

—Joseph Tan with Fay Cobb Payton

Foundation Concepts of Health Management Information Systems

Health Management Information Systems: A Managerial Perspective

Joseph Tan

CHAPTER OUTLINE

Scenario: *Key Trends Contributing to the Merging of Enterprise and Health Information Exchange Models*

Scenario: Key Trends Contributing to the Merging of Enterprise and Health Information Exchange Models[1]

Informatics Corporation of America (ICA), with its website (www.icainformatics.com) offering insightful materials for the interested readers, is a health information technology (HIT) organization whose mission is to provide clinicians and healthcare providers with more or less seamless access to information extracted from various uncoordinated systems for patient diagnosis and evaluation. Recently, ICA sent out a press release to various stakeholders in the healthcare informatics (HI) community outlining five key trends shaping the development of health information exchanges (HIE) among large healthcare organizations:

1. The growing impetus for healthcare provider connectivity.
2. An increasing focus on the need to manage chronic diseases.
3. Increased patient expectation of personal involvement in the care process.
4. Market pressures for improved hospital–physician alignment.
5. Advances in technology facilitating system interoperability.

With an increasing number of baby boomers and the elderly constituting the U.S. population, it is envisaged that these trends will become more prevalent for U.S. healthcare services organizations in the near future.

"These trends highlight the benefits which community-based healthcare models can offer all constituents—physicians, patients, and healthcare providers across the continuum of care," says Gary M. Zegiestowsky, chief executive officer (CEO) of ICA. "The gap between traditional enterprises and HIE is closing, with growing connectivity for physicians and ultimately the entire healthcare community in certain cities or regions. We believe this is signaling a paradigm shift that has both near- and long-term implications for healthcare and HIT."

"In order to keep pace with these trends," Zegiestowsky continues, "physicians in every community first need intuitive, proven technology solutions aligned with clinical workflow to speed the adoption of electronic health records. Moving toward patient-centric care will be possible when all providers across the broad spectrum of care are able to access and utilize a unified patient record in combination with tools that enable better care."

ICA's response to this growing trend is the use of an exchange platform created for both enterprise and HIT systems, such as the A3Align Solution™. For 10 years, practicing physicians and informatics professionals from Vanderbilt Medical Center have developed this technology, which has eventually been installed at Bassett Healthcare's enterprise comprising four hospitals and 27 clinics in Cooperstown, New York. A3Align Solution will also be implemented by both the Montana and Northwest Healthcare for HIE. In addition, Vanderbilt distributed this same technology across its 40 facilities in the Mid-South eHealth Alliance, a successful HIE in western Tennessee.

With these major trends encouraging HIE among healthcare services organizations, what do you believe are the benefits of having all of your health information made freely accessible and interchangeable among all of your caregivers? What would be your worst fear?

I. Introduction

As we enter this world, how did we become aware and conscious of who we are, and of things that surround us? How did we learn about the myriad ideas, sights, sounds, and smells and the many events that we see, hear, feel, and witness in the surrounding space in which we live and breathe for each day of our lives? Aren't "data" and "information" the essential constructing blocks in our lives? Isn't "knowledge" the central intellectual core that links everything else to form meanings, interpretations, and actions? Aren't "information systems" innate in each and every one of us as human beings who find it so very natural to process incoming streams of "stimuli" continuously, seamlessly, and automatically—irrespective of how cognitively complex these stimuli may at first appear to be? Seemingly, all of us have already been introduced some-what to the subject of health management information systems (HMIS) even from the first day of birth as we "woke up" from our "deep sleep" inside our mother's wombs, most likely, within the confines of a healthcare or maternal health-related facility.

The field of HMIS is inherently complex. Take the myriad terminologies employed in this text as an example. There are subtle differences even with major terminologies used to describe the field. For instance, *health management information systems (HMIS)*, which is the term used liberally throughout the first edition of this text, has, in and of itself, a managerial slant, and whereas *healthcare information technology* (HCIT or *health IT–HIT*) has a technology slant, *health information systems (HIS)* or *healthcare information systems (HCIS)* may be interpreted as the umbrella term with a systems or information systems connotation. *Informatics* is another commonly used term among European researchers, and *health informatics* or *clinical informatics* generally refers to the application of data methods in medicine, healthcare services, and clinical practices. For this reason, some authors, as will become apparent in the latter part of the text, use the terms *health informatics (HI)* and *medical informatics (MI)* as well as *e-health (electronic health)*. Thus, in this edition of the HMIS text, for the sake of simplicity and to further reduce complexities for less sophisticated readers, we allow the usage of these several and diverse termi-nologies to be more or less interchangeable among the works accumulated by the different con-tributing authors and accompanying editors. Also, to ease the disruption in the readings and simplify the editing process, we have generally dropped the "s" that is typically appended to many of these acronyms to create the plural sense and simply use these acronyms in more or less the plural sense unless it is specifically preceded with an article such as "a" or "the" when attach-ing a verb to the specific acronyms or using it as a descriptive adjective, as in "the HMIS" field.

More importantly, the HMIS conceptualization we have drawn in this text comes from an eclectic well of traditionally established as well as newer disciplines. Academic researchers, edu-cators, and practitioners from diverse disciplines—including, but not limited to, electrical and computing engineering, industrial engineering, clinical and management engineering, nursing and allied health, health informatics, health management, organizational behavior, computer science, and cognitive science—have all contributed, in one form or another, to the develop-ment and accumulation of HMIS knowledge domains.

Indeed, as early as the 1960s, cognitive scientists have modeled the human cognition as an information processing system. Here, the human brain is perceived to act just like the computer, and experiments conducted on the human stimuli-response system inform us of the familiar story of how different external stimuli (information) can exert different patterns of resulting or induced behaviors among the human observers. In other words, the information systems within humans are exemplified by the cognitive activities recurring within the human brain. In the HMIS analogy, the information processors are likened to the eyes and minds of the health organization.

In this newly revised edition, the term *adaptive HMIS* has been used specifically to emphasize the need for a flexible approach to health information administration and management. HMIS students must learn how to apply information science, information systems, and health informatics concepts from an adaptive but integrated health management perspective. More generally, this text aims to provide the students with a state-of-the-art managerial perspective of health information technological systems in the coming years so that they are well prepared to face the many challenges of acquiring and applying new forms of HCIT for healthcare services management purposes in this century and beyond. In this first chapter, we briefly cover the HMIS evolution, its underlying architecture, and its basic functions. We then close the chapter with a brief survey of the role HMIS technology plays in driving today's healthcare and healthcare-related businesses.

II. Evolution of HMIS

In its broadest sense, HMIS encompasses diverse concepts, methods, and applications from many related fields. Its genesis may be traced to multiple roots, including general systems thinking, information economics, management science, information systems development methodologies, software engineering, computer science and communication theory, medical computing, health organization behavior, health management, policy, and health services research. From a practical viewpoint, the evolution of HMIS over the past several decades has been largely driven by strategic, tactical, and operational applications of various information technology (IT) and advanced systems concepts for healthcare services delivery within an individual, group, and, more appropriately, an organizational perspective. The regional or even national health coalitions are also on the horizon, enabled by the establishment of electronic health information exchange infrastructures.

In a world where growing competition for healthcare services delivery is defined by rapidly changing technology and maturing organizational arrangements, it is critical to understand how evolving HMIS technologies operate and how HMIS interact within all key aspects of an organization. In other words, it is important to know how HMIS are developed or procured; how they are managed and maintained; how their functions are executed to support daily operations and more advanced activities, such as continuous quality improvement programs and medical research; and finally, how to evaluate their performance and cost-effectiveness. More importantly, with globalization and the emergence of large-scale computing systems such as electronic health records (EHR) and innovative business-driven applications such as enterprise resource planning (ERP), customer relationship management (CRM), supply chain management

(SCM) systems, and patient-centric applications such as personal health records (PHR), the resulting landscape for future-oriented HMIS is bound to change quickly.

New advances in HMIS are vital to our society because these technologies guide our everyday lives; without them, life would be rather difficult. Imagine, for example, while visiting with your doctor today, you find him or her searching busily through a mountain of incoherent, unorganized, and piecemeal data about you for all of the different visits that you may have made to the different clinics that may now be part of a merged health maintenance organization (HMO), or, what if your doctor has to spend most of his or her time making clarification phone calls to laboratories and pharmacies to gather information rather than focusing on diagnosing and treating your illnesses? Imagine also that these data were recorded using various data-coding schemes by different clinicians with different recording media (such as paper records, tapes, and film images) and stored in multiple locations. How different would it be for your doctor to manage you and your information if these data had been "digitally" captured in standardized formats on nano-chips and could now be easily recombined, reorganized, and made securely accessible and available to him or her quickly even before meeting with you?

Indeed, past technologies such as file folders, paper-and-pencil entries, tape recordings, and X-ray films are both physically limited and very restrictive in terms of keeping secure, accessible, portable, and available records about you and capturing progressive changes to your health and wellness status each time you visit with one of your care providers, who may be practicing in different hospitals and clinics associated with your HMO. These traditional recording methods are limited because the captured data and information can only be kept largely in a "physical" form and not easily accessible, transportable, or available "virtually" or "digitally" to other expert clinicians or even to you, who may decide to travel to another country seeking a second opinion, or who may have been placed in emergencies outside the state of your residence. New forms and modes of HMIS technology such as wearable devices and embedded chips promise to give you the ability to access such recorded information that has been accumulated over the years both conveniently and securely at any time, anywhere. In the foreseeable future, you will also be able to control and access your own personal health records stored online and contributed by all of your care providers. As amazing as new technologies can be, it is important to first understand the type(s) and basic functions of HMIS technologies that currently exist and how these technologies will likely evolve due to increased globalization, continuous healthcare reforms, the corporatization of medicine, and other major trends such as the formation of new alliances and consolidations among healthcare provider organizations.

Apparently, the emergence of satellite-based, wireless, user-friendly portables; the proliferation of cellular networks; new computing privacy and security technologies; and new implementation of various powerful network-based systems such as sensor networks and Internet-based data warehouses are now in the order of multimillion-dollar projects to serve large populations with massive capabilities of automated collection, manipulation, and analysis of multidimensional data sets. These emerging trends are now pressuring senior healthcare executives and managers to become seriously interested in understanding and endorsing cost-beneficial, integrative, and innovative HMIS solutions.

III. HMIS Components and Basic Functions

Publicly, as health consumers become more aware, more informed, and better trained in accessing electronic and social media and as they become more intelligent in evaluating alternative healthcare services (such as using Leapfrog's hospital ratings), engaging in online forums for health information sharing, and participating in physician/hospital referrals among patients and/or virtual marketing using social network sites, consumers are exerting greater pressures for a revolution in HMIS technological applications. With the expansion of the aging baby boomer generation and the accelerating growth in U.S. healthcare expenditures, we can confidently expect the continuing growth of HMIS applications during the coming decades to have a significant impact on primary healthcare, pharmaceutical, rehabilitative, palliative, and home healthcare services. Therefore, management should not and cannot afford to leave the job of designing, developing, and implementing network-based, integrated HMIS in the hands of IT experts or commercial vendors alone. Instead, they must now take a personal interest in paving the way for new generations of HMIS technology—technology that satisfies both organizational requirements and patient needs. As such, the importance of using an adaptive managerial perspective in HMIS design and development within an organizational context for the coming decades cannot be overly emphasized. Let us now turn to an overview of the basic HMIS components and functions.

HMIS Components

An understanding of the adaptive but integrated HMIS begins with differentiating among its five major components and their interrelationships:

1. Data/information/knowledge component.
2. Hardware/software/network component.
3. Process/task/system component.
4. Integration/interoperability component.
5. User/administration/management component.

The data/information/knowledge component forms the central core, the content, of all HMIS. It encompasses the specification of, organization on, and interrelationship among data, information, and knowledge elements required of integrated HMIS.

Raw data form the basic building blocks for generating useful information that is to be stored in any HMIS; processed data are transformed into information that serves as useful output for HMIS end-users to make informed and intelligent decisions. Some pieces of data about your child may be that of his or her demographics or the medication that he or she is allergic to (e.g., penicillin). Another example would be his or her childhood vaccination records. Here, the data would be immunization dates and type. Putting all these data together to form a view of a child's immunization schedule derives information. Determining whether the child is due for a vaccine requires knowledge, specifically, the captured experience and knowledge of the attending physician, which could further be stored and recorded into existing HMIS and passed on to another care provider for future care delivery.

The combination of effective data, information, and knowledge resource management involves designing the critical databases and instituting various intelligent data-mining algorithms, rule engines, and online analytical processing (OLAP) tools to manage the increasingly complex and information-intensive care decision situations physicians are facing in this day and age. In other words, organized information and captured experience will, in turn, yield the essential knowledge and business intelligence for guiding healthcare services for the individual care provider, a group of care providers managing related health problems, or an entire health provider organization trying to deliver healthcare services. Figure 1.1 shows the conceptual flow of the data/information/knowledge paradigm within the HMIS organizational and healthcare provider decision-making context.

Ultimately, the HMIS used to support key decision-making functions of healthcare providers and administrators within the organization must be reformed to achieve greater integration of data, information, and knowledge across organizational stakeholders. ICA's newly proposed A3Align Solution, discussed in the chapter-opening scenario, is an example of how innovative HMIS applications can better integrate enterprise databases (such as EHR) and other uncoordinated data systems [such as computerized physician order entry (CPOE) and clinical decision support systems (CDSS)] and to support integrated healthcare delivery at a regional level. In an integrated and well-designed HMIS, the goal is to distribute these information-related elements efficiently, effectively, and appropriately throughout the organization for enriching learning among organizational users and for enhancing the delivery of healthcare services among care providers.

The next critical component within "information systems," aside from the "information" core, is the "technology" layer. Here, the hardware/software/network component features prominently as it entails the choice deployment of various information and computing-related technologies to support HMIS applications and use. Briefly, this component involves configuring various hardware, software, user interface, and communication-enabling infrastructures, associated devices, and applications in such a way as to best achieve efficient and effective information services integration throughout while connecting individuals, groups, and organizations.

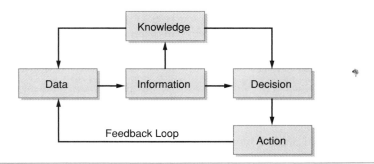

FIGURE 1.1   A Data/Information/Knowledge Decision System.

ICA's A3Align Solution, for example, is an exchange platform created for integrating data and information from both enterprise and HIT systems. It would be important to ensure that all connected devices can access the HMIS applications seamlessly; better yet, these devises can access an adapted version of an application customized to a device platform. In this sense, for any healthcare organization, the technology layer must be supportive of the people (internal users), aiding the performance of tasks to be accomplished by these users and helping them to thrive in the resulting technology-driven environment. Furthermore, new and emerging HMIS technologies and methods play an increasingly significant role in enhancing healthcare organizational delivery of patient care–related services. This brings us to the third basic HMIS component.

The process/task/system component exemplifies the routine and internalized driving engine for HMIS. Here, our focus should be on the cohesion to be achieved within established "local" processes, tasks, and applications. In other words, existing administrative-based HMIS, such as financial information systems, human resources information systems, facility utilization and scheduling systems, materials management systems, facilities management systems, and office automation systems, as well as clinical-based HMIS applications such as EHR, CPOE, and CDSS, must be designed to collect relevant data and accumulate useful information for organizational task-processing and decision-making activities. It is possible, too, that over time organizational structural and procedural changes and/or regulatory changes may require certain different routine processes that have been instituted previously to be changed or completely deleted, yielding room to new processes, tasks, and applications. Therefore, a systems perspective is critical in order to achieve optimal functionality among the different task processes and applications.

Surely, the integration/interoperability component is a key determinant of HMIS success from an enterprise view. Often, the key to positioning today's healthcare services organizations for future success is the interoperability of systems used in managing existing and ongoing healthcare information services vis-à-vis its competitive marketplace environment. The "interoperability" for much of the computerized information processing within the organizational framework must be upheld both internally and externally to achieve efficient, effective, and excellent delivery of healthcare services. This requires not only an elaborate understanding of evolving technological innovations and changing needs in organizational task processes, but also knowledge of the market structure and changing characteristics of the healthcare services industry and how the different current systems should be designed to fit well with every other HMIS application to achieve an integrated, enterprisewide HMIS.

In fact, as early as 1980, Lincoln and Korpman recognized the difficulties with computer applications in healthcare services delivery.[2] In their classic paper, "Computers, Healthcare, and Medical Information Science," they argued that the goals for medical information science, although easy to state, are difficult to achieve for several reasons. First, adapting well-tested information processing procedures and methods from other fields into medicine is difficult because of the uncertainty and sophistication surrounding the medical context; the wide spectrum of medical data; and the vagueness, disparity, and variation of organizational healthcare objectives. Second, this difficulty is further exacerbated by the apparent dissonance between the often-embedded ambiguity in medical data structure and the rigidity of computer logic structure. Specifically, in medicine, the materials cover the entire range of patient care data and the methods used span a wide range of disciplines, including the management, behavioral, and fundamental sciences, not just information processing and communications.

This brings us to the final but most critical HMIS component, the users. The user/administration/management component brings together and intelligently coordinates all of the other HMIS components. Based on a shared technological infrastructure, for example, various users are, in turn, empowered to perform designated tasks and activities that will support the overall business goals of the organization—that is, to serve their clients both inside and outside the organization in the most efficient, productive, and effective manner. The function of this critical user component, when blended appropriately with all the other HMIS components, is to engender a holistic conceptualization that absorbs the many insights and interactions inherent in any organizational HMIS endeavor.

Altogether, an adaptive, managerial HMIS perspective encompasses a combined interaction of data-related elements, appropriate technologies and methods, designated task processes, and intended users to gather, store, manipulate, and supply the needed information to support key organizational decision-making activities. The HMIS is an integral part of the organizational system, a mechanism that is central to integrating the enterprise and its various components. Every unit of that enterprise, which presumably is interrelated, must necessarily complete its purpose by working in unity. Like a jigsaw puzzle comprising a mass of irregularly shaped pieces that form a picture when fitted together, an adaptive, integrated HMIS emerges when the different components of the enterprise fit together. Still, the HMIS must fit in with the existing culture and organization work environment. An adaptive, integrated HMIS approach therefore exemplifies a holistic conceptualization of the fit among various enterprise components within the context of an adaptive, integrated management perspective. The relationships among these major enterprise components are illustrated in Table 1.1, which may be further used to outline the different parts of this text.

Part I, comprising Chapters 1 through 3, emphasizes HMIS foundational concepts. Chapter 1 provides an overview of HMIS from the health managerial perspective. Chapter 2 highlights the roles and responsibilities of chief executive and chief information officers in healthcare services organizations followed by *Research Brief I*, discussing how a personal digital assistant (PDA) can enhance data collection efficiency for wait-time reductions in emergency departments. Chapter 3 discusses online health information–seeking behavior among Internet users, accompanied by *Technology Brief I*, which focuses on the fundamentals of Internet and associated technologies for healthcare services organizations.

Part II, comprising Chapters 4 through 7, surveys the technology and application layers of HMIS. Chapter 4 focuses on HMIS enterprise software, the new generation of HMIS administrative applications, accompanied by *Technology Brief II*, a refresher overview of basic hardware, software, and interface design concepts. Chapter 5 concentrates on community health information networks (CHIN) to interconnect healthcare provider organizations and build virtual communities. *Technology Brief III*, focusing on HMIS telecommunications and networks, follows this chapter. Chapter 6 familiarizes readers with three key patient-centric management

Table 1.1   HMIS Text: Content and Organization

Part I **Foundation Concepts** **of HMIS**	Chapter 1. HMIS: A Managerial Perspective *Joseph Tan*
	Chapter 2. HMIS Executives: Roles and Responsibilities of Chief Executive Officers and Chief Information Officers in Healthcare Services Organizations *Joseph Tan*
	Research Brief I: Personal Digital Assistants Enhance Data Collection Efficiency during a Study of Waiting Times in an Emergency Department *N. Elkum, W. Greer, and A. Al-Madouj*
	Chapter 3. Online Health Information Seeking: Access and Digital Equity Considerations *Fay Cobb Payton and Joseph Tan*
	Technology Brief I: Fundamentals of Internet and Associated Technologies for Healthcare Services Organizations *Joshia Tan*
Part II **HMIS Technology and** **Applications**	Chapter 4. HMIS Enterprise Software: The New Generation of HMIS Administrative Applications *Joshia Tan with Joseph Tan*
	Technology Brief II: Basic Hardware, Software, and Interface Concepts for Healthcare Services Organizations *Joshia Tan and Joseph Tan*
	Chapter 5. CHIN: Building Virtual Communities and Networking Health Provider Organizations *Jayfus T. Doswell, SherRhonda R. Gibbs, and Kelley M. Duncanson*
	Technology Brief III: Telecommunications and Network Concepts for Healthcare Services Organizations *Joseph Tan*
	Chapter 6. Trending toward Patient-Centric Management Systems *Joseph Tan with Joshia Tan*
	Technology Brief IV: Database, Data-Mining, and Data-Warehousing Concepts for Healthcare Services Organizations *Joshia Tan and Joseph Tan*
	Chapter 7. HMIS Integration: Achieving Systems Interoperability with Web Services *J. K. Zhang and Joseph Tan*
Part III **HMIS Planning and** **Management**	Chapter 8. HMSISP/IR: Health Management Strategic IS Planning/ Information Requirements *Jon Blue and Joseph Tan*
	Chapter 9. HMIS Development: Systems Analysis and Development Methodologies *Joseph Tan*
	Chapter 10. Data Stewardship: Foundation for HMIS Design, Implementation, and Evaluation *Bryan Bennett*

(continues)

Table 1.1   *(Continued)*

	Chapter 11. Managing HMIS Projects: HMIS Implementation and IT Services Management *Joseph Tan*
Part IV **HMIS** **Standards, Policy,** **Governance, and Future**	Chapter 12. HMIS Standards: Standards Adoption in Healthcare IT *Sanjay P. Sood, Sandhya Keeroo, Victor W. A. Mbarika, Nupur Prakash, and Joseph Tan*
	Policy Brief I: HIPAA, Privacy, and Security Issues for Healthcare Services Organizations *Joseph Tan and Fay Cob Payton*
	Chapter 13. HMIS Governance, Policy, and International Perspectives: HMIS Globalization through E-Health *Anantachai Panjamapirom and Philip F. Musa*
	Chapter 14. HMIS Innovation: HMIS Innovation Diffusion in Healthcare Services Organizations *Tugrul U. Daim, Nuri Basoglu, and Joseph Tan*
Part V **HMIS Practices and Cases**	Case 1. Emergency Medical Transportation Resource Deployment *Homer H. Schmitz*
	Case 2. The Clinical Reminder System (CRS) *Kai Zheng*
	Case 3. Integrating Electronic Medical Records and Disease Management at Dryden Family Medicine *Liam O'Neill and William Klepack*
	Case 4. Delivering Enterprisewide Decision Support through E-Business Applications *Rajiv Kohli and Henry J. Groot*
	Case 5. Mapping the Road to the Fountain of Youth *Joshia Tan*

systems, namely, EHR, CPOE, and CDSS. *Technology Brief IV*, focusing on the fundamentals of HMIS database, data warehousing, and data-mining concepts, accompanies this chapter. Lastly, Chapter 7, which centers on the idea of achieving HMIS integration with systems-interoperable Web services, provides closure to Part II.

Part III, which encompasses Chapters 8 through 11, concentrates on HMIS planning, design, and management issues. Chapter 8 covers HMIS strategic planning and methods to elicit organizational information requirements. Chapter 9 presents HMIS analysis and development methodologies, whereas Chapter 10 offers practical advice on HMIS design, implementation, and evaluation from a data stewardship perspective. Chapter 11 then closes Part III by reinforcing the concepts of HMIS implementation from the perspective of IT project management as well as IT service management concepts.

Part IV, which covers Chapters 12 through 14, acquaints the readers with HMIS standards, policy, governance, and the future. Chapter 12 presents HMIS standards and is augmented with *Policy Brief I*, focusing on the Health Information Portability and Accountability Act

(HIPAA), privacy, and security issues that govern HMIS design, deployment, and use; Chapter 13 opens up the scope of earlier discussions by transitioning into HMIS governance, policy, and international perspectives based on emerging trends of globalization and the e-healthcare paradigm; and Chapter 14 jumps forward with a look at the future of HMIS by dwelling on innovation diffusion.

This ushers us into the final part of the text, Part V, which is devoted completely to selective cases intended to pull together parts and pieces of HMIS concepts, methods, and applications as presented throughout the different parts of this text. Briefly, five selective contributions of HMIS applications cases are covered in Part V. Case 1, which focuses on strategic planning for HMIS in the context of an emergency medical transportation (EMT) setting, opens the case discussions for examining the applications of HMIS solutions to real-world problems. Case 2, "The Clinical Reminder System," offers insights into the development, utilization, and acceptance of a patient-oriented system to aid clinical workflow activities and routine decision making. Interestingly, Case 3, "Integrating Electronic Medical Records and Disease Management at Dryden Family Medicine," zooms in on HMIS implementation within a small physician group practice, while Case 4, "Delivering Enterprisewide Decision Support through E-Business Applications," shows how different generations of decision support evolved for a large-scale healthcare services delivery system. Case 5, "Mapping the Road to the Fountain of Youth," is an accumulation of the concepts covered in the cases in Part V and brings a closure to the entire text. With this overview, it is important to get back to the fundamental conceptualization of an HMIS and what are its basic functions.

HMIS Basic Functions

It is critical that beginning HMIS students achieve a good grasp of the basic functions of an information system. Historically, all information systems, including HMIS, are built upon the conceptualization of three fundamental but iterative information-processing phases: data input, data management, and data output. The data input phase includes data acquisition and data verification. The data management or processing phase includes data storage, data classification, data update, and data computation. Finally, the data output phase includes data retrieval and data presentation. Altogether, these eight elements and three phases define a typical information system as represented schematically in Figure 1.2.

Data acquisition involves both the generation and the collection of accurate, timely, and relevant data. Data are the raw materials needing verification, organization, and transformation before they can be useful information. The process of data generation in HMIS is normally achieved through the input of standard coded formats (e.g., the use of bar codes), thereby allowing rapid mechanical reading and capturing of data. The process of data collection differs from that of data generation in that data can be entered directly at the source (e.g., the use of a point-of-care bar code scanner), thereby enhancing data timeliness, validity, and integrity. Data verification involves the authentication and validation of gathered data. It is generally known that the quality of collected data depends largely on the authority, validity, and reliability of the data sources. The garbage in garbage out (GIGO) principle is an important factor to consider in this process; that is, data containing inaccuracies and inconsistencies should be detected as

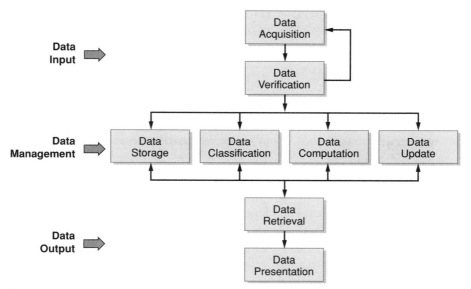

FIGURE 1.2   Basic Functions of a Health Management Information System.

early as possible in the system to allow immediate correction and minimize the eventual costs of system output errors.

The preserving and archiving of data may be regarded as part of the data storage function. Memory (i.e., a physical storage system) and indexing (i.e., the selection of key words to determine major subject areas) are primary means of amassing data. When accumulated data are no longer actively used in the system, a method to archive the data for a certain period is usually advisable and may sometimes be mandatory, as when it is required by legislation. A closely related element to data storage is data classification (or data organization). It is a critical function for increasing the efficiency of the system when the need arises to conduct a data search. Moreover, imposing a taxonomy on the data that have been collected and stored provides greater understanding of how the data can be reused. Most data classification schemes are based on the use of certain key parameters. For example, data referring to a patient population may be classified and sorted according to various diagnostic classification schemes, such as the widely accepted ICD-9-CM, a clinical modification of the original ICD-10 system developed by the National Center for Health Statistics (NCHS). More recently, the ICD-10-PCS (the International Classification of Diseases, 10th Procedure Coding System) has replaced volume 3 of ICD-9-CM.[3,4] While ICD-10-PCS is yet to be implemented, awaiting propagation from the World Health Organization (WHO), such an organized patient data system is useful for conducting a case-mix analysis because it comprises a set of diagnostic codes of thousands of patient classifications. Each code has seven alphanumeric characters, including section, body system, root operation, body part, approach, device, and qualifier. Indeed, the particular taxonomy employed will have a powerful influence on the way the data can be subsequently used.

This is because a high degree of semantics is implied in any particular data classification. Crowe and Avison noted that if the wrong classification is chosen, a great deal of potentially useful information could be lost.[5] This, however, is not a problem that can be easily resolved due to the lack of standardization among competing taxonomies. System integration and data interoperability have, therefore, been an enduring challenge for HMIS researchers and practitioners.

New and changing information is accounted for through the element of data update. The dynamic nature of such data modification calls for constant monitoring. For HMIS to maintain current data, mechanisms must be put in place for updating changes in the face of any ongoing manual or automated transactions. The concept of processing a transaction (i.e., whenever an event alters the current state of the system) is critical for ensuring data timeliness. Such updates can be either online (real-time) or batch processed sequentially. Due to legal and ethical considerations, archiving and tracking each data update can be a critical requirement in designing and implementing HMIS. Data computation involves various forms of data manipulation and data transformation, such as the use of mathematical models, statistical and probabilistic approaches, linear and nonlinear transformation, and other data analytic processes. Computational tasks allow for further data analysis, synthesis, and evaluation so that data can be used for strategic decision-making purposes other than tactical and/or operational use.

Data retrieval is concerned with the processes of data transfer and data distribution. The data transfer process is constrained by the time it takes to transmit the required data from the source to the appropriate end-user. A key problem in data transmission is the existence of noise (i.e., distortion) that could be both internal and external to HMIS. The data distribution process ensures that data will be accessible when and where needed. There must also be ways to ensure that unauthorized users are denied access to sensitive data in the system. This is normally achieved through the institution of data security and access control mechanisms, such as the use of firewalls, passwords, user authentication, and other forms of user identification. One significant criterion to be considered in the data retrieval function is the economics of producing the needed information. Many early systems (particularly stand-alone hospital information systems) were far too costly to operate, and the costs were simply not justified relative to the value of information that was finally produced. This situation has largely changed with advancing HMIS techniques and technologies available at decreasing costs.

Finally, data presentation has to do with how users interpret the information produced by the system. In situations where only operational or even tactical managerial decision making is expected, summary tables and statistical reports may suffice. However, certain managerial decision making involves strategic thinking and active collaboration. The use of presentation graphics for higher-level managerial decision analysis is particularly encouraged because these appear to provide a better intuitive feel of data trend. Tan and Benbasat[6] and Tan[7] have presented a theory to explain and predict the human processing of graphical information, which is valuable to guide HMIS designers in the matching of presentation graphics to tasks.

To illustrate these various HMIS data phases, we can use the case of a computerized patient health records system for inpatients, which is usually supported with bedside terminals. In this system, data acquisition comprises the generation and gathering of daily notes on symptoms, treatments, diagnoses, progress notes, discharge summaries, registration of orders for laboratory tests, operations, anesthesia, and other sources of information such as patient demographics and physicians' findings. The data may also come from other interconnected HMIS through live or batched data feeds. The data to be coded and automated are usually formatted into specific and normalized elements, fields, and records.

Figure 1.3 illustrates an abstract of a patient health record that could be implemented as a Web-based system for monitoring patient medical conditions and treatments in a healthcare services organization. As for data verification, the system relies on the ease with which the coded data may be mechanically processed and properly decoded. In many cases, standard forms and standard terms are used in recording patient data to ensure data integrity and consistency. Most computerized patient record systems have built-in capabilities to reject invalid data inputs through the use of range checks (e.g., specifying a patient's age to fall within a verifiable

```
┌─────────────────────────────────────────────────────────────────────────────┐
│  1. Patient Medical                    3. Date of Admission:    /    /         │
│     Insurance Number: _____                                             │
│                                                                                │
│  2. Patient Name: _____       4. Date of Discharge:    /    /         │
│                                            Mo/Day/Yr:                          │
├──────────────────────────┬───────────────────────────┬───────────────────────┤
│  5. Sex:                 │ 12. Discharge Status:      │  PROCEDURES           │
│     __ Male              │     Alive:                 │                       │
│     __ Female            │       __ With Approval     │  15. Principal Procedure:│
│                          │       __ Against Notice    │      a. _____ Date:  /  / │
│  6. Birthdate:   /   /    │                            │                       │
│                          │     Death:                 │  16. Additional Procedures│
│  7. Tel. No.:__ __ __     │       __ Autopsy           │      a. _____    │
│                          │       __ No Autopsy        │      b. _____    │
│  8. Next of Kin: _____  │                            │      c. _____    │
│                          │     Transfer to:           │                       │
│  9. Address: _____     │       __ Other Institution │  17. History/Physical:│
│                          │       __ Home              │                       │
│  10. Admission Source:   │                            │      _____       │
│                          │  13. Type of Death:        │                       │
│     __ Admitting         │     __ Anesthesia          │  18. Laboratory:      │
│     __ Emergency         │     __ In Operating Room   │                       │
│     __ Outpatient        │     __ Postoperative       │      _____       │
│                          │     __ Other               │  19. Radiology:       │
│  11. Location            │                            │                       │
│      of Patient: _____  │  14. General Remarks:      │      _____       │
│                          │      _____            │                       │
├──────────────────────────┴─────────┬─────────────────┴───────────────────────┤
│  PHYSICIANS                         │  DIAGNOSIS                               │
├─────────────────────────────────────┼──────────────────────────────────────────┤
│  20. Principal Specialist: _____   │  21. Principal Diagnosis: _____         │
│                                     │  22. Additional Diagnoses:               │
│      Second Specialist: _____      │      a. _____                       │
│                                     │      b. _____                       │
│      Family Physician: _____       │      c. _____                       │
└─────────────────────────────────────┴──────────────────────────────────────────┘
```

FIGURE 1.3   A Sample Abstract for a Computerized Patient Medical Record System.

range of classification) and other means (e.g., using batched totals). After data input, the data are kept securely (data storage) in a database, a central data repository. This is to ensure that the data are accessible to the healthcare services providers on any subsequent visits by the same patient. A unique patient identifier and a master patient index (MPI) are used to identify the exact locations of all related records of a specific patient. This type of data organization also allows for easy processing and regular updating by care provider organizations.

Updating and maintenance of the data (data update) to ensure timeliness and integrity can be carried out either on a daily basis (i.e., routinely) or interactively (real-time). For example, some hospitals collate their daily census through batch processing around midnight. Additional data-processing functions include data analysis and synthesis to transform and combine various elements of the input data into useful and meaningful information (data computation). The data retrieval function ensures that the appropriate end-users (e.g., physicians, nurses, quality improvement managers, and medical researchers) have access to accurate, timely, and relevant information from the system. The distribution of information to end-users typically occurs through Web-based services, where appropriate users can be authenticated whenever they want to abstract certain views of the stored data or perform queries. Ultimately, data presentation in the context of the preceding example is concerned with generating reports that are easy to read and interpret for use in informed patient care or related decision making.

IV. HMIS Cultures

Why do HMIS cultures matter? A health information system exists as part of a larger system to support one or more of a combination of administrative, financial, clinical, research, or managerial activities occurring within a health organization. Yet, it is the culture of the health services organization that largely determines the appropriate product mix, roll out, and use of HMIS solutions within the organization. More likely than not, existing and traditional HMIS applications often tend to be disintegrated so that critical information embedded in the different parts of the organization is not going to be transparent among employees of the organization.

In terms of HMIS cultures, based on what we now know about successful and effective IS/IT (information systems/information technology) leadership, a healthcare services organization may intentionally or unintentionally adopt and nurture one of four types of cultures: an information-functional culture, an information-sharing culture, an information-inquiring culture, and an information-discovery culture.[8] Understanding the different characteristics of each of these cultures is important to guide managers, administrators, and systems analysts in generating appropriate HMIS solutions for the organization.

An information-functional culture essentially takes the traditional view that information is power and that giving up information means giving up the power of controlling others. It also follows that as most organizations are structured functionally, information-functional culture therefore limits the flow of information within a functional area such as human resources, accounting and finance, sales and marketing, and IT. For example, nurses in an emergency department of a healthcare services organization adopting an information-functional culture will attempt to safeguard their own use of patient-gathered information as well as limit the sharing of patient records as a way of exerting power over nurses in other departments. Thus, whenever nurses from the acute care units or other departments need to schedule a care routine of a discharged patient from the emergency department, they would have to involve the emergency department nurses.

In contrast, an information-sharing culture promotes trust among employees of different departments within the same organization. While needing to be sensitive as to the privacy, confidentiality, and security of particular information under his or her safeguard, it is important that nurses, physicians, and others be able to share certain types of information with fellow employees for the benefit of the entire organization. For example, the chief medical officer (CMO) of a hospital who wants to see that his or her direct reports work collaboratively to benefit the efficient and effective running of the entire hospital must not only encourage sharing of information among individual physicians, but he or she should also focus on making information—especially on procedural problems and patient care process failures—transparent among the individual physicians in the hospital.

An information-inquiring culture essentially makes transparent the core values, beliefs, and purpose of the organization and ensures that critical information about the due processes, procedures, and functioning of the organization is easily accessible for all employees throughout the organization. Employees are also encouraged and trained to actively monitor such information and to align their daily actions and behaviors with the trends and new leadership directions of the organization. For instance, all nurses and doctors of a healthcare provider organization could be asked to greet and politely interact with incoming and discharged patients to promote its reputation as an organization focused on patient care and customer satisfaction. All employees are also clear about how conflicts should and can be resolved quickly and the due procedures for attending to patient complaints.

Finally, an information-discovery culture entails that the organization is able to share insights freely and encourages its employees to collaborate in offering new products and/or services that meet the needs of existing and new clients. Employees throughout the organization are also provided with a comprehensive view of how the organization functions and how it will support them in their attempt to deal with crises and radical changes and/or finding ways to achieve competitive advantages against its competitors. For healthcare organizations, it is difficult to imagine the adoption of an information-discovery culture, especially among the physicians, because of these organizations' strong traditional roots in which physicians are accustomed to make their decisions independently about the patients under their care, even though they are affiliated with the organizations in which they practice.

Understanding HMIS applications begins with having an appreciation of how health organizations function and how IT is used in these organizations. The complexity of healthcare organizations and the intricacy of its myriad processes often is the root cause of IT failures in health care. Many health executives thought that slapping a complex HMIS on top of the problems encountered in a healthcare organization would resolve its woes when, in many cases, it not only worsens it, but adds unnecessary expenses when the root causes of these problems are not well understood. It is far more important to map out the processes, simplify the complexity, consolidate the needs, and identify the core IT requirements. From here, management has to nurture, cultivate, and respect the working of the HMIS culture and implement appropriate HMIS solutions accordingly.

V. Conclusion

This chapter started out with a real-world scenario describing the challenge of HMIS integration within a healthcare organization. It briefly highlighted the roots and evolution of HMIS discipline. The basic components and functions of a health management information system were further contemplated. It is clear that in order to understand HMIS, students should appreciate the functioning of a healthcare organization, such as the HMIS cultures, before HMIS solutions can be efficiently and effectively deployed in the organization and used to their full capacity.

In the next chapter, we highlight the roles of the chief information officer/chief executive officer for healthcare services organizations. Understanding these roles is critical for managing and designing future HMIS. Following this, we close Part I of this text with a chapter on how users are individually seeking health information on the Internet, selecting the best healthcare providers, and learning to become better-informed consumers. It is hoped that instructors will find these three foundational chapters in Part I helpful in encouraging students to become excited about the world of HMIS. The scenario at the beginning of each chapter and the minicases, *Research Briefs, Technology Briefs, Policy Briefs*, additional readings, and discussion questions that are offered at the end of the chapters are ways to motivate the students' learning—as well as to help them seek answers to many more new questions about HMIS—as new knowledge and technological breakthroughs in HMIS-related fields continue to emerge in a rapidly changing world.

Notes

1. http://www.digitalhcp.com/2008/05/27/dc-rhio-sets-ambitious-plans.html, accessed May 27, 2008.
2. T. L. Lincoln and R. A. Korpman, "Computers, Healthcare, and Medical Information Science," *Science* 210, no. 4467 (1980): 257–263.
3. ICD-9 is a U.S. Public Health Service official adaptation of a system for the classification of diseases and operations. The original system was developed and updated periodically by the World Health Organization for indexing hospital records. See T. C. Timmreck, *Dictionary of Health Services Management* (Owings Mills, MD: National Health Publishing, 1987): 306.
4. ICD-10-PCS is purported to be a replacement code set for ICD-9-CM. See http://www .inhcc.com/Standardization/coding _systems.htm, accessed June 1, 2008.
5. T. Crowe and D. E. Avison, *Management Information from Data Bases* (New York: Macmillan Press, 1980).
6. J. K. H. Tan and I. Benbasat, "Processing Graphical Information: A Decomposition Taxonomy to Match Data Extraction Tasks and Graphical Representation," *Information Systems Research* 1, no. 4 (1990): 416–439.
7. J. K. H. Tan, "Graphics-Based Health Decision Support Systems: Conjugating Theoretical Perspectives to Guide the Design of Graphics and Redundant Codes in HDSS Interfaces."

In J. K. H. Tan with S. Sheps, *Health Decision Support Systems* (Gaithersburg, MD: Aspen Publishers, 1998): 153–173.

8. Booz Allen Hamilton, *Information Sharing* (New York: HarperCollins, 2006). See also www .boozallen.com.

Chapter Questions

1–1. How does HMIS affect or influence the different departments within a healthcare services organization?

1–2. Why is it difficult to integrate IT and medicine? Discuss the need for an integrated management perspective of HMIS.

1–3. List the five major components of integrated HMIS. Discuss which component deserves the most attention in today's HIT environment and why. Provide specific examples of each component in the context of your work.

1–4. If you were a CIO, which of the four types of IT cultures would you pursue, and why?

1–5. List and illustrate the basic functions of an HMIS. How may these basic functions be extended to accommodate complex health information processing tasks such as medical diagnosis and teleconsultation?

Mini-Case: MinuteClinic

MinuteClinic, owned by pharmacy giant CVS, is a retail healthcare provider with more than 500 locations established throughout the country. The centers are designed to treat patients with minor injuries or sicknesses, and more than 1.8 million patient visits have been documented since the company's inception in 2000. By creating a healthcare delivery model that responds to consumer demand, MinuteClinic makes access to high-quality medical treatment easier for more Americans.

As more patients used MinuteClinic resources, one issue the company faced was how to pass medical information to primary care physicians. As Cris Ross, chief information officer of MinuteClinic, explains, "There are a number of things we do very well with physicians, except connect electronically. We've been looking for a business-to-business exchange."

As a solution to this problem, MinuteClinic recently turned to ePrescribing connectivity network SureScripts to facilitate this exchange. It is the first time the SureScripts network has been used for anything other than pharmacy orders and related transactions.

"The idea is that we already have pharmacies connected," acting SureScripts CEO Rick Ratliff told Digital Healthcare & Productivity by telephone. "We have an ability to identify a physician uniquely on the network."

As part of this connection, MinuteClinic will convert records from its proprietary electronic medical records system into Continuity of Care Record (CCR) standard format. Ratliff adds that this record "can be moved around almost like a piece of mail" from provider to provider, and into personal health records (PHR).

Now with every visit, MinuteClinic practitioners stress the importance of maintaining a medical home for each patient by making information accessible to primary care providers. If a patient doesn't have a primary care provider, MinuteClinic provides a list of physicians in the area who are accepting new patients. Practitioners are then able to use a multipurpose software-based approach at the conclusion of each visit that generates educational material, an invoice, and a prescription (when clinically appropriate) for the patient, as well as a diagnostic record that is automatically sent to the patient's primary care provider's office (with the patient's consent) to facilitate continuity of care.

Mini-Case Questions

1. How might embracing the CCR standard benefit and/or damage MinuteClinic's overall profitability?
2. Why does MinuteClinic choose to promote the patient/primary care provider relationship?
3. What patient issues might MinuteClinic face in implementing an electronic record that can be easily transferred from clinic to physician?

Health Management Information System Executives:
Roles and Responsibilities of Chief Executive Officers and Chief Information Officers in Healthcare Services Organizations

Joseph Tan

CHAPTER OUTLINE

Scenario: *Managing Waiting Time in Emergency Rooms*

Notes
Additional Readings
Chapter Questions

Mini-Case: *Predicting Future HMIS Trends by Chief Information Officers*

Research Brief I: *Personal Digital Assistants Enhance Data Collection Efficiency during a Study of Waiting Times in an Emergency Department*
   N. Elkum, W. Greer, and A. Al-Madouj

Scenario: Managing Waiting Time in Emergency Rooms[1]

For the most part, patients entering the emergency room (ER) will not know what treatment they need or the specific department they should be admitted into; often, they are largely dependent on the ER to quickly and effectively diagnose their illness so as to get them transferred into the right department for optimal care and treatment. Some patients, for example, should be transferred to the intensive care unit (ICU), others should proceed to the operating room (OR), and some others to the recovery room (RR) waiting to be enrolled into possible long-term rehabilitation programs.

In November 2006, Beatrice Vance of Chicago, Illinois, was experiencing chest pains and quickly found her way to a local hospital ER. Hours later, she apparently died of a heart attack. The coroner's report concluded that the length of her wait time in the ER was partly responsible for her death because she died of congestive heart failure—the inability of the heart to pump the required amount of blood to her body due to a weakened muscle. At 10:15 P.M., she was already checked into the ER but was told to wait her turn for a doctor. At 12:25 A.M., she collapsed and died.

As Carol Haraden from the Institute for Healthcare Improvement noted, "The dangers are that the person's condition may escalate . . . (during) . . . waiting time in the ER." With wait time in the ER averaging 3 hours and 47 minutes nationally in the United States, it is clear that something should have been done. When an inquiry into a case such as that of Beatrice Vance is made, senior executives of the healthcare organization, including the chief executive officer (CEO) and others such as the chief information officer (CIO), may be held partly responsible. Thus, it is critical nowadays for healthcare organizations to shorten ER waiting times and be fully prepared to deal with differing needs of patients being admitted.

Indeed, the number of U.S. emergency departments has fallen by about 425, or about 12 percent from 1993 through 2006, while 26 percent more (or 114 million patients) have sought ER care during the same period. Hospitals across the nation are being pressured to find new ways of coding and assessing patients to keep the ER services efficient and effective by attending to admitted patients within 30 minutes. At the very least, the hospital should provide accurate and timely services to their patients who come to the ER for care. An ER triage system, for instance, is essential for the prompt recognition of urgent cases.

Imagine yourself to be one of these patients who would like to see changes to the ER waiting times. Do you feel this might be an opportunity where it would be beneficial for appropriate IT solutions and effective leadership in healthcare services organizations to come into play? What could, or would, you do to fix the situation, if you were given a leadership role by the Chicago hospital where Beatrice Vance was admitted?

I. Introduction

For years, practicing physicians in urban areas, especially those catering primarily to under-served communities, have struggled with patients who frequently miss scheduled appointments. With the national no-show rate in 2000 averaging 5.5 percent, many physician offices have now adopted a double-patient booking schedule in order to remain productive and financially viable. In other words, two patients are scheduled every 15 to 20 minutes at the physician's office, resulting in patients having to wait their turn even if they arrive on time. This then puts a lot of stress on the system as office staff struggles to balance between patient flow and flaring tempers, greatly increasing the potential for staff frustration and patient dissatisfaction.

To further aggravate the situation, physicians also have the habit of placing patients on a wait list that may be months away. Typically, these physicians would advise their patients to go to the ER if it is something for which the patients cannot wait. With ER services, no appointments are maintained, so situations can be even more demanding because federal law dictates that no patient can be denied needed treatments when showing up at an ER. As with challenges encountered in many critical business operations, where scheduling, queuing, and waiting time create problems, one way of resolving the ER challenge in the U.S. healthcare system is the adoption and implementation of appropriate health management information systems (HMIS). This opens up discussion of the critical roles played by the chief executive officer (CEO) and the chief information officer (CIO) in healthcare services organizations. These executives are responsible for providing an appropriate vision for future HMIS directions. They are responsible for aligning IT departmental goals and strategies with corporate goals and strategies, and they are also responsible for strategizing appropriately, executing intelligently, and evaluating wisely on the system's performance of healthcare services delivery with the application of effective and efficient business processes and information technologies throughout the corporation.

II. Vision

The role of the CEO or CIO to oversee the use of HMIS in any healthcare services organization requires that the individual has at least been trained and has experienced and mastered a certain set of strategic, tactical, and operational IT competencies. Just as with any business organization, every healthcare services organization drastically needs such an individual to be visionary in providing future directions with respect to the organizational HMIS infrastructure, product life cycle management, and innovations. Aside from being visionary, the CEO or CIO is expected to be goal-directed in resolving HMIS performance in different parts of the organization on the one hand and to be emphatic in dealing with HMIS staff and daily customer complaints on the other.

Imagine that with the shortage of administrative and clinical staff members hired to man ER services, you, as the appointed CEO or CIO, have been asked to execute and implement a triage system and other critical clinical database and reminder systems for the ER to monitor the flow of patient traffic and ER scheduling information. What will be your role and responsibilities? How would you go about aligning the IT goals and strategies to be pursued for the ER with the greater organizational mission, goals, objectives, and strategies?

Essentially, senior executives who are directing organizational information systems or technology development efforts are expected to think quickly and strategically, solve problems intelligently in many areas of IT specializations, and advocate influentially on the use of available and advancing technologies to close the gap between departmental HMIS strategies and "the business" strategies. In a healthcare services organizational context, the mission, goals, and objectives of the health organization determine how HMIS should be incorporated throughout an organization. Oftentimes, not only is senior management expected to be responsible for immediate challenges facing the organization due to a breakdown of computing services, but more importantly, top management is often looked upon to take the lead in championing existing and new HMIS services. Among the most important roles, then, is having a vision—a vision that involves the creation of scenarios and possibilities to drive needed directions for future organizational HMIS growth and investments. For the CEO, the end result of this visioning process may be an enterprisewide business plan; for the CIO, it is more likely to be an IT plan aligned with this corporate business plan.

Backtracking to our ER example, for instance, one vision of the CEO/CIO may be the deployment of IT systems to ensure that all future incoming patients who are being transported via the hospital ambulance service are assessed even while en route to the hospital through the use of tele-medical devices, thereby shortening the assessment wait time for other incoming patients. Furthermore, installation of courseware for self-help and patient education can further help to reduce wait time. A targeted wait time for incoming patients can also be effectively cut down by ensuring that any available treatment records of new and previously admitted patients be abstracted electronically and in real time to all attending ER physicians and nurses; the entire ER patient record systems could also be wirelessly connected to all local area hospitals, and patients who banked their personal health records (PHR) with any secured health information agencies can then download their records conveniently and/or allow the reading and updating of their records by the attending ER physicians and nurses.

In practice, however, crafting such a "vision" is a long-drawn-out process whereby a set of shared and related notions in the form of a vetted "proposal" or "business plan" supported by top management in the organization is generated. Presumably, there is an assumed need to sell both the professional staff and other employees within the organization on the vision in one fashion or another. This means that a large majority of the organizational members should become aware of it, must be willing to support it, and must be able to participate in it in some fashion to bring about the realization of that vision. Surveys of management, professional staff, and other employees are some of the ways to promote an understanding and keen awareness of such a corporate view.

Strategic IT planning sessions could also be held on a continuous basis. These sessions need to be attended and supported by the key stakeholders across the organization, with the possibility of instituting changes as new ideas are introduced. Top management of the organization must also approve the finalized proposal, because future directions of the organization should extend the major thoughts captured by that proposal. It is also important to generate a business plan clarifying the strategies, policies, and procedures connected to unfolding the vision—one that is shared and supported by the majority of the organizational stakeholders. Essentially, this articulation should bring together all the pieces of HMIS components related to the organization: data, people, hardware and software, network requirements, and functional tasks to be supported.

While the CEO/CIO may not yet find complete answers to many of the questions raised by such a visioning process, having a well-consolidated plan is better than having none at all. After all, if you don't really know and can't articulate where you are heading, any road will lead you to it. This simply means that the next best thing to do may just be to do nothing because there will be no significant difference if you take (or don't take) actions without first having a strong conviction about the purpose for doing so.

Key questions to be answered by the CEO/CIO in such a business plan include:

1. What is the core mission of the IT department vis-à-vis that of the organization?
2. What are the major IT department goals to be accomplished in the longer term?
3. What are the specific objectives relating to each of these major, longer-term goals?

To turn the vision into reality, however, top management will need to take a practical approach to understanding and detailing the "strategies" in the context of unfolding the business plan.

III. Strategy

Whereas vision is concerned primarily with future directions and mission with a sense of purpose, "strategy" is concerned with how we go about achieving that vision and/or mission. For all intents and purposes, there are several levels of strategies, which should not be confused with those at the tactical and/or operational levels that pertain to shorter-term or more immediate goals and objectives, respectively. Among major groups of strategies with which top management should become fully acquainted are corporate strategies, competitive strategies, and functional strategies, as depicted in Figure 2.1.

Developed through a detailed scanning of the corporate environment at its highest level, in which the threats and opportunities of the external environment are assessed with respect to internal corporate strengths (core competencies) and weaknesses (inadequacy of corporate resources), corporate strategies may be further categorized into four major groups: growth, diversification, turnaround, and defensive strategies.

FIGURE 2.1   Taxonomies of Strategies.

Growth strategies, in the form of product and market development, mergers, acquisitions, and/or internal ventures, are aggressively followed when the healthcare organization's internal resources and competencies serve identified market opportunities readily. With a growing population of baby boomers, seniors and elderly persons facing the challenges of increased physical limitations and mobility, and increased chronic ailments, it may signal a time of growth for tele-home healthcare services. Moreover, with increased fuel and public transportation costs, an aggressive entry into the mobile healthcare market opportunities such as the promotion of tele-home care products and services may also be justified. Several national pharmaceutical chains in the United States and Canada (such as London Drugs) are already pursuing this strategy. Examples of such products and services include wearable medical devices; in-home, medical tele-consultation; and in-home, real-time monitoring care services via secured electronic networked devices.

Diversification strategies represent an approach to risk management. These strategies are often adopted when the existing healthcare organizational business portfolio is threatened; for example, delays in the reading of digitized images taken for ER patients may be a problem if other competitive healthcare services organizations are able to provide one-stop comprehensive ER services due to the availability and round-the-clock accessibility of in-house radiological services. One diversification strategy in this instance may be for the CEO/CIO to increase outsourcing of digital imaging services through the value chain by adding tele-radiological services to assess ER patient conditions quickly.

Turnaround strategies essentially take advantage of situations to retrofit the organizational strengths and internal capabilities to market opportunities that may still be available and waiting to be served. Typical approaches pursued in turnaround situations may be those of outsourcing, organizational restructuring, business process reengineering, budgetary cost-cutting measures, assets reallocation and reduction, or even service downsizing. One example here may be the introduction of expert-based courseware in integrative medicine to combat the strong growing market forces in the complementary and alternative medicine services for educating ER patients in follow-up and self-care services to reduce the need for time-consuming patient education by the attending ER physicians and nurses.

Finally, *defensive strategies* come into play when the stage of the industry and/or product life cycle is experiencing a steady decline due to its ongoing maturity. Here, several approaches that are typically used include divesting and liquidating to reduce the losses sustained by unproductive and increasingly inactive engagements as well as exiting the oversubscribed industry niches and/or practices. As an example, traditional paper-based patient records and paper-based prescribing are difficult to maintain but still used by many physicians across U.S. healthcare systems. These practices will eventually decline in popularity as competitive clinics move to electronic patient records and e-prescription services—and gain a larger percentage of the market share of patients. Part of the role and responsibilities of the CEO/CIO is then to employ defensive strategies to move the organization to a 21st-century healthcare services organization by replacing these paper-based medical records and drug prescribing systems with server-networked electronic health records (EHR) and/or e-prescription systems.

Based on Porter's classical work on competitive advantage strategies, for a healthcare services organization to stay competitive, commonly employed strategies include cost leadership, differentiation, and innovation strategies. In *cost leadership*, cost advantage is gained through economies of scale and cost-effectiveness as well as other cost-cutting measures. *Differentiation* highlights the uniqueness of certain aspects of the business activities maintained by the organization in a competitive marketplace. Lastly, *innovation strategy* for an organization is to be constantly at the leading edge of its product offering and service development. We illustrate the applications of these various strategies in terms of how a specific health maintenance organization such as Blue Care Network (BCN) can stay competitive in the marketplace so as to provide its clients with greater benefits as well as continuing to attract new subscribing members.

BCN, an affiliate of Blue Cross Blue Shield (BCBS), for example, is relatively successful in attracting new clients in the Detroit metropolitan area. Their clientele include neighboring state universities and other major corporate employers such as the University of Michigan, Michigan State University, Wayne State University, General Motors, Ford One, and Chrysler Corporation. Their competitors operating in the same regional area are less competitive because of somewhat higher co-payment options for active and nonmedical retirees; less benefit coverage; greater limitations for servicing active subscribers; and/or less comprehensive and competitive benefits for emergency, diagnostic, and preventive services.

With regard to differentiation strategy, what distinguishes BCN from its competitors here is the sheer growth in the number of its subscribing physicians, all of whom practice in the surrounding area and will thus be able to accept new patient-subscribers. Not surprisingly, their less competitive counterparts may have a relatively limited list of available general practitioners and specialists. Other factors distinguishing BCN from its competitors may involve BCBS and its affiliates' voluminous purchasing power, rapid third-party service reimbursement schemes, and effective supply chain management. Many third-party healthcare provider organizations would gladly work with BCN subscribers due to easy third-party reimbursement payment schemes. For instance, Dynamics, a Michigan company specializing in neck-and-back pain therapies for accident victims, will readily accept subscribers of BCBS of Michigan, BCN of Michigan, and Community Blue PPO (another affiliate of BCBS of Michigan), but may have difficulty accepting patient-subscribers of less known health maintenance organizations (HMOs) because of challenging third-party service provider reimbursement schemes. Finally, new-product developments and wellness programs such as smoking cessation, nutrition, and other health preventive measures are being actively propagated and introduced to BCN subscribers in order to stay competitive in the HMO marketplace.

Functional strategies, another set of strategies typically employed at the more operational level of managing the healthcare services organization, are nonetheless still critical for success in the longer-term and intermediate-term time frame. These strategies include marketing strategy, financial strategy, operation strategy, and human talent management.

Marketing strategy has to do with how the products and services are being propagated and promoted in the marketplace. BCN, for example, may decide to join forces with other competing HMOs to provide educational seminars and presentations to major corporate employees who represent the bulk of potential new HMO subscribers on a yearly basis. Financial strategy has to do with the intelligent use of financial information to make key decisions on resource allocation and financing of new programs within the organization. In an attempt to understand how chief executives use HMIS for strategy implementation in hospitals, David Naranjo-Gil and Frank Hartmann surveyed 218 public hospital CEOs in Spain and noted that executives with a "predominant administrative" background tend to be more effective in "establishing cost-reduction strategies, through their larger inclination to emphasize financial information in combination with a diagnostic use of the MIS" whereas executives with a "predominant clinical" background will "focus more on nonfinancial information for decision making and prefer an interactive style" of using HMIS, which tend toward use of flexibility strategies.[2] The latter, it appears, has to do more with operation strategy where quality improvement and greater efficiencies become the key focus for achieving greater patient satisfaction in healthcare services organizations. Thus, both financial and operation strategies are important for senior executives of BCN to implement appropriately and intelligently to achieve immediate, intermediate, and longer-term goals in the face of competitive challenges in the healthcare marketplace. Above all, human talent management is critical to determine the success of any organization because it is the people who work for the organization who portray the organization—they are the ones who put a face to how the organization really is perceived by its customers, third parties, and external relations.

IV. Execution

The McKinsey 7-S framework was developed by McKinsey & Company to guide the evaluation and implementation of organizational strategies. The underlying premise is that all seven elements of this model—strategy, structure, systems, style, staff, shared values, and skills—

should be moving in the same direction in order to achieve a "strategic fit" for the organization. In other words, the strategy of the organization "fits" with every other variable within the 7-S organization framework[3] of strategy, structure, systems, style, staff, shared values, and skills as illustrated in **Figure** 2.2.

Strategy is the set of activities or actions targeted at achieving a competitive edge in the marketplace through organizational process improvements, intelligent capital management application, and systemic resources allocation. *Structure* is the reporting hierarchy of the organization as determined by the placement of personnel within the organization and the accompanying division and/or integration of organizational tasks, roles, and responsibilities to be accomplished on a daily and longer-term basis. *Systems* are the task and informational processes and workflow that together determine how the organization conducts its daily affairs. Examples include information systems, healthcare delivery systems, performance evaluation systems, quality control systems, and capital budgeting systems. *Style* refers to the way management behaves within the organization, not just what is being communicated—the tangible evidence of how the organization spends time, pays attention, and performs collectively. *Staff* refers to the human resources—the people hired by the organization to perform its daily functions—although it is important to

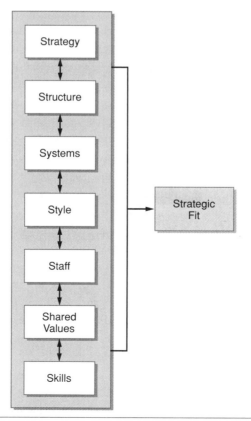

FIGURE 2.2   McKinsey's 7-S Strategic Fit Framework.

think of this not in terms of individuals, but of corporate demographics. *Shared values* portray the common goals, objectives, and beliefs of most members of the organization and may be indicative of both the organizational identity and corporate destiny. Finally, *skills* may be conceived as the total competencies of the organization due not simply to individual expertise in isolation, but more appropriately, to the interactive coordination among the hired employees. In essence, it is a derivative of the other six organizational elements noted in the 7-S framework.

Ginter, Swayne, and Duncan[4] used the case of Allegheny General Hospital (AGH) as sourced from David Burda's article[5] in *Modern Healthcare* to illustrate the McKinsey 7-S framework as applied in a healthcare organizational setting. Today, as a top-performing, tertiary-care hospital and academic medical center serving Pittsburgh and the surrounding five-state area with 724 beds,[6] AGH competes in an extremely sophisticated healthcare marketplace against the background of other highly performing, tertiary-care competitors. These competitors include the 729-bed St. Francis Medical Center, the 583-bed Presbyterian-University Hospital, the 500-bed Mercy Hospital of Pittsburgh, and the 452-bed Western Pennsylvania Hospital. Without a proper strategic fit, AGH would not have been able to excel in one of the country's most challenging and competitive tertiary-care marketplaces.

Strategically speaking, AGH has, over a critical period of time, been able to establish itself as a significant regional level-1 resource trauma center in Pennsylvania for tertiary-care services, with added recognition in pediatric trauma. Services offered by AGH include specialized patient care, resident physician teaching, and research administered collaboratively by more than 850 physicians and 4,000 employees. Located in the North Side section of Pittsburgh, AGH admits more than 29,000 patients and registers no less than 450,000 outpatient visits annually.

In term of its structure, AGH is strongly linked both professionally and academically. Not only is it affiliated with the Medical College of Pennsylvania, which has significantly strengthened its resident physician teaching mission, but it has significantly augmented its research mission through the ASRI (Allegheny Singer Research Institute). ASRI has an annual research budget of more than $30 million and conducts research in many clinical areas, including cardiology, cardiothoracic surgery, diagnostic radiology, gastroenterology, nephrology, neurology, neurosurgery, obstetrics/gynecology, oncology, ophthalmology, orthopedic surgery, pediatrics, psychiatry, pulmonary medicine, and transplant surgery.

Management style at AGH is known to be both aggressive and direct. AGH management is externally oriented and is prepared at all times to take the challenge of meeting the tertiary-care needs of the region. More recently, the hospital has focused on providing comprehensive care to those with behavioral disorders in their central nervous systems through the Allegheny Neuropsychiatric Institute (ANI). By emphasizing service quality, operational efficiencies, and individual productivity with a strong internal orientation, AGH management is highly committed to the excellence of the hospital's overall performance and to becoming the region's top hospital.

AGH also employs a variety of systems to guide future directions for the hospital progress and for new services and technology. For example, a system of objectives and strategies is maintained for implementing organizational policies and procedures, an advanced system is used for matching referring physicians to specialists, and plans are available for medical staff development and clinical services development.

Shared values of AGH's medical staff and employees reach above and beyond the highest level of community involvement, advanced technology deployment, and service excellence. The aim is to promote employees' commitment through supporting development and training programs as well as gain-sharing programs.

Staffing at AGH, as noted previously, comprises more than 850 physicians and 4,000 employees. These include more than 565 medical staff members, more than 1,350 registered and practicing nurses, and other personnel. AGH's residency program for junior and senior Medical College of Pennsylvania students is well managed, with a reputation that attracts fully qualified practicing specialists who love to teach and practice high-quality medicine. The hospital runs a medical staff development plan that emphasizes the training of the medical staff to meet the medical needs of the community.

Finally, skills and competencies at AGH are the sum derivatives of all the other elements within the 7-S strategic framework. AGH not only employs highly qualified experts, specialists, and staff members, but also promotes a learning environment throughout the organization to ease the flow of key clinical and nonclinical procedures, processes, and services. Both the public and its referring physicians are well aware of AGH's high-performing and accreditation standing and professional marketing strategies.

At this point, we move on to discuss the differing roles and responsibilities of the various senior executive positions within a healthcare services organizational context. For HMIS to make a significant contribution and impact on the organizational performance, understanding the role and responsibilities of the CIO is most critical, which is where our discussion is concentrated. In an organization where a CIO has not been appointed, the CEO or another designated senior officer is expected to step in and take on the CIO role and responsibilities.

V. Senior Executives in Healthcare Services Organizations

Among the highest-ranking officers appointed in a healthcare services organization is the president and chief executive officer (CEO). This individual is largely responsible for articulating the organizational vision and mission, specifying the core competencies of the organization, and delineating its strategic plan and directions typically with the aid of an appointed high-level board of governors. It is also often the case that this individual is elected as the chairman of the board.

The CEO is also expected to appoint and oversee the meetings involving all other senior executives of the organization. These senior executives may include a chief financial officer (CFO); a chief operations officer (COO); a chief marketing officer (CMO); and other IT-related strategic appointments such as a chief information officer (CIO), a chief technology officer (CTO), a chief security officer (CSO), a chief privacy officer (CPO), and a chief knowledge officer (CKO). For small businesses and start-ups, the CEO may be the only person who takes on the roles and responsibilities of all these different executive functions. In healthcare organizations, a chief medical officer (CMO) is also appointed. Table 2.1 provides brief definitions of the different roles and responsibilities of these various executive officers.

Table 2.1   Executive Roles and Responsibilities for Healthcare Services Organizations

Executive Designation	Executive Role and Responsibilities for Health Services Organizations
Chief executive officer (CEO)	Articulates corporate vision, mission, and strategy; chairs senior executive meetings and conducts performance evaluation of top management personnel; oversees corporate growth and development; and ensures the realization of strategic business goals and objectives over time.
Chief financial officer (CFO)	Oversees the financing function, budgeting, and funding of the health services organization's operating programs and services, including advising the CEO and other senior executives on strategic capital investment decisions, capital expansion projects, market competition, and organizational revenue-generation strategies.
Chief operations officer (COO)	Oversees the daily healthcare services delivery operations, business processes, policies, and procedures of the health services organization's care delivery, including advising the CEO and other senior executives on strategic business process reengineering; human resources development and productivity improvement projects; operational and clinical efficiency and effectiveness enhancement projects; scheduling, facility, and inventory management; logistics; and changes in daily organizational production functions.
Chief marketing officer (CMO)	Oversees the marketing and promotion operations, business processes, policies, and procedures of marketing and promoting the health services organization's care delivery, including advising the CEO and other senior executives on strategic marketing opportunities, purchasing and external relations projects, customer relation and satisfaction ratings, and changes in daily organizational marketing functions.
Chief medical officer (CMO)	Oversees the decisions and operations of physicians and other clinical personnel providing services within the context of a health services organization.
Chief information officer (CIO)	Oversees all HMIS applications and technology procurement, acceptance, and adoption practices throughout the healthcare services organization; responsible for the alignment of corporate and HMIS strategic goals and objectives, including use of IT to improve administrative efficiencies and clinical productivity and effectiveness.
Chief technology officer (CTO)	Oversees the throughput, accuracy, speed, availability, and reliability of an organization's HMIS; improving the efficiency of IT systems; and the appropriate implementation of hardware, software, communication, and network technology solutions.
Chief security officer (CSO)	Oversees the security and backup of HMIS applications and developing strategies, including safeguarding HMIS technology applications against attacks from hackers and viruses.
Chief privacy officer (CPO)	Oversees the ethical and legal dimensions of organization information use and releases; sets policies, standards, and procedures for privacy and confidentiality of health information release in compliance with HIPAA rules and standards.
Chief knowledge officer (CKO)	Oversees the gathering, maintenance, and dissemination of the health organization's knowledge; designs the organizational programs and systems to ease the reuse of knowledge among organizational employees, with the aim of creating a knowledge-enabled organization.

In this discussion, our focus is on the overall roles and responsibilities of the CIO for a health services organization because these functional duties are representative of the key duties to be performed by a single individual or a combination of senior officers who are asked to take charge of the procurement, development, use, and servicing of health management information systems within the organization. As we know, when a company does not have a CIO or any other senior officer appointed to be in charge of HMIS, it would be included as part of the role and responsibilities of the CEO. In this instance, the CEO in the healthcare services organization would be responsible for aligning the HMIS mission and goals with the enterprisewide mission and goals.

Before spelling out the specific roles and responsibilities for the CIO with respect to HMIS strategic planning and service management, it is critical to note that most senior executives share some important functions and should have a number of key traits in order to successfully carry out their share of duties. These important characteristics include being (1) a trustworthy leader, (2) an inspirational manager and motivator of others, and (3) an effective communicator.

A Trustworthy Leader

Regardless of the senior executive appointments, trustworthiness is an essential trait of effective leadership. Because "trust" is the essence of leadership effectiveness, extraordinary leaders must have the ability to exude trust from their direct reports and corresponding followers. As leaders, senior executives should be able to command the highest respect from their subordinates. In other words, for this trustworthiness to be sustained, it cannot simply be one-sided. The development of a mutual trust and respect over time between the superior and his or her direct reports is key to building a lasting and successful working relationship. This is true for a CEO, CKO, CTO, CSO, or any other executive officer (such as a CIO asked to take charge of HMIS).

Closely related to trustworthiness and respect is the concept that leaders should not upset their followers with any unannounced surprises—which requires that they stick to their principles, keeping precisely to what they have articulated or promised, with a clear and open attitude about how and why certain things are or are not being executed. Effective leadership can then result naturally in having the highest trust and respect from others. For a CIO, this means being consistent in everything that he or she does, showing good judgment on equality and equity issues, and providing equal opportunities for the advancement of subordinates.

At times, some employees may become frustrated because there is more work to be completed than there are people assigned to the task—due, perhaps, to budgetary constraints, regulatory changes, and/or economic downturns. This frustration may result in employees having difficulty understanding where they should focus their time. It is the job of an effective CIO, then, to prioritize tasks for the employees: framing major issues, simplifying complex assignments, and spelling out what is the most to the least important. By eliminating the unnecessary distractions to employees and focusing on what should be the central issue, the employees will be less frustrated with their work. Not only will they become more satisfied, but they will also be more creative and productive in achieving the key goals set for them by the CIO.

An Inspirational Manager and Motivator of Others

As a manager, the CIO wants to ascertain that all HMIS projects are delivered on time and within budget. This requires the CIO to provide in-depth inspiration and self-motivation as well as to be a motivator of others. *Motivation* is the art of inspiring others, giving them a sense of confidence and/or the desire to accomplish certain goals. Because it is an "art" form, motivation requires that the CIO have special skills and elevated expertise before he or she can effectively manage and inspire others.

How, then, is the CIO able to effectively motivate others? Among the first critical steps is effective communication, which is discussed more fully later. Here, rather than making generalizations, effective managers should be as specific as possible when detailing the goals and objectives for their employees. A follow-up point is that when goals are set, the employees must be sold on the feasibility of achieving those goals, and how best to reach them. Once the employees are clear about what is expected of them and realize how the goals may be achieved, they can then be inspired to do so.

Another characteristic of an effective manager and motivator of others is that not only is the CIO able to position specific individuals who are capable of accomplishing the different tasks in the appropriate spaces throughout the organization, but when all tasks are fully accounted for as a whole, the CIO can expect his or her subordinates to have reached key goals of the organization at an even higher level. In addition, it is the job of the CIO to support his or her subordinates to become skilled and ever ready to complete the most challenging tasks at hand. Above all, instituting a collaborative spirit with a strong sense of team belonging and task information sharing among subordinates is critical to success when faced with executing any complex HMIS-related project goals.

Another very important step in motivating others is measurement; that is, for subordinates to remain motivated, not only must they have a clear grasp of their assignments, but they must also be clearly informed on how they are performing at any given time. Providing constructive feedback as opposed to micro-managing and unnecessary criticisms is therefore the key to successful goal attainment among employees. Conversely, employees often need to be encouraged and recognized for their achievements, which would give them a sense of being valued while they seek to improve further. Without individualized recognition, the employees are not motivated to do their best—to work past their potentials and to reach out for the top or to perform to the best of their abilities.

An Effective Communicator

Effective communication is essential for forming all kinds of work relationships. It is especially important for building strong social networks among key stakeholders, whether it is to be executed through e-mail, one-on-one meetings, bulletin boards, Weblogs (or blogs), or other more formal means of communication. Communication is, in fact, the core of effective management. Without it, chaos and dissatisfaction can emerge and evolve over time.

Clearly, one-sided communication is ineffective, which means that it is essential for a CIO to learn to "listen." What is the difference between just "speaking" and "speaking and listening" to others? To ensure that subordinates understand what is being communicated, it is critical for the CIO to remain open and "listen" to his or her subordinates. Listening requires patience. It is having eye contact with others; spending time to acknowledge what others have articulated with appropriate gestures; and being able to provide feedback, whenever necessary, by rephrasing what others may have articulated to achieve clarity of thoughts. This will then begin to build a good rapport between the conversing parties. Listening also allows the CIO to relate the concerns of the subordinates to those key points he or she wishes to communicate to them.

As well, effective communicators are media-sensitive. Understanding the media used in the communication is important because different types of information may be received under each setting. For example, certain means of communication, such as television and radio broadcasting or even a newspaper press release, may be appropriate for specific or more formal messages to be conveyed, whereas other means such as e-mail and telephone communications are useful for informal, humorous, and/or lighthearted exchanges.

Moreover, having specific knowledge about your audience or those to whom you will be communicating is critical in effective communications because every audience is different with different needs to be satisfied. Among senior-level colleagues, for example, the CIO must advocate and articulate the HMIS vision and strategy through developing and maintaining cohesive executive relationships. He or she has to communicate the same message, but in a very different way, to his or her direct reports internally and/or to the customers and third parties externally.

VI. Specific CIO Role and Responsibilities

Broadly speaking, the CIO role is to provide strategic HMIS vision and leadership for integrating IT initiatives in a healthcare services organization. As most healthcare services organizations are increasingly dependent on IT to improve on service quality, enhance efficiencies, and productivity, as well as to reduce human errors, a CIO is expected to work intelligently in a growing political environment.

Today, the CIO job has become increasingly stressful, more business oriented, and less hands-on. For example, he or she directs the planning and implementation of enterprisewide HMIS in order to improve health information exchanges within the organization and enhance overall cost-effectiveness, operational efficiencies, and healthcare services delivery quality. This individual is clearly responsible for all aspects of the organization's HMIS functions and applications. In addition, most CIO responsibilities now have expanded beyond the traditional role to include concerns about enhancing "customer satisfaction" and being "customer-centric."[7]

The formal education and on-the-job training for a CIO can differ significantly, but having a university degree in a related field such as industrial engineering, computer science, and/or business administration is a very good start. A CIO must be able to execute strategic as well as tactical HMIS planning effectively. He or she must have knowledge and experience in managing and directing increasingly sophisticated HMIS operations, and possess acumen in routine business operations, periodic performance evaluation activities, and strategy and human resource management. The CIO is expected to demonstrate the ability to apply HMIS concepts in real-world business problem-solving situations. He or she is also largely responsible for negotiating, outsourcing, and/or managing vendor contracts on HMIS products, services, and other related projects (such as ensuring the compliance of the health organizational information systems with HIPAA rules and standards).

Overall, the key role of a CIO is the need to develop and preserve tight integration between HMIS decisions and corporate business goals. The CIO must have superior understanding of both the organization's and HMIS departmental goals and objectives so as to align these goals and objectives seamlessly. This single set of responsibility calls upon every CIO's political, negotiation, and project management skills.

In response to an increasingly hyper-competitive HMIS marketplace, the CIO of a healthcare services organization today has to learn to focus on external relations such as customer satisfaction concerns, HMIS security issues, technology acceptance and evaluation ratings, budgeting, staffing, outsourcing, hosting, and return on investment (ROI) analysis. With advancing technology and a more computer-literate U.S. population, the role of a CIO will continue to evolve over the next several years; most likely, the future CIO will be expected to act as a change agent and as a business change leader. The traditional HMIS functions will move from internal-focused tactical operations to more global-oriented strategic functions. For example, if an HMO decides to branch out to a different country such as Mexico, then the HMIS department must necessarily support the Mexican operations. Indeed, globalization and advancing technology are "flattening" the competition among multi-provider organizations in the healthcare services industry and are breaking down traditional barriers to business, which will impact significantly on the evolving role of the CIO.

Ultimately, CIOs must combine strong technological and business skills with leadership, persuasion, and communication skills to be successful at their jobs. Over the years, chief information officers have helped many different companies to succeed as well as fail. Lac Van Tran, former CIO at Children's Hospital Boston, has now relocated to join Houston-based Methodist Health Care System. His new role and responsibilities as senior vice president and CIO at Methodist Health Care System will be to boost e-health development, solicit and establish business partnerships, and promote standardization and common practices.[8] Danny Shaw, the first chief knowledge officer at Children's Hospital Boston, for example, has helped integrate information from diverse sources and systems to enable analysis of both the hospital's administrative and clinical operations.[9] Beginning with a series of small HMIS integration efforts, Shaw quickly demonstrated value, which eventually led to increased operational efficiencies, clinical effectiveness, and improved quality of the hospital's care delivery systems. Building on past successes, Shaw was able to create a knowledge-enabled organization out of Children's Hospital Boston. The CEO/CIO of Green Valley Hospital, discussed in one of the cases presented in the previous edition of this text, failed the hospital miserably by relying on personal friendships to decide vendor outsourcing of the hospital's HMIS services. Thus, if a healthcare services organization does not have a good strategy or a good CIO, it can be devastating for the organization. Even successful businesses can fall behind if there is lack of leadership to guide IT development for the organizations.

VII. Conclusion

Management students should pay particular attention to the role and responsibilities of senior healthcare executives if they want to follow in their footsteps. This is why such a topic has been placed near the beginning of this text. Senior health executives must not only have a strong vision and an awareness of different types of strategies, they must also be able and ready to execute such strategies to ensure that any obstacles encountered while achieving the ultimate organizational vision and mission can be wisely eradicated. This is one difficult challenge for many budding executives to overcome.

Moreover, real-world practices are not easily replicated and cannot be learned by merely reading published theories or cases in textbooks. Successful practices have to be learned on the job, hands-on, and must be orchestrated in a variety of social settings. Hence, the use of the word *inspiration* in this chapter does a great justice to the idea. It is vital that senior managers are "inspirational" and "on fire," doing what the employees are not able to "articulate" clearly for themselves; these executive leaders must be the "mouthpiece" of the organization in crafting the organization's future visions, strategic directions, and strategic thinking. They must meet and talk with everyone who is a part of the organization, both at the top and on the front line. It is the inspiration from senior executives that will ultimately make a difference in transforming the organization. For the CIO, this inspiration has to be transcribed into words, articulated, and produced as an active HMIS plan, in alignment with the overall corporate plan. The corporate plan must then be rolled out into actions, thereby subsequently realizing the key goals and objectives that have been envisioned.

An effective leader and manager must also possess several specific characteristics, each of which significantly affects the performance of subordinates. The abilities to communicate effectively, to motivate others, and to lead followers are all essential for being a good leader. By earning the trust and respect of their employees, these senior executives help and allow their subordinates to work to the best of their abilities. This not only generates personal success for the employees but, ultimately, for the organization. Another essential point is the importance of continuing to "sharpen the saw" when it comes to effective management skills.[10] We have to be willing to learn from our own mistakes and understand that learning is a part of the total process of becoming an effective manager. It is not possible to always get things right the first time; thus, good managers learn from their own mistakes, turning those mistakes to their advantage at the earliest points of opportunity.

Finally, one of the most important steps that an effective CEO/CIO should take is seeking feedback from his or her direct reports. Using such feedback to turn the CEO/CIO's noted weaknesses into additional strengths makes the CEO/CIO that much more effective. In other words, being an effective leader is a continuous process. By possessing and continuing to sharpen those effective management skills, the CEO/CIO can positively affect the morale of the organization's employees. It also naturally enlarges the CEO/CIO's circle of influence, and the less senior managers can then be inspired to follow through with the outstanding model exemplified by the senior management team. Effective management inspires everyone from your employees (who will manage successfully in the future) to other managers (who will immediately manage more effectively). By effectively managing people, the CEO/CIO is ensuring the success of his or her subordinates, which will ultimately translate into the organization's success.

In summary, senior executives play critical roles in organizational success. The overall performance standard of a healthcare services organization, in particular depends not only on the quality and work productivity of its employees, but also on the training, quality, and active participation of the administrative and professional staff in supporting the services of the organization. It also depends on the extent to which IT support has empowered and enabled these various individuals to perform as productively as possible. The sharing of a technology vision among top management team members, professional staff members, and employees within the organization is also critical in determining the success of the HMIS leadership. The culture of a healthcare services organization can transform because of changes in HMIS implementation, as well as the extent to which employees are accepting the HMIS innovation and working collaboratively with each other, and with the organization's customers. In healthcare services organizations, these customers are those patients who are helping the organizations generate much-needed revenues. Under the supervision of a proactive, productive, and politically astute CEO/CIO, the health organizational HMIS support and services can grow and expand effectively and quickly, leading to a transformed organization and the envy of all its competitors.

Notes

1. MSNBC. (2006). "Tired of Waiting for the Doctor? You're Not Alone." Retrieved March 18, 2008, from http://www.msnbc.msn.com/id/15487676/.
2. David Naranjo-Gil and Frank Hartmann, "How CEOs Use Management Information Systems for Strategy Implementation in Hospitals," *Health Policy* 81 (2007): 29–41.
3. Robert H. Waterman, Jr., "The Seven Elements of Strategic Fit," *Journal of Business Strategy* 2, no. 3 (Winter 1982): 69–73.
4. Peter M. Ginter, Linda M. Swayne, and W. Jack Duncan, *Strategic Management of Health Care Organizations*, 2nd ed. (Malden, MA: Blackwell Publishers, 1998).
5. David Burda, "Allegheny: A Tertiary Titan with All the Right Moves," *Modern Healthcare*, February 12, 1990: 50–58.
6. http://www.wpahs.org/agh/about/index.html, accessed June 28, 2008.
7. Cindy Waxer, "The 2008 State of the CIO: The Imperative to Be Customer-Centric IT Leaders." Retrieved June 28, 2008, from www.cio.com.
8. Retrieved June 28, 2008, from www.cio.com.
9. Ibid.
10. Stephen R. Covey, *The 7 Habits of Highly Effective People*. (New York: Free Press, 1989).

Additional Readings

Sam Geist, "Are You a Boss or a Leader?" *Super Vision* 67 (January 2006).
Paul Glen, "Developing the Managerial Mind," *Computer World* 40 (January 9, 2006).
Stephen R. Robbins, *The Truth About Managing People . . . And Nothing But the Truth*. (Upper Saddle River, NJ: Prentice Hall, 2003).
Jack Welch and Suzy Welch, "The Leadership Mindset," *BusinessWeek*, January 30, 2006.

Chapter Questions

2–1. Imagine you came into a company without an organizational IT strategy. Describe in detail how you would develop an IT strategy. Some questions to consider are:
   a. Who would be involved in the strategy meeting?
   b. How would you involve participants in developing a strategy? What questions would you ask?
   c. How would you get participants to adopt your shared vision?

2–2. In your own words, what are the role and responsibilities of a CIO? What would be the difference between the role and responsibilities of a CEO versus a CIO in a healthcare services organization if both of these executives were appointed? Who would the CEO pick to be the most appropriate senior executive responsible for HMIS in the absence of a CIO? Why?

2–3. What are the three most important traits of a CIO? On a scale from 1 to 10, rank yourself in each of these categories. For each trait, give an example of a time that you did and did not demonstrate this trait effectively. How might you improve your score in each category?

2–4. How does an executive such as a CIO become an effective leader? What will be the greatest challenges in a healthcare services organizational context?

Mini-Case: Predicting Future HMIS Trends by Chief Information Officers

Quammen Group, an Orlando, Florida–based consulting firm, co-sponsored the *Health Data Management* 2008 CIO Survey and found CIO and HMIS executives to be optimistic on many aspects of future HMIS growth, including real-time claims adjudication and clinical decision support.

When asked, "How do you expect your organization's total IT budget to change in your next fiscal year?", 37 percent rated it to grow between 5 and 10 percent, 23 percent felt it would grow less than 5 percent, 20 percent expected it to exceed 11 percent or more, 13 percent did not expect a change, and only 4 percent claimed there would be a decline—leaving 2 percent for all other rating categories. More generally, the survey found that most healthcare services organizations expect this growth to be fueled by greater information access needs for clinicians, especially in the form of electronic and personal health records (EHR).

In short, most chief executive officers and other IT executives indicated that the top priority for the coming year for healthcare services organizations is implementing EHR. The full survey results are given at http://www.healthdatamanagement.com/CIO_Survey/.

Mini-Case Questions

1. Why do you think a CIO survey is important for the HMIS industry?
2. Predict what type of hardware investments would be considered key to HMIS future. Then check out the full survey results, and compare your prediction to the actual results.
3. Why do you think the results showed investment in EHR to be a top priority for CIOs in the coming year?

Personal Digital Assistants Enhance Data Collection Efficiency during a Study of Waiting Times in an Emergency Department

N. Elkum, W. Greer, and A. Al-Madouj

ABSTRACT

Objectives

To explore the suitability of the personal digital assistant (PDA) as the primary vehicle for data collection within the context of a clinical research study and to quantify the improvement in performance compared with a conventional paper-based approach.

Methods

This investigation was an adjunct to a study of waiting times in the emergency department (ED) of a large, tertiary-care hospital. Medical charts were randomly selected for those patients who had been recently triaged in the ED. In addition to patient identification and demography, five principal variables were collected: day of arrival, registration time, triage level, room assignment time, and MD time (time physician spent with the patient). A database application was developed for the PDA. When the PDA was subsequently connected to a desktop computer, the data were automatically synchronized with the PC-based Access database. The data for each patient were captured in two different ways: using the PDA and using the traditional paper-based approach. For each method, the data-collection time was recorded for each patient.

Results

Using the traditional paper-based approach, the average time per patient for data capture was 226 seconds, whereas using the PDA, average time was significantly reduced to only 78 seconds.

Conclusions

The PDA is a superior alternative to traditional methods for data collection in simple clinical research studies. PDAs are more convenient and diminish overall data-collection time by 60 to 70 percent, thereby significantly reducing the cost of clinical research.

Introduction

Data collection is the spine of most medical research studies. The ideal data-collection methodology should be inexpensive, easy to use, and applicable to widely varying types of studies. Paper forms have traditionally been used to record these types of data. However, these forms can lead to a number of different errors, such as ineligible scripts, undefined codes, and illegal or inappropriate dates. It can also make it difficult to obtain complete answers to questions within the time allocated for the patient interview or chart review. Furthermore, data collected in this way are often subsequently entered into a computer database, which can introduce additional sources of error. Problems associated with the paper-based method can be minimized by improving the quality of the training given to data-entry personnel and by performing double data entry, but this incurs a larger cost to the research project.

Electronic methods of data capture have been available for many years. Mark sense technology, for example, uses "marks" (usually shaded boxes) at predefined locations on specially prepared sheets of paper to store information.[1] This approach is very successful when the data can be easily categorized into a small number of categories (such as multiple-choice examination questions) but becomes unwieldy for continuous data or when a large number of categories are involved. A more recent electronic alternative is to use optical character recognition (OCR) technology to "read" data directly from paper-based questionnaires and automatically transform the contents into electronic form.[2]

Although OCR software can achieve excellent results when the data have been typed using predefined fonts, the fidelity of the recognition process leaves much to be desired when handwritten text is involved and would not normally be considered for clinical research studies. In any case, any electronic scanning approach requires the raw data to be stored on loose (and losable) sheets of paper; it therefore offers no advantage with respect to missing pages, data storage space, or confidentiality issues. The extra cost of the technology can also be prohibitive.

One relatively recent electronic alternative is the personal digital assistant. Personal digital assistants (PDAs) are already being used throughout clinical medicine to deliver information at the point of care in such diverse areas as anesthesia,[3] surgery,[4] pediatrics,[5] general practice,[6] obstetrics,[7] evidence-based medicine,[8] and public health.[9] They are also being used to collect patient information and improve clinical records for administrative functions such as electronic prescribing,[10] coding and tracking,[11] and medical education.[12] This research brief explores the suitability of the PDA for the collection of clinical research data.

King Faisal Specialist Hospital and Research Centre (KFSHRC) maintains many disease registries, such as the National Cancer Registry[13] and the Congenital Heart Defects Registry,[14] which routinely require detailed patient interviews and structured data abstraction from medical charts. There are also a large number of scientists and clinicians who regularly conduct research projects involving the collection of large amounts of data.

The cost of recording, entering, and cleaning these data consumes a significant part of the budget of every research project. A systematic approach to data capture, which would reduce this cost and improve the accuracy of the collected data, would therefore be welcomed by our research community.

To this end, we conducted a study to investigate the advantages and disadvantages of using a PDA during a typical clinical research study. This was developed as an adjunct to a pilot study of the distribution of waiting times experienced by patients at our emergency department (ED). This is a key entry point to the healthcare system at our institution, and having patients wait for excessive periods of time prior to treatment may negatively color their perception of the care provided by KFSHRC. The specific objective of this study was to compare the data-collection efficiency of the PDA-based method with the more traditional approach comprising standard paper forms and subsequent computer data entry. To our knowledge, this was the first research study at this hospital to be conducted using a PDA-based data-entry system.

Methods

Medical charts were randomly selected for those patients who had been recently triaged in the ED during the period of the study. In addition to patient identification and demography, five principal variables were collected: day of arrival, registration time, triage level, room assignment time, and MD time. The triage nurse and the evaluating physician(s) recorded the various times required by the study in the charts.

A trained research assistant captured the data for each patient in two different ways: (1) entering data directly into a PDA database and (2) manually recording data on case report forms and subsequently typing these data into a PC-based Microsoft Access database. These methods were applied "one-after-the-other," so that each patient's data were recorded twice. To avoid observer bias, the order of the methods was randomly changed between patients. For a given patient the same research assistant was responsible for applying both methods. For each method, the time spent in collecting data for every chart was also recorded. A Palm Pilot (Compaq Inc., Houston, Texas) was selected as the PDA for this study. The PDA database application was developed using the Data-on-the-Run database system (Biomobility Inc.). This permits databases to be developed directly on the PDA and is designed to integrate seamlessly with Microsoft Access on the PC; when the PDA was connected to a PC, the databases were automatically synchronized. We further replicated the database on an SQL server so that multiple users via the hospital's intranet could access it.

The difference in the time taken for data capture between the two methods was assessed using the paired t-test within the SPSS statistics package (SPPS Inc.). This study was approved by the Research Advisory Council (Institutional Review Board) of our hospital.

Results

During the period of the study, charts were randomly selected from the medical records for those patients who were triaged in our emergency department. Using the traditional method, the average time for data capture was 226 seconds, whereas using the PDA approach, the average time was significantly reduced to only 78 seconds ($p < 0.0001$); this difference is illustrated in Figure RB1.1.

Discussion

The application of PDAs within clinical research studies can lead to substantial cost savings by directly reducing the duration of the data-capture period. Based on our results (and depending on the specific study design) a PDA-based approach can reduce the duration of the data-capture phase by as much as 60 to 70 percent in comparison with paper-based alternatives.

Using a PDA may also improve the quality of the data because it eliminates the need for a paper intermediary between the recording of the data from the patient's interview or medical chart and the final entry of these data into a database. Further gains in usability and efficiency (Table RB1.1) can also be found through the easy data-storage and downloading capabilities in

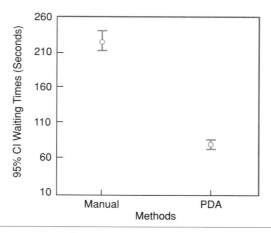

FIGURE RB1.1   Comparison of Mean Waiting Times (with Their 95% CIs) between the Two Different Methods Used in the Study.

Table RB1.1   Comparison of Data Collection Methodologies

	Paper Forms	Mark Sense Forms	Optical Character Recognition	PDA Forms
No manual data-entry cost	–	+	+	+
Multicenter trials: No shipping/faxing	–	–	–	+
Tracks response times	–	–	–	+
Easily handles complex skip patterns	–	–	–	+
Prevents incorrect responses	–	–	–	+
Images, videos easily incorporated	–	–	–	+
Speed of completion	–	–	–	+
No computer skills required	+	+	+	–
Automatic desktop synchronization	–	–	–	+

combination with fast data processing; these enable the researcher to more easily perform analyses while the study is in progress. Furthermore, the ability of the PDA to create electronic documents eliminates printing, binding, and shipping costs and provides a reduction in storage space at research locations.

The choice of a database system is crucial to the effectiveness of the PDA in the clinical research context. Using the data-on-the-run package, we were guaranteed a user-friendly, networked environment, which provided frequent data backups and which could make use of the SQL databases on our Windows servers.

Increasing responsibilities and other demands on researchers' time necessitate more and more reliance on technology. The personal data assistant provides an effective answer to the problem of efficiently capturing, storing, and retrieving large volumes of medical research information within reduced timescales. PDAs offer a superior alternative to traditional methods for data collection in clinical research studies.

Notes

1. *IBM Reference Manual*, "Reproducing Punches," pp. 513, 514, October 1959.
2. H. F. Schantz, *The History of OCR, Optical Character Recognition* (Manchester Center, VT: Recognition Technologies Users Association, 1982).
3. Q. Fu, Z. Xue, and G. Klein, "Using Mobile Information Technology to Build a Database for Anesthesia Quality Control and to Provide Clinical Guidelines," *Studies in Health Technology and Informatics* 95 (2003): 629–634.
4. T. V. McCaffrey, "Using Hand-Held Computing Devices in the Practice of Otolaryngology-Head and Neck Surgery," *Current Opinion in Otolaryngology & Head and Neck Surgery* 11 (2003): 156–159.
5. C. G. Weigle, B. P. Markovitz, and S. Pon, "The Internet, the Electronic Medical Record, the Pediatric Intensive Care Unit, and Everything," *Critical Care Medicine* 29, no. 8 (2001): N166–N176.

6. M. Greiver, "Evidence-Based Medicine in the Palm of your Hand," *CMAJ: Canadian Medical Association Journal* 164, no. 2 (2001): 250.

7. S. Joy and G. Benrubi, "Personal Digital Assistant Use in Florida Obstetrics and Gynecology Residency Programs," *The Southern Medicine Journal* 97, no. 5 (2004): 430–433.

8. G. M. Leung, J. M. Johnston, and K. Y. Tin, "Randomised Controlled Trial of Clinical Decision Support Tools to Improve Learning of Evidence Based Medicine in Medical Students," *British Medical Journal* 327, no. 7423 (2003): 1090.

9. I. Abubakar, C. J. Williams, and M. McEvoy, "Development and Evaluation of a Hand Held Computer Based On-Call Pack for Health Protection Out of Hours Duty: A Pilot Study," *BMC Public Health* 5, no. 1 (2005): 35.

10. B. C. Grasso, R. Genest, K. Yung, and C. Arnold, "Reducing Errors in Discharge Medication Lists by Using Personal Digital Assistants," *Psychiatric Services* 53, no. 10 (2002): 1325–1326.

11. J. Luo, "Portable Computing in Psychiatry," *Canadian Journal of Psychiatry* 49, no. 1 (2004): 24–30.

12. S. Fischer, S. E. Lapinsky, J. Weshler, et al., "Surgical Procedure Logging with Use of a Hand-Held Computer," *Canadian Journal of Surgery* 45, no. 5 (2002): 345–350.

13. Registry NC, *Cancer Incidence Report Saudi Arabia 2001* (Riyadh, Saudia Arabia: Ministry of Health, 2005).

14. King Faisal Specialist Hospital and Research Centre, *Congenital Heart Defects Registry: Annual Report* (Riyadh, Saudi Arabia: Ministry of Health, 2005).

Online Health Information Seeking:
Access and Digital Equity Considerations

Fay Cobb Payton and Joseph Tan

Editor's Note: Readers of this health management information systems text should be aware of the growing force that the Internet has exerted on the masses, in particular, how it affects health consumers in term of their health information searches. Apparently, the Internet is beginning to change the way medicine is going to be practiced as more and more computer-literate health consumers, armed with the latest research information on their particular illnesses, shop around for the best doctors. This chapter prepares the readers to predict the next major HMIS evolution. Legacy systems used in healthcare services organizations for isolated routine information processing will soon become obsolete given the rapid advances in HMIS applications and technologies (Part II), Similarly, how we perform HMIS planning and management (Part III) will have to change to accommodate new policy, governance, and regulatory changes as well as globalization (Part IV). While bringing a close to Part I, the knowledge acquired in Chapter 3 is intended to stimulate us to explore more fully the other parts of the text.

CHAPTER OUTLINE

Scenario: *A New RHIO in DC*

Scenario: A New RHIO in DC[1]

With $11,000,000 of seed funding from the District of Columbia's government, the District of Columbia Primary Care Association (DCPCA) has launched a new regional health information organization (RHIO) in the nation's capital to improve healthcare services delivery for the city's poor and underserved population.

RHIO aims to reform health management information systems (HMIS) in the coming decade by deploying integrated electronic medical records (EMR) solutions among six community-based health centers in the District to better serve DC's poor and uninsured populations. It is envisioned that the EMR will link these centers to major DC hospitals such as the Washington Health Center and Georgetown University Hospital. Although there is a high degree of difficulty for cash-strapped health centers to adopt this type of technology, the six organizations that decided to jump on board felt that the need for an integrated EMR justified the added stress of additional staff and resources.

Sharon Baskerville, DCPCA's CEO, notes that the proposed RHIO differs from past isolated and stove-piped systems oriented toward low-income populations because with "siloed care, problems go unidentified. Our way of addressing the problem is different from any approach . . . (in that) . . . the safety net group is leading the pack. We're going to try to take lessons from . . . (past failed RHIO efforts) . . . and focus our energy on things like governance and a long-term business plan for sustainability. . . . I do hope that this becomes a model, not just for communities but for payers and the government. It needs to be clear that there must be incentives and large-scale programs that enable these kinds of providers to be involved."

Apparently, the newly proposed DC RHIO will network the district's community health centers. Its EMR vendor, eClinicalWorks, will customize the system to the needs and special requirements of these centers. Baskerville noted that the mental health module for eClinicalWorks did not provide sufficient capacity to account for the large volume of patients. As a result, the company crafted an expanded version of the software. The current plan is to have EMR solutions installed at all six centers with at least three functional in 2008. The enhanced version of eClinicalWorks will first be piloted with the local hospitals. DCPCA is hopeful that robust and continuing support from diverse sources will help them avoid many of the same technological and economic threats that have overwhelmed past RHIO efforts.

Could the RHIO initiative be expanded to help other healthcare consumers, aside from focusing on the underserved and underinsured? What is the significance of improving health information accessibility, availability, and connectivity? How can initiatives such as RHIO be linked to Internet use among consumers searching for health information?

I. Introduction

Undoubtedly, the Internet has become a significant and powerful mechanism in the dissemination of health information. Over the years, researchers as well as healthcare educators have employed Web-based courseware to advise select populations on every conceivable subject in the medical field, including identifying symptoms of common illnesses, advising on key rehabilitative procedures to promote self-care, and sharing practical strategies about preventive medical or health promotional activities (such as healthy lifestyle alternatives and wellness maintenance).

Online health information seeking should be of concern for health administrators for myriad reasons. The management and dissemination of health information via the Internet engages the faster diffusion of medical findings, improves consumer empowerment, reduces social isolation often associated with stigmatizing medical conditions, improves patient–physician interactions, and provides efficiencies in the health insurance and registration processes, just to name a few.[2] Consequently, these outcomes affect the demand for medical services, resource utilization, and, ultimately, costs.

Not surprisingly, online extraction of relevant health information by both experts and laypersons have proliferated due to advances in Web-based interface technology; improved computing literacy; and greater availability, affordability, and accessibility of the Internet and other information and communications technologies (ICT). It is further anticipated that the growing community of Internet users will continue to expand globally in the coming years, especially for rapidly developing countries and emerging markets such as Brazil, Tanzania, Russia, India, and China. More users can now easily access the Internet via smart phones as well as other cellular and wireless devices while these hand-held technologies are increasingly disseminating health information to health consumers. For example, in South Africa, the Cell-Life project connects HIV/AIDS patients with the public health system to monitor treatment plans, drug therapy and interactions, and dietary compliance. According to the 2007 African Global Innovation Report, "In five years, the service has grown from one site with 200 patients to 11 sites with more than 15,000 patients . . . with improved health, there is greater opportunity for improved wealth and quality of life."[3(p. 29)]

Among the myriad prospective advantages that arise from use of the Internet and other ICT are cost reductions, minimal time and spatial barriers, increased access, rapid diffusion of medical research, improved patient empowerment, reduced social status cues, and improved provisions for peer group support. Participants who are normally reserved during face-to-face interactions now have a medium in which they can freely express their thoughts and desires without fear of public speaking or physically encountering socially challenging moments. Those who are unable or unavailable to participate physically on site may now do so virtually.

Nonetheless, the Internet is not void of particular weaknesses, including fragmentation of health information, continual digital and health inequities among underrepresented populations, lack of data quality in health information, iron-clad security, and inappropriate access to third parties.[4] Oftentimes, it is up to individual Internet users to distinguish whether the information they receive is trustworthy or not. It is also difficult for laypersons to determine the authentication of the experts claiming to post certain information.

Health information seekers, according to the Pew Internet and American Life Project release, are "Internet users who search online for information on health topics" whether they take on the role of consumers, caregivers, or e-patients.[5] Given its ubiquitous nature, the Internet continues to be a key source of health information among health seekers. Specifically, the Pew Internet data indicate that 8 of 10 Internet users, or roughly 113 million adults, have sought health information online. The question is, What type of health information do these Internet users want or need? In 2006, 66 percent of all health seekers searched for information on a specific disease or medical problem for themselves, family members, or friends. Based on this metric, the Pew study committee concluded that health searches have reached parity with common uses of the Net, such as electronic bill paying, blogging, or directory lookups for addresses and telephone numbers.

II. Emotional Support and Empowerment of Health Information Seekers

As Internet use continues to help inform a variety of decisions challenging experts and laypersons, breakthroughs in the application of such Internet use are mounting. One of the most important breakthroughs thus far is the emotional support and empowerment of health information seekers. The Internet and other ICT have granted all such seekers a convenient and easy means of access to available health information and social networks. For instance, patients who are faced with debilitating diseases and chronic ailments are experiencing a new dimension of social networking and support via the Internet.

The Internet has facilitated the use of ICT to educate, guide, and sustain patients with a variety of illnesses. Specifically, for those affected by Alzheimer's disease,[6] smoking addiction,[7] and AIDS,[8] researchers have found that the use of the Internet can further reduce social isolation and increase emotional support. In fact, each of these recently published U.S.-based studies implemented homecare health information networks to meet the needs of patients. The varying needs meant that patients were able to participate in different levels of services: decision support, nurse moderation, e-mail, and discussion boards. These services were found to have empowered participants with information beneficial to the understanding of new developments in the treatment of their diseases, and, more importantly, researchers were able to determine which computer-supported services were most utilized by patients based on their individual medical and emotional concerns.

In the case of Alzheimer's, Payton and Brennan[9] reported that over an 18-month period 30 percent of the caregivers accessed the system more than 100 times while one individual accessed ComputerLink 868 times. Users accessed the ComputerLink functions 3,926 times based on total frequency of use of each system function. Users accessed the bulletin board and read messages 2,095 times (which appears to be the most used service), and this substantial figure was attributed to the social interaction among users as they formed electronic support groups and communities to cope with the challenges associated with caregiving. The question-and-answer utility represented 24 percent of the total frequency of use and clearly points to the critical role of the nurse-moderator, who received private, direct inquiries from caregivers. The decision-making module was the second least accessed (218 times, or 5 percent of the total frequency) system function. The electronic encyclopedia depicted the least used ComputerLink function, with least number of accesses shown for both the self and disease-related services. The authors concluded that these findings were a function of caregivers seeking to communicate with those in similar circumstances or socialization to overcome isolation rather than decision-making assistance concerning care delivery.

With regard to cancer patients, for example, the Internet has proven to be a valuable communication source for patients and their families. Several researchers have argued that computer-mediated communities supporting cancer patients foster emotional support and empowerment,[10] in addition to providing a vehicle by which patients and family members can acquire familiarity with the disease and its stages.[11] As the number of worldwide cancer deaths escalates to 7.6 million people, based on World Health Organization (WHO) data,[12] the role played by computer-mediated communities is seen to be even more critical.

One such online community is CarePages, accessible via www.carepages.com. CarePages is a blossoming social networking site for patients with various ailments. Patients of sponsoring hospitals, as well as their families, can create an account, which provides them with a personal page. On this page are various features, including a blog and comment page. Both the patient and his or her family members can write updates in the blog for friends and caring strangers alike to follow. Visitors create their own accounts and can leave personal comments on the patient's page, whether they are reactions to the blog or simple messages of support. This way, patients can seek emotional support through friends, strangers, or even other patients. A simple tour of the website reaffirms the notion that many patients find this an excellent coping mechanism—and a place to discover hope and understanding.

Again, for breast cancer patients who may have distinct needs for care and coping, several researchers have also found that these patients actively engage in online and interpersonal interactions via support groups and seek information regarding treatment plans and medical progress.[13,14] Interestingly, differences in race, ethnicity, education level, and cultural backgrounds are found to be significant; any one factor, or a combination of them, can alter the prospective psychological benefits of using the Internet, or any other means of communication, for interactions among women with breast cancer.

III. Profiling Health Information Seekers

While Internet use has increased among all demographic groups, access has been found to be greatest among those with higher education and incomes. Moreover, this access is least significant among African Americans and Latinos, who both continue to trail whites and Asian Americans.[15] This phenomenon contributes to the digital divide, or exclusion, and stands to affect education and health quality, equity, accessibility, affordability, and availability.[16–19] According to the National Telecommunications and Information Association,[20] Internet use and online activities have significantly increased between 2001 and 2003. While the primary use of the Internet is e-mail, users tend to engage in myriad online activities. These activities can be clustered into four major areas of interest: communications, entertainment, transactions, and information, as shown in Figure 3.1.

Figure 3.1 indicates that overall, the percentage of users seeking health information grew from 34.1 percent to roughly 41.6 percent between September 2001 and October 2003. This trend is consistent with the increased use of the Internet for seeking other forms of information,

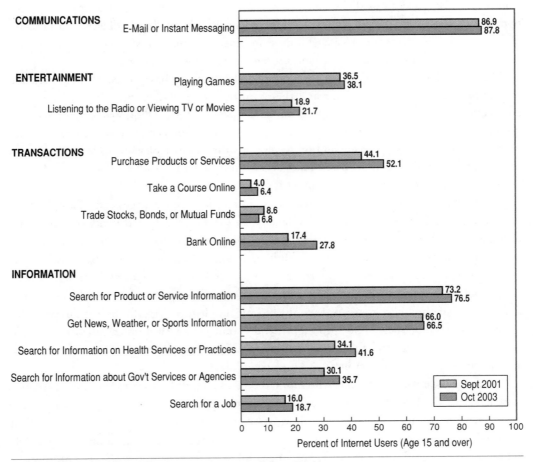

FIGURE 3.1   Online Activities, 2001 and 2003 (Percent of Online Activities for Internet Users Age 15 and Over). *Source:* National Telecommunication and Information Administration (2004).

including extraction of general products and services information, online searches for information on government services and agencies, and Web mining for job-related information.

As stated earlier, the 2006 Pew Internet and American Life Project survey indicated that 8 out of 10 Internet users seek health information online. This statistic is surprisingly high even for America as a developed country. Of those participants surveyed by Pew, 82 percent of the users were women and 75 percent were men. Table 3.1 offers a detailed profiling of the health information seekers as informed by the 2006 Pew survey. Seventy-eight percent of the surveyed sample were between ages 50 and 64, while 71 percent had a high school education or less. Again, these statistics portray a relatively high level of computing literacy among the baby boomers and seniors, most of whom may have significantly fewer opportunities to become educated during these times as compared with children of this generation.

Using the Pew Internet and American Life data from 2006, several key observations can be noted about Internet use for health information seeking (Table 3.2):

- Of the 537 survey participants in the study, 79 percent of Internet users investigated at least 1 of 16 health topics.
- In comparison to 60 percent of the men surveyed, 71 percent of the women participants probed for a specific disease or medical problem.
- Women sought more information related to depression/stress/mental illness and smoking cessation than did men.
- Internet searches on a specific disease or medical condition were significant and comparable among those with some college education and those who have completed college.

Table 3.1   Health Seekers from Pew Internet and American Life Project

Demographic Group	Percent Who Have Looked for Health Information Online
Online women	82%
Online men	77
Internet users ages 18–29	79
Internet users ages 30–49	84
Internet users ages 50–64	78
Internet users ages 65+	68
Internet users with a high school diploma or less	71
Internet users with some college education	80
Internet users with a college degree	89
Internet users with 2–3 years of online experience	62
Internet users with 6+ years of online experience	86
Internet users with a dial-up connection at home	75
Internet users with a broadband connection at home	86

Source: Pew Internet and American Life Project, August 2006 survey (*n* = 1,990).

Margin of error for the entire sample of Internet users is ±3 percent. Margins of error for comparison of subgroups are higher.

Table 3.2 Health Topics Searches from the 2006 Pew Internet and American Life Project

In all, 80 percent of Internet users have looked online for at least 1 of 17 health topics. Certain subgroups reported significantly higher interest in some topics and are marked in bold type. For example, when compared with online men, online women reported significantly more interest in information about specific diseases, certain treatments, diet, and mental health.

Health Topic	All Internet Users (n = 1,990)	Online Women (n = 1,116)	Online Men (n = 874)	Ages 18–29 (n = 333)	Ages 30–49 (n = 751)	Ages 50–64 (n = 579)	Ages 65+ (n = 277)	High School or Less (n = 614)	Some College (n = 510)	College Graduates (n = 853)
Specific disease or medical problem	64%	**69%**	58%	61%	67%	64%	54%	52%	65%	**74%**
Certain medical treatment	51	**54**	47	45	**56**	51	40	41	**51**	62
Diet, nutrition, vitamins	49	**53**	45	45	**55**	19	29	40	52	56
Exercise or fitness	44	46	41	**55**	47	35	24	35	**47**	51
Prescription or over-the-counter drugs	37	39	35	29	42	**40**	30	29	38	45
A particular doctor or hospital	29	31	27	27	**33**	26	18	21	**25**	40
Health insurance	28	27	29	23	**34**	27	12	20	28	37
Alternative treatments or medicines	27	29	25	25	29	29	14	22	**29**	31
Depression, anxiety, stress, or mental health issues	22	**26**	17	25	24	20	7	21	24	22
Environmental health hazards	22	21	22	25	23	22	10	16	**23**	26
Experimental treatments or medicines	18	18	19	18	**18**	18	14	15	**21**	20
Immunizations or vaccinations	16	15	17	**18**	**18**	12	7	13	15	**19**
Dental health information	15	14	15	17	16	12	6	13	14	**16**
Medicare or Medicaid	13	13	13	10	11	**15**	22	12	14	13
Sexual health information	11	11	12	**21**	10	7	2	10	**15**	10
How to quit smoking	9	10	8	**13**	8	9	3	11	10	7
Problems with drugs or alcohol	8	9	8	**14**	6	7	2	8	**10**	7

Source: Pew Internet and American Life Project, August 2006 survey (n = 1,990).

Margin of error for the entire sample of Internet users is ±3 percent. Margins of error for comparison of subgroups are higher. Significant differences between demographic groups are in **bold** type.

Table 3.2 highlights additional significant differences among demographic groups based on the reported data from the 2006 Pew Internet and American Life Project.

IV. Accessing Health Information beyond the Internet

While the Internet has proven to be a means of health information dissemination and a commonly used tool among health seekers, there are populations that are best reached via other communication modalities or that choose not to engage in online use. In a survey of 3,553 Americans, the 2003 Pew Internet and American Life Project[21] identified the profile of Internet users and nonusers.

While issues associated with digital divide, divide inequity, and social exclusion[22,23] have been used to rationalize the resistance among non-Internet users for going online, interesting facts exist to demonstrate the need for targeted strategies. In a survey of 3,553 participants, women are more likely to be nonusers than men by a margin of 8 percent. With regard to race and ethnicity, African Americans comprise 11 percent of the overall U.S. population. Yet 14 percent of non-Internet users surveyed are African American, while the figures for Hispanics remained constant at about 10 percent.

The largest group of nonusers (32 percent) ranged in age from 30 to 49. Interestingly, Internet users did not show a gradual increasing pattern relative to income level, even though this is not true with the pattern shown by nonusers. That is, those with lower incomes were more likely to be nonusers (41 percent); this figure declines to 6 percent at an income level greater than $75,000 per year.

V. Alternative Means of Accessing Health Information

Interestingly enough, alternative means of communication and health information dissemination can capture the diversity of social, economic, ethnic, racial, gender, and educational backgrounds of the healthcare populations in a specific region or community. For instance, the Metamorphosis Project[24] has targeted the Los Angeles Hispanic community to engage in and promote early childhood development from prenatal stages to age 5.[25]

In a survey of 327 Hispanics alongside a series of planned focus group interviews, the researchers determined the top 10 ways the targeted Los Angeles Hispanic community seeks health information. From these data, they also determined the most cited referral sources. The statistics of their findings break down as follows: (1) more than one-third of the Hispanics in the study received their health and medical care information via television, (2) discussions with family/friends via the telephone are pivotal, (3) a smaller sample of about 22 percent consulted with healthcare providers, and (4) radio and print media (newspapers, magazines) should not be ignored. More importantly, Latino men play a pivotal role as influencers in women's lives and should not be ignored. Accordingly, the researchers concluded: "increased education while maintaining control by the men may influence increased support of early detection and medical care of Latina women."[26]

Still others have investigated the relationship between race and use of health information resources. In a random-digit dialed survey of 509 women (341 white, 135 African American, and 33 of other races), Nicholson, Grayson, and Powe[27] investigated the independent effect of race on women's use of health information resources. Print, news, broadcast media, Internet, health organizations, and organized health events were among the sources of information in their study. Women with higher education levels tended to use print health or news media, broadcast media, health policy organizations, and organized events 2.0 to 2.4 times more than less educated women (high school education or less); these findings, however, were not statistically significant. Interestingly, more than 40 percent of white women used the Internet compared to 20 percent of African American women. Whites, however, used health policy and other organizations three times more than African Americans.

VI. Future Directions

The literature demonstrates that implementation of multiple access points to health information is critical. Health administrators must recognize and act upon the unbounded nature of health information seeking among consumers. This action on behalf of the consumers creates greater equity in health dissemination, democratizes the healthcare process, and empowers users. Despite the proliferation of the Internet, administrators should implement multiple communication modalities (i.e., mobile phones, television, print, and radio should not be eliminated), which then provides the opportunity to reach diverse socioeconomic, cultural, and global populations. The profile of the health information seeker/participant in medical studies, particularly longitudinal investigations, has an essential role in the interpretation of health outcomes: reducing health disparities and health dissemination. One communication mode or approach will and does not attract diverse populations to medical studies and clinical trials. Digital equity is pivotal to this notion, along with awareness of culturally competent approaches to healthcare delivery. Social networking among online healthcare support groups is on the rise. While Google Health and Microsoft HealthVault are working to assist patients to electronically share their own medical information, social networking ventures, such as Trusera (invitation only), DailyStrength, PatientsLikeMe, and Caring.com, enable storytelling and blogging among their users. Determinants of success rest with a triad of theory, research, and practice.[28]

Notes

1. Maureen D. C. McKinney, "RHIO Sets Ambitious Plans." Accessed May 27, 2008, from http://www.digitalhcp.com/2008/05/27/dc-rhio-sets-ambitious-plans.html.
2. M. Mureo and R. E. Rice, *The Internet and Health Care: Theory, Research and Practice* (Mahwah, NJ: Lawrence Erlbaum Associates, 2006).
3. *Africa: A Global Innovation Report 2007* (Armonk, NY: IBM, 2007).
4. Ibid.

5. Pew Internet and American Life Project. Online Health Search 2006, p. 1 (2006). Accessed June 10, 2007, from http://www.pewinternet.org/pdfs/PIP_Online_Health_2006.pdf.

6. F. C. Payton and P. F. Brennan, "How a Community Health Information Network Is Really Used," *Communication of the ACM* 42, no. 12 (1999): 85–89.

7. K. Bosworth and D. H. Gustafson, "CHESS: Providing Decision Support for Reducing Health Risk Behavior and Improving Access to Health Services," *Interfaces* 21, 3: 93–104, (May-June 1991).

8. P. F. Brennan, "Use of a Home-Care Computer Network by Persons with AIDS," *International Journal of Technology Assessment in Health Care* 10, no. 2 (1994): 258–272.

9. Payton and Brennan (1999).

10. J. W. Turner, J. A. Grube, and J. Meyers, "Developing an Optimal Match within Online Communities: An Exploration of CMC Support Communities and Traditional Support," *Journal of Communication* 51 (2001): 231–251.

11. S. Ziebland, A. Chapple, C. Dumelow, J. Evans, S. Prinjha, and L. Rozmovitis, "How the Internet Affects Patients' Experience of Cancer: A Qualitative Study," *Briti* (2004).

12. World Health Organization. (2006). Accessed July 2, 2007, from http://www.who.int/media centre/news/releases/2006/pr06/en/.

13. J. Fogel, S. M. Albert, F. Schnabel, B. A. Ditokk, and A. I. Neugut, "Racial/Ethnic Differences and Potential Psychological Benefits in Use of the Internet by Women with Breast Cancer," *Psycho-Oncology* 12 (2003): 107–117.

14. G. A. Barnett and J. M. Hwang, "The Use of the Internet for Health Information and Social Support: A Content Analysis of Online Breast Cancer Discussion Groups." In M. Mureo and R. E. Rice (Eds.), *The Internet and Health Care: Theory, Research and Practice* (Mahwah, NJ: Lawrence Erlbaum, 2006).

15. National Science Board. *Science and Engineering Indicators* (Arlington, VA: National Science Foundation, 2006).

16. C. Zarcadoolas, A. Pleasant, and D. S. Greer, *Advancing Health Literacy: A Framework for Understanding and Action* (San Francisco: Jossey-Bass, 2006).

17. F. C. Payton, "Rethinking the Digital Divide," *Communication of the ACM* 46, no. 6 (2003): 89–91.

18. L. Kvasny and F. C. Payton, "Minorities and Information Technology: Critical Issues and Trends in Digital Divide Research." In M. Khosrow-Pour (Ed.), *Encyclopedia of Information Science and Technology*, 2nd ed. (Hershey, PA: IGI Global Publisher, 2007).

19. Payton (2007).

20. National Telecommunications and Information Administration, "A Nation Online: Entering the Broadband Age" (2004). Accessed June 22, 2007, from http://www.ntia.doc.gov/reports/anol/NationOnlineBroadband04.doc.

21. Pew Internet and American Life Project. "The Ever-Shifting Internet Population: A New Look at Internet Access and the Digital Divide" (2003). Accessed June 10, 2007, from http://www.pewinternet.org/pdfs/PIP_Shifting_Net_Pop_Report.pdf.

22. F. C. Payton, "Digital Divide: Other Considerations?" (2008). In W. Darity (Ed.), *International Encyclopedia of the Social Sciences*, 2nd ed., 9 vols. (Detroit: Macmillan Reference USA, 2008).

23. Kvasny and Payton (2007).

24. See www.metamorph.org.

25. P. H. Cheong, H. A. Wilkin, and S. Ball-Rokeach, "Diagnosing the Communication Infrastructure in Order to Reach Target Audiences." In P. Whitten and D. Cook (Eds.), *Understanding Health Communication Technologies* (San Francisco: Jossey-Bass, 2004).

26. D. O. Erwin, V. A. Johnson, M. Trevino, K. Duke, L. Feliciano, and L. Jandorf, "A Comparison of African American and Latina Social Networks as Indicators for Culturally Tailoring a Breast and Cervical Cancer Education Intervention," *Cancer Supplement* 109, no. 2 (2006): 375.

27. W. K. Nicholson, H. A. Grason, and N. R. Powe, "The Relationship of Race to Women's Use of Health Information Resources," *American Journal of Obstetrics and Gynecology* 188, no. 2 (2003): 580–585.

28. G. A. Barnett, "Communication and Organizational Culture." In G. M. Goldhaber and G. A. Barnett (Eds.), *Handbook of Organizational Communication* (Norwood, NJ: Ablex, 1988): 101–130.

Chapter Questions

3–1.   What are the anticipated shifts in service utilization due to consumer health information seeking?

3–2.   How are these shifts likely to differ among the population being targeted by DCPCA?

3–3.   Describe the emerging trends in consumer health information seeking.

3–4.   In the 1990s, community health information networks flourished. By the early 2000s, these technology-enabled models were termed health information networks. How do these networks compare with RHINs relative to service provided, consumer influence, and health administration?

3–5.   What are the (non)technological barriers DCPCA must address in its implementation of its RHIN?

3–6.   How can Web 2.0 (social networking) influence consumer health dissemination? Describe the anticipated advantages and disadvantages.

3–7.   Given the trends in the Pew Health data, how can the trends shift among consumers seeking health information?

Fundamentals of Internet and Associated Technologies for Healthcare Services Organizations

Joshia Tan

Introduction

Generally speaking, the *Internet* may be thought of as a complex web of networks.[1] Briefly, Internet services include electronic mailing (e-mail); newsgroups; file transfer protocols (FTPs); and other information transfer and exchange services, including, notably, the access of the World Wide Web (WWW) through browser software (e.g., Mozilla Firefox, Safari, and Microsoft Internet Explorer). Currently, within the context of healthcare services organizations, this technology architecture has become a vital interactive research and communication tool—one that aids both medical professionals and health consumers in search of health-related information and knowledge.

The massive, indispensable Internet we know today had humble beginnings as a military project, the ARPANET.[2] Funded by the U.S. Department of Defense (DOD) through the Advanced Research Projects Agency (ARPA), its initial goal was to be a bombproof means of communication. This, however, inevitably propagated the idea of dynamic message routing (i.e., automatically rerouting the initiated communication through alternative pathways in the network, should a certain part of the communication network be attacked or destroyed). Severely underestimated by technology companies, the earliest users of the Internet were restricted to university scholars and military personnel. Today, however, the Internet boasts more than a billion users, as well as several regulating bodies, including the Internet Engineering Task Force (IETF),[3] Internet Architecture Board (IAB),[4] and Internet Engineering Steering Group (IESG).[5]

So what exactly is the Internet? In the United States, the physical backbone of the Internet was constructed by NSFNET[6] (a hub infrastructure sponsored by the National Science Foundation). It consisted of several supercomputer installations servicing as major "hubs," collaborated by a few key universities and commercial undertakings. Today, it is a universal network of smaller computer networks that send and receive information from each other, open to everyone. Certain standards, or protocols, managed by the IETF, define various rules and the format of data that must be adhered to while passing from one network to another.

Fundamentally, intranets and extranets are extensions of the Internet concept because they all use the same hardware and software to build, manage, and view websites. Unlike the Internet, however, these virtual private networks (VPNs) are protected by security software known as "firewalls" to keep unauthorized users from gaining access. In essence, an *intranet* is a private computer network built for the purpose of providing Internet-based services only to inside organizational members. Similar to the intranet concept, an *extranet* offers network access privileges to certain external parties, giving them access to selected areas inside the VPN, thereby creating a secure customer or vendor network.

World Wide Web

When the World Wide Web (WWW) appeared, the Internet started down a different road altogether. With the hypertext transfer protocol (HTTP), which supports the transmission of data on the universal hypertext system that is the WWW, individuals could now place hyperlinks in WWW files through the use of universal resource locators (URLs)—locators that may be employed to obtain resources anywhere in the networks of the Internet.

A user would use a browser, or Web client, to send a request for certain information; the process through which the request is sent is specified by the HTTP. A program constructed to reply to HTTP requests, or a Web server, would then offer the requested information. The aforementioned hyperlinks are used in this manner: the user clicks a certain hyperlink, sending a request, and receives a second document.

Soon, hypertext markup language (HTML) was developed. In this language, browsers receive the HTML text and translate it into a Web page for users. HTML allows for much more than simple text to appear on Web pages, including sound and even video files. It could also include links in a page that would permit a user to rapidly switch from one document to another—even if the document has been stored in separate computers.

Web 2.0 and 3.0

Web 2.0,[7] the next revolution in the Web, is not a simple technological update, as the name might suggest. It is, instead, a new approach to using the Internet. With more than a billion users; the continuous mass proliferation of never-off, high-speed broadband connections; and the rising popularity of mobile Internet-access devices, the Internet has been building itself up for a change. Web 2.0 will transform how business is done, changing the Internet from simply being user-friendly to user-driven. With such radical changes, and Web 3.0[8] on the horizon, the Internet is constantly gravitating toward being open to everyone across the globe.

As for Web 3.0, different writers have used the term in dissimilar manners. The primary idea is that of an evolving and expanded Web, in which artificial intelligent technologies, semantic, and three-dimensional (3D) orientation can transform Web usage. This has numerous advantages for the user:

1. It serves as a virtual database, in the form of linkable Web pages, in which content access may be shared by multiple nonbrowser applications. This is due to the Web's increasing propagation as a medium for storing and sharing information that can be queried with standard query language.

2. The application of powerful Web-mining strategies, based on previous patterns of Web usage, represents the integration of Web with artificial intelligence technologies; this results in the prediction of new and interesting search paths for the users.

3. An evolution into the semantic Web extends the usefulness of WWW by giving structured meanings to information. It also permits the automation of data and software in a format to be read, shared, and used by intelligent software agents.

4. The concept of service-oriented architecture (SOA) offers an interchangeable bundle of services to create competitive advantage; this is produced by reengineering the existing business and IT processes of its Web services, especially for organizations connected through a value chain.

4. The evolution of the WWW into a series of shared 3D spaces means that a new vision of the Web could allow many dimensions of services and resources to be innovatively integrated.

Applications of Internet-Related Technologies in the Healthcare Services Industry

There are many published examples of Internet use, within the context of healthcare services organizations, providing relevant health information and services. A simple strategy is offering access to online insurance service data to users such as patients, physicians, hospitals, and others. Offering electronic claims for insurance benefits is a simple cost-cutting measure for the HMO and its network of hospitals, physicians, and corporate clients. The network-based services improve access, convenience, and usability for members. It also cuts agency and other labor costs while providing insight into healthcare trends and medical practices.

For example, Blue Cross Blue Shield (BCBS) of Massachusetts employs WWW server and onsite multimedia kiosks, equipped with modem connections to the insurance carriers' customer service operations, to enhance access to online insurance services. Apart from real-time access to information about particular BCBS services, the Internet services also provide users with healthcare and medical updates. Furthermore, the website provides a front end for medical information available at other points on the Internet, such as OncoNet,[9] a repository for data on treatments for cancer patients. It is also possible to access the Internet via kiosks; this allows users to extract, query, and print physician and hospital database information as well as to peruse drug and treatment alternative information as part of BCBS services. In addition, these kiosks provide telephone links to customer service representatives and member services. Corporate customers have claimed that being able to provide services and information to users directly over the Internet and via kiosks can significantly reduce the cost of in-house insurance support and education.

Intranet and extranet architectures have also been profusely applied across a growing number of hospitals for in-house and external health data and information sharing and distribution. Aetna/US Healthcare[10] of Hartford, Connecticut, for example, allows members to change their primary care providers online via an extranet service. The EZenroll application handles the critical process of adding, dropping, or changing health plans. Members gain access to the system with a user name and password supplied by their employer, who also approves the transactions online through their intranet–extranet architectures. Implementation of electronic health records via this same technology has been shown to be generally reliable and secure. Web-based transactions also provide the potential to reduce some of the inherent inefficiencies of paper forms and faxes and to circumvent the postal mailing system.

Group Health Northwest (GHNW),[11] another HMO, has been among the first to tap the potential of intranet and Web technology in aiding cost-effective sharing of information in a user-friendly fashion. For example, it has Web-enabled the organization's patient accounts data to give users at outlying physicians' offices the ability to query the data. Using a client server architecture, where clients can access data from a database, GHNW's intranet and Web applications not only provide a better solution than previously used legacy systems, but also improve the quality of patient care. Previously, much of the information had been disseminated in paper form.

Geisinger Health Care System[12] of Danville, Pennsylvania, the largest U.S. rural HMO, is seen as applying Internet-related technologies to reinvent health care. Its system concept includes replacing isolated legacy systems with a universal workstation concept, resulting in a patient-accessible intranet supported by an Ethernet backbone. Through this, Geisinger is able to offer innovative services such as Tel-a-Nurse, where nurses, who have access to relevant information and expert knowledge through the intranet, answer medical questions that users call in with. Geisinger's physicians can also use digital cameras to take pictures of patient injuries, making these pictures accessible via the intranet. Geisinger's intranet is also being used to support patient education. The radiology department, for example, which performs diagnostic procedures such as X-rays, mammograms, and magnetic resonance images, has a kiosk in its waiting room. Through this kiosk, patients can access the radiology home page and retrieve a list of the various departmental procedures.

The Detroit Medical Center (DMC) Virology Lab,[13] a world leader in identifying and treating different strain of the HIV-1 virus, has used DNA sequencing to prescribe medication for patients. In recent years, with the implementation of a semantic Web solution to replace legacy systems, the new software tools have helped doctors gather information of the sample workflow in the HIV virology laboratory system. Moreover, by tracking any changes that may have affected the HIV strains, these tools further enhance patient care by also allowing the doctors a better overview of patient history.

Finally, Google has been developing a 3D satellite-based application, Google Earth, to help capture data and images that are not possible with basic guidance systems. A possible future application would be for an emergency call center to track the status, type of services needed, and urgency of the situation for a patient by simply zooming in on a 3D image of the patient requesting assistance.

Indeed, with the continuous development of groundbreaking technology, the healthcare services industry will soon be significantly more effective, efficient, and user-friendly.

Notes

1. A. T. Stull, *On the Internet: A Student's Guide* (Upper Saddle River, NJ: Prentice-Hall, 1997).
2. Michael Hauben, "History of ARPANET: Behind the Net—The Untold History of the ARPANET, or—The 'Open' History of the ARPANET/Internet," accessed June 23, 2008, from http://www.livinginternet.com/i/ii_arpanet.htm.
3. Internet Engineering Task Force (IETF), http://www.ietf.org/, accessed June 23, 2008.
4. Internet Architecture Board (IAB), http://www.iab.org/, accessed June 23, 2008.
5. Internet Engineering Steering Group (IESG), http://www.ietf.org/iesg.html, accessed June 23, 2008.
6. B. Chinoy and Hans-Werner Braun, "NSFNET: The National Science Foundation Network," accessed July 1, 2008, from http://moat.nlanr.net/Papers/nsfnet-t1-technology.ps.
7. Tim O'Reilly, "What Is Web 2.0? Design Patterns and Business Models for the Next Generation of Software," accessed July 3, 2008, from http://www.oreillynet.com/pub/a/oreilly/tim/news/2005/09/30/what-is-web-20.html.
8. Cade Metz, "Web 3.0," *PC Magazine*, accessed July 3, 2008, from http://www.pcmag.com/article2/0,1759,2102852,00.asp.
9. B. Blobel, "OncoNet: A Secure Infrastructure to Improve Cancer Patients' Care," *European Journal of Medical Research* 5, no. 8 (August 2000): 360–368.
10. Aetna/US Healthcare of Hartford, www.aetna.com/news/1997/pr_19971112.htm, accessed July 3, 2008.
11. Group Health Northwest (GHNW), www.ghc.org, accessed July 3, 2008.
12. Geisinger Health Care System, www.geisinger.org, accessed July 3, 2008.
13. Detroit Medical Center (DMC) Virology Lab, http://www.dmc.org/univlab, accessed July 3, 2008.

Health Management Information Systems Technology and Applications

Health Management Information Systems Enterprise Software: The New Generation of HMIS Administrative Applications

Joshia Tan with Joseph Tan

Editor's Note: Isolated legacy systems—such as hospital financial and payroll systems, nurse scheduling systems, admission-discharge-transfer systems, purchasing and inventory control systems, facility planning systems, and the like—used for decades in healthcare facilities will soon give way to emerging business-oriented systems, namely, supply chain management, customer relationship management, and enterprise resource planning. These systems are believed to be emerging as the next-generation enterprisewide HMIS administrative applications that will significantly affect the future quality of healthcare services delivery. Chapter 4, therefore, begins our discussion of HMIS applications and technologies. Chapters 5, 6, and 7 will then continue this line of thought by highlighting applications such as community health information networks (CHIN), regional health information organizations (RHIO), electronic health records (EHR), computerized physician order entry (CPOE), clinical decision support systems (CDSS), and integrated HMIS via Web services technology. Put together, Chapters 4 through 7 offer readers a wide-ranging survey of HMIS applications and technologies. The knowledge acquired in Chapter 4 therefore prepares students to face new and emerging challenges in the evolving HMIS field.

CHAPTER OUTLINE

Scenario: *Customer Relations Management with Blue Cross Blue Shield of Minnesota*

Notes
Chapter Questions

Technology Brief II: *Basic Hardware, Software, and Interface Concepts for Healthcare Services Organizations*
  Joshia Tan and Joseph Tan

Scenario: *Customer Relations Management with Blue Cross Blue Shield of Minnesota*[1]

In 2001, Blue Cross Blue Shield (BCBS) of Minnesota sought to persuade executives at the consumer goods giant General Mills to join its regional health plan. These executives decided they would switch health plans on one condition: BCBS of Minnesota needed to install a Web-based customer service system that would allow subscribers to manage their health profiles and benefits online. BCBS of Minnesota consented, and the task of building a customer relationship management (CRM) system that would live up to General Mills's assurances fell upon John Ounjian, then senior vice president and CIO of BCBS of Minnesota.

From the very beginning, Ounjian clearly understood the requirements imposed by General Mills: to give subscribers the ability to select health plans tailored to their individual needs and budgets, to calculate their own contributions to their coverage, to research information on prescription drugs and other treatments, to locate nearby participating physicians, and to check the status of their claims at any time of the year. Before such a system could be implemented, however, Ounjian needed to create a brand-new infrastructure that linked website and call center operations with timely, accurate information. In addition, he needed to transfer gigabytes of data from back-end databases to the Web so that it could be accessible and meaningful to consumers. It was a very challenging assignment with limited time and budget.

In the end, Ounjian pulled it off. But how did he do it? The difference, Ounjian liked to think, was in the planning. From the outset, Ounjian had a data management strategy. He likened constructing an online customer self-service system without this type of strategy to building a bridge without support. "If you don't have a data management strategy, then you're only building half the bridge," he reasoned. Thus, he and his staff began the project by attempting to develop a new infrastructure to record, over the Internet, automated interactions that had previously taken place over the phone. They then proceeded to pursue a strategy that would overcome many of the problems that could arise from converting raw data from back-end systems to consumer-accessible information on the Web. Had Ounjian been restricted to moving data back and forth, customers would end up looking at information that was essentially outdated, inaccurate, or not synchronized with other company information channels.

Once its website was ready for beta testing, Ounjian and his staff invited a focus group of customers to evaluate it. The customers were initially unimpressed, mainly because they found the site to be lacking a consumer-friendly interface. Specifically, BCBS-hired engineers discovered that they needed to redesign the layout of pull-down menus that guided viewers around the site. The interface was eventually improved with added features; as a result, customers were able to access information in a more efficient and relaxed manner.

As of 2003, 61 employers (including Northwest Airlines, 3M, and Target) have used the system—more than 450,000 individual employees in total. This number has also been projected to grow as more companies and individuals adopt this consumer-driven approach. Ounjian used a car metaphor to describe the flexibility of his new system: "We have the chassis on which to build our investments from year to year. If my transmission needs to move from a three-speed to a five-speed, I don't have to redesign the whole car."

Now, imagine you are the next CEO of General Mills and would like to build a strong information systems department to do in-house systems development with the criteria of these systems being customer-friendly. What do you think would be some examples of such systems? Would Ounjian be a person you may want to consider hiring to be in charge of the IS department of General Mills? If so, why? Otherwise, why not?

I. Introduction

In Part I, we learned that health management information systems (HMIS) combine people, data, processes, and health information technologies to collect, process, store, and provide needed results—all in support of a healthcare services organization's different departmental functions and task activities. This is the foundational knowledge to prepare us on how to go about managing HMIS within healthcare services organizations as complex adaptive systems so that these organizations can thrive in an intensely competitive and increasingly demanding marketplace.

Part II of this text covers HMIS technology and applications. At this point, we need to specify the type of HMIS applications, in today's healthcare services organizations, in which strategic and operational initiatives may be championed to yield competitive advantages. Our focus here is on HMIS administrative applications at the enterprise level. At this level, the overall performance of the organization depends on effective communications among its members; the building of an interoperable, interconnected HMIS architecture; and, finally, the implementation of effectively integrated enterprise software to connect the existing legacy administrative systems that support the organization's routine functions and activities.

As we move steadily toward globalization; e-commerce; knowledge asset management; collaborative partnerships; total quality management; and greater expectations for the security, privacy, and confidentiality of patient data, HMIS must evolve into an integral part of any healthcare services delivery system. To sustain an intense competitive edge and promote strategic initiatives, several high-profile enterprise software systems have emerged in the HMIS landscape. Key among these include:

- Supply chain management (SCM).
- Customer relationship management (CRM).
- Enterprise resource planning (ERP).

These enterprise software systems play numerous important roles, including supporting and enhancing (among key stakeholders inside and outside of the networked enterprise) communication, coordination, collaboration, information exchange, and resource management sharing. The successful implementation of these systems also ensures that every internal enterprise unit is somehow interrelated and interoperable and, furthermore, able to link with external support infrastructure systems. Just as a jigsaw puzzle, comprised of a mass of irregularly shaped pieces, forms a total picture when fitted together, these strategic HMIS initiatives combine effectively to help integrate the enterprising functions and task activities among the various constituencies. They will also link to external entities to provide seamless high-quality healthcare services delivery, as is expected by today's healthcare consumers.

These enterprise software systems primarily target large-scale health maintenance organizations (HMOs) and integrated healthcare services delivery systems to satisfy the need for economies of scale; the increasing volume of daily purchasing, claims, and information exchange transactions; the trend toward increased growth, acquisitions, and merger arrangements; and globalization. Therefore, discussion of these systems takes center stage in this text, rather than the disparate legacy administrative systems such as hospital financial systems, material purchasing systems, nursing scheduling systems, facilities management systems, and many other systems that are typically covered in most published standardized and more traditionally oriented HMIS texts.[2-4] We believe that the major HMIS enterprise applications presented here will soon become the next-generation administrative applications for most, if not all, healthcare services organizations.

II. Supply Chain Management

Owing to escalating costs, advances in medical devices, innovations in health technology, new discoveries in prescription drugs, and increasing demand for quality services in the U.S. healthcare marketplace, large-scale HMO and multi-provider healthcare organizations must now begin to evaluate their supply chain management (SCM).

The design of an effective SCM system essentially involves an understanding of how to manage the information flow throughout a supply chain (SC) so that the total SC effectiveness is maximized.[5-7] In other words, the primary goals of SCM are (1) to optimize service quality in terms of an organization's internal information flow processes, while reducing costs and delivery time, and (2) to achieve increased efficiencies with regard to information flows and exchanges between the organization and its external parties, including all its vendors and suppliers.

Take the case of the materials purchasing and handling department of a health maintenance organization that oversees, on a daily basis, the purchasing and inventory of supplies from a multitude of suppliers for several HMO-affiliated hospitals. First, it is almost always a challenge to predict, at any one time, the composition of patients in the different affiliated hospitals and, ultimately, their supply consumption of medical equipment or devices, prescriptions, ambulances, and office supplies, such as computer hardware and software. Second, different vendors and suppliers may behave very differently with differing systems, policies, and procedures for fulfilling orders. These vendors and suppliers can change from time to time, and depending on their efficiencies, some orders may be misfiled, shipped to the wrong places, or even lost in the process—any of which would lead to unsatisfactory backlogs and further logistical delays. Poor inventory management and inadequate quality control on the part of any of the suppliers, as well as on the part of the materials purchasing and handling department of the HMO, will also significantly affect subsequent costing and budgeting, as well as delivery time or recalls of these supplies. Many of these events will, in turn, affect the availability and eventual pricing of certain products and, ultimately, the customers' perceived product and service quality.

The deployments of e-commerce enterprisewide software, such as electronic data interchange (EDI) or Web services, are examples of SCM solutions. Having the materials purchasing and handling department set up and send electronic orders to all the vendors and suppliers in a preauthorized standardized format not only reduces errors in manual paperwork, lessens inconsistencies among disparate legacy systems, minimizes mail order delays, lowers costs, and increases the overall efficiency achieved in order procedures, but it also reduces the need to spend time chasing unfilled orders or canceling orders. Moreover, information flow among manufacturing, purchasing, and acquiring parties on quality control can easily be an added component in the system.

SCM also ensures readily available access to electronic order information, such as order tracking, at any time and anywhere the e-commerce application is operable. It even grants the materials purchasing and handling department the ability to confirm approximate delivery time and availability of products—such as the type, number, and functionalities of wheelchairs at order placement. Moreover, staffing in the materials purchasing and handling department may also be reduced. Electronic healthcare requisition, or e-procurement, therefore, saves tremendous logistics costs, with the added possibility of instituting a just-in-time (JIT) inventory. JIT is a strategy used by many businesses to improve the return on investment (ROI) by reducing in-process inventory and its associated costs. Demand printing, such as the publication of required health information brochures, is an example of JIT because only the number of ordered brochures is printed for delivery as orders are received. It is expected that the HMO's process efficiencies, service quality, and performance effectiveness will dramatically improve if JIT inventory can also be implemented as part of the SCM strategy.

Over the years, the healthcare industry has lagged in terms of innovative HMIS implementations and IT applications compared with banking, manufacturing, and many other service industries. As the next-generation HMIS enterprise software strategy, SCM provides the healthcare industry with an opportunity to systematize materials purchasing and handling processes. In fact, there is the possibility that globalization will soon transform SCM for healthcare supply purchasing into global sourcing.

With an increasing global population, healthcare services organizations—although long recognized to have thrived as one of the most established industries—are also now predicted to become the world's fastest growing industry sector. Because the supply chain is being identified as a means of equating supply and demand in terms of the high daily volumes of information that are exchanged between suppliers and customers, the management of healthcare services organizations should not analyze a single department, or even a single enterprise. Instead, these organizations should collaborate and, perhaps, integrate purchases by applying SCM philosophy for networks of healthcare services organizations and partnering HMOs. Not only will this lower the cost of SCM investments, it will also increase SCM efficiencies and promote cost-effectiveness in the building of supplier–customer relationships. As a result, both the primary and support activities levels will see greater competitive advantages among the partners with shared infrastructure. To this extent, it could be demonstrated that outsourcing may be the next growth-strategic initiative for many HMO and healthcare services organizations, so that the current borders in the relationship between suppliers and customers are expanded. Evidently, the traditional approach of "make or buy" is rapidly approaching extinction, yielding to transformational outsourcing as an SCM strategy in redesigning traditional links. This would allow healthcare services organizations to focus on their core businesses and core competencies, which are, essentially, patient care.

To further illustrate the SCM concepts for healthcare services organizations, we present two relevant cases drawn from different vendor-published websites. The first is Marion Area Health System (MAHS) of north-central Ohio's Caduceus Material Management Information System (Caduceus MMIS)[8]; the second is a press release of Andersen's pharmaceutical, biomedical, and health services (PBH) supply chain practice on its attempt to project, in the IT industry, the valuation of future, achievable, e-commerce benefits.[9]

MAHS, whose affiliates include the Marion Area Health Center, Smith Clinic, and Marion Ancillary Services, recently licensed the Caduceus MMIS for implementation throughout its system. The Caduceus MMIS involves more than 70 physicians, whose specialties range from minor illnesses to full-blown surgery. Because of its sheer size, a new technological approach to managing its inventory and records was needed. Rick Brunswick, the director of materials management at MAHS, believes the system will fill this need by "automat[ing] a wide range of supply-related processes and eliminat[ing] a series of manual tasks." Such processes and tasks include the ability of electronically managing purchasing contracts, invoices, and financial records.

Using wireless technology and automatic updating, Caduceus MMIS seeks to cut costs by managing inventory and finances in a comprehensive manner. This extinguishes any superfluous or redundant practices and diminishes the risks associated with human error and safety hazards. MAHS physicians and clinicians will then have more time to personally care for patients without having to worry about locating and correcting misplaced or mislabeled supplies. As the system is developed with a scalable and receptive architecture, existing systems can be incorporated into Caduceus MMIS. Not only will this reduce the funding needed to replace existing systems, but it will also save implementation time.

Ed Lane, the president and CEO of Caduceus Systems, has faith that "the Caduceus MMIS will equip MAHS with the capabilities to realize significant efficiency improvements, cost savings, accurate charge generation, and improve communication with their suppliers and trading partners while positioning MAHS with a strategic software platform for managing their internal supply chain operations."

A study by Andersen's PBH supply chain practice found that the future value of e-commerce is predicted to fall between 2 and 10 percent of total benefits for members of the healthcare industry supply chain. Providers would receive 1 or 2 percent of the benefit, while suppliers would obtain the remainder. These values were calculated from interviews and activity-based costing methods, involving both tangible and intangible future values of e-commerce. These included improvements in procuring products, managing orders, invoice processing, integrating systems, managing contracts, and operational efficiency.

However, the largest benefit has been purported to be from controlling redundancy, such as overpayment and rework. Furthermore, as administrative issues can now be handled with less effort through e-commerce, and real-time information is easily accessible and available, salespeople now have more time to focus on completing sales transactions and garnering new clients. "This study quantifies the future state of the healthcare industry through the use of e-commerce," said Ramona Lacy, partner with Andersen's PBH supply chain practice. "It will be a roadmap for all parties involved in the supply chain."

III. Customer Relationship Management

Customer relationship management (CRM) is another major HMIS enterprise software system that is emerging in the healthcare IT marketplace. As noted in the beginning scenario of this chapter, the responsibility eventually rests on BCBS of Minnesota's CIO, John Ounjian, to implement Web-based CRM software so that executives at General Mills are convinced to join BCBS of Minnesota's health plan. Such software would permit subscribers to manage and personalize their healthcare services benefits online. In brief, the system will enable them to customize their plans to their individual needs and budgets, locate participating and select highly recommended physicians and specialists, decide on their own coverage contributions, check on the status of their submitted claims, and uncover the research information on prescription drugs and/or other recommended treatments at their own convenience.

How, then, would having CRM software distinguish BCBS of Minnesota from its competitors? Although CRM applies to organizations of every market, John Ounjian claimed that healthcare organizations such as BCBS are ready for such a system and would find it to be extremely beneficial in retaining its customers. Evidently, in order to maximize revenue generation and maintain customer loyalty, BCBS of Minnesota, as a leading-edge HMO, must be ready to implement such a solution and use it to carefully manage all of the customers' associations with the organization—this is exactly what customer relationship management is all about, and what BCBS of Minnesota's competitors have yet to discover.

With CRM, BCBS of Minnesota customers can now communicate with the HMO through numerous means and at different times. An archetypal CRM scheme would record each interaction a customer has had with the HMO and allow all the different departments of BCBS of Minnesota to access this record. In so doing, the HMO can garner valuable perspectives on both the effectiveness of its current systems and the preferences of any individual customer. Furthermore, with this knowledge, BCBS of Minnesota can save considerable cost by eliminating corporatewide inefficiencies. Customer satisfaction will also be improved, because the treatment of each individual client can be further personalized, given that BCBS of Minnesota can access the record of interactions the customer has had with it, and then offer, accordingly, only the services and information that the customer seeks. Targeted mailing of information will also reduce waste. With reduced inefficiencies leading to reduced costs, and increasing customer loyalty leading to augmenting sales, BCBS of Minnesota can then, as a result of implementing powerful and unique CRM software, maximize its revenue generation.

Still, in order to design the most appropriate CRM software, the HMO or healthcare services organization must have an in-depth recognition of its customers' specific needs. Accordingly, Shams and Farishta[10] argue that the application of CRM philosophy is based on understanding the communications architecture of the healthcare services organization. The communications architecture should include a center core communications piece, augmented by branding and strategic communications. In terms of core communications, the patient's profile, which includes a synopsis of his or her physical demographics and other treatment-specific information (such as gender, age, allergies, and so forth) would be used to further trigger event-specific communications. In terms of branding communications, the messages will be used to distinguish the type and quality of products, programs, and services that the health organization in question is able to offer from its competitors in the regional, or even global, healthcare marketplace. Finally, strategic communications refer to the enhancement of existing programs and services, as well as to the development of new programs and creative services that would progress and fulfill the organizational long-term goals.[11,12]

Ultimately, the CRM being designed should first capture and generate customer profile data. With the core communications architecture in place, it should then allow an authorized employee or affiliate of the healthcare organization to offer, at the patient's convenience, appropriate information on treatments in a relatively shorter span of time. With the additional branding and strategic communications layers implemented, CRM would further allow the healthcare organization to reach its target audience for specific programs, such as immunizations, by contacting only those patients whose profiles suited the need. The CRM would also be able to communicate to the selected customers specifically why these services or programs are unique and competitively desirable, compare these services and programs to other apparently similar programs and services available in the healthcare regional marketplace, and offer special and personalized packages to the customers. Not only would such a system save the healthcare organization significant funds from general advertising and marketing costs, but it would also, indubitably, recover the cost of its implementation over the long run. Moreover, it will increase patient retention by offering customers a personalized relationship with tailored suggestions that other health organizations are not yet able to offer.

IV. Enterprise Resource Planning

Enterprise resource planning (ERP) is the final, major, enterprisewide software system to be highlighted in this chapter. As with many businesses, legacy systems in healthcare services organizations require employees to post different departmental financial, purchasing, and other service-oriented data in separate systems. These systems may not be consistent with each other, thereby encouraging the proliferation of islands of HMIS. Posting is the essence of manual operations. In an integrated environment, all that is needed is a "view." For instance, a patient's claims and claims reimbursement filing forms are just different views of the same data set in different order.

In this regard, Duncan et al.[13] observe that the integration of intraorganizational processes can significantly affect strategic management. Linked inventory control, if it exists, can be updated every time a drug, special diet, medical device, or other item is ordered; the cost of the item can then be added electronically to the patient's claims and claims reimbursement filing forms, thereby improving efficiency and reducing costs. Extending this linkage externally, the process of reordering items from designated suppliers, so that sufficient safety stock is maintained, can also be automated. With SCM, suppliers can be linked to customers in real time for electronic order processing, third-party payors can be linked to health providers for billing and claims reimbursement procedures, government regulators can be linked to providers for documentation, and researchers can be linked to all of the various stakeholders for the purpose of conducting studies.

In essence, the ERP philosophy is an attempt to integrate all departmental and functional processes throughout the enterprise into a single, integrated HMIS, enabling enterprisewide information management and decision making on all organizational operations. If the entire organization is not sold on the philosophy of change accompanied by the use of ERP applications, for example, unintended and highly disruptive consequences may result. Existing ERP packages include SAP, R/3, Baan, PeopleSoft, and Oracle.[14]

In the same context as the assembly of isolated legacy systems into an integrated system with real-time access of different views (allowing decisions to be made intelligently across the enterprise) is the idea of reducing, or possibly eliminating, all paper-based forms for which healthcare services organizations are especially vulnerable. If all transactions between customers and providers can be captured online and directly via CRM, then all the troubles of any manual follow-up that may be needed could be avoided. With CRM and SCM in place, ERP can provide management quick access to enterprisewide resource planning summaries, such as the generation of enterprisewide purchasing aggregate reports, shipping status reports, and revenue-generation reports from all related services, programs, and investments.

Yamanouchi Pharmaceutical Co. Ltd. and Fujisawa Pharmaceutical Co. Ltd. merged in April 2005 to form Astellas Pharma Inc., ranking among the top 20 global pharmaceutical companies. Astellas Pharma US Inc., headquartered in Deerfield, Illinois, represents the U.S. Astellas operation.[15] Previously, Yamanouchi Pharmaceuticals, with sales at $3.9 billion, was also the third-largest pharmaceutical company in Japan. It has made information systems the key component in improving the timeliness and quality of answers to customers' tough questions.

Product support personnel at Yamanouchi can immediately answer half the questions that come in from the doctors or pharmacists. To find answers to more difficult questions, they have access to Yamanouchi's Web-based PRoduct INformation CEnter Supporting System (PRINCESS).[16] With the help of JRI Consulting, Astellas Pharma was able to further integrate both Yamanouchi's and Fujisawa's systems to quickly achieve stable operations within a short period of time. The Astellas ERP system is based on SAP R/3 products with business processes in accounting, production, sales and distribution, purchasing, and personnel from both companies integrated.[17]

Still, ERP is not a panacea. Take, for instance, a typical healthcare services organization today, where management, employees, or customers need specific answers to important product order or service information. There are also the related questions about suppliers, shipping status, and sales status, causing the front offices of these healthcare services organizations to typically scramble behind the scenes for answers. The inconsistency across disparate databases and business operations in legacy systems often make it difficult for conflicting data sets to be reconciled. These cannot be used to provide straight answers, either, to many of the questions pertaining to the provided services. Moreover, it will always be complicated to provide straight answers for such questions as, "How long does it take to perform a knee replacement operation today?" or "How much does it cost the HMO to schedule a knee replacement operation today?" The HMO can generate the answers only after that knee replacement operation is completed—its expenses depend on, among other things, who performs the surgery, how is it performed, when is it performed, the patient's insurance subscription and the extent of its coverage, the length of the patient's postoperation stay in the hospital, and any complications arising from the operation(s). Administrators of healthcare services organizations can only provide a smile as service until their employees and subordinates have had sufficient time to deal with addressing many of these questions. Operational practices within healthcare services organizations and subcomponents are diverse and sometimes unique. Software development has to be done on a project-by-project basis, because the service processes are often nonstandardized. Developing ERP software, or even customizing and implementing some off-the-shelf packages, is, therefore, a very lengthy, risky, and difficult venture. In this sense, the information architecture that can be achieved through the integration of core business processes and requirements will sometimes be limited, complex, and expensive.

The goal for ERP, then, is to achieve single data-entry points throughout the organization so that the goal of enterprise data modeling can be realized wherever possible. Today, this is becoming a more attainable goal with the adoption of data and process standardization, advances in business process reengineering, and the willingness of healthcare professionals and employees to streamline processes and operations. When standardization goes beyond the basic data levels to a service process level, invoices and paper-based orders can be eliminated, and payments or services can be made without the need for a paper trail. Often, the major issues are not technical, but process reconceptualization and educational issues. Overcoming these issues is key to making intra- and interorganizational systems work together. Simply put, ERP software can be used to facilitate data integration by amalgamating existing business processes in an organization. ERP implementation for an integrated delivery system

(IDS) essentially connects the different pieces of existing HMIS applications in the system to fit into the ERP centerpiece software.

Figure 4.1 shows how the ERP replaces the existing islands of HMIS for an IDS with a resulting centerpiece ERP application, which allows sharing of core administrative data. It is important to note that not all services and functions currently performed in healthcare services organizations can be easily integrated.

The service process model for healthcare services proposed in the previous edition of this text is the beginning of an ERP conceptualization for healthcare services organizations. It is an attempt to reconceptualize and streamline all services and processes transpiring within these organizations into an integrated model. We briefly summarize the approach here; those who are enthusiastically interested can seek out further details by consulting the previous edition of this text, as referenced.[18]

All organizations, including healthcare services organizations, provide services. The service process is therefore a common link among organizations, subsets of organizations, and various people who work for these organizations. All service processes have three common basic elements: a customer, a service that is provided, and a provider. Information pertaining to these

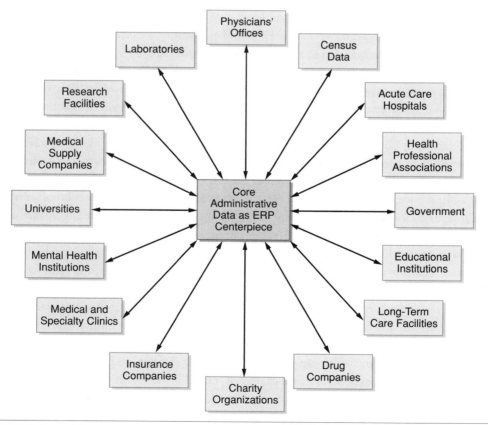

FIGURE 4.1   The Enterprise Resource Planning (ERP) Conceptualization.

elements may be maintained as servicing records in master tables. Service processes are simple and very consistent; in general, most organizational services can be classified into three levels, each having a few major types. Uniformity in service processes is essential because it shortens the customization and implementation time for an integrated ERP application.

Service transactions occur at three levels within a unit: (1) external services, (2) internal services, and (3) procured services. *External services* are services provided by the unit or persons to external units or persons. *Internal services* are services provided within the unit by one person or unit to another person or unit. *Procured services* are services procured by units or persons from external units or persons. Within each of these three levels, service processes of (or for) units or individuals can be classified as consultative, procedural, material (consumable), facility (use of hard or soft assets), monetary, or information (maintenance). In healthcare services organizations, *consultative services* involve logical interactions between customers and providers; these include services provided by doctors, management consultants, and clinical specialists. *Procedural services* involve physical interactions between customers and providers. This type of service may also involve the use of equipment, such as a hard or soft instrument. *Material services* transfer the ownership of hardware or software from providers to customers. These services result in debits or credits to the material accounts of providers and customers. *Facility services* involve the blocking and releasing of assets used. In this case, the service providers typically limit the use of their hardware or software to the customers. Examples are use of hospital beds (hard assets) or Internet services (soft assets). *Monetary services* are either independent or reciprocal of other service types. For example, money is transferred from customers to providers by various negotiable instruments, resulting in debits and credits to monetary accounts of customers and providers, respectively. *Information services* merely involve updating the service master tables after transactions. The customer, provider, and service master tables are results of such service transactions, and the structure of these service master tables depends on the type of the service provided.

IDS can easily customize the layout of data on these services into service master tables, depending on their needs and information requirements. Services of all types within each level are processed with multiple steps. At least four of these steps are common to most service processes: request for service, acknowledgment of request, service delivery, and confirmation of service delivery. Figure 4.2 shows how these steps can be sequenced and analyzed along a value-added chain, resulting in a service outcome. Services can sometimes, alternatively, be processed with a single step, or multiple steps can be merged into a single step. It is also possible for these steps to take place all at the same time. First, a service process is initiated through a request for service. Numerous forms have been used in the manual process for making requests (e.g., drug prescriptions and test orders). Apart from other attributes, these service request forms commonly identify the customer, the service to be provided, and the provider—that is, the basic elements of the service process. The manual forms necessitated a docket number (header) and a detailed type of reference system, which are not necessary in our standardized model. Abolishing this concept of header and details requires a change of the old mind-set for many health professionals. This also means abolishing the names used for identifying all the different request forms. In the integrated, computerized model, each record consists only of one customer, one deliverable item of service, and one provider.

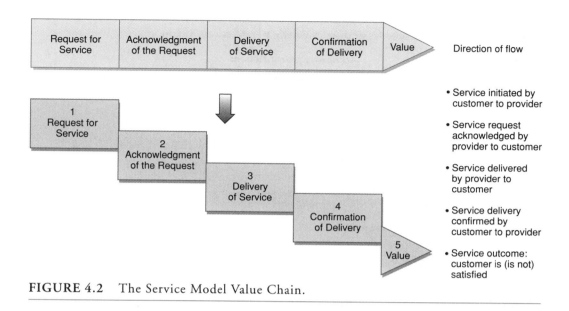

FIGURE 4.2   The Service Model Value Chain.

In general, requests are generated one at a time. However, it is possible for group requests to be made for several services ganged together. Moreover, requests may also be prescheduled with a start time, end time, and follow-up periods. Requests for a particular service may also be automatically generated for a predefined condition by activating it through a triggered built-in logic when a change in certain fields is registered. For example, a purchase request for an item can be generated automatically when the reorder level is reached. This type of request is unnecessary in an integrated environment, because the provider who is sharing the data will supply the item with an automated built-in request. In this case, what should have been a reorder level would now become a supply level. Also note that requests and services flow in opposite directions between the various request levels and that external and procured services are usually accompanied by reciprocal monetary transactions.

Following the service request, the acknowledgment screen of the service provider is updated with the new request. The service provider then acknowledges the request by some preliminary action. For example, in the case of a laboratory test request arising within a hospital, the phlebotomist will have to collect the required blood sample. In the case of a machinery breakdown, the request is made to the service engineer to carry out a preliminary inspection of the equipment. Table 4.1 shows the "acknowledgment actions" of the different requests, as noted on the system by the provider. The system also notes the user identity of the person acknowledging the request and the date and time of acknowledgment. After the acknowledgment is registered, the person actually responsible for delivering the service is notified through an automatic update of this person's pending actions list. Services are then delivered and the records of "delivery actions" are updated electronically by the providers or, subsequently, by individuals acting on their behalf, as shown in Table 4.2. Again, the identity of the person updating the records and the date and time are noted by the system.

Table 4.1   Services Processes and Acknowledgment Actions Taxonomy

Types of Service Processes	Acknowledgment Actions
Consultative	Confirmation that the provider and the customer are both ready
Procedural	Pre-procedure preparation carried out by the system
Material (consumable)	Transportation of material
Facility (use of hard or soft asset)	Reservation/allotment of facility
Monetary	System checks to ensure that the service is deliverable and instruments are acceptable
Information	System checks to ensure that all information required for master updating is available

Table 4.2   Services Processes and Delivery Actions Taxonomy

Types of Service Processes	Acknowledgment Actions
Consultative	Recording the outcome parameters
Procedural	Recording the procedure outcomes
Material (consumable)	Transfer of ownership of material to the customer; stock records update
Facility (use of hard or soft asset)	Physical occupation of the facility
Monetary	Transfer of money to the customer; financial records update
Information	Master update

The last step is confirmation of the service provided, that is, an acceptance or approval of the service by the customer. As noted, all services have outcomes; for example, a service may be completed to satisfaction or below satisfaction. The consultative and procedural services may have outcome values for various parameters, as recorded by their providers. An outcome may also be the identity of another service request. Moreover, a service may be canceled or rolled back at any stage. Hence, if the service is accepted, the system merely updates the acknowledgment; otherwise, a feedback occurs, and the "chain" of service activities is repeated accordingly. Following the service delivery, the transaction data are archived into a service data archival table or the service database.

It is possible that services may be grouped and ordered together by a group name, and a hierarchy pattern of multiple levels of groups thus enables rapid ordering of related services.

V. Conclusion

Only the primary features underlying the service process model have been presented so far to give the reader a sense of the benefits of what process standardization can provide. In other words, standardization can incur benefits at levels beyond data codes, data schema, and data exchange formats; in fact, significant efficiencies can be recovered from standardizing the service processes. Standardization of all these levels, if pursued appropriately and vigorously, holds great potential for reduced costs, diminished complexity, greater security control, and better data management—a systems philosophy that prepares the organization to move into an SCM, CRM, and ERP environment. Adoption of HMIS standards is discussed in Chapter 12.

In closing, here are some pointers toward achieving HMIS integration in an IDS context. The first significant change, as was noted throughout many of the illustrations covered in the chapter, is increasing awareness of the organization to reconceptualize its business and services processes as well as the need to adopt a new corporate culture of data sharing. This culture needs to be supported across all organizational units and departments. In this light, SCM, CRM, and ERP play key roles in supporting meaningful sharing, integration, and exchange of data; such software systems allow enterprisewide views of the organization, thereby ensuring efficient and effective interorganizational cooperations and intraorganizational collaborations. For such interorganization and intraorganizational linkages to succeed, Sprague and McNurlin[19] note that all linked programs and processes should be expandable to other links in the future, whether these are at community, regional, state, national, or international levels. This can only be possible if an enterprise view, process standardization, and a data-sharing culture are upheld and if stakeholders and users are educated about the significance of the standardization process (the subject of Chapter 12). In an IDS context, the more technologically advanced partners will typically have to pull the others along, whether it is through education or some other means. Standardization also requires the cooperating organizations to be involved in the ongoing development of standards. Government agencies, regulators, and third parties are often also involved. Standards task forces can be formed to operate as electronic intermediaries, facilitating the flow of information. In hammering out a consensus among the stakeholders involved in a standardization process, a change in one of the cooperating systems often must be coordinated with all others.

Finally, as illustrated by the Yamanouchi-Fujisawa case, applications of the HMIS enterprise software will, sooner or later, allow individual organizations to go beyond their limitations as such software systems require the participation of other organizations before total efficiencies and effectiveness can be achieved. As long as organizational employees and staff are ready to share views, and management is open to high-performance changes, new enterprise software can be instituted to add value to the organization's growth and development. Along this line, we close this chapter by summarizing a press release on the combination of ERP and SCM solutions for pharmaceutical distribution channels across Europe.

Frost & Sullivan[20]—a global innovative growth strategies consulting company—proposes, in one of its press releases through its London office, the use of ERP and SCM solutions to ease the flow of pharmaceutical distribution channels across Europe. The company argues that ERP and SCM solutions will ease integration of processes across various functional areas and streamline related functions of key stakeholders in the pharmaceutical distribution channel, resulting in rapid and secure delivery of pharmaceutical products. Rahul Philip Mampallil, a Frost & Sullivan research analyst, claims that "with these IT solutions, manufacturers and other participants in the distribution channel can track the flow of drugs from pharmacy shelves and replenish accordingly to avoid stock outs. . . . Moreover, companies can monitor the movement of stocks and detect the illegal intrusion of batches into the distribution channel." The challenge, he believes, lies in correcting the current lack of understanding about specific business requirements that organizations have when implementing particular add-on ERP modules, and when these modules do not support those requirements. Andersen[21] projected that these solutions will generate revenues of $1.835 billion by 2013, given the high market potential, in the European pharamaceutical sector, for these technologies to diffuse. The application of IT solutions such as SCM, CRM, and ERP will translate into new efficiencies, new boundaries, and new possibilities.

Notes

1. http://www.cio.com/article/31903/Blue_Cross_and_Blue_Shield_of_Minnesota_s_Success_With_CRM/4, accessed June 29, 2008.
2. J. Tan (Ed.), *Health Management Information Systems: Methods and Practical Applications*, 2nd ed. (Gaithersburg, MD: Aspen Publishers, 2001).
3. C. J. Austin and S. B. Boxerman, *Information Systems for Health Services Administration*, 5th ed. (Chicago: AUPHA/Health Administration Press, 1998).
4. K. LaTour and S. Eichenwald Maki (Eds.), *Health Information Management: Concepts, Principles, and Practice*, 2nd ed. (Chicago: AHIMA, 2006).
5. H. L. Lee, V. Padmanabhan, and S. Whang, "Information Distortion in a Supply Chain: The Bullwhip Effect," *Management Science* 43, no. 4 (1997): 546–558.
6. J. W. Forrester, "Industrial Dynamics: A Major Breakthrough for Decision Makers," *Harvard Business Review* 38 (July–August 1958): 37–66.
7. C. Bechtel and J. Jayaram, "Supply Chain Management: A Strategic Perspective," *International Journal of Logistics Management* 8, no. 1 (1997): 15–34.
8. http://www.caduceussystems.com/news-marion-selects-caduceus-systems.html, accessed May 27, 2008.
9. M. Pastore, *The ClickZ Network*. Accessed June 27, 2001, http://www.clickz.com/showPage.html?page=792781.
10. K. Shams and M. Farishta, "Knowledge Management." In K. LaTour and S. Eichenwald Maki (Eds.), *Health Information Management: Concepts, Principles, and Practice*, 2nd ed. (Chicago: AHIMA, 2006).
11. N. Paddison, "Benefits of Event-Driven CRM in Healthcare, Part 1," *DM Review*, January 26, 2001.
12. N. Paddison, "Benefits of Event-Driven CRM in Healthcare, Part 2," *DM Review*, February 2, 2001.
13. W. J. Duncan et al., *Strategic Management of Health Care Organizations* (Oxford, UK: Blackwell Business Publications, 1996).
14. G. Koch and K. Loney, *Oracle: The Complete Reference* (NY: McGraw-Hill, 1996).
15. http://www.astellas.us/press_room/docs/launch_release033105.pdf.
16. B. Gates, *Business at The Speed of Thoughts* (NY: Time Warner, 1999).
17. http://www.jri.co.jp/english/press/press_html/2005/050624.html, accessed July 2, 2008.
18. Tan (2001).
19. B. C. McNurlin and R. H. Sprague, Jr., *Information Systems Management in Practice,* 2nd ed. (Englewood Cliffs, NJ: Prentice-Hall, 1989).
20. http://www.frost.com.
21. http://www.itconsulting.com/press-releases/european-pharma-streamline-112006/, accessed July 3, 2008.

Chapter Questions

4–1. What are some of the major HMIS enterprise software systems? Discuss the need for a data-sharing culture in implementing the various HMIS enterprise software systems.

4–2. Why would it be (or not be) beneficial to combine SCM and CRM into a single system for healthcare services organizations? What about combining SCM with ERP, or other combinations of HMIS enterprise software systems for healthcare services organizations?

4–3. How should one go about standardizing service nomenclature, such as the process service names and outcomes, in order to achieve a level of ease with implementing enterprisewide software? Why must people be sold on the software and be ready to change before moving ahead with a large-scale implementation such as ERP?

4–4. What do you see as the trend of healthcare services organizations with the applications of HMIS enterprise software?

Basic Hardware, Software, and Interface Concepts for Healthcare Services Organizations

Joshia Tan and Joseph Tan

Introduction

Health management information systems (HMIS) are the result of blending healthcare business operations and processes with informational, technological, and human resources. To understand the role and capabilities of technology architecture in the healthcare environment, it is necessary to have a working knowledge of the various hardware, software, and interface concepts. It is assumed that most readers already have a basic understanding of many of these technological concepts in this age of information and knowledge explosion.

Hardware

Hardware includes all physical devices (machines, storage, and input/output devices) that constitute a computer system. A computer system is a subsystem of an organization's HMIS and is an assembly of physical devices connected to at least one processing mechanism, the central processing unit (CPU).

Central Processing Unit

Often referred to as the "brain" or "heart" of the computer, the CPU is the primary core of a computer system. The CPU consists of three associated elements: the control unit (CU), the arithmetic/logic unit (ALU), and the registers.

The CU accesses program instructions, decodes and interprets these instructions, and then issues to other parts of the computer system the necessary orders to carry out the functions. The CU coordinates the flow of data in and out of the ALU, registers, primary storage, secondary storage, and various input and output devices. The ALU receives instructions from the CU and then performs the necessary mathematical calculations and logical comparisons. The registers are used in the CU or the ALU. Registers are high-speed temporary storage areas used to hold small units of program instructions and data temporarily, immediately before, during, and after execution by the CPU. The CPU is designed so that data can be placed into or removed from a register faster than from a location in the main storage area. The CPU has the ability to process raw data into information and execute directions and instructions in a program. The execution of an instruction is known as a machine cycle. The machine cycles, which determine the speed of modern computer processing, are measured in nano- (one-billionth) and pico- (one-trillionth) seconds. Bus lines, which are the physical wires connecting the various computer system components, transfer data from the CPU to other system components. The number of bits that a bus line can transfer at any one moment is the bus line width, which should be matched with CPU word length. Word length is the number of bits a CPU can process at any one time.

Multiprogramming involves executing more than one program at a time. The memory is divided into segments or partitions, each of which holds a program. Virtual storage is an extension of multiprogramming, in which, instead of storing a complete program in memory, the computer stores in memory only a small part of the program at a time while the rest is stored on disk. Thus, the entire program is not needed because the computer is executing only a few instructions at a time. The CPU is therefore less likely to be waiting for programs to be transferred from disk to memory. This reduces idle CPU time and increases the number of jobs that can be completed within a given time span.

Primary and Secondary Storage

Primary storage, or main memory, is closely associated with the CPU. Primary storage holds program instructions and data immediately before or after the registers and provides the CPU with a working storage area for program instructions and data. All programs and data must be transferred to primary storage by way of an input device or secondary storage before programs can be executed or data can be processed. Types of primary storage include random-access memory (RAM), read-only memory (ROM), programmable ROM (PROM), and erasable PROM (EPROM).

RAM is used for short-term storage of data and/or program instructions. It is the memory in which a program is stored when it is presently active in the computer. RAM is volatile because it requires a continuous application of power to retain data and programs: if the power is turned off, everything in RAM is lost unless it is first saved or stored. Two types of RAM chips are dynamic RAM (DRAM) and static RAM (SRAM). The main difference between them lies in how often each needs to be refreshed or recharged per second. DRAM needs to be refreshed thousands of times per second, whereas SRAM needs to be refreshed less often. ROM is used for the permanent storage of program instruction, such as standard instructions. ROM can only be read, not changed or erased, and is nonvolatile. The information it stores is not lost when the power to the computer is interrupted. PROM is a memory device in which the memory chips can be programmed only once and are used to store instructions entered by the purchaser. Once a program is written into PROM, it is permanent. EPROM is a device whose memory chips can be erased and reprogrammed with new instructions.[1]

Secondary (external) storage supplements main memory by holding data and instruction in machine-readable format outside the computer. It offers the advantages of nonvolatility, greater economy, and greater capacity than primary storage. Common forms of secondary storage are floppy disks, magnetic tape and disks, optical disks, optical or laser cards, and smart cards.

Small areas or spots of magnetized particles are used to represent bits on magnetic tapes or disks. Two types of access to the information stored on the magnetic media are available. Direct access allows the computer to go directly to any desired piece of data, regardless of its location on the magnetic medium, such as a floppy disk (which is a flexible disk inside a plastic sleeve). Sequential access, on the other hand, can only read and write data in sequence, one data item after another (e.g., a cassette tape).[2]

Operating like a compact disc (CD) player, an optical disk device uses laser beams to store and retrieve data. One advantage of optical disk storage is its ability to withstand wear, fingerprints, and dust. Two of the most common optical disc storage systems are compact disc–read only memory (CD-ROM) and digital versatile discs (DVDs). Data are stored on these discs by burning small crevices into their coatings. This allows another laser device to read the disc by measuring the difference in the reflected light caused by the crevices on the disc. Each crevice represents the binary digit 0, and the smooth surface area represents the binary digit 1. Storage capacity in DVDs can be several times that of a typical CD-ROM.

Typically, each side of a compact disc is capable of storing 800 or more megabytes of information, which may include text, sound, and pictures. A DVD has the ability to hold a massive amount of information (e.g., an encyclopedia or even a series of movies). Write once, read many (WORM) format allows users to record data only once on a customized basis and then access it whenever needed. WORM discs are nonerasable and are often used to store original versions of valuable documents or data (e.g., archives).

Finally, optical or laser cards and smart cards are the emerging, secured secondary storage medium for many commercial applications. Resembling plastic credit cards, the only difference between these cards has to do with their storage (and processing) capacity. Smart cards have the added capability of "intelligent" processing. As the use of these cards proliferates in commercial and healthcare applications, the cost of manufacturing and supporting their applications will soon become very attractive.

Input/Output Devices

A number of devices can be used to input or enter data into a system. For larger computer systems, key-to-tape and key-to-disk devices have been used, which allow data to be keyed directly onto a secondary storage device. Personal computers are often used for initial entry, editing, or correction of data before the data are downloaded to a larger system for processing.

Keyboards are inexpensive and easy-to-use devices that enter alphanumeric data. Some keyboards allow special character data input at the same time. Online data-entry and data-input devices are connected directly to the computer system by phone lines or cables. The mouse, a pointing device, is another example of an input device. Light pens and track balls, both of which evolved from the mouse concept, are becoming popular for use with portable and handheld devices. Voice recognition systems are used to capture and respond to human speech. Scanning devices, such as direct magnetic ink character recognition (MICR) systems, allow data printed in a special magnetic ink to be read by both humans and computers; the bottom part of a check is an example.

Optical scanners and data readers are used to read characters directly from a page without using special ink. Optical character recognition (OCR) equipment can read alphabetic, numeric, and special characters (i.e., bar codes). Image-processing systems use scanners to input an image into memory. Scanned images can then be manipulated by using graphic software and reprinted as desired. Other input devices include handwriting recognition devices, data tables, and touch screens.

There are many forms of computer output media, including ink-jet and laser printers, video display terminals (VDTs), plotters that draw graphics on paper, computer output microfilm (COM) devices, and voice output devices.

As we move into the future, the miniaturization trend of hardware will reduce the size of peripheral equipment, CPUs, storage, and other computer components. With an increasing reduction in hardware size and increased hardware processing capabilities, costs of computer hardware will continue to drop.[3] This will generate faster, greater volume, and more accurate information for the user.[4,5]

Software

Over the decades, software and user interface technologies have gained a larger share of total system costs.[6] Advances in hardware have dramatically reduced costs; however, prices in software and user interface have increased. Currently, software encompasses 75 percent or more of the costs of an organization's computer system.[7] Increasingly complex software systems require more time, memory, and money to develop and, in turn, increase the demand for the product and the salaries of developers. Systems management software and applications software are two classes of software used routinely.

Systems Management Software

Systems management software refers to machine executable programs designed to supervise and support the overall functioning of the computer system, independent of any specific application area. Systems software manages computer resources, such as the CPU, printers, terminals, communication links, and peripheral equipment. Three main categories include operating systems (OS), language translation programs (LTP), and utility programs (UP).

OS, written for specific computers and usually stored on disk and transferred to memory when a computer is "booted" (i.e., turned on), run the computer hardware and interface with applications software. Examples include Mac OS V10.5 (Leopard), Windows Vista, and Windows Server 2008. LTP convert statements from high-level programming languages into machine code. The high-level program code is referred to as the source code and the machine language code as the object code. To perform such a conversion, a compiler is used. An interpreter executes each machine language statement, discards it, and then continues to translate the next statement. UP perform specialized functions directly related to the actual computer operation. They are considered part of systems software and are used to prepare documents, merge and sort files, keep track of computer jobs being run, manage printers and disk drives, recover lost programs, and lock confidential files.

A mainframe is a large computer that has access to large amounts of data and is capable of processing these data very quickly. Mainframes have now been replaced with supercomputers. Online and real-time processing involves the running of a program whenever data are collected and entered into the computer system. Online processing is possible because terminals and other devices are directly connected to the main computer; as a result, data files are kept as current as possible. Batch processing is done at the end of the day, mostly to back up transactions and other data types.

Applications Software

Applications software, designed to handle the processing for particular tasks, refers to programs written to solve specific domain problems and cannot be used without the system software. A company can develop applications software in house (make), use existing off-the-shelf software (buy), or outsource part of their data processing (contract). Microsoft Office 2008, Adobe Flash, and Macromedia Dreamweaver are some of the more popular applications software systems.

A programming language is a set of symbols and rules used to write program code. There have been at least five identifiable "generations" of programming languages. First-generation, or machine, language is the most basic level of computer operation. It uses binary coding and addresses to execute instructions and is difficult to write because of its binary representation of information as 1s and 0s corresponding to "on" and "off" electrical states of the computer. Second-generation, or assembly, language is a low-level symbolic language, unique to a specific computer. It replaces binary digits with understandable symbols to ease programming. Third-generation, or procedure-oriented, language uses structured English-like statements in the coding of program instructions. Each instruction is equivalent to multiple machine-level instructions. Examples include Cobol, Fortran, Pascal, C, C++, Visual Basic, and Java.

Fourth-generation language (4GL), or very high-level language, is nonprocedural and more English-like than any previous generation language. Its distinctive features include high-level queries for direct database access; interactive dialogs; simple-to-learn, helpful error messages; and use of defaults and relational database management systems. However, these application generators, as 4GLs are sometimes called, are often less efficient in terms of computer running time than earlier-generation languages. Examples include database query languages such as SQL, data analysis such as SAS, and report generators such as Oracle Reports.[8] Fifth-generation languages, or artificial intelligence, include expert systems and natural language interfaces. Research in this domain has also advanced the knowledge of user–computer interface.

User–Computer Interface

When the concept of interface emerges, it was commonly understood as "the hardware and software through which a human and computer could communicate."[9] Over time, the concept has broadened to include "the cognitive and emotional aspects of the user's experience as well."[10] From a user's perspective, an interface is a discrete and tangible thing that can map, draw, design, implement, and attach items to an existing bundle of functions. Interfacing allows users to interact with the computer to perform various interactive functions.

Two main types of user–computer interfaces are action and presentation language.[11] In action language, the user instructs the computer to take a series of actions; it is the way in which the user's intentions are translated into syntax that the machine understands. A simple example is the use of a touch screen or an icon. Presentation language is the way in which the computer communicates with the user, for example, by the use of color and graphics.[12] Four main designs for user–computer interface are graphical, iconic, direct manipulation, and group interfaces.

A graphical interface is associated with presentation languages, whereas an iconic interface relates to action language. Graphical interfacing allows tables and numbers to be converted and represented spatially. Common examples include lines, bar graphs, and scatter plots. These interface architectures enable visual representations of trends, taxonomies, statistical summaries, forecasting patterns, and performance reports—generally giving the user an increased understanding of data patterns and trends.[13] Iconic interfaces use pictures or images to represent commands and objects that can be invoked by users.[14] They allow for improved performance and learning and help eliminate unnecessary errors. Icons allow for easy recognition and categorization and are usually faster to absorb than words. A key disadvantage of iconic interfaces is that it is often difficult to convey the desired meaning to the user without sometimes invoking other undesirable properties and connotations. Three different classes of icons are representational icons (or metaphor graphics), abstract icons, and arbitrary icons.

Representational icons or metaphor graphics[15] are prototypical images of a specific class of physical objects. These types of icons correspond to real-world objects, thereby enabling the user to recognize the icons and make some inferences based on them. Examples of representational icons are file folds, trashcans, and document images. Abstract icons convey a specific concept using a visual image. Examples of abstract icons are warning labels on household products. Arbitrary icons have a meaning assigned to them; however, they are often difficult to interpret. For these types of icons to be meaningful and useful, there needs to be some standard definition.

Another design of user–computer interface is direct manipulation, which involves communication between a system and a user through the physical manipulation of object representations using a device, such as a mouse. The general characteristics of direct manipulation interfaces are a continuous representation of the object of interest; physical actions instead of complex syntax; and rapid incremental reversible operations, whose impact on the object of interest is immediately visible.[16] In general, direct manipulation incorporates the concept of an analogy between the system and a problem domain. Through direct manipulation, the users feel as if they are working on the actual problem of interest rather than interacting with an abstract, computer-based model.

Finally, the complexity of the user interface increases as HMIS become more complex and there is a need for communication and collaboration between several individuals. Malone defines a "group" interface as an organization interface (i.e., the parts of a computer system that connect human users to each other and to the computing capabilities provided by systems).[17] A group interface provides a flexible interface that allows different individuals to communicate with one another efficiently and effectively.

To tie in the discussion of hardware, software, and interface concepts with healthcare services organizations, we proceed with a real-world scenario where the applications of these concepts can improve organizational efficiency.

How Hardware/Software and Interface Design Affect the Healthcare Services Industry

During the 1980s, Harvard Pilgrim sought to expand its business presence through purchasing a number of healthcare services organizations. After 13 years of acquisitions, Harvard Pilgrim had accumulated more than 55 separate core HMIS applications that were not integrated with each other, including four claims-processing systems that failed to track claims or set accurate insurance premiums. The situation became critical in 1999, when the health maintenance organization (HMO) reported an astonishing $54 million net loss and an operations loss of $94 million. A new management team was hired, and Louis Gutierrez, the new CIO, blamed part of this mess on the lack of Harvard Pilgrim's systems integration.

Immediately, Gutierrez looked for ways to improve IT operations. He decided to outsource both claims processing and the technology functions, which included data center operations, network infrastructure, and programming. In October 1999, the HMO signed a $700 million, 10-year contract with Perot Systems as an answer to the company's massive IT problem. Unfortunately, the next year showed additional losses of between $60 and $70 million, and Harvard Pilgrim was forced into temporary receivership by the courts, effectively putting the organization into state control to keep it from going bankrupt.

Searching for solutions, Gutierrez and Perot Systems decided to tackle the claims-processing mess first. They narrowed the problem to four outdated hardware and software systems that were unable to handle the heavy load of daily transactions. The team eventually kept only a single HMIS, upgraded it, and added a more durable hardware platform. They brought in Cap Gemini consultants to help install Oracle financials, human resources, and payroll systems, in an effort to consolidate all operational data from claims systems, pharmacies, and other third-party service providers.

Since implementing these new systems, Harvard Pilgrim's situation has stabilized, and the financial outlook gradually improved. During the turnaround, Harvard Pilgrim spent $75 to $80 million on HMIS investments alone. Surprisingly, Gutierrez credits much of the success to overall cost cutting rather than implementing new HMIS solutions. "Many of the key levers were decidedly nonsystems fixes," he claimed. "A lot of the progress was in tighter management and better business processes. I learned a lot from that. We were very smart about what we did to clean up on the IT side, but it's just not the case that one can point to massive new systems as the solution here."

Notes

1. K. C. Laudon and J. P. Laudon, *Business Information Systems: A Problem-Solving Approach* (Hinsdale, IL: Dryden Press, 1991).

2. J. O'Brien, *Introduction to Information Systems in Business Management*, 6th ed. (Homewood, IL: Richard D. Irwin, 1991).

3. T. K. Zinn, "HIS Technology Trends," *Computers in Healthcare* (February 1991): 46–50.

4. C. Dunbar, "It Comes Down to Managing Minutes," *Computers in Healthcare* (March 1992): 6.

5. S. L. Mandell, *Dr. Mandell's Ultimate Personal Computer Desk Reference* (Toledo, OH: Rawhide Press, 1993).

6. P. J. Hills, *Information Management Systems: Implications for the Human-Computer Interface* (Toronto: Ellis Horwood, 1990).

7. J. Burn and E. Caldwell, *Management of Information Systems Technology* (Orchard, Oxfordshire, UK: Alfred Waller, 1990).

8. J. K. H. Tan, "An Introduction to Health Decision Support Systems: Definition, Evolution and Framework." In J. K. H. Tan with S. Sheps (Eds.), *Health Decision Support Systems*, (Gaithersburg, MD: Aspen Publishers, 1998): 25–32.

9. I. Benbasat et al., *The User-Computer Interface in Systems Design* (British Columbia: Faculty of Commerce and Business Administration, University of British Columbia, 1993).

10. B. Laurel (Ed.), *The Art of Human-Computer Interface* (Reading, MA: Addison-Wesley Publishing Co., 1992).

11. Benbasat et al. (1993).

12. J. K. H. Tan, "Graphics: Theories and Experiments," *Computer Graphics Forum* 11, no. 4 (1992): 261.

13. J. K. H. Tan and I. Benbasat, "Processing of Graphical Information: A Decomposition Taxonomy To Match Data Extraction Tasks and Graphical Representations," *Information Systems Research* 1, no. 4 (December 1990): 416–439.

14. D. Gittens, "Icon-Based Human-Computer Interaction," *International Journal of Man-Machine Studies* 24 (1989): 519–543.

15. W. Cole, *Metaphor Graphics and Visual Analogy for Medical Data, Section on Medical Information Science* (San Francisco: University of California at San Francisco, 1988).

16. Benbasat et al. (1993).

17. T. Malone, "Designing Organizational Interfaces," *Proceedings of CHI'85* (1985): 66–71.

18. W. Raghupathi and J. K. H. Tan, "Strategic Uses of Information Technology in Health Care: A State-of-the-Art Survey," *Topics in Health Information Management* 20, no. 1 (1990): 1–15.

19. S. Patton, "Turnaround Strategies: Harvard Pilgrim Health Care Finds a Remedy." Accessed July 7, 2008, from http://www.cio.com/article/31506.

Community Health Information Networks:
Building Virtual Communities and Networking Health Provider Organizations

*Jayfus T. Doswell, SherRhonda R. Gibbs,
and Kelley M. Duncanson*

Editor's Note: Building virtual community networks involves the use of a combination of the Internet and associated technologies *(Technology Brief I)*; hardware, software, and computer-user interface design *(Technology Brief II)*; as well as telecommunications and network technologies *(Technology Brief III)*. Its primary concern is the integration of community organizations as partners for healthcare services delivery. This represents an expansion of concepts discussed in HMIS administrative applications and technologies (Chapter 4), patient-centric management systems (Chapter 6), and/or Web services applied for healthcare services delivery (Chapter 7). Community organizations will always play a significant role in the development and application of HMIS foundational concepts (Part I); technologies and applications (Part II); planning and management (Part III); and policy, governance, and globalization (Part IV). The knowledge acquired in Chapter 5 will, therefore, be useful and important to aid in the understanding of many other parts of this text.

Scenario: Designing an Intelligent Community Health Information Network[1]

Imagine that you have been asked to oversee the design of a new community health information network (CHIN) that would electronically link information from various "smart spaces" in a community ranging from homes, parks, fitness centers, and restaurants to available health provider networks and other community services such as police, fire, and ambulatory care.

Depending on age, prior health condition, genetic profile, and current prescribed medications, intelligent and noninvasive sensors may be employed remotely to monitor your health in a home environment, where personalized medicine is being propagated. While asleep, your bed may be equipped with sensors to monitor vital physiology to determine current health status against optimal health. When you wake up and brush your teeth, the toothpaste may be equipped with nano-particles to automatically eliminate tartar, and the toothbrush may include nano-electronics to collect information about critical plaque areas. Data collected from the toothbrush may wirelessly communicate incidences of periodontal disease, which has direct correlation to heart disease. At the same time, a mirror may use intelligent software agents to visually recognize skin and eye abnormalities and determine severe incidences of stress, natural aging, or the consequences of poor nutrition. When you urinate, sensors in the toilet may automatically analyze nutritional deficiencies and incidences of disease progression and update your health profile, all in real-time. Your genetic profile may automatically be registered when you go to the hair salon or barber shop when equipment, used to cut the hair, has embedded sensors to collect hair samples and process them using on-board "lab-on-the-chip" before sending data to the centralized CHIN repository.

All information collected and processed using artificial intelligent algorithms may be filtered and then transmitted to the CHIN grid, where a collection of community-volunteer computer processors interpret the information and consequently reduce community healthcare costs. From a public health perspective, human healthcare data may be continually collected in parks, fitness centers, supermarkets, homes, and schools to monitor the overall health of various communities around the nation and the world to prevent illness, injury, and disease at an affordable cost to the community.

Imagine no more—the future of intelligent CHIN is here!

I. Introduction

A community health information network (CHIN) is a combination of telecommunication and networking capabilities that links healthcare stakeholders throughout a community. It is what Ernst and Young Health Care practices describe as "interorganizational systems using information technologies and telecommunications to store, transmit, and transform clinical and financial information."[2] This information can be shared among patients, providers, employers, pharmacies, and related healthcare entities within a targeted geographical area.[3]

The rapid advancements of e-commerce and managed care placed new demands on the healthcare industry in the 1990s to establish information infrastructures that facilitate timely, accurate, secure, and interoperable patient information across the continuum of care.[4] Integrated healthcare delivery systems and managed care organizations responded by developing health information networks within their organizations to support required internal information.[5] Hospital information systems have evolved from mainframe legacy systems to complex, integrated, PC-based administrative, clinical, and financial decision support systems. In the late 1990s, the paradigm of dot-com start-ups has led to several online medical records solutions for healthcare providers unable or not wishing to support electronic medical records (EMR) internally. With the exception of Internet-based EMR, clinical and financial information was trapped within each organization's system and could not be shared through the continuum of care or with business partners.[6]

Data in EMR often could not be shared beyond the provider, and electronic data sharing was not possible between competitors even for the purpose of continuity of care. By 2002, the government recognized the inability of healthcare service organizations to effectively communicate healthcare information across disparate networks and consequently endorsed the National Health Information Infrastructure (NHII). The fundamental objective of the NHII is to bring timely health information to, and aid communications among, those making health decisions for themselves, their families, their patients, and their communities. Individuals, healthcare providers, and public health professionals are key NHII stakeholders and users, and the applications that meet their respective needs are distinct dimensions of the infrastructure.

As a result of problems in data standards, patient restrictions in healthcare information access, and poor interoperability among healthcare systems, the concept of CHIN emerged. Specifically, the CHIN concept grew out of grassroots community efforts to streamline information among myriad partners with the end goal of better integration of care, increased cost savings, and efficient data interoperability.[7] Many definitions are offered to describe CHIN. Common elements from these definitions include:

- Interorganizational information systems for data and information exchange among participants in the local healthcare delivery system. Members include physicians, clinics, hospitals, payors, managed care companies, community health centers, public health, laboratories, diagnostic/testing companies, pharmacies, and educational entities (including universities).
- Improved efficiency and effectiveness of healthcare services delivery.
- Independent operation of member organizations, often initiated by grassroots or community-based not-for-profit organizations.
- Resources and educational tools for the community and disease management and case management modules.

II. Previous Community Health Information Networks

Various types of CHIN have emerged in the past, ranging from home healthcare delivery and voluntary care to enterprise- and telephone-based networks. For example, telephone-based networks (funded by organizations such as ComputerLink) have emerged as a type of CHIN offering a relatively inexpensive alternative to those involving a full-function centralized computer network. In early CHIN implementations, telephones provide community links through a low-cost, widely used alternative to care delivery. Used to address public health needs, telephone technology can help deliver medical, prevention, and patient self-care services through conference calling, patient education, support groups, voice-mailing, referral information, announcements, and services. Even with the promise of improved healthcare delivery, very few CHIN implementations survived. Notable survivors include the Wisconsin Health Information Network (WHIN; www.whin.net) in Milwaukee and the London and Regional Global Network (LARG*net).

The WHIN is an open system design intranet used to track, access, and distribute voluntarily provided patient and medical information.[8] WHIN offers services such as eligibility verification, electronic claim submission, benefits review, and prescription-refill authorization. These services focus on the health transactions needed by healthcare professionals to tend to their patients. It also delivers access to application, human, financial, and time resources to support the CHIN initiative. WHIN operates independently of its member organizations as a for-profit organization that, in part, derives revenue from electronically processing healthcare transactions. WHIN is made up of three independent components working together to make the flow of information possible:[9]

- WHIN connect software to give users access to the network.
- WHIN processor interface software to connect provider and health information.
- WHIN switch to route request for information and corresponding responses between users and providers, besides managing the network security.

Some CHIN have focused on the efficient care for uninsured community residents.[10] Others like the Vermont Health Information network[11] provides a Web interface to assist consumers in finding quality medical and healthcare information on the Internet. Because of the Health Insurance Portability and Accountability Act of 1996 (HIPAA), new iterations of CHIN have emerged with a better chance at success because of environmental factors such as increased data and transaction standardization. These factors simplify data exchange and promote Internet utilization for platform-independent applications and tools that will be more widely available to the community.

III. From CHIN to RHINO

Community health information networks have evolved into what researchers and practitioners now call regional health information networks (RHIN) or regional health information organizations (RHIO), hereafter referred to as RHINO. As evolutions of CHIN concepts, RHINO are quickly becoming the organizational structure of choice for many healthcare organizations and networks. As discussed, the funding support for previous CHIN implementations was limited due to reliance on cumbersome pre-Internet technology, lack of standardization of data, and insufficient funding sources. With the advent of advanced health data exchange methods from Health Level 7 (HL7); the adoption of NHII standards; and the work performed at the American Public Health Association health informatics/information technology special interest groups (SPIG), Healthcare Information and Management Systems (HIMSS), and the American Telemedicine Association, on-demand and client-governed healthcare delivery may now be achieved.

More recently, Thielst defined RHINO as "a network of stakeholders within a defined region who are committed to improving the quality, safety access and efficiency of healthcare through the use of HIT (health information technology)."[12,13] RHINO involve a complex amalgamation of communitywide collaborations and the creation of sustainable organizational structures. They are designed to move healthcare information efficiently and inexpensively. RHINO usually proceed through a series of life cycle stages consisting of *start-up* (recognition of need, stakeholder consensus building, creation of organizational structure, governance, and acquisition of financial support and resources), *transition* (implementation under way, personnel expansion, beta and pilot testing, and Web presence), and *production* (live data processing, adding new partners, and administrative routine). RHINO are typically not-for-profit organizations, although some are now adopting for-profit status. To successfully implement a

RHINO, stakeholders must bring together competitors to share a common vision and goals. Key barriers[14] to RHINO implementation include:

- Cost of development (46 percent).
- Lack of organizational leadership (2 percent).
- Lack of clinical nomenclature (19 percent).
- Concerns about data security (10 percent).
- Unknown (2 percent).

At the same time, successful RHINO focus on the delivery of relevant information to clinicians at the point and time of care and clinical decision support (to help process vast amounts of data and benchmarking to save time and eliminate redundancies).[15] HIPAA is also touted as being an enabler of RHINO through its requirements for privacy and security regulations that permit electronic health record (EHR) diffusion.

There are three types of RHINO structures: federation, co-op and hybrids. According to Thielst[16]

1. *Federation.* RHINO structure includes multiple independently strong enterprises in the same region, which are self-sufficient but that agree to share access to information maintained on a peer-to-peer basis. This is facilitated through a system of indexing (e.g., regional or statewide master patient index).
2. *Co-op.* RHINO structure also consists of multiple but smaller enterprises that agree to share resources and create a central utility. Within this structure, technology and administrative overhead are shared.
3. *Hybrid.* As the name implies, hybrid structures contain both federation and co-op networks. The model allows aggregation within and across healthcare organizations in large regional areas, statewide regions, or multistate regions.

IV. Prospects for RHINO

Ultimately, the primary goal for the CHIN evolution and the RHINO movement is the subsequent establishment of a national health information network (NHIN). NHIN, which will be supported by new U.S. federal governmental initiatives, will comprise a network of RHINO. While progress toward this goal is still in the infancy stage, forums are taking place with discussions concerning connecting provider EHR and consumers' personal health records (PHR) as well as state, regional, and nongeographic health information exchanges and specific network functions such as clinical laboratory records, disease registries, and beyond.

To achieve the steps toward establishing a NHIN, practitioners must first address broader challenges faced in the healthcare competitive marketplace. These challenges relate to major issues such as:

- Competition.
- Internal policies.
- Consumer privacy.

- Uncertainties regarding liabilities.
- Difficulty reaching multi-enterprise agreement on information sharing.
- Economic factors.
- Incentives.
- Interoperability.
- Security testing, authentication, and auditability.

In a recent article, Feris[17] notes that RHINO are struggling to survive, despite the intentions of U.S. Department of Health and Human Services (HHS) policy makers for RHINO to serve as the building blocks for a national system. A total of 145 RHINO were known to exist nationwide during their first inception. However, a recent Harvard University study showed that currently only 20 of these are functioning at a modest scale with just 15 of them tending to a broad set of patients. Nearly 25 percent of RHINO existing in mid-2006 have now gone defunct, suggesting an increased difficulty for achieving a nationwide electronic clinical data exchange.

Key barriers to RHINO implementations are financial sustainability and partnering to increase membership. This seems to suggest that problems may exist in terms of championing by governmental and healthcare leaders. RHINO cannot succeed without the joint funding and sharing of resources from governmental, public, and private sector organizations. Consequently, healthcare leaders from the aforementioned networked organizations must lend their full support to RHINO. In recognizing this need, Frisse[18] also argues that sustained leadership, a review of best practices in other regions, and an assessment of regional needs and capabilities are all key to the long-term success of RHINO alliances. Frisse's work concludes that over the long term, a truly interoperable health information infrastructure depends on the extent to which the alliances demonstrate value to consumers and practitioners.

V. HL7 Standard Health Data Exchange

The new CHIN will have to rely on standard health data exchange in order to achieve the health system data interoperability goal of the National Health Information Infrastructure. HL7 is a collaboration in health data standardization that would help to realize this goal.

HL7—an international community of healthcare subject matter experts and information scientists who collaborate to create standards for the exchange, management, and integration of electronic healthcare information—promotes the use of health data standards within and among healthcare services organizations to increase the effectiveness and efficiency of healthcare services delivery. It focuses on developing coherent, extendible standards that permit structured, encoded healthcare information of the type required to support patient care to be exchanged between computer applications while preserving meaning.

The stated goals of HL7 collaboration are to:

- Develop coherent, extendable standards that permit structured, encoded healthcare information of the type required to support patient care, to be exchanged between computer applications while preserving meaning.

- Develop a formal methodology to support the creation of HL7 standards from the HL7 Reference Information Model.
- Educate the healthcare industry, policy makers, and the general public concerning the benefits of healthcare information standardization generally and HL7 standards specifically.
- Promote the use of HL7 standards worldwide through the creation of HL7 International Affiliate organizations, which will, in turn, participate in developing and in implementing HL7 standards locally as required.
- Stimulate, encourage, and facilitate domain experts from healthcare industry stakeholder organizations to participate in the HL7 healthcare information standards developmental process in their area of expertise.
- Collaborate with other standards development organizations and national and international sanctioning bodies such as the American National Standards Institute (ANSI), International Organization for Standardization (ISO), and others in both the healthcare and information infrastructure domains to promote the use of supportive and compatible standards.
- Collaborate with healthcare IT users to ensure that HL7 standards meet real-world requirements and that appropriate standards development efforts are initiated by HL7 to meet emergent requirements.

HL7 Version 3 is an HL7 messaging standard that has been developed. Version 3 uses a Reference Information Model (RIM) as a common source for the information content of specifications. As part of Version 3, the HL7 Vocabulary Technical Committee developed methods that allow HL7 specifications to draw upon codes and vocabularies from a variety of sources. The V3 vocabulary work ensures that the systems implementing HL7 specifications have an unambiguous understanding of the code sources and code value domains that are being used by those who adopt HL7 standards.

The HL7 Version 3 development methodology is a continuously evolving process that seeks to develop specifications that facilitate interoperability among healthcare systems. The HL7 RIM, vocabulary specifications, and model-driven process of analysis and design combine to make HL7 Version 3 one methodology for development of consensus-based standards for healthcare information system interoperability.

Community Management Systems

New CHIN need to implement community management systems that operate from a central information hub. This "hub" connects to practice management systems, personal medical records, and novel health data collection devices around a community.

For practice management systems delivered from private healthcare organizations and hospitals, electronic billing and patient scheduling are being developed to reduce time for data entry and increase the accuracy of billing/coding, patient scheduling, and reporting to healthcare insurance companies through registered clearinghouses. Practice management systems do not work alone but are accompanied by electronic records that are increasingly complementing and, in some cases, replacing physical charts. Earlier versions of electronic medical records are limited mostly to gathering patient data only in a single-provider clinical environment—the data therefore, would, not be easily shared with other providers.

Owing to reported medical errors arising from restricted sharing of critical healthcare information, policies are now being addressed on the need to apply HL7 to facilitate the exchange of EMR across healthcare providers and managed through practice management systems. This observed trend in data sharing, as discussed, provides the benefits of improving the quality of care services to patients, who are potentially consumers in a community. As well, the new HL7 standardized data system will provide a trajectory record of patient historic data and prescriptions to yield better accuracy in portraying a person's health state at any time.

Unfortunately, there still is a lack of health decision support systems that will be referenced on the recorded data to help healthcare providers improve their quality of decision making with respect to optimizing care for the patient. In this sense, new CHIN are being developed with artificial intelligent (AI) algorithms embedded. The application of such intelligent CHIN will not only enhance the analysis of patients' health profiles, but also provide continuous monitoring of their lifestyle changes (e.g., nutrition and exercise). Moreover, for the purpose of public health reporting, these intelligent CHIN will permit the use of predictive models to further determine health risk and the onset of adverse health impact to both the individuals and the community.

A good example of a community health exchange system would be that of HealthBridge. HealthBridge, a not-for-profit health information exchange center, primarily serves Cincinnati, Ohio, and the surrounding area. The organization is noted as being one of the nation's largest, most advanced, and most financially successful community health information exchanges. HealthBridge provides connectivity for more than 4,400 physicians; 29 hospitals; 17 local health departments; and dozens of physician offices and clinics, nursing homes, independent labs, and radiology centers, as well as connectivity for others in the healthcare community. Through the clinical messaging system, HealthBridge is able to deliver more than 2.4 million laboratory, radiology, transcription, and Admission-Discharge-Transfer (ADT) results to physicians every month. Currently, HealthBridge represents nearly 95 percent of the hospital sector activity in the Cincinnati region.[19]

HealthBridge's exchange system is driven by software developed by the Axolotl Corporation. According to CEO Ray Scott, this is how the system works: (1) Each hospital pushes out reports from its own systems to a local Axolotl server. (2) In turn, periodically the local server pushes aggregated data to a central HealthBridge server. (3) From there, reports are collated from the various hospitals and sorted by patients against a community index that the software maintains. (4) Then, organized around the physician of record, these "messages" are distributed to physicians electronically, via fax, or through the regular mail. Many physicians receive the messages electronically but print out the results they need for their own charts. This, in turn, benefits the hospitals since they no longer must mail and track reports being generated by multiple departments. Furthermore, by organizing data around physicians, HealthBridge side-steps sticky privacy issues.[20]

HealthBridge has overcome major milestones with regard to its clinical messaging feature. At the beginning, physicians were constrained by the company's "pull" technology. Eventually, the messaging system gained the capacity to "push" information out to the hospitals. And for the first time, they could justify HealthBridge through a more definitive return on investment formula. Now with the ability to use a common tool to distribute lab results, radiology reports, transcribed documents, and admission-discharge-transfer summaries, hospitals could identify savings.

VI. Mayo Clinic CASE Study

At this point, it should be noted that the possibilities for enhancing an interoperable CHIN are limited only to our imagination as described in the opening scenario of this chapter. We close the chapter with a case study on the Mayo Clinic. In this case study, the organizational structure described closely resembles that of a hybrid RHIO—or a RHINO—functioning in two ways: utility versus neutral/convener/facilitator. Whereas the *utility* works using a centralized database and serves as a patient information exchange, clearinghouse, and location, the role of the *neutral/convener/facilitator* is to partner competitive enterprises and bridge multiple RHINO through an open-standards approach. Indeed, the latter of these two roles is more difficult to implement, although it may be ideal for laying the foundation to establishing a National Health Information Network.

In recent years, an increasing number of healthcare organizations began efforts to create more efficient, integrative communication and information systems infrastructure and architecture. For instance, to increase its effectiveness and to affect surrounding communities with its capabilities, the Mayo Clinic has pursued an aggressive strategy of complementation using a number of communication configurations, including both hub-and-wheel and group community support systems.

The Mayo Clinic, which is most renowned for its outpatient clinic, is a diverse and complex organization. Today, the Mayo Clinic network spans far beyond its outpatient facilities to include multiple hospitals, research facilities, a medical university, affiliated partner clinics and hospitals in surrounding states, and independently run hospitals and clinics in places such as Arizona and Florida. Affiliated hospitals and clinics are located in smaller communities in southern Minnesota, northern Iowa and western Wisconsin. All facilities within the network are able to provide better patient and community care because they benefit from the vast resources, knowledge, and technological capabilities of the Mayo Clinic. Through shared resources (e.g., clinicians, researchers, and information systems), smaller hospitals and clinics are able to offer specialized radiological services or cancer treatments to patients.

While many of the affiliate and independently run hospitals maintain their own centralized EMR, patient medical history is shared through a centralized EMR database maintained by

Mayo. At the same time, affiliate hospitals and clinics can access Mayo's centralized EMR to monitor the health care of their patients at other Mayo facilities. Mayo's visionary leadership and its integrated IT systems group enabled this strategy of collaboration. The IT group used the Tandem platform and GE Carecast software to develop Mayo's centralized, comprehensive EMR system that now contains data from all providers within Mayo's network. Through this system, Mayo is able to maintain an EMR system that provides unprecedented access to patient history and medical information.

EMR for patients seen at affiliates within the Mayo network can be retrieved by authorized network providers by way of a master patient index (MPI) linked to the centralized EMR system. Mayo employs electronic data interchange (EDI) using HL7 messaging to facilitate data sharing among affiliates whose EMR systems may operate on diverse platforms such as the IBM mainframe, Sun OS, AIX, AS/400, or Linux. Even within Mayo's main campus facilities, researchers and clinicians enjoy cross-platform access to shared departmental resources, directories, and server-based applications. This is due in part to Mayo's unique RHINO implementation.

Mayo's information infrastructure allows for the integration of disparate platforms and systems, giving network providers maximum flexibility in resource selection. Mayo's research computing facility,[21] for example, utilizes Red Hat Linux high-powered computing systems to perform large computations for research. In contrast, Mayo's on-campus hospitals may opt to maintain EMR on the IBM platform, while specialty areas such as radiology may use the Sun OS. Despite the diversity in systems, through HL7 EDI, patient medical data are continually sent to the integrated, centralized EMR system via the MPI and standard system interfaces. This eliminates the need for cross-training on multiple systems and enables better decision making on the part of the care providers. Health care becomes more efficient by providers having access to their own system as well as the centralized EMR. Theoretically, a patient's complete medical history could be available to any Mayo network care provider. The RHINO implemented by Mayo is particularly important for healthcare organizations that (like the Mayo Clinic) are frequented by patients from other cities, states, and countries. Figure 5.1 illustrates Mayo's health information network and depicts the various components of its communications systems infrastructure.

Mayo offers a fully integrated intranet that allows providers access to shared information and Web-based applications. Patients and potential patients also have access to research and information disseminated by Mayo care providers through the Mayo Clinic consumer information website.[22] Soon, Mayo Clinic patients will be able to make Web-based calls into a separate customer-centric website, where patient portals allow customers to view their bills and information online while speaking with their physicians. Mayo is also taking the lead by tapping into multimedia technologies that offer simulation-based education to medical students and residents.[23] Although integration and collaboration dominate current planning efforts at Mayo, research performed in specialized fields such as genetics may exist external to the infrastructure described.

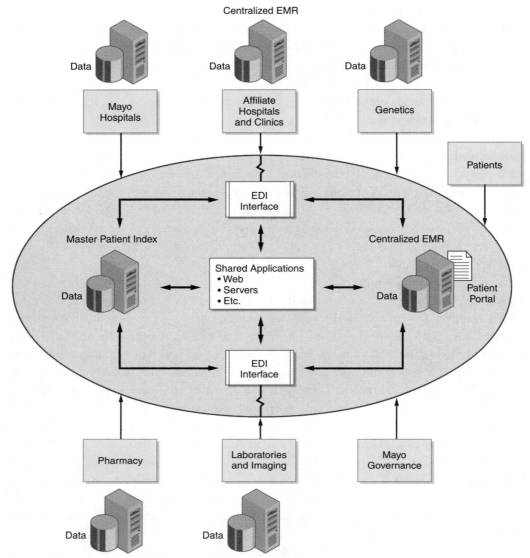

FIGURE 5.1   Mayo Clinic Health Information Network.

VII.   Conclusion

While the Mayo model is reflective of current healthcare trends, like many healthcare institutions, change is painstakingly slow, whereby new technology and innovative methods for delivering patient information are provided only after its effectiveness and efficiency have been proven. Current efforts toward cost minimization and improved patient care are starting to affect this brontosaurus-like movement. However, technological challenges and policy-related issues may continue to stall RHINO implementations so long as information infrastructures are governed by well-intentioned committees concerned with the effects of network innovations on established policies and procedures. In cases where technology adoption and network collaboration decisions are dictated by a single decision maker or specially appointed teams, more innovative and expedited choices can be made. Whether the larger community accepts the resulting RHINO and adopted technologies has yet to be further evaluated.

Other issues that may arise with a RHINO setup like the Mayo Clinic's include problems with data shadowing and the need for creating interfaces to communicate among disparate platforms and software. These problems are, in part, controlled by implementing HL7, which enables messaging and data interchange among systems. Also, the continuing need for CHIN data storage, backup, and replication on all platforms must be accommodated with a failsafe for system outages and during times of inclement weather. Timing is another cause for concern because patient test results may be delayed or dated depending on the accuracy and speed of the RHINO EDI. Reciprocal access is another potential problem that has to be addressed. While Mayo's centralized EMR is available to affiliates, the same access to affiliates' EMR may not be available to Mayo's main campus providers. At the same time, Mayo allows network providers limited access to patient EMR while technical issues, security protocols, and agreements are resolved. The governing bodies of organizations within the network must decide the scope and level to which access (and reciprocal information sharing) is given to other network providers that will allow the best patient care possible.

RHINO or CHIN like the Mayo Clinic were set up to improve the quality of health care, support provider decision making, and facilitate cost reductions.[24] They allow physicians to make better judgments concerning patient care, which saves lives, time, and money. To truly benefit from a CHIN, hospitals must closely align their centralized systems with key business processes and strategies. The systems will then generate strategic output, whose uses allow CHIN providers to enjoy an advantage over competitors. As is the case with the United Kingdom national healthcare model, most hospital systems are moving toward CHIN/RHINO, where all affiliated healthcare facilities can feed to and read from a centralized "spine" that houses all patient data. Eventually, it is expected that more use of wireless technologies will factor into CHIN/RHINO when issues such as learning curves and compatibility can be overcome.

Notes

1. F. Payton and P. Brennan, "How a Community Health Information Network Is Really Used," *Communications of the ACM* 42 (1999): 85–89.
2. Ibid.
3. F. Payton, P. Brennan, and M. Ginzberg (1995). "Needs Determination for a Community Approach to Health Care Delivery," Special Issues Series on Management of Technology in Health Care, *International Journal of Technology Management* 1, no. 1 (1995): 157–173.
4. P. Soper, "White Paper: Realizing the Potential of Community Health Information Networks for Improved Quality and Efficiency through the Continuum of Care: A Case Study of the HRSA Community Access Program and the Nebraska Panhandle Partnership for Health and Human Services," WHP023A, December 2001.
5. C. J. Austin and S. B. Boxerman, *Information Systems for Health Services Administration* (Chicago: Health Administration Press, 1997): 359–381.

6. Soper (2001).
7. Ibid.
8. Payton and Brennan (1999).
9. J. Tan, *Health Management Information Systems: Methods and Practical Applications*, 2nd ed. (Gaithersburg, MD: Aspen Publishers, 2001).
10. Soper (2001).
11. http://library.uvm.edu/dana/vthealth/.
12. C. B. Thielst, "Regional Health Information Networks and the Emerging Organizational Structures," *Journal of Healthcare Management*, 52 (2007): 146–150.
13. C. B. Thielst and L. E. Jones, *Guide to Establishing a Regional Health Information Organization* (Chicago: Healthcare and Information Management Systems, 2007): 1.
14. www.himss.org/content/files/vantagepoint/vantagepoint_200604b.htm, Vantage Point, 2006.
15. Thielst (2007).
16. Ibid.
17. N. Feris, "RHINOs Fail to Thrive, New Study Finds," *Government Health IT*, December 11, 2007, www.govhealthit.com/online/news/350142-1.html, accessed December 12, 2007.
18. M. E. Frisse, "State and Community-Based Efforts to Foster Interoperability," *Health Affairs* 25 (2005): 1190–1196.
19. http://www.healthbridge.org/index.php?option=com_content&task=view&id=5&Itemid=6, accessed October 29, 2008.
20. http://www.healthbridge.org/downloads/HealthLeaders-2005-07.pdf, article published May 2005.
21. http://mayoresearch.mayo.edu/mayo/research/rcf/crick.cfm, accessed October 1, 2007.
22. www.mayoclinic.com.
23. http://www.mayo.edu/simulationcenter, accessed October 9, 2007.
24. R. Wullianallur and J. K. H. Tan, "Strategic IT Applications in Health Care," *Communications of the ACM* 45 (2002): 56.

Chapter Questions

5–1. In the future, with advanced EMR and CHIN, public health experts will be able to monitor health levels of the masses of populations and certain at-risk groups. Comment and discuss the implication of this statement.

5–2. How is data sharing different between previous CHIN, RHINO, and something like the Mayo Clinic?

5–3. Interoperability is facilitated through the use of HL7 for standardization among healthcare systems. This protocol was not previously available among other systems. Additionally, wireless technologies and better visualization systems are advances in health IT. Sensors are also used for better data collecting. What do you see as the trend of RHINO or the potential of an NHIN?

5–4. Advances in technology and multidisciplinary thinking have driven the evolution between previous and current CHIN. Healthcare informatics takes stored data about a population of people's health and analyzes the data to retrieve current reality and trends occurring within certain groups. Physicians realized that better and more accurate care could be provided through electronic data interchange of patient information between providers. This sparked the creation of electronic medical records and the concept of a centralized IT system. Provide a rationale for the noted evolution.

Telecommunications and Network Concepts for Healthcare Services Organizations[1]

Joseph Tan

Introduction

Telecommunications has been conceptualized since the mid-1800s, when the telegraph, telephone, and teletypewriter all emerged. Since the 1960s, it has become one of the world's fastest growing areas of technology as its applications allow individuals, as well as businesses, to access information near-instantaneously from anywhere in the world. Metcalfe's law, $N(N-1)$, where N refers to the number of nodes on the network, expresses the value of a network to a business; apparently, as N grows, the number of connections tends to grow exponentially.

In *Technology Brief I*, we covered the fundamental concepts of network technologies such as the Internet, intranets, and extranets. Here, we expand the discussion to look at how network and telecommunications technologies relate to the transformation of healthcare services organizations. To date, many of these organizations have all been reconstituted under one of two arrangements: consolidation or complementation.[2] Each of these two different arrangements eventually suggest the relevant administrative and appropriate technological requirements that can help them achieve their intended goals of functioning as a merged organization.

Consolidation versus Complementation

Consolidation, sometimes purported as a "market-sheltering activity," occurs when two or more comparable healthcare services organizations combine to augment or preserve market power. The merger leads to reduced price competition and aggregated economies, as well as operational efficiencies, which, in turn, will result in a quasi-monopoly or local market dominance.[3–5] A health maintenance organization (HMO), where the player with the most money rules, is a good example. By instituting uniformity across specialties in local and regional hospitals, the now-defunct Columbia/HCA had consolidated to gain a dominant market position.[6,7] This, in turn, helped the HMO to gain leverage on local pools of physicians who wished to gain practice privileges on multiple sites, as well as to benefit from operational efficiencies in managing their overlapping services.[8]

The development and implementation of a common managerial system (CMS) is a key administrative necessity for consolidation. Instituted through a formal managerial process, CMS provides a shared platform for guiding policies and procedures, standard business practices, and performance evaluation.[9,10] For instance, Columbia/HCA's CMS streamlines overlapping activities offered by the original separate units in the same neighborhood and concentrates all the previously nonoverlapping activities of various geographically dispersed units into a single operation. Not only were administrative overheads drastically reduced, but allocation and sharing of resources were also economized. From a corporate perspective, the Columbia/HCA network, during its rise to popularity, was able to achieve greater economic benefits while simultaneously developing superior enterprise resource planning, allocation, and management.

Complementation occurs when two or more healthcare organizations with contributing production/service expertise selectively merge. Such a union capitalizes on transactional economies, expands both the scope and area of services for an individual-partner organization, and reduces costs via symbiotic interdependence.[11] Such a partnership is analogous to supplier–retailer value chain integration, as illustrated by the merger of Vencor and Hillhaven, which resulted in the nation's second-largest nursing home chain. As Osterland notes, "Vencor treats chronically ill patients, particularly those with respiratory problems, through a network of 36 hospitals, while Hillhaven provides nursing home care and rehabilitation service. . . . Therefore, if Hillhaven patients get sick, they can be placed in Vencor hospitals. If Vencor patients improve, they can be referred to less intensive Hillhaven facilities."[12(p.20)]

The Vencor–Hillhaven case also contrasts the main rationale of consolidation versus complementation. That is, consolidation typically occurs with healthcare organizations competing in different locations of the same market, whereas complementation increases the scope or area of cooperational services in a region by unifying partner organizations with complementary production or service expertise. Therefore, the implementation of cooperative data interchange systems to oversee the supplier–retailer value chain, such as the Vencor–Hillhaven's cross-referral system, is a key administrative necessity for complementation. With regard to computing architecture, contemporary client–server-based IT can bridge disparate systems and manage the distribution of transaction-oriented functionality.[13]

Key Healthcare Communication Configuration and System Architecture

Several categories of health communication configuration and system architecture can be used to support consolidation and/or complementation: (1) the hub-and-wheel (H&W) communication configuration, (2) open systems and intranets, (3) groupware and group communication support systems (GCSS), (4) executive information systems (EIS), and (5) others. Given that *Technology Brief I* already covered open systems and intranet architecture, we will briefly touch on these topics while focusing primarily on H&W, GCSS, EIS, and other configurations.

Hub-and-Wheel

Hub-and-wheel topology comprises (1) the hub, which enables centralized system control or monitoring among inter-unit exchanges, and (2) the wheel, which includes systems that support and respond to local requirements and functional linkages between and among units.[14]

Unlike peer-to-peer (P2P) networks, where central file servers are not used and all networked computers are automatically opened for accessing any publicly stored files, H&W employs client–server computing. Client–server computing supports the hub configuration through its architecture, in which a specific application is partitioned among multiple processors (clients) that combine the process in a single, unified task (server).[15] Essentially, a hub network system sustains a many-to-many system linkage by using a local area network (LAN), metropolitan area network (MAN), or wide area network (WAN) to connect the geographically dispersed clients and servers. Conversely, end-user computing supports the wheel configuration by featuring applications administered by local unit, often involving LAN-based connections.[16]

The H&W topology typically exhibits a two-tier network configuration. For one layer, a client–server-based distributed network, which serves as a control and coordination channel, is commonly installed between headquarters and the remote units. This "hub" configuration, with an implemented CMS that employs resource sharing and elimination of redundancies to consolidate all activities into a single operating framework, supports the expansion of healthcare services organizations via consolidation. The other layer, supported by a number of LAN-based installations, is of the "wheel" configuration. Here, the inter-unit linkages are typically achieved via a private access-protected WAN. Alternatively, links between far-flung local area networks, among other links, can be achieved by a proprietary organizationwide network using a satellite-based WAN, as opposed to the H&W configuration.

Healthcare services organizations expanding via complementation will therefore also find H&W a necessity and a preferred configuration because it supports the linkages between heterogeneous systems, which are common to partnering specialty healthcare services organizations. In summary, H&W does not only empower headquarters as the core resource coordinator/controller by providing the units access to the LAN-based bulletin board systems or the corporate databases, it also allows the remote units to be more efficient and responsive to local situations.[17]

Open Systems and Intranets

Open systems, as characterized by the Internet, electronic data interchange (EDI), and extranets, provide a supportive computing architecture to an HMO expanding via consolidation or complementation. They offer two-way access for external agencies, provide for the exchange of standard-formatted transactions, and support electronic ordering and invoicing through EDI. As these Web-based open-system networks gradually become the mainstream of emerging technologies, they heighten the ability of healthcare services organizations to share information both within and across organizational units.

Moreover, intranets provide unmediated reticular linkages for exchanging information between corporate headquarters and their units. The architecture also promotes additional communication support for the expansion of healthcare services organizations, specifically for operations transforming via complementation. This mode of expansion demands a more efficient informal channel for coordination and collaboration of integral activities, which, in turn, require input from both formal and informal sources. This is especially true when intersecting activities require inter-unit relational linkages or involve quasi-autonomous units, such as those between two specialized hospitals. Technologically, intranets also complement the previously introduced H&W communication configuration by increasing the effectiveness of local responses, especially in sharing know-how information on research and development (R&D). It is also an important supportive communication system for healthcare services organizations expanding via consolidation, because it can facilitate the development of a common operating framework for the consolidated functions or services. To illustrate, Koala, a corporate intranet of Columbia/HCA, provides a common intracommunication network for delivering patient care among the local units while consolidating various services.[18]

Finally, intranets provide support for intelligence, the tool for capturing and sharing corporate knowledge. This knowledge-sharing capability makes it easier for a healthcare services organization to market new services better than its competitors, thereby meeting or exceeding the expectation of its customers. Traveling health executives can also use the corporate intranet as a means of keeping in touch with headquarters and staying abreast of late-breaking company information. Essentially, intranets support free access to internal online databases, corporate grapevine communications, and information interchanges among dispersed units.[19] Healthcare organizations have used intranets to distribute information, computing applications, and everyday communications (such as online medical newsletters), and even as virtual meeting places for work groups. In summary, the intranet architecture is essential for complementation, but supportive for consolidation, because it allows for efficient and effective supply chain management and collaboration across networked partnering organizations.

Group Communications Support Systems

Group communications support systems provide a platform for group cooperation and collaboration. The architecture will affect the way people work and, eventually, the reporting and power structure of the organization.

GCSS support real-time communication among distant locations via a public or proprietary WAN and provide a common and shared interface with representational capability. In other words, GCSS can use information control to facilitate cooperative work and group collaboration, support communication processes among group members, and reduce group communication barriers such as distance, cultural, and linguistic differences.[20] GCSS can also generate collective wisdom, knowledge, and better interpersonal communications; these can then be applied to increase productivity, reduce costs, and improve services or product quality. GCSS, ultimately, offer the opportunity for interaction among remote units and are, specifically, capable of collecting and exchanging different inputs or decision predicates from widespread sources. From this perspective, GCSS establish the communication basis for supporting both the relational linkages among subsidiaries and the interactions between quasi-autonomous corporate units. It is expected that GCSS use will improve decision-making quality, enhance user satisfaction, and increase the efficiency of group meetings. Common examples include the use of videoconferencing, electronic messaging systems, electronic boardrooms, and local group networks.

GCSS will, therefore, offer a communications solution for complementation, because healthcare services organizations expanding via this mode require the establishment of cooperation-oriented processes to support the intersecting activities between their quasi-autonomous corporate units.

Executive Information Systems

Executive information systems enable headquarters to monitor the operational performance of remote units. The architecture provides senior managers with critical aggregate information to facilitate coordination on key strategic decisions.

EIS collect, filter, and extract a broad range of current and historical information from multiple applications and multiple data sources, both internal and external to an organization. EIS functions are deemed essential for healthcare services organizations expanding via consolidation, because the concept involves the extension of organizational communications systems to widespread healthcare units or networks. The technology benefits those healthcare services organizations, specifically, that demand process consistency and coordination.

Finally, the EIS architecture is complementary to the H&W configuration. EIS can assist top management in extracting, filtering, compressing, and tracking critical data from dispersed corporate units, while providing online access, trend analysis, exception reporting, and drill-down capabilities.[21,22] Drill-down is an exceptional capability of EIS; it allows top management at headquarters to access or track a remote unit's detailed operational status and performance indicators by conducting a reverse exploration of a critical data point. By monitoring the indicators preset by top executives, EIS can also quickly and automatically identify the unit that has not met corporate performance benchmarks. Top healthcare executives receive needed information from many sources, which may come in the form of memos, periodicals, letters, telephone calls, meetings, social activities, or reports produced either manually or electronically. With the growth in the use of electronic devices such as personal digital assistants (PDAs), executives nowadays rely on paper-based sources and electronic means equally to meet their information needs. Therefore, for EIS to become truly useful and practical in this day and age, these systems must be linked to data from multiple sources and permit the exchange of data with diverse electronic devices, such as PDAs, at any time.

Other Configuration

Several other network configurations may be used to support information flow and e-commerce exchanges when healthcare services organizations merge. In this sense, the use of hybrid and wireless topology are two potential network configurations.

Combining the bus and H&W configurations, hybrid typology can be used to satisfy the administrative requirements of an HMO expanding via either consolidation or complementation. The bus (or backbone) typology dictates that all connected devices be linked to a central cable and is the easiest or least expensive network typology to install. When combining the bus with the H&W typology, the enhanced hybrid network will be flexible in supporting the data-sharing, intersect-transaction processing, and information exchange needs of both centralized headquarters and its dispersed but affiliated units.

Similarly, wireless typology can also be used to support either a consolidated or complemented HMO expansion. With wireless networks, devices are connected by a receiver/transmitter to a special network interface card that transmits signals between a computer and a server, all within an acceptable transmission range. Wireless typology can be used in a LAN-based, MAN-based, or WAN-based network. A MAN-based network provides connectivity of data communication services for healthcare services organizations within a geographic area or region larger than a LAN-based network but smaller than the area covered by a WAN-based network. This is usually within the confines of a metropolitan region, whereas LAN connections span mostly roundabout a localized area, such as nearby buildings within a university and WAN could cover as far as the four corners of a nation like the United States. At this point, we move to a case on wireless applications for healthcare services delivery.

A Case of Wireless Networking in the Ingalls Health System

Ingalls Memorial Hospital, a renowned community medical center located south of Chicago, is taking a technology lead among its competitors. As a 564-bed private facility operating within the Ingalls Health System, it is consistently ranked among the top 50 hospitals by *US News and World Report*. According to a February 2008 press release, Ingalls recently engaged ARINC to design and implement a wireless network system for positioning its physicians, nurses, and other clinical staff to gain rapid access to medical data.

The newly planned system is designed to support a virtual private network (VPN) of the newest Wi-Fi standard—802.11N—for fast, secure wireless transmissions. Such a move could simultaneously reduce paperwork and increase the dependability of medical records, resulting in improved clinical efficiencies and effectiveness. In addition to installing private network access points throughout the hospital's campus and other Ingalls facilities in nearby areas, ARINC also plans to offer complimentary Wi-Fi access in its public areas.

"We are moving forward as the technology permits to ensure patient safety and enhance the quality of care Ingalls provides," stated Vince Pryor, the CFO for Ingalls.[23] "One of Ingalls's core values is to seek innovative approaches to delivering high-quality patient care for the communities we serve, by leveraging technology in our healthcare environment."

One immediate application of the ARINC-installed network will be to track the distribution of medicine to patients. It is envisaged that bar codes and scanners will provide an electronic means of collecting data about the types, times, and dosages of medications administered, resulting in the elimination of potential human errors.

Moreover, the new Ingalls system will be designed to enable the introduction of voice over Internet protocol (VoIP) technology—a technology that will provide a means of relatively inexpensive, quick, and clear communications across the hospital's campuses. Other future updates of the system anticipated include such ancillary support systems that will allow physicians access to medical information from the patient's bedside, automated physician-submitted medication orders, and electronic file documentation. Such flexibility is further expected to maximize Ingalls's preparedness for future health IT strategies and applications that may develop, ensuring that it remains among the top-ranked hospitals in America.

Notes

1. The content of *Technology Brief III* presented here is based largely on the published work of Wen et al. on the same topic, appearing in J. K. H. Tan, *Health Management Information Systems: Methods and Practical Applications*, 2nd ed. (Gaithersburg, MD: Aspen Publishers, 2001).

2. R. C. Coile, "Health Care Outlook 1997–2005: Transitions, Transactions, and Transformations," *Journal of Lending & Credit Risk Management* 79, no. 8 (April 1997): 18–22.

3. H. Leibenstein, "X-inefficiencies Xists—Reply to an Xorcist," *American Economic Review* 68 (1978): 203–211.

4. W. G. Shepherd, *On the Core Concepts of Industrial Economies, in Mainstreams in Industrial Organization*, J. W. DeJong and W. G. Shepherd, Eds. (Boston: Kluwer Publications, 1986).

5. J. Hopping, "The Layered Look," *Health Systems Review* 30, no. 3 (May/June 1997): 24–25.

6. J. Morrissey, "Columbia Wraps up Mass. Venture," *Modern Healthcare* (May 6, 1996): 26.

7. S. Lutz, "Columbia Completes Deals in N.C., Texas," *Modern Healthcare* (May 6, 1996): 26.

8. "University Hospital Blurs Richmond, Va., Battle Lines," *Modern Healthcare* (April 22, 1996): 40–41.

9. B. R. Robinson and W. Peterson, *Strategic Acquisitions: A Guide to Growing and Enhancing the Value of Your Business* (Burr Ridge, IL: Irwin, 1995).

10. P. McKiernan and Y. Merali, "Integrating Information Systems after a Merger," *Long Range Planning* 28, no. 4 (August 1995): 54–62.

11. O. E. Williamson, *The Economic Institutions of Capitalism: Firms, Markets, Relational Contracting* (New York: Free Press, 1985).

12. A. Osterland, "Acquire, then Digest: Vencor—Specialty Hospital Chain Acquires Nursing Home Operator Hillhaven," *Financial World* 164, no. 14 (June 20, 1995): 20.

13. J. Smith, "There's More Than One Road to Client-Server," *Computing Canada* 18, no. 16 (August 4, 1992): 40.

14. J. H. M. Tarn, *Exploring the Impact of Geographic Dispersion on Information System Requirements* (Richmond, VA: Virginia Commonwealth University, 1998). Dissertation.

15. B. H. Boar, *Implementing Client/Server Computing* (New York: McGraw-Hill, 1993).

16. E. A. Regan and B. N. O'Connor, *End-User Information Systems: Perspectives for Managers and Information Systems Professionals* (New York: Macmillan, 1994).

17. J. Diamond, "Modem Sharing and Collaborative Computing," *Network World* 12, no. 19 (May 8, 1995): 35.

18. "Intranet Lexicon," *Business Communications Review* 26, no. 6 (1996): 8.

19. L. Fried, "Advanced Information Technology Use: A Survey of Multinational Corporations," *Information Systems Management* 10, no. 2 (Spring 1993): 7–14.

20. A. Pinsonneault and K. Kraemer, "The Effects of Electronic Meetings on Group Processes and Outcomes: An Assessment of the Empirical Research," *European Journal of Operational Research* 46, no. 2 (May 25, 1990): 143–161.

21. H. J. Waston, R. K. Rainer, and C. E. Koh, "Executive Information Systems: A Framework for Development and a Survey of Current Practices," *MIS Quarterly* (March 1991): 13–30.
22. P. Palvia, A. Kumar, N. Kumar, and R. Hendon, "Information Requirements of a Global EIS," *Decision Support Systems* 16, no. 2 (February 1996): 169–179.
23. Annapolis, MD: Brand Management & Communications, February 21, 2008, http://www.arinc.com/news/2008/02-21b-08.html, accessed July 11, 2008.

Trending toward Patient-Centric Management Systems

Joseph Tan with Joshia Tan

Editor's Note: Among the most popular HMIS applications and technologies employed in today's healthcare services organizations are electronic health records (EHR), computerized physician order entry (CPOE), and clinical decision support systems (CDSS), which are the topics of this chapter. As noted in the chapter title, these applications may be seen as a movement toward patient-centric management systems because they are ultimately designed to elevate patient care by providing the caregivers with relevant, current, accurate, reliable, and complete information. Therefore, the significance of these systems for benchmarking both administrative and clinical performance across healthcare services organizations cannot be overemphasized. *Technology Brief IV*, focusing on database, data-mining, and data-warehousing concepts for healthcare services organizations, has been appended to this chapter to augment the readers' understanding not only of the internal structure, content, and functionalities of these systems, but also to provide insights as to the enabling and empowering nature of these systems for the end-users. Finally, the benefits and challenges of these systems are discussed in the context of electronic health records, which is the cornerstone of the U.S. and Canadian healthcare services delivery systems.

CHAPTER OUTLINE

Scenario: *Google Health, a Portal for Personal Health Records and Health Decision Support*

Scenario: Google Health, a Portal for Personal Health Records and Health Decision Support[1]

Google Health, an Internet portal where patients can collate their personal data previously entrusted to various care providers, pharmacies, insurers, and even laboratories in a single repository upon consenting, is a site that planned to compete with existing vendors supporting the storage and tracking of personal health records (PHR).

In contrast to competitors such as Dr. Koop, HealthCentral, and Revolution Health (which require their subscribers to key in their own personal health information), Google's PHR system aims to permit subscribers to upload their previously captured records from care providers such as Cleveland Clinic, PatientSite, Longs, MEDCO, Beth Israel Deaconess Medical Center (BIDMC), Minute Clinic/CVS, Quest Laboratories, RxAmerica, and Walgreens. With the patient's agreement, their records can be conveniently uploaded directly into Google Health—they do not have to gather any of these data manually or risk entering their private personal health information erroneously. Once their records have been uploaded, health decision support and knowledge services such as drug monographs, drug-to-drug interaction advice, reference materials on diseases, and other health information will become available and accessible to the subscribers. Another prominent feature of Google Health is that subscribers can link with applications of other third parties who have partnered with Google Health, share their health information with these third parties if they so wish, and receive even more specialized health decision support and knowledge services.

Google Health pays particular attention to security and privacy issues. The privacy policy, for example, clearly restricts the transmission or release of the subscriber's information to third parties without the subscriber's consent. Just as with the Microsoft HealthVault policy, subscribers will have complete control over the content of their records and will have the option to delete or destroy their stored information at any time. In terms of security standards, Google Health uses digital certificates, IP address restrictions, and encryption technology to manage information exchange between Google Health and its partners, as well as temporarily storing or "caching" of retrieved health data on desktop computers and workstations. To enhance interoperability, data standards adopted by Google Health and its decision support partner, Safe-Med, include CCR/G (Continuity of Care Record/Google), SNOMED CT, LOINC, NDC, RxNorm, and ICD-9. Over time, Google Health aims to empower subscribers by providing them with connectivity and interoperability with as many well-recognized third-party caregivers as possible.

The message that BIDMC dispatched to patients and clinicians is as follows: "Over the past year, BIDMC has worked with Google Health to integrate PatientSite and Google's new patient portal. It is an Opt-In service and the patient controls every aspect of the Google Health site. . . . Patients who use PatientSite will now be able to upload their records about diagnoses, medications, and allergies from PatientSite to Google Health, and then also use Google's specialized medical knowledge features—online reference materials about medical conditions, information about drug safety, questions to ask your doctor, and more . . . patients with a Google Gmail e-mail address will have a new link in PatientSite called Google Health that will enable them to optionally use these Google features. . . . At no time will BIDMC share your data with Google without your consent. . . ." At this time, BIDMC expects to empower 5,000 patients with existing Google Gmail accounts by connecting them to the Google Health link.

Imagine trusting all your personal health records with a carrier such as Google Health. Remember that giant commercial partners such as Microsoft and Google are new to the e-healthcare marketplace but are entering into the business of safekeeping one's personal health records (PHR) because of its potential for profitability. Such an approach can indeed cause quite a bit of apprehension for some health consumers. As these organizations lack a history of involvement with healthcare services businesses prior to their offering of PHR systems, what if the information could be sold to, or mined by, people from organizations that are unknown to the patients? What is the chance or potential for security breaches and privacy compromises with the patient health information captured in Google Health? Take a minute to reflect on these possibilities and debate the various probable scenarios.

I. Introduction

The past few decades have seen continuing cost acceleration, advancing technologies, and growing competition challenging the healthcare marketplace. To adapt, healthcare services organizations have become increasingly more eager to change from relying on traditional paper-based health data and information processing systems to newer forms of electronic health recording practices so as to ensure greater efficiencies in health data management and effectiveness in clinical decision making. While patients have voiced major concerns over the security, privacy, and confidentiality of their health records being captured electronically, their ultimate objective remains unchanged: to receive high-quality healthcare, with easily accessible and available records for preauthorized care providers and referral specialists, especially in emergencies.

Accordingly, the need for electronic data gathering, tracking, and coordinating systems that can provide caregivers with timely, reliable, and secured access to a patient's files—such as his or her complete medical history, laboratory test results, and radiological images—cannot be overly emphasized. An ideal network of health data-entry, storage, and reporting systems should achieve interoperability among themselves, as well as with all of the legacy systems. Such is the concept of electronic health records (EHR), a system that will allow doctors and nurses to access conveniently accurate health records, reduce the need for unnecessary duplication of patient data, and give clarifications to clinicians performing follow-up care, to whom a patient's previous treatment or medical information is often needed. Without knowing a patient's history, practitioners—especially in the case of an emergency—will have to blindly perform treatments on such a patient in hope of saving his or her life. It is apparent that the quality and speed of care can be enhanced, in many cases, if only the appropriate and relevant patient information were available, accessible, and verifiable.

Three major patient-centric management systems have evolved in the healthcare services industry that will continue to affect patient care and the performance of care providers in the coming years: electronic health records (EHR), computerized physician order entry (CPOE), and clinical decision support systems (CDSS). Among these, the EHR system is the most inclusive and important for direct patient care because it typically also encompasses the other two patient-centric management systems. Therefore, our discussion of CPOE and CDSS will be embedded partly in the larger EHR context for delivering error-free and quality patient care. Tan[2] addresses the concerns of those who would like to have a more detailed understanding of these different systems, their historical developments, applications, and cases, especially for EHR and CDSS implementations. Meanwhile, a brief review and empirical evidence on the acceptance of CPOE among physicians may be found in Liang, Xue, and Wu.[3]

Here we begin our limited review by first defining and reviewing the historical evolution of these three patient-centric management systems.

II. Definitions of EHR, CPOE, and CDSS

Electronic health records (EHR)[4] comprise, essentially, the health information of an individual patient that exists as part of a complete history; such records are, furthermore, designed to provide clinicians with a comprehensive picture of the patient's health status at any time. Today, the EHR term has largely replaced older terms such as "computerized patient records" and "electronic medical records." Specifically, the U.S. Department of Veterans Affairs defined computer-based patient records (CPR) as records that are stored in decentralized hospital computer software, whereas electronic medical records (EMR) may be conceived as an enterprisewide system where patient medical histories are captured in a single repository. The EHR term has taken on an even wider connotation in that these systems are also meant to automate and streamline the clinician's workflow, besides having the ability to independently generate a complete record of clinical patient encounters, sourcing data from various care episodes over the lifetime of a patient. In other words, these patient-centric, electronic database management systems capture, using all available patient–provider encounters in a longitudinal fashion, both the historic and current records of a patient's health information. Altogether, the system may contain various patient demographics and patient history information, such as progress notes, medical diagnoses, prescriptions, vital signs, immunization records, laboratory test data, and radiology reports.

Closely related to, and often functioning as part of, EHR, a *computerized physician order entry (CPOE)*[5] system is basically an automated order-entry system that captures the instructions of physicians with regard to the care of their patients. Physicians enter orders in the EHR using CPOE, which has been shown to increase patient safety and improve the quality of care. The system also provides clinical guidelines for physicians and prints summaries of visits for patients, among other services. CPOE orders are disseminated, via computer networks, throughout various parts of a healthcare services facility, such as pharmacy, laboratory, or radiology, as well as to other care providers, including nurses, therapists, and other consulting medical professional staff, who will then follow up on the orders.

Finally, *computer-based decision support systems (CDSS)*[6] are medical information processing systems that are designed to aid clinicians in making complex and/or less-than-complex clinical-based decisions. CDSS provide data banks, alerts and reminders, algorithms, analytic or pathophysiologic models, clinical decision theoretical models, statistical pattern recognition methods, symbolic reasoning, and/or expert knowledge bases to enhance the diagnostic, therapeutic, and prognostic-thinking and cognitive-reasoning strategies of expert and amateur clinicians alike.

Healthcare managers, administrators, and executives hoping to perform well in complex healthcare services organizations must become thoroughly familiar with all of these patient-centric management systems. These are the three major systems that drive the majority of diagnostic, therapeutic, and prognostic decisions made for patients attending the different care facilities of a health maintenance organization. These systems have evolved over the years and have drawn significant influence from the early developments and history of computer-based patient records and hospital information systems. We turn now to look briefly at the historical developments of these systems.

III. Historical Evolution of EHR, CPOE, and CDSS

Computer-based patient records, according to the 1997 National Academy of Sciences Institute of Medicine (IOM) report,[7] are systems specifically designed to aid clinical users in assessing patient information. Such information typically includes complete and accurate patient history, alerts and reminders, clinical decision support models, guides and links to medical knowledge bases, and other references and informational resources (such as a referencing drug database). The evolution of computer-based patient data systems such as EHR, CPOE, and CDSS is best understood in terms of the historic evolution of hospital information systems (HIS), artificial intelligence (AI) in medicine, health decision aids, and electronic patient records.

The genesis of HIS dates back to the early 1950s, when only mainframes were available and when even the processing of a batch of patient-related information required considerable time, knowledge, and expertise. From the 1960s to the 1970s, a new era of HIS emerged when "pioneering" American and European hospitals joined forces to eventually develop a successful patient information management system prototype, named the Technicon system. It is this prototype that laid the foundation for many of today's working hospital patient information systems throughout North America and Europe. The major lesson learned was the need to focus on users' information needs and the need to change the attitudes of the users, particularly those of physicians, nurses, and other clinicians.

During the early and mid-1970s, computerization was pinpointed as the source of the evident gains in productivity and increased efficiency, prompting the diffusion of large-scale data-processing applications in medicine and health record systems. With the emergence of minicomputers and microcomputers during the 1980s, physicians and clinical practitioners soon began to realize the speed and astounding harnessing power of computers. During this time, interest in the application of AI in medicine expanded and soon contributed to the development of CDSS.

In 1999, the IOM reported a disturbing statistic—each year, in the United States, medical errors were responsible for up to 98,000 unnecessary hospital patient deaths. An urgent call was immediately made for healthcare services organizations to reduce this exorbitant level of medical errors.[8] Several institutions took up the challenge; Palo Alto Medical Foundation (PAMF), for example, became one of the earliest adopters of EHR, replacing paper charts with electronic records, thereby allowing physicians and clinical staff direct and very convenient access to patient information. The adoption not only eliminated the hectic scramble to locate paper records, but also led to a reduction in medical errors. Similarly, in 2004, three suburban Chicago hospitals reported a 20 percent drop in medication errors and the complete elimination of transcription errors with their EHR implementations. Against this background, Arsala et al.[9] believe that we have undergone four generations in the evolution of computer-based patient records in overcoming the medical error challenge and will soon move into fifth-generation EHR by 2010.

During the first generation of computer-based patient records (CPR), hospitals relied heavily on the clinical data repository (CDR); in fact, the adoption of a single, comprehensive repository for clinical information during the 1960s to 1970s was said to have eliminated about 15 percent of preventable medical errors in hospital-based patient care. From the 1970s to 1980s, the next generation of CPR development was noted to have the added capability of documenting clinical activities, as well as the ability to tailor the IT report for the use and needs of specific caregivers. This resulting improvement was estimated to have garnered up to another 25 percent reduction in medical errors. Moreover, CDSS implementation during this period was thought to have further reduced error rates with their automated intelligence. The combination of these augmented capabilities thus amounted to a 40 percent level of reduction in preventable errors.

Third-generation CPR/EHR development, during the 1980s to 1990s, involved the combination of an improved CDSS with the use of a controlled medical vocabulary to standardize medical concepts and the availability of a CPOE system, thus allowing a more effective management of the physician ordering process. It was envisaged that this increased level of automation helped to realize up to a 70 percent preventable error reduction as compared with the systems capabilities of the previous generations. During this generation, it became progressively critical for workflow capabilities to emerge as tools for supporting the optimal delivery of patient care.

The fourth-generation EHR, which are expected to reduce preventable errors by up to a 90 percent level, have now been realized. These systems are considered to have an improved CDSS function capable of providing a detailed portrait of each patient and automated support for care management protocols. These systems are claimed to be flexible so that clinician users can tailor them for individual patients; they are also capable of knowledge management so that continual improvement in care delivery can be provided; they are supposedly geared with formal workflow capability so that the consistencies of medical practices can be balanced as needed for optimal care outcomes.

The next-generation EHR are projected to have complex CDSS functionalities, to have a networked CPOE, and to be supportive of natural language interfaces. In this sense, EHR software will enable automation of the care processes with preprogrammed alerts and reminders. With CPOE interfacing capability, the future EHR software will not only aid caregivers in obtaining complete, real-time updates of patient information at all times, but also offer caregivers the ability to disseminate their orders efficiently and effectively. These fifth-generation systems are, therefore, expected to aid clinicians intelligently, especially in the caring of patients who may demand real-time monitoring, and even those with multiple, concurrent medical conditions. Finally, with mobile and sensor networks on the rise, these systems should also support interfaces to wireless health data networks, enhance mobile healthcare services, and provide secured linkages to sensor-based tracking and health monitoring devices.

IV. Electronic Health Records

For decades, healthcare services organizations have invested millions of dollars in the research and development of a system that can computerize patient records, thereby satisfying the information needs of care providers who deliver high-quality patient care. Despite the noted progress, even until today, some healthcare facilities are still relying on traditional paper-based recordkeeping systems. This may be due, in whole or in part, to the high cost of implementing computerized patient records; the expressed concerns of patients over privacy, confidentiality, and security issues with computerized records; and the lack of government and private funding to support computerized healthcare databases administration, research, and development.

As previously noted, many terms have been used interchangeably to describe how patient records are captured electronically, and these terms have often resulted in some confusion—and a lack of strategic vision alignment and conceptual integration among healthcare administrators and health IT managers. Specifically, computer-based patient records (CPR) may be regarded as records that are stored in decentralized hospital computer software systems, whereas electronic medical records (EMR) refer generally to an enterprisewide system capturing patient medical histories in a single repository. The EHR term has a wider connotation, encompassing automation and streamlining of the clinician's workflow besides being capable of independently generating, by sourcing data from various care episodes throughout a patient's life, a complete record of clinical patient encounters. In addition, EHR will support other care-related activities, including, but not limited to, clinical decision support, care delivery quality management, and clinical reporting.[10] According to Dickinson,[11] the EHR should serve diverse purposes such as assisting direct patient care, improving routine reporting on the care processes, aiding the processing of claims reimbursement, credentialing care providers, providing an audit trail for care processes, ensuring quality, preventing medical errors, satisfying public health needs, enhancing education, supporting research, and satisfying the legal needs of healthcare services organizations. Ultimately, these incredibly powerful systems are intended to improve physician practices as well as increase health organizational competitiveness and profitability.

An integrated EHR will link all electronic patient records and critical patient care systems so that patient data can be shared and disseminated among authorized clinician users. In general, such an integrated system comprises six primary modules or components working in unison, most of which have already been alluded to in earlier discussions. Specifically, these components include (1) a CDR, which offers a comprehensive source for storing and retrieving relevant, reliable, and accurate clinical information; (2) a CDSS, which provides rule-based alerts such as warning messages against potential harmful drug interactions when patients are inadvertently placed on two or more potentially interactive medications; (3) a clinical documentation module, which can inform the caring clinician of specific activities taken by other clinicians in managing a particular patient; (4) a CPOE, which will electronically capture the attending physician's instructions so as to help eliminate errors caused by illegible handwritten orders; (5) a controlled medical vocabulary (CMV) module for ensuring that information sourced from various clinical repositories can be easily compared, making it easier to generate proper clinical rules for achieving quality patient care; and (6) a workflow controller module, which manages clinical care processes so that these processes may be sequenced appropriately, executed properly, and executed without omissions.[12]

Other systems that can be integrated with the EHR, but that are discussed later, include laboratory information systems (LIS), pharmacy information systems (PIS), and radiological information systems (RIS).

By implementing an integrated EHR, a healthcare services organization is therefore expected to gain data management speed and accuracy, enhance patient safety and clinical workflow efficiencies, reduce medical errors, and control administrative and medical cost. Not surprisingly,

EHR technology is quickly replacing paper-based systems as well as legacy EMR in many healthcare services organizations today.[13]

V. Computerized Physician Order Entry

A CPOE system, as noted in earlier discussions, is often implemented as a component of the EHR. This accompanying system must be able to communicate orders to other connected systems within the EHR. These include ancillary support systems such as laboratory information systems (LIS), where laboratory results are captured; pharmacy information systems (PIS), where medication information is captured; radiology information systems (RIS), picture archiving and communications systems (PACS), where radiological reports and images are captured; and electronic document/content management (ED/CM) systems, where form documents are captured, streamlined, and managed. Medical records scanning is often a solution when such data are entered manually into forms and need to be archived, stored, and/or shared electronically.

When combined with various other workflow tools, CPOE can also be useful in providing information about patient scheduling, wait times, referral networks, physician work patterns, and disease management. Similarly, the CPOE system may be enabled via PIS for presenting clinical drug choices to the ordering provider. The key success factor for implementing CPOE is overcoming user resistance, particularly the resistance from physicians who may be accustomed to giving verbal or written orders.

Accordingly, acceptance of CPOE by physicians can induce numerous benefits, including decreased delays in order completion and reduced errors from handwritten or transcribed orders. It will also allow order entry at point-of-care or off-site, provide error checking for duplicate or incorrect medication doses or tests, and simplify inventory and posting of charges. A successfully implemented CPOE system can therefore improve the quality of healthcare services delivery and significantly cut healthcare costs.

VI. Clinical Decision Support Systems

At this point, we turn our attention to the last patient-centric managment systems in the group, the clinical decision support systems.

In this age of healthcare reform, health administrators and clinicians, with their increasingly complex decision-making activities, are in need of advanced methodological and technological support tools to enhance their effectiveness. CDSS are computer-based information-processing and decision support tools that are intended to serve as aids in the rationalization of the clinical decision-making process and/or justifying final choices the clinicians have advocated for their patients. Indeed, these systems are not meant to replace the clinical decision makers. Specifically, if clinicians are armed with CDSS containing computerized models, alerts, reminders, and critical sets of data—all of which will contribute in one way or another to analyzing the probability of the onset of certain acute or chronic illnesses for a particular patient—it is anticipated that these clinicians, assisted by the CDSS, will exercise better diagnostic, therapeutic, and/or prognostic judgments. In order words, they would not simply jump to conclusions about the complex data set based on the shortsightedness of their self-evaluations, their limited cognitive reasoning power, or even their intuitive feelings.

Use of CDSS interrelate and span almost every conceivable area of healthcare administrative and clinical decision-making activities. Key components to the building of CDSS include database management subsystem, model management subsystem, knowledge bases, inference engine, intelligent graphical interfaces, and any other modules that may enhance the functionalities of the CDSS. In this sense, clinicians can use CDSS to query general and specific questions about the conditions of their patients based on data that have been collected, stored, organized, manipulated, and retrieved appropriately from its database management subsystem. The model base management component in the CDSS permits clinicians to infer and/or forecast resulting outcomes, based on various mathematical computations and analytic model fittings of collected data about the patient's conditions. The knowledge base component of the CDSS typically contains rule-based knowledge, case reasoning, neural networks, artificial intelligence, and/or other expert diagnostic consults for the clinicians. The inference engine component then integrates these different components to arrive at the computed alternatives and/or choice outcomes for the decision makers. It is the intelligent graphical interface that will finally translate and interpret resulting choices in either graphical forms or images to support the decision makers' varying perspectives.

Today, CDSS have evolved to support many administrative and medical specialties—examples include nursing decision support systems, pharmacy decision support systems, health executive decision support systems, and specialty medical expert systems. The major cases provided in Part V at the end of this text provide a further examination of EMR and DSS functions. For the next part of this chapter, we review the key benefits and challenges of EHR. As previously stated, with CPOE and CDSS being typical parts of EHR system installments nowadays, readers can safely assume that the discussion on EHR benefits and challenges apply similarly to the other two patient-centric management systems.

VII. Benefits and Challenges of EHR, CPOE, and CDSS

Healthcare is an industry that is, apparently, very data intensive; the complexity of healthcare data cannot—and must not—be overlooked. Imagine what impact human-induced medical errors can wreak on the quality of life and safety of patients and what benefits systems such as EHR, CPOE, and CDSS can have in reversing the adverse effects of these errors.

Paul Tang, the chief medical information officer for the Palo Alto Medical Foundation (PAMF) and chair of the IOM's Committee on Data Standards for Patient Safety,[14] notes that electronic health records such as PAMF's system can cut healthcare costs, enhance the quality of healthcare services delivery, and significantly lower the risk for medical errors. He believes that providing physicians with convenient and direct access to the information they need for making patient care decisions will automatically raise the bar for ensuring patient safety to a higher level, or "new standard of care."

Aside from the benefits of using EHR and other patient-centric computerized management systems, there are still many challenges in implementing these systems. These benefits and challenges are discussed next.

Benefits

One of several key benefits of using EHR, CPOE, and CDSS is that they allow direct sourcing and capturing of patient data, which, in turn, can be used flexibly for myraid purposes. Some of the more important purposes, aside from direct patient care, include continuing patient care, follow-up treatment protocols, medical education for nurses and resident physicians, and research. Many resident physicians, for example, are learning from interacting with these systems on job sites and taking orders when caring for particular patients by automatically extracting captured instructions left for them by mentoring physicians. More importantly, the combined usage of these systems will eventually lead to a noticeable reduction in medical errors, preventing potential patient deaths and possible legal repercussions for clinical malpractices such mistakes may cause. These systems, therefore, will also assist with legal compliance, cut costs, and improve patient safety by performing such tasks as providing an audit trail for treatment protocols or alerting physicians of potentially adverse drug reactions.

Indeed, the acceptance and regular use of these systems promises to yield the primary benefits of cost cutting. This will be accomplished through lowering costs related to personnel, paper storage, processing, and treatment delays; enhancing safety of patient care; reducing medical errors; and controlling quality to eliminate poor or inadequate care. And because patient data and images can be conveniently accessed with the click of a computer mouse via one or more of these systems, physicians and other healthcare providers no longer have to search for misfiled paper charts or wait for another healthcare facility to send duplicate copies of patient records and/or images. Moreover, these systems can even source data from the patient bedside, if necessary, and furthermore provide a common platform for coordinating patient care across multiple care providers. This permits caregivers a common understanding of a patient's health condition, thereby preventing unnecessary treatments and/or omissions of critical treatments.

Use of these systems will also provide doctors and nurses with decision support capabilities. For example, laboratory and X-ray results can be sent electronically, immediately after completion, to a physician for prioritized interpretation, diagnostic analysis, and decision making regarding treatment alternatives. The EHR installed at PAMF, for example, enables caregivers to document interactions with patients, improve on physician–patient relationships, ease the charge-capturing process, eliminate repetitive tests, allow hospital personnel to view patient medical history and insurance information, assist in making referrals, and speed up prescription orders through electronic requests to pharmacies. PAMF's EHR also incorporated a computerized physician order entry (CPOE) system, which provides resident physicians and nurses with clinical guidelines and patients with printed summaries of visits and other services.[15] The EHR system is also cost-effective, scalable, and flexible in the sense that new security features, improved CDSS capabilities, and other ancillary support systems can be added at any time to enhance future healthcare services delivery.

Finally, the benefits of using an integrated EHR system must be contrasted with the many challenges that also come with its implementation, which is the topic of discussion.

Challenges

Several major challenges, with respect to the acceptance and adoption of EHR in healthcare services organizations, have been noted in the extant literature.[16–20] These include confusion about the concept; the cost of implementing EHR or customizing EHR to a particular healthcare services organization; the lack of standardization; and other challenging issues such as the reliability, privacy, confidentiality, and security of patient data housed by the system. There is also a lack of motivation in creating interoperability among the connected systems of competing care provider organizations. This is due to uncertainties about the direct benefits the care providers of one healthcare facility can reap by coordinating patient care and sharing patient data versus the benefits another facility can sow.

First, EHR software can be complex—the technology is known by various names, each indicating a specific vision that differs from the others. For example, as previously indicated, the vision of the computer-based patient record (CPR) was popular for a while, albeit more than a decade ago. Eventually, the idea of enterprisewide electronic medical records (EMR) replaced the limited CPR concept. Subsequently, a migration to the EHR philosophy seems to have gained worldwide acceptance as the preferred, generic term of use in describing the vision of how the electronic records of a patient should contain information, such that it would allow the trajectory of patient care in the patient's lifetime to be traced. Yet some authors continue to use terms such as CPR, EPR (electronic patient records), and EMR interchangeably, which has, inevitably, added to the confusion.[21]

EHR will be one of the most costly project expenditures that a healthcare services organization will undertake, with regard to the investments of time and money and the resultant challenge of returns on investments (ROI). This is because the significance of the returns to be realized from an EHR implementation remains a concern for many healthcare executives. Not only will the initial outlay be significant and extremely challenging, but equally difficult tasks lie in trying to customize the system, linking it with existing legacy systems, and garnering acceptance from the user community. Understanding the needs and wants of healthcare professional users is unlike building an automobile; therefore, drilling into the requirements and specifications for EHR means that either technical people will have to speak a layperson's language, or healthcare professional users must change the way medicine is practiced. Patient examinations and procedures have to be differently structured by the care providers before data can be entered into the EHR, which is completely different from what these professionals practiced when using a paper-based medical record system. In addition, some familiarity with the "EHR" procedures is needed; otherwise, the clinical users will soon become frustrated with using the system, as it certainly does not align easily with what physicians and/or nurses believe to be the typical way of practicing medicine.

While the vision of EHR is theoretically possible, it is difficult to realize in practice. EHR would portray a lifetime record of every health encounter between the patient and all of his or her caregivers, regardless of which clinic or hospital the episode was recorded in, and regardless of who the healthcare provider was—a dentist, family physician, physiotherapist, cancer specialist, or nurse. Interestingly, there are good reasons as to why sharing patient data by creating interoperability among systems belonging to competing clinics or hospitals is not practical, even if direct benefits can be obtained with interoperable patient information systems that cut across organizational boundaries. The responsibility of housing patient data in EHR is one that each clinic or hospital would prefer to bear independently. Major gains from implementing EHR are therefore confined within the boundaries of a single enterprise. In this manner, patient safety, care efficiencies, and clinical decision effectiveness can be clearly demonstrated, and the motivation to share patient data among competing HMO can, as a result, be diminished. Moreover, EHR require practitioners to perform more computer entries and less handwriting, which is often counterintuitive to practitioners in terms of being productive—a computer order entry may, for example, take twice as long as writing or dictating an order, and practitioners who are not familiar with how the EHR-embedded CPOE functions may experience anxiety, thereby finding difficulty in reviewing his or her instructions stored in the system in front of a co-worker or patient. Worse still, some practitioners are not in the habit of sharing their analysis of patient data with other practitioners or would prefer to privately review their own notes before opening them for distribution. Such practitioners would not want to see their detailed progress notes automatically stored in a system that other practitioners can freely access.

The lack of standardization has been a major barrier to linking different EHR systems and related components. These standards can range from how patient information is stored or the terminology used to store the information to the procedures for exchanging information among the different systems. Major areas where the lack of standards prevent interoperability and data sharing include information content (e.g., uniformity or comparability); input procedures (e.g., direct sourcing); representational format (e.g., data coding); clinical practice (e.g., treatment protocols); decision support (e.g., reminders and alerts); performance metrics (e.g., quality assurance); and security, confidentiality, and privacy (e.g., compliance with the Health Insurance Portability and Accountability Act of 1996, or HIPAA).

Indeed, one of the most formidable challenges for EHR technology adoption involves HIPAA's privacy and security ruling. HIPAA rules prohibit the disclosure of patient health information, except where it is specifically permitted with the patient's consent. HIPAA violations can result in civil sanctions (entailing a limited fine, which varies for individuals and organizations) or criminal liability (entailing fines of $50,000 to $250,000, or 1 to 10 years of imprisonment).[22] In any case, training authorized personnel, instituting appropriate organizational policies, and having effective audit processes are all critical factors for properly securing the EHR information and accomplishing a successful EHR implementation.

VIII. Conclusion

Despite rapid and continuing growth in the healthcare services industry, the application of health management information systems (HMIS) in enhancing organizational efficiency and effectiveness has been slow. Technologies, such as EHR, need to be appreciated (and accepted) by both healthcare administrators and practitioners before EHR can significantly affect the performance of healthcare organizations. As previously discussed, considerable benefits can be gained from the electronic processing of a patient's records, because they will then be made accessible and available to the treating physician and other caregivers. New EHR features will also enable physicians to monitor their patients' responses to treatment interventions quickly and will improve their ability to manage patients with chronic illnesses. Perhaps it is time for EHR technology to replace many of the fragmentary data repositories used in legacy systems throughout the healthcare services industry. This move will eradicate unnecessary redundancies, unwanted anomalies, and unacceptable errors in patient records, all of which can only contribute to poor quality in healthcare services.

Upham[23] argues that substantial administrative and clinical benefits can be achieved, should a universal EHR system be finally realized. His list of benefits include (1) easy dissemination of critical patient information to other care providers for follow-up assessments; (2) rapid accessibility of patient records universally; (3) fewer documentation errors, less paperwork, and less filing of paperwork; (4) more efficient navigation through patient records; (5) no misfiled or lost charts; (6) standardization of care procedures among providers; (7) ease of clinical data management; (8) shared coding; (9) greater awareness of medical errors, possible drug interactions, and inherent patient allergies; and (10) ease of performing quality, risk, utilization, and ROI analyses due to the improved accessibility and availability of clinical data. Of course, as noted, these benefits must still be weighed against the challenges of implementing EHR.

At present, much of a patient's health information acquired from a specific healthcare facility stays within the facility; it is not routinely shared with other clinics or healthcare providers. This has been a significant problem, especially for patients who happen to require emergency treatment. To eliminate this predicament, future patient records should use EHR technology to provide connectivity, reliability, flexibility, efficiency, security, mobility, availability, and accessibility. Ideally, the EHR should be receptive to continuous updates. Newer functions—such as statistical reporting for varying purposes, wireless links to other databases and systems, and the incorporation of advanced decision support and graphical imaging tools for shortcutting the clinical decision processes—will further enhance the quality of patient care. Other features and connecting devices—such as Web-based personal health records (PHR), radio-frequency identification (RFID), virtual medical patient records (VPR), and smart cards—will combine with EHR to empower patients and providers. The ultimate aim is to ensure the highest quality of patient care provided always and everywhere.

A Web-based PHR system will, for example, empower patients with access to their own records and help them take a more active role in managing their own health. They will be able to check these records, ensuring that they are receiving appropriate care in a safe and effective manner. A Web-based PHR will organize the patient's private health information, allow them to restrict certain caregivers to particular views, and allow them to efficiently communicate with their caregivers about test results and follow-up plans. Older patients may be able to add remote patient-monitoring tools so their caregivers are kept abreast of possible warning symptoms, thereby managing their chronic states of health, from anywhere in the world, in a more effective manner.

RFID[24] is an unusual form of health IT; based on the VeriChip system, an RFID microchip can be implanted under the skin, granting instant access to a patient's records. Developed by

Applied Digital Solutions Inc. of Delray Beach, Florida, this VeriChip system works by transmitting a unique code to a scanner, permitting caregivers to confirm a patient's identity and extract detailed patient information from a connected database. The implant will only provide the identification so that the system will remain limited to hospitals, doctors, and patients who have access to the scanner.

VPR,[25] another approach to the access of patient medical records (in which data from all the different sources are merely linked electronically as and when needed), allow integration of patient information from all sources, including data from the many ancillary health information systems used in enhancing patient care. VPR are electronically created, edited, and stored in electronic digitized media, just as traditional patient records were done with the medium of ink on paper.

A smart card is an integrated circuit card that can retain a patient's vital medical information. The information can then be easily retrieved, after entering the necessary security information, by swiping the card through a reader. The technology is also compatible with mobile healthcare computing, so that products, medical treatments, or alternative medical therapies can be purchased wherever a card reader is available.

More research and development is needed to ensure that future EHR systems meet the needs of patients, providers, administrators, researchers, and policy makers. Pressing issues relating to reliability, privacy, confidentiality, and security also need to be resolved. The need to protect patient privacy must be balanced by the need for efficient access to data from multiple sites. It is therefore necessary to find the solutions that will reduce the barriers in implementing and developing EHR. If all of the challenges and concerns are resolved, future EHR will quickly propel the healthcare services industry to new heights and possibilities.

Notes

1. Google Health, accessed Monday, May 19, 2008, from http://geekdoctor.blogspot.com/2008/05/launch-of-google-health.html.
2. J. Tan, *E-Health Care Information Systems-An Introduction for Students and Professionals* (San Francisco, CA: Jossey-Bass, 2005).
3. H. Liang, Y. Xue, and X. Wu. "User Acceptance of Computerized Physician Order Entry: An Empirical Investigation." *International Journal of Healthcare Information Systems & Informatics* 1, no. 2 (2006): 39–50.
4. *Wikipedia*, http://en.wikipedia.org/wiki/Electronic_health_record.
5. *Wikipedia*, http://en.wikipedia.org/wiki/CPOE.
6. J. Tan, with S. Sheps, *Health Decision Support Systems* (Gaithersburg, MD: Aspen Publishers, 1998).
7. Institute of Medicine, *The Computer-Based Patient Record: An Essential Technology for Health Care* (1997), from http://www.nap.edu/openbook.php?isbn=0309055326.
8. M. Arsala, N. Rosenblatt, S. Singer, and L. Slouffman, "EHR History and Technology" (2005), accessed June 1, 2008, from http://www7.kellogg.northwestern.edu/techconcepts/Winter2005Projects/healthcaresoftware/techhome.htm.
9. Arsala et al. (2005).
10. HIMSS EHRVA, "Definitional Model and Application Process" (2006), Accessed June 15, 2007, from http://www.himssehrva.org/docs/EHRVA_application.pdf.

11. G. Dickinson, "HL7 EHR System Functional Model and Standard" (2003), accessed June 15, 2007, from http://www.himss.org/Content/Files/EHR_Functional_Model_Ballot.pdf.
12. Arsala et al. (2005).
13. CTEC, "Glossary of Telemedicine and eHealth" (2006), accessed June 15, 2007, from http://www.cteconline.org/terms.html.
14. Palo Alto Medical Foundation, "EHRs Revolutionize Care for Patients, Physicians" (2006), accessed June 15, 2007, from http://www.pamf.org/news/2006/0706ehrs.html.
15. Ibid.
16. A. Melczer, "Background on Electronic Health Records" (2005), accessed June 15, 2007, from http://www.providersedge.com/ehdocs/ehr_articles.
17. "Electronic Health Record," accessed June 15, 2007, from http://findarticles.com/p/articles/mi_hb4365/is_200602/ai_n18950965.
18. M. Amatayakul, "Electronic Health Records." In K. M. LaTour and S. Eichenwald-Maki (Eds.), *Health Information Management: Concepts, Principles, and Practice*, 2nd ed. (Chicago: AHIMA, 2006): 211–237.
19. P. Waegemann, "Healthcare Informatics Online (EHRs vs. CPRs vs. EMRs)" (2003), accessed June 15, 2007, from http://www.providersedge.com/ehdocs/ehr_articles/EHR_vs_CPR_vs_EMR.pdf.
20. P. Waegemann (2004). "EHR vs CCR: What Is the Difference between the Electronic Health Record and the Continuity of Care Record?" (2004), accessed June 15, 2007, from http://www.providersedge.com/ehdocs/ehr_articles/EHR_vs_CCR-What_is_the_difference_between_the_EHR_and_the_CCR.pdf.
21. Waegemann (2003; 2004).
22. *Wikipedia*, Computer physician order entry.
23. R. Upham, "The Electronic Health Record: Will It Become a Reality?" (2004), accessed June 15, 2007, from http://www.hipaadvisory.com/action/ehealth/EHR-reality.htm.
24. P. Fuhrer and D. Guinard, "Building a Smart Hospital Using RFID Technologies (2006), accessed June 15, 2007, from http://diuf.unifr.ch/people/fuhrer/publications/external/RFIDECEH.pdf.
25. F. Malamateniou (2007). "A Workflow-Based Approach to Virtual Patient Record Security" (2007), accessed June 15, 2007, from http://ieeexplore.ieee.org/xpl/freeabs_all.jsp?arnumber=735778.

Chapter Questions

6–1. What is the rationale for classifying EHR, CPOE, and CDSS as patient-centric management systems?

6–2. Why might it be important to link EHR to CPOE and/or CDSS? What about linking EHR to LIS, PIS, RIS, and any other clinical-based IS? What about linking it to a physician PDA?

6–3. Why is user resistance—particularly from physicians and nurses—often considered the greatest obstacle to successfully implementing patient-centric management systems?

6–4. What are the benefits for healthcare consumers of PHR versus EHR? Does this imply that EHR can simply be replaced with PHR or that both systems may be necessary? Why or why not?

Database, Data-Mining, and Data-Warehousing Concepts for Healthcare Services Organizations

Joshia Tan and Joseph Tan

Introduction

A healthcare services organization is essentially a collection of interacting subsystems, one of which is its health management information system (HMIS). A key part of HMIS is the database, which is the focus of this technology brief.

Healthcare Data and Data Sources

According to Kroenke, a *database* is a "model of a model," a self-describing repository of integrated records.[1] In other words, a health database contains healthcare data such as patient demographics (socioeconomic data), patient billing and accounts information (financial data), patient Social Security number (a master index or other personal identification data), and patient treatment data and progress notes (clinical data) to support the delivery of healthcare services.

Three categories of healthcare data are required, almost universally, by healthcare services organizations for supporting their planning and decision-making activities: health status statistics, health resource statistics, and environmental statistics.[2] *Health status statistics* include population, vital, and morbidity statistics. Population statistics are invaluable in planning and delivering community healthcare services, identifying high-risk groups, locating local and regional services demands, flagging potential problems, and evaluating the effectiveness of existing programs. Examples include the size, composition, and growth of the population. Vital statistics like mortality–morbidity rates provide important indicators about the prevalence of specific diseases, or the incidence of ill health in the population. These data facilitate the identification of high-risk groups, who can then be reached through special programs. *Health resource statistics* are concerned with the availability of healthcare personnel, facilities, and services. These data are useful for manpower planning and other resource allocation decisions. *Environmental statistics*, or public health statistics, provide critical data for the prevention of public health problems.

Data and data sources must first be recognized as the fundamental basis for generating meaningful information, because they are the primary drivers of a healthcare enterprise's operation, control, and management. Therefore, the quality of the data being collected is very important. If the data cannot be understood or are inaccurate, it will be a significant impediment to generating the needed information for setting healthcare organizational policies and decisions.

Healthcare Databases

Healthcare databases have been in existence for as long as there have been data storage devices. Even so, the volumes of patient files lining the shelves of a physician's clinic may be considered a physical "database" of patient records. It must, however, be clarified that the database term applies typically in a computer data-processing context.

Databases are essentially collections of data, organized in software, that can be easily accessed, managed, and updated just like an electronic file system. Therefore, instead of paper filing, the data are organized in fields, records, and files in a database. A file is a collection of records, and a record is a complete set of fields. Fields contain individual data elements; for instance, a patient record can be organized into fields of information relating to individual patients. Database management systems (DBMS) are software employed to manipulate (enter, reorganize, and retrieve) data into or from a database.

Depending on how the data are organized, users will extract information from databases by using a query language as part of the DBMS. SQL, which can be formulated in the form of a question, is an example. If a physician is looking for a prescribed medication given to a patient on a certain day, he or she can use SQL to retrieve the information by inputting the patient name or the prescription date. In fact, with the appropriate question framed in SQL, information on all of the patients given a certain medication on the same day may also be extracted. The DBMS architecture can affect how quickly and/or flexibly one can extract the information from the database. There are different data models by which DBMS organize information, the most common ones being relational, network, flat, and hierarchical, all of which are discussed later in the section on data models. At this point, we highlight a commonly used graphical tool for database design, the E-R model.

E-R Model

The entity–relationship (E-R) models are among the most popular means of depicting the data architecture of healthcare services organizations and other data-intensive organizations. E-R models[3] concentrate on highlighting the data structure underlying the information processes, whereas E-R diagrams may be used to model these processes or flows. More specifically, E-R models can be used to show entities and relationships among them for any simple or complex network of entities within a system.

Key elements of the E-R model include entities, relationships, and attributes. An entity is a "thing" that can be identified in a workplace—common examples include patients and physicians. An entity of a given type may be grouped into entity classes: the "volunteer" entity class is the collection of all volunteers. Each entity class can have many entity instances; for example, John and Peter may be instances of the "patient" entity. In the E-R model, a relationship, or an association between entities, can be one-to-one (1:1), one-to-many (1:N), and many-to-many (N:M) relationship. For example, the statement, "Dr. Nolan 'treats' John," portrays a 1:1 relationship between a single-entity instance of one type to a single-entity instance of another type. If Dr. Nolan also "treats" Peter, then the relationship becomes a 1:N (one physician, many patients) relationship. Also, if John and Peter are referred by Dr. Nolan to Professor Chen and both these referrals are also Professor Chen's patients, then it is a N:M (many physicians, many patients) relationship. The determination of these relationships depends largely on the user's and designer's perspectives. Attributes, meanwhile, are the properties of an entity class and are descriptions of the entity's characteristics. In the E-R models, entities are conceptualized as having various attributes. One such attribute, or a certain combination of them, serves as the entity's unique identifier, or "key," allowing it to be distinguished from the other entity instances. For example, John's personal health number, name, age, and gender are attributes of the patient instance, John. The unique identifier, which is the personal health number, can be used to differentiate among the patient instances.

E-R diagrams—by focusing on "things" about which data must be recorded (entities), the relationships among the entities, and their attributes—provide a high-level architectural view of any health database. Moreover, these diagrams can also assist in identifying various ways of dividing the database into subject databases so that they can be used in distributed systems. If changes are made, E-R diagrams can therefore offer great assistance in redesigning the data architecture and will be helpful tools for logical modeling of HMIS problem solutions. An example of an E-R diagram for a community health promotion project (CHHP) is given in Figure TB4.1.

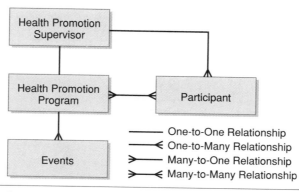

FIGURE TB4.1   An Example of an Entity–Relationship Diagram for the Multicommunity Health Promotion Project.

Data Models

Data models are ways of conceptualizing how information is organized and how it can subsequently be extracted from a database. Among the different record-based logical models, the hierarchical, network, and relational models are most widely used. For the database designer, the use of these models depends chiefly on the user's perspective and interpretation of their organizational structure and processes. *Hierarchical models* are those in which the structures are organized in a top-down, inverted tree-like structure. Health data are stored as nodes in a tree structure, with each node having one "parent" node and perhaps multiple "child" nodes, which may or may not contain health data. For instance, health data about a CHPP, run by staff from a community hospital, may follow the hierarchical model shown in Figure TB4.2.

At the top of the tree hierarchy is the root segment of an element of the tree that corresponds to the main record type, which, in this case, is the CHPP. Below the root element is a subordinate level of health data elements, possibly the walking or restaurant program, each directly linked to the root. Health data elements at each subsequent (subordinate) level are linked to only one element above, but they may be linked to more than one element below; this is demonstrated in our example by the various events of Programs 1 through N. Accordingly, E1 and E2 may refer to the Walkathon event and the Walk-for-Life event of the Walking Program (Program 1). The hierarchical organizational structure is best suited to situations in which the logical relationship between data can be properly represented with the one-to-many approach—that is, where subordinate levels of health data can sufficiently define all relevant attributes of the superior data element. In our case, the CHPP has several programs, which, in turn, are filled with numerous events. In a hierarchical health database, data are accessed logically (navigated) by going through the appropriate levels of data elements to reach the desired data element. There is usually only one access path to any particular data element.

Network data models are logical extensions of the hierarchical models. Instead of having various levels define one-to-many relationships, the network structure represents a network of "many-to-many" relationships, as shown in Figure TB4.3.

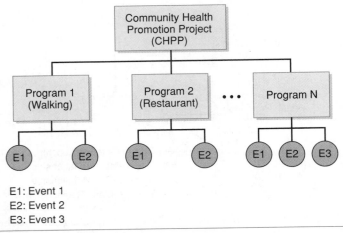

E1: Event 1
E2: Event 2
E3: Event 3

FIGURE TB4.2   An Example of the Hierarchical Model.

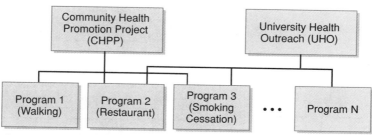

FIGURE TB4.3   An Example of the Network Model.

Here, the CHPP and the University Health Outreach (UHO) project, for example, may require work from two or more programs: walking, restaurant, smoking cessation, and so on. Although all three of the programs mentioned here are involved in the CHPP project, only the latter two are part of the UHO project. Lines joining the responsible programs with the respective projects indicate these relationships. In a network health database, there is often more than one navigational path through which a particular health data element can be accessed.

Unfortunately, health databases structured according to either the hierarchical or the network data model suffer from the same deficiency. Once these relationships are established between data elements, it is difficult to modify them (modification/update anomalies), either by adding new relationships (addition anomalies) or by removing old ones (deletion anomalies). For these reasons, the relational structure has gained popularity among database designers and users over the past several years. *Relational data models* are those in which all health data elements are placed in two-dimensional tables that are the logical equivalent of files. The purpose of the relational structure is to describe health data by using a standard tabular format. As long as the tables share at least one common health data element, any health data elements in these tables can be linked, and the desired data elements subsequently generated in a usable fashion. The health data in the relational model, in most cases, can be linked according to the actual relationship of the various health data elements (i.e., one-to-one, one-to-many or many-to-one, and many-to-many). In the relational tables, each row, called a "tuple," normally represents a record or collection of related facts. The attributes are represented by the table columns, with each attribute only capable of taking on certain values. The allowable values for these attributes or columns constitute the domain. The domain for a particular attribute indicates what values can be placed in each of the columns in the relationship role. The concept is analogous to a series of vectors.

Figure TB4.4 provides an example of how a relational health database may be organized and accessed for the evaluation of the CHPP case. A health program evaluator may, for instance, wish to determine the performance of a particular program's leader (say, of the walking program) under the previously mentioned CHPP and the number of events for that program that have been held by this supervisor to date. The evaluator would make an inquiry to the health database via, say, SQL or another query facility linked to the DBMS. DBMS are software for accessing and processing databases and applications. The query facility provides end-users with a structured tool for searching and making changes to the database. In this case, the query

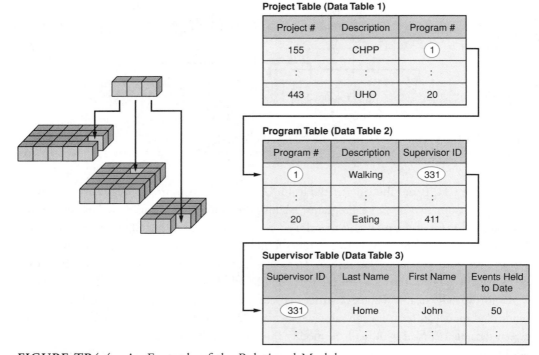

FIGURE TB4.4   An Example of the Relational Model.

would start with the project description and search the Project Table (Data Table 1) to find the appropriate program number, then use the number to search the Program Table (Data Table 2) for the project leader's employee identification number. This identification number, in turn, would be used to search the Supervisor Table (Data Table 3) for the name and other attributes of this supervisor. From here, the evaluator can tell, as a response to the query, if there were 50, or however many, events held to date by this supervisor.

Normalization

Normalization is a process for standardizing relations. A *relation* is defined as a table where all of its cells are single valued with no repeating groups and all entries in any column (attribute) are of the same kind. Data Tables 1, 2, and 3 in Figure TB4.4 are all relations. Essentially, normalization converts problematic relations or tables into desirable and well-structured ones. Thus, highly normalized relations are designed to avoid addition, deletion, and anomalies in updates. This means that the structure of normalized relations is designed to support data integrity, consistency, comparability, and reliability, apart from achieving physical and logical data independence; that is, data can be manipulated freely in the database without the need to revise linked application programs.

Although a discussion of the various normal forms is beyond the scope of this technology brief, Figure TB4.4 summarizes five important normal forms (NF) and the famous domain/key normal form (DK/NF). Fagin[4] argues that a DK/NF relation has no modification anomalies and that, conversely, any relation having no modification anomalies is a DK/NF relation. In other words, the highest normal form that a relation needs to achieve is DK/NF, which, with very few exceptions, is a desirable standard data schema for database designs.

Despite promises for the standardization of relations and automation of database design, many end-users continue to find concepts of normalization difficult to grasp. Readers who are interested in further details on data normalization should consult Silberschatz et al.[5] or any other recently published text on database management.

Data Mining

For decades, different companies have used *data mining*, or "data dipping," to uncover hidden knowledge or patterns from massive data. To understand data mining, the reader should first understand *data warehousing*, which essentially refers to the amassment of enterprise-related data for strategic decision support analysis and knowledge discovery.

Hospital CEOs now realize that the only way to survive and grow in a managed care market is to gain significant expertise in managing information, knowledge, and documentation. Thus, many workers in the medical field are searching for quick and affordable ways to tap into available information banks of detailed patient records. The data-warehousing concept is crucial, because the healthcare industry is moving from a revenue-based business model to one focused on cost-outcomes information management. Many hospitals need data-warehousing architecture to handle the tedious process of analyzing and comparing massive patient treatment outcome information. Johnson Medical Center in Johnson City, Tennessee, needed a data warehouse for studying the historical records of patient treatments and spotting trends or anomalies. Its aim was to help create report cards about physicians, thereby measuring the cost of each doctor's services at the hospital; this was measured by the types of treatments used, total time spent with patients, and other factors. Also, the data gathered could be used to analyze cost of each treatment vis-à-vis the amount of money paid for by insurers. This architecture, then, permits comparison of information among the various departments to show the profitability of each individual operation.

More recently, HIC, the Australian federal agency that processes all medical claims, began using data-mining software to discover subtle patterns, useful for making strategic business decisions, by sifting through seemingly unrelated data. Given the breadth of its transactions, HIC is a classic example of an organization that could benefit from the data-warehousing technology architecture. The staff traditionally relied on paper reports to ensure that medical services were appropriately prescribed and billed. However, with HIC conducting more than 300 million transactions and paying out $8 billion annually to physicians and hospitals, the ability to monitor everything was almost impossible. By using various data-mining tools, HIC's staff can now track areas never before possible. For instance, the different ordering habits of physicians in similar clinical situations can be analyzed so that best practices for various treatments can be established. Often, the key challenge is to know what information to tap into and to ensure that the information tapped will be reliable and valid.

There are different data-mining techniques, such as artificial neural networks (ANN), decision tree analysis, genetic algorithms, and rule induction. *ANN* is a nonlinear predictive model that learns through training and resembles biological neural networks in structure. ANN are expensive due to their need for extensive training, although they are compatible with all data types. *Decision trees* are tree-shaped structures that entail an analytic drill-down process when examining a given decision task's best alternatives. *Genetic (evolutionary) algorithms* are essentially iterative procedures for evolving new populations of structures; this is done through reproduction, cross-over, mutation, and natural selection methods in order to effect the best solutions (chromosomes) to specific domain problems. Finally, *rule induction* is the extraction of useful if–then rules from statistically significant data, accommodating all forms of numeric as well as nonnumeric (symbolic) data.

Conclusion

Frontiers of the medical field are advancing at an escalating pace; parallel to this, the amount of patient information required by healthcare services organizations, in order to achieve high-quality care, has also soared. At the same time, stringent budgetary measures have put enormous pressure on the healthcare industry to tighten cost-control mechanisms and form new alliances. These changes have, in turn, dramatically increased the need for an integrated HMIS approach that can produce the relevant information; with numerous desirable characteristics, the appropriate information would reduce the need for duplicated services in the healthcare system. This technology brief has introduced the basic concepts of healthcare data, databases, DBMS, and various other aspects related to databases, such as health data-mining and data-warehousing methods.

Data mining is an influential business intelligence technology with great potential for rapid growth. Data-mining tools predict the future patterns and behaviors of employees and clients alike; help guide managers to arrive at rational and sensible decisions; and can be applied to answer complex questions that, without extensive research, may not be easily addressed within a short and rapid time period. As an example, a telxon, which is a 900-MHz wireless hand-held terminal equipped with a barcode scanner, is sometimes used to locate specific items. In some organizations, when these products are scanned, the inventory database will be automatically updated; using preprogrammed electronic orders automatically sent to the suppliers, items in need of reordering would also be replenished. In essence, data mining automates the process of finding predictive information in large databases. Similarly, data mining is a powerful technology that will help many healthcare services organizations focus on the most important information in their databases. Data-mining programs can be installed, with relative ease, on existing software and other hardware platforms, and result in instant added value to the healthcare services organization's information resources. Nearly every healthcare facility has massive quantities of data on patients and the many different services each patient has received over the years, but a good number of these facilities lack the tools to fully utilize the information they have toiled so hard to acquire. We end this discussion with an illustration.

A pharmaceutical company can analyze its recent sales force activity and their results—and use these results to improve the targeting of high-value physicians—while simultaneously determining which marketing activities will have the greatest impact in the next few months. The data need to include competitor market activity, as well as information about the local healthcare systems. The results can be distributed to the sales force via a wide area network (WAN), enabling the representatives, as the key attributes in the decision process, to review the recommendations. The ongoing, dynamic analysis of data warehousing allows best practices from across the organization to be applied in specific sales situations.

Notes

1. D. M. Kroenke, *Database Processing: Fundamentals, Design, and Implementation*, 6th ed. (Upper Saddle River, NJ: Prentice Hall, 1998).
2. G. Thompson and I. Handelman, *Health Data and Information Management* (London: Butterworth Publishers, 1978).
3. P. Chen, "The Entity-Relationship Model: Toward a Unified Model of Data." *ACM Transactions on Database Systems* 1, no. 1 (March 1976): 9–36.
4. R. Fagin, "A Normal Form for Relational Databases That Is Based on Domains and Keys," *ACM Transactions on Database Systems* (September 1981): 387–415.
5. A. Silberschatz et al., *Database System Concepts*, 3rd ed. (New York: McGraw-Hill, 1997).
6. Kurt Thearling, "An Introduction to Data Mining" (2008a), accessed February 11, 2008, from www.thearling.com.
7. Kurt Thearling, "Data Mining and Customer Relationships" (2008b), accessed April 6, 2008, from http://www.thearling.com/index.htm#wps.

Health Management Information System Integration:
Achieving Systems Interoperability with Web Services

*J. K. Zhang and Joseph Tan**

Editor's Note: Chapter 7, which focuses on the topic of HMIS integration, concludes the Part II discussion on HMIS technology and applications. Apparently, maintaining legacy systems in healthcare services organizations can be both costly and increasingly cumbersome due to the lack of interoperability among disparate applications. Indeed, these isolated systems will eventually result in unsatisfactory delays to patient care and will continue to take a toll on both clinicians' and employees' time and productivity. The application of Web services as a way to transform healthcare organizational HMIS into seamless integrated systems is certainly a major step that promises to benefit the healthcare services organizations in the longer term, not just temporarily. Therefore, the technology discussed in Chapter 7 is an innovative one. Not only would this technology help prepare the readers to move away from islands of legacy systems in light of the rapid advances in HMIS technology and applications, but the message conveyed could also help open the readers to adopt new HMIS thinking through careful analysis, planning, design, and management (Part III) as well as help them take the next steps to move into higher and wider perspectives regarding HMIS (Part IV). Altogether, the knowledge acquired in Chapter 7 will assist the readers in relating to the other parts of the text much more comprehensively.

---
*The authors would like also to acknowledge specifically the contribution of Ms. Ai Li Mao, a data analyst at Airinmar Ltd, UK, for her valuable assistance in improving the content of several parts of this manuscript.

Scenario: The SAPHIRE Project[1]

Interoperability is concerned primarily with the challenge of linking software and systems being developed and implemented with diverse platforms and languages when required information has to be shared conveniently and securely among multiple providers and users. For example, it is typical for medical and clinical users to derive information embedded in heterogeneous and independent health management information systems (HMIS), most of which are often supported traditionally with the use of specialized clinical hardware and applications. In other words, people with varying levels of expertise and needs typically use different parts of a large-scale HMIS supported by different vendors, who will also adopt different standards, technological architecture, and information formats. Once these interoperability problems are tamed, it is believed that large-scale HMIS can be more easily implemented and maintained with the benefits of reusing previously captured data, adopting well-tested programming codes, and diffusing proven and related applications.

In the United States, Europe, and elsewhere, growing demands for health care due to an aging population and the slowing down in mortality rate among older adults over the last few decades have led to further growth and development of wearable medical devices, sensor-based monitoring technology, and mobile health care. Advanced IT, network, and Web technologies must now be combined to offer support to healthcare professionals in delivering healthcare services at a distance. With these advancing HMIS capabilities, it is anticipated that the quality of health care will be further enhanced, thereby letting people live longer than they are used to. Owing to the increasing percentage of elderly people in Europe, the SAPHIRE Project was launched.

The aging population trend basically means that a growing number of people will need to become more aware of the basic and clinical research on disease pathophysiology and treatment. Coupled with increased demands on healthcare services delivery systems, this rapid growth has made the future practice of medicine even more complex. Essentially, using an interoperable and integrated platform to connect between the hospital information systems and the wireless medical devices, SAPHIRE aims to build an intelligent healthcare monitoring and health decision support system (HDSS) to address the challenge of growing workload intensity in medicine.

Clinical decision support systems (CDSS) are used to provide clinicians or patients with clinical knowledge and patient-related information, intelligently filtered and processed to enhance patient care. The healthcare community response to the complex challenge of modern medical practices is through developing clinical practice guidelines to simplify and improve healthcare services delivery. Although there are many clinical standards and practice guidelines, it is easier for healthcare professionals to access and apply these guidelines if computerized HDSS (automating these clinical guidelines to support the health professionals) are readily available. When developing computerized HDSS, one of the major challenges is to retrieve patient-specific information from the many disparate data sources. There are a large number of legacy clinical systems that have been independently created and administered; they do not, therefore, physically or logically provide support for interoperating and sharing information. In addition, most of the healthcare systems in Europe are built with various computer technologies (e.g., different system platforms supported by diverse vendors and using various database management systems). Moreover, most HMIS applications supplied by local and national service providers are introduced alongside existing departmental applications such as laboratory information systems and mental healthcare record systems.

In the SAPHIRE platform, the solution to tackling the interoperability problem is to expose the data coming from sensors as well as the data stored in medical information systems as semantically enriched Web services. Data from both of these sources and their functionalities could then be combined into different Web services through standard-based ontologies. With the support of Web services, different platforms would be enabled to exchange information and share the functions.

Apparently, the interoperability problem is significant and central for the development of an effective intelligent healthcare monitoring tool. The key challenges have to do with the fact that the data coming from the wireless medical sensors are either (1) in proprietary format, or (2) when it conforms to a standard, the interoperability challenge remains or could not be completely solved because there are numerous standards being adopted. For electrocardiogram data, the available standards include SCP-ECP, U.S. Food and Drug Administration FDA/HL7 Annotated ECG, I-Med, and ecgML. If these data are to be combined with those stored in electronic healthcare records (EHR), the problem would become more complicated due to the fact that hospital information systems are mostly isolated; even when these systems do conform to an interface standard, there still will be the challenge of different standards (or different versions of the same standards). Specific examples include HL7v2.x, HL7v3 CDA, CEN ENV 13606, EHRExtract, and openEHR archetypes. Therefore, the existence of these differing standards does not achieve the aimed interoperability. Besides, interoperability of data coming from different wireless medical sensors is critical to infer information by integrating data coming from various sensors.

By examining the guideline models that are used in SAPHIRE, an understanding of the interaction with the clinical workflow running in the hospital is a necessity. For example, "aspirin should be prescribed to the patient" could be decided on one of the guideline models. For this type of interactions, medical Web services are used to store such medication and procedure orders to the available hospital information system. These kinds of orders are usually implemented as asynchronous Web services to increase the performance.

As the result of a European commission–funded project, IST-1-002103 Artemis, the SAPHIRE project is being developed. IST-1-002103 Artemis developed a semantic Web service-based P2P infrastructure for the interoperability of medical information systems. With the support of Artemis project, the Healthcare Institutes are able to exchange EHR in an interoperable manner through semantically enriched Web services and semantic mediation. These results are well used by the SAPHIRE project for the integration of the patient data collected through wireless medical sensor devices with hospital information systems. This infrastructure comprises the interoperability base for the intelligent healthcare monitoring system.

Imagine a world where everyone speaks the same language—the international language. How easy would it be for people to exchange ideas—and understand each other? Trading among world partners would occur in a snap, and there would be reduced costs for everything, including paperwork, whether manual or computerized. That, in essence, is interoperability. Why is interoperability an important milestone for HMIS integration in a healthcare services organization? What would be the rationale for some people to be against such an idea?

I. Introduction

Characteristically, healthcare information is highly complex, heterogeneous, dynamic, and time-oriented. These features, together with the need to satisfy increasingly stringent regulatory and medico-legal requirements, make healthcare management information systems (HMIS) a costly investment. HMIS cost has been projected to comprise 25 to 39 percent of total healthcare costs.[2]

The traditional healthcare services organizations are expected to be transformed in the coming years, extending from their traditional hospital base to include the home, and from focusing on the treatment of acute and chronic diseases to general patient well-being and improvement of the quality of life. This translates to massive amounts of information to be communicated and shared. With advances in information technologies and greater HMIS complexity, many healthcare institutions have developed systems[3] to manage and process these large amounts of medical information. While the accuracy and performance of health information processing have significantly improved, in order to support massive information exchange and medical knowledge sharing, healthcare providers have to integrate their systems' functions and data. This desire raised some concerns, such as data security, data transmission and network limitation, and system interoperability.[4]

In this chapter, our focus is on *system interoperability*, a major barrier for HMIS integration. In the United Kingdom, for example, most legacy systems are isolated in that data cannot be shared among them. Hence, if a patient needs to change his original general practitioner (GP), the patient's information cannot be immediately moved to the new GP's system until his original GP transfers the information. Technically, these systems were developed using different languages such as Java, Visual Basic, and C++; different system platforms such as the Microsoft Windows operating systems (OS), Linux OS, and Macintosh OS; and different database management systems (DBMS) such as Microsoft SQL server, Oracle, and Microsoft Access.[5–7] The use of a distributed middleware technology, or Web service, is one solution.

Traditionally, the middleware is a convenient means of dealing with the interoperability problem. Distributed object middleware provides the abstraction of an object that is remote; yet, its methods can be invoked, just like those of an object in the same address space as the caller. Distributed objects make all the software engineering benefits of object-oriented techniques—encapsulation, inheritance, and polymorphism—available to the distributed application developer. Developers have used distributed middleware technologies like CORBA (Common Object Request Broker Architecture)/DCOM (Distributed Component Object Model)—both of which incorporate software such as I-HER,[8] BHS,[9] and Hospital Information System[10]—to tackle the issue of system and language interoperability. Yet, CORBA/DCOM solutions, which are largely applied in complex systems context based on Internet environment, are unsuitable because of shortcomings in the firewall crossing and wireless environment.[11–13] In contrast, Web service, as a new distributed middleware technology, can overcome these CORBA/DCOM shortages. It will also successfully address the system-language interoperability issue. However, this new technology has not been formally applied to HMIS domains. Unlike most commercial systems, HMIS involves many more users and entails more historical data and legacy systems. Therefore, the influence of interoperability issues in HMIS is much more apparent. Moreover, Web service technology and Microsoft .NET (a platform for developing Web services applications) are still relatively young.

Guah and Currie[14] state that "Web service architectures are the key to unlocking the full business potential of any Internet-based strategy" and argue for its application into HMIS. Another HMIS researcher notes that "Microsoft .NET platform is a very promising solution but it was not fully available. . . ."[15] Others observe that flexible Web-based services in e-health care are a result of the recent Microsoft .NET developments and that these solutions are probably more flexible, more dynamic, and easier to implement than CORBA-based systems. Our focus here, therefore, is to address the interoperability issue with the Web service technology in the healthcare arena. A small-scale but real-world Web service–based integrated healthcare information system (WSIHIS) designed for the osseointegration project at Queen Mary's Hospital is presented at the end of the chapter to demonstrate and assess such an HMIS integration solution. Although this case study is based specifically in the United Kingdom, its application is similarly significant for healthcare services organizations in the United States, given the abundantly complex and heterogeneous information systems employed in the U.S. multi-provider healthcare delivery systems.

II. Current HMIS Interoperability Issue

The intention of nationalizing and even globalizing healthcare systems through IT has become a very common talking point. Since the end of 2003, the British government started to develop a computerized healthcare system on a national scale, namely, the National Program for IT (NpfIT). NpfIT aims to integrate most of the healthcare systems and services based in England and Wales. However, this project was severely delayed for years because of various issues, such as data transmission, network limitation, data security, and the disincentives for medical staff to cooperate with each other.

Today, the issue of system interoperability appears to have become increasingly critical because there are a considerable number of hospitals in England and Wales that run on different healthcare IT servicing models. Many of these hospitals have also built up their own HMIS and DBMS. This situation is disconcerting because it may easily result in one individual patient having multiple medical records in different hospitals or even in different departments within a single hospital. In addition, most hospital legacy systems have been developed using different computer languages, compiled on different platforms, executed on different hardware—thereby supporting different data structures, types, and formats. The diversity of these systems was not the result of a well-planned development effort nationwide, but it has simply evolved, as autonomous and heterogeneous systems proliferated due to changing institutional needs. Eventually, these islands of HMIS function independently and do not share their data and process. Meanwhile, computer technologies have advanced and the needs for systems that will be able to share information across organizational units have changed. If systems are designed inadequately and with poor interoperability planning for future connectivity—as with the increasing demands from healthcare employees, caregivers, and patients living in today's healthcare services organization environment—a small mistake in early HMIS design and developmental efforts could easily stop these systems from working properly the next time around.

Interoperability, a critical HMIS issue,[16,17] may thus be defined as "the capability with which two or more programs can share and process information irrespective of their implementation language and platform."[18] Connecting for Health, as a single IT provider for the National Health Services (NHS), identified the interoperability challenge as the need to interconnect heterogeneous HMIS to share information easily, seamlessly, and securely whenever and wherever information sharing is needed. As noted, most clinical applications are determined by a huge variety of heterogeneous and independent workplaces, and most of them are also equipped with specialized clinical hardware.[19] Moreover, people with varying levels of expertise and needs typically use different parts of a large-scale telemedicine system. These systems may also be from different vendors, who adopt different standards and information formats, as in the case of NpfIT.[20] Once the interoperability problem is resolved, it is believed that the development and maintenance of large-scale telemedicine systems (or any other large-scale HMIS) can be streamlined with data reuse, code reuse, and application reuse.

Several major HMIS interoperability challenges have been noted to date:

1. *Database (DB) system interoperability.* Patient records are often located in different databases[21]; however, data stored in different database platforms using Microsoft SQL server, Oracle, and Microsoft Access cannot be exchanged among the different systems nor be used by applications based on different DBMS.

2. *Language interoperability.* Different HMIS have been designed and developed by different IT providers, as is the case with patient record systems under the NHS system,[22] where developers make use of different programming languages such as Java, Visual Basic, C++, and C# to build their HMIS. This inevitably makes reusing and sharing of applications nearly impossible because of the programming language incompatibility.

3. *System platform interoperability.* This equates to operating system (OS) interoperability, although over the past few years the Internet browser has, in and of itself, emerged as a platform.[23] As different HMIS applications emerged based on different development platforms (e.g., Microsoft Windows OS, Linux systems, IE Web browser, and Avant Web browser), most of these HMIS applications will only work on certain system platforms. For example, if the HMIS were built based on a Windows system platforms, it would restrict the software to run also on another platform such as Linux.

4. *Semantic interoperability.* Many interoperability problems arise because of semantic differences. Semantic interoperability assumes that the components of the distributed application will have different interpretations of the data. For example, the same term may have different meaning contents in different countries, or different terms could have the same meanings. Such situations are common in medical information systems, and human intelligence is often required to resolve such semantic interoperability issues.

HMIS integration is necessary when two previously independent organizations (such as NHS trusts) merged—each of which not only has its own IT architecture but also promotes different ways of recording, sharing, and accessing information. Somehow, these merged organizations have to unify core applications, such as patient administration systems, so that the staff can continue to use both the newly installed system and the legacy system.

More recently, the NHS has proposed the NpfIT, which is aimed at integrating HMIS under the NHS in England and Wales.[24] Unfortunately, a large number of legacy clinical systems, which do not provide the support for interoperating and sharing information either logically and/or physically, have been independently created or administered in the NHS. In addition, most of the healthcare systems in England and Wales are built with different system platforms and DBMS, and most HMIS applications supplied by local and national service providers are introduced alongside existing departmental applications like laboratory information systems (LIS) and mental healthcare record systems. As a result, the interoperability issue was a major challenge for the NpfIT when it was proposed in 2002.[25,26]

Put together, the NpfIT interoperability issue is largely a result of several factors:

1. *Interoperable business processes.* There are thousands of hospitals under the NHS adopting different business processes with different health systems, which makes NpfIT more complex to interoperate.

2. *Changing interoperability requirements among NpfIT systems.* For example, Electronic Transmission Prescription, one of the systems delivered by NpfIT, was envisaged originally as a separate system, but the program is now required to be integrated with another software system, NHS Care Records Service.[27]

3. *Diverse patient record systems in use across the NHS.* The challenge of integrating records is augmented largely by diverse NHS patient record systems contracted to isolated software vendors.

4. *Need to interoperate with systems on doctors' desktops.* NHS Care Records Service, as one of NpfIT's services, will need to interoperate with doctors' desktop systems. The challenge for NpfIT is not really building systems from scratch, but having to deal with many existing hospital and GP systems to be connected to the "spine," which is a newly developed NHS database system.[28]

5. *Two separate Scottish and English NHS systems.* Because Scotland and England are using two different NHS systems,[29,30] both of these places are also developing two different HMIS with different IT providers, potentially leading to future interoperability between systems.

6. *Localized systems.* Under the NHS system, most existing IT systems in trusts are localized and do not typically support information sharing across buildings and departments. Consequently, within a single organization, several records are often created for the same patient. In primary care, individual practices also have their own IT applications and databases, so patient records are not easily transferred to other practices or care providers.

III. Web Services: The Interoperability Solution

Integrating with seamless interoperability among applications and data from different systems is a very challenging task. As noted, the achievement of a good interoperability strategy is significantly constrained by many restrictions in traditional CORBA or DCOM implementations.[31,32] Fortunately, Web services have emerged as the next-generation HMIS integration technology.[33] Based on open standards, Web services permit any piece of software to communicate with any other in a standardized XML messaging system, resolving the constraints with DCOM/CORBA.

As a modular, self-describing type of software service, Web services are self-contained applications that can be published, located, and dynamically invoked across the Web. The Web services technology is built on the foundation of open standards and common infrastructure, comprising three areas: communication protocols, service descriptions, and service discovery, of which each is specified by an open standard.[34] In general, Web services consist of two major technologies—XML (eXtensible Markup Language) and SOAP (Simple Object Access Protocol)—and two assistant technologies—WSDL (Web Services Description Language) and UDDI (Universal Description, Discovery, and Integration).

The specifications of services can be described using WSDL. WSDL is a general framework (based on XML) for describing network services as collections of communication endpoints capable of exchanging messages. It describes where a service is located, what operations are supported, and the format of the messages to be exchanged based on how the service is invoked. WSDL does not mandate a specific communication protocol used.

The Web service vision foresees a proliferation of services, which in turn requires the availability of public directories that can be used for the registration and finding of services. UDDI provides a mechanism for service providers to advertise their services in a standard form and for service consumers to query services of interest, thereby paving the way for interoperability between services. A UDDI entry consists of white pages (e.g., address, contact information), yellow pages (e.g., industrial characterization based on standard ontologies), and green pages (e.g., references to specifications of services).

Focusing on the core technology of Web Services, SOAP is a platform-independent protocol that uses XML to make remote procedure calls over HTTP. SOAP message is written in an easy-to-understand and platform-independent XML. HTTP was chosen to transmit SOAP because HTTP is a standard protocol for sending information across the Internet. The use of XML and HTTP enables different operating systems to send and receive SOAP messages. As well, Web services allow client and server implementations to construct their distinct but equivalent representations of any data structures. Web services that use SOAP support a wider variety of data types, including most basic data types as well as Dataset, DateTime, XMLNode, and several others. SOAP also permits the transmission of arrays of all these types.

Figure 7.1 indicates how Web services works. First, Web service providers make use of WSDL to describe their Web services. Following this step, Web service providers register and

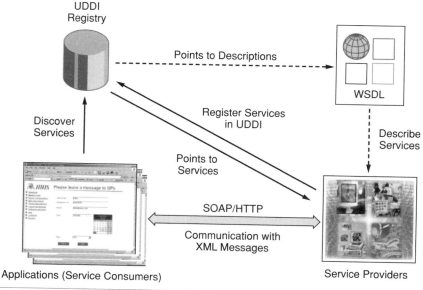

FIGURE 7.1   A Detailed Architecture of Web Service.

publish their services in UDDI. In this way, applications or service consumers are then able to find or locate the services that interest them via UDDI, which directs these service consumers to relevant services according to the description of Web services. With regard to the last step just discussed, applications or service consumers are able to invoke relevant Web services using SOAP transmitted via HTTP on the Internet.

When Web services are encoded in XML, SOAP then provides a way to facilitate communications between applications developed with different programming languages and/or running on different operating systems. In fact, Web services provide a distributed computing technology environment for integrating HMIS applications on the Internet using open standards and XML encoding. The use of standard XML protocols makes Web services platform-independent, language-independent, and vendor-independent. In light of this, Web services will provide an ideal solution for use in HMIS application integration. Figure 7.2 depicts how applications work with Web services.

With respect to Figure 7.2, applications or service consumers send requests and responses to and from Web services via SOAP. When any piece of software system invokes a Web service method, the request and all relevant information are packed in a SOAP message and sent to the appropriate destination. When the Web service receives the SOAP message, it triggers an automatic processing of the contents (called the SOAP envelope), which specifies the method that the client wishes to execute and the arguments the client is passing to that method. After the Web service receives this request and parses it, the proper method is called with the specified

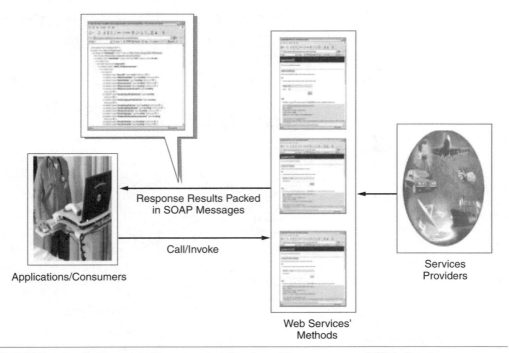

FIGURE 7.2   Interaction between Applications/Consumers and Web Services.

arguments (if there are any), and the response is then sent back to the client in another SOAP message. Conversely, the client parses the returned response to retrieve the result of the method call.

As illustrated in the second half of this chapter, an integrated HMIS Web service (or WSIHIS) can be developed and its performance assessed using different OS platforms, programming languages, and DBMS. The result of assessment showed that Web services enabled WSIHIS to work on cross-system platforms, make use of functions and applications developed by different programming languages, and exchange the data across database systems. It can therefore be argued that the Web service–based solution could help existing and future HMIS to reduce significant effort in overcoming the interoperability challenge today and in the future.

IV. WSIHIS Case

Evidently, system interoperability has become critical for NpfIT or any large-scale HMIS to share information. To this end, HMIS developers have used CORBA/DCOM, a traditional distributed middleware technology approach, which is unfortunately relatively complex to handle without specialized expertise. Given that any large-scale systems are challenging to develop and maintain, it is all the more critical that these systems should be technically easy for longer-term development and maintenance requirements.

Web services were touted here to address the interoperability issues. Compared with CORBA/DCOM, Web services could reduce development and deployment time, lessen system implementation costs, reduce the maintenance complexity, and lower HMIS project failure risk. These features make Web services suitable for large-scale projects such as NpfIT. Simply put, *Web service*, as a new distributed middleware technology, promises to address the HMIS interoperability challenge. Yet, the technology has not been formally applied to HMIS, unlike known successful applications in e-business. To illustrate Web services conceptualization, a small-scale but real-world Web service–based integrated healthcare information system (WSIHIS) designed for the osseointegration project at Queen Mary's Hospital, was designed and developed based on the Web service technology, using flowcharts and object-oriented system development methodology. In this section, we present a case description of the necessary knowledge and technologies for implementing WSIHIS.

Background of WSIHIS

Many people around the world become amputees due to warfare, traffic accidents, and the progression of diseases such as diabetes. Traditionally, these amputees would have to be treated with conventional socket techniques. With the development of new medical technologies, however, new treatment techniques for amputees, based on the osseointegration technique discovered by Professor Branenmark in the 1990s, have emerged.

Basically, Professor Branenmark's osseointegration technique makes use of a titanium implant as the attachment site for the artificial limb. The first osseointegration surgery performed was a dental implant.[35] Professor Branenmark further applied the osseointegration technique in orthopedics. In 1997, he decided on Queen Mary's Hospital as the site for the clinical trial outside of Sweden.

Because osseointegration is an entirely new technique, patients have to be selected carefully. A scheme called OPRA (Osseointegration Programme for Rehabilitation Amputee) was developed in Sweden that consists of patients' selection and recruitment, surgical plan after surgeon retirement, and rehabilitation. The whole procedure of osseointegration—from the operation to the rehabilitation of patients—can last several years. Overall, this process would involve doctors, patients, surgeons, prosthetic clinicians, and rehabilitation clinicians. All relevant information must be recorded and documented for progress review. Patients' files are also required if the infection is developed at a later stage. An integrated HMIS would be needed to manage and process the massive health data to be exchanged and processed accordingly at each stage, because the patient, the hospital, the rehabilitation center, and the prosthesis are not normally in same location. The data exchange between the systems would be very important. Consequently, WSIHIS is proposed to computerize all documents and data and offer a secure and stable environment for the communications between doctors and patients across the Internet.

WSIHIS Interoperability

On the basis of the need to integrate and share information about the patients among caregivers, it is not difficult to surmise that WSIHIS would also face most, if not all, of the interoperability challenges affecting any other HMIS.

Principally, WSIHIS interoperability issues could be purported as follows:

- *System interoperability.* Based on the background description, WSIHIS would be required to link with various medically relevant caregivers such as the GP, surgeon, prosthetic clinician, and rehabilitation clinician, who might be using different systems on their desktops to access WSIHIS for different purposes. To accommodate the needs of these caregivers, WSIHIS would require the capability to interoperate among different systems such as Microsoft Windows Systems, Linux, and other operating systems. Additionally, some parts of patient records may have to be extracted from legacy systems used by some medical staff (such as the GP) or be derived from data previously captured in existing legacy systems. As with the data-sharing purpose, WSIHIS would need to interoperate with different DBMS such as Microsoft SQL server, Oracle, and Microsoft Access.
- *Language interoperability.* WSIHIS will have to integrate with functions of existing and future healthcare systems. Generally speaking, different systems are developed using different technologies, particularly the use of different programming languages. For example, the NHS houses many different patient record systems in use across units that were developed by independent software providers. To enable WSIHIS to be compliant with the functionalities of different systems, WSIHIS would have to interoperate with applications developed in different programming languages such as Java, Visual Basic, C++, and C#.

Web Service–Based Solution for WSIHIS Interoperability

As a solution to resolve the interoperability challenges noted earlier, WSIHIS was developed with the support of Web service. Currently, there are two major application platforms—Microsoft .NET and Java 2 Enterprise Edition (J2EE)—that can be applied to create Web services.

Microsoft .NET is selected as the major platform for developing the proposed system because it would be more suitable than J2EE in terms of certain features from the NHS perspective, including overall maturity, interoperability, scalability, and cost.[36,37] Besides, several HMIS developers have expressed interests in Microsoft .NET for health IT development even before Microsoft .NET packages were marketed. Consequently, Microsoft .NET has been selected as the platform for building the proposed system. Figure 7.3 illustrates the general conceptualization of a Web service–based solution of WSIHIS.

User Interfaces

WSIHIS provides front-end users with convenient and easy-to-use interfaces. Medical content provided through these interfaces is generated dynamically based on a specific patient's medical profile. To get access to these interfaces, patients or relevant medical staff members are required to log in by entering the user name, password, and identity code.

Data Repository

The WSIHIS data repository holds medical data and knowledge. The WSIHIS data repository has been developed to store all of the data related to patients' medical profiles and information about the progress and status of treatment. In addition, all data in the WSIHIS data repository come from various DBMS.

WSIHIS Core System

A Web service–based middleware, the WSIHIS core system, encapsulates business logic in a shared middle tier. As such, all of the different client applications will access the same middle tier, avoiding the redundancy of duplicating business rules for each one. Additionally, the WSIHIS

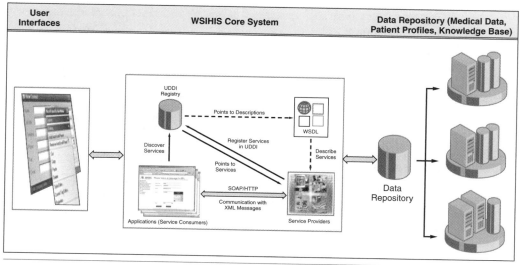

FIGURE 7.3   General Concept of a Web Service–Based Solution for the Interoperability Issue of WSIHIS.

core system can render data from different DBMS readable and understandable to client applications.

Within WSIHIS, Web service plays the role of middleware that hides all these differences in system platforms, programming languages, and DBMS to both users and developers. Accordingly, from the users' perspective, they would be oblivious to the differences in their system platforms because these were able similarly to get access to WSIHIS. From the developers' perspective, they can invoke or reuse WSIHIS applications in their systems with the support of Web services.

On the one hand, Figure 7.3 illustrates a general conceptualization of Web service–based solution for WSIHIS interoperability. On the other hand, Figure 7.4 explains how Web service and Microsoft .NET technology are applied in WSIHIS. WSIHIS is built upon the Microsoft .NET platform, and Web service plays the role of middleware. Web services can be exposed from and consumed by any platform that can format and parse an XML message due to the use of XML for the formatting of requests and responses. This allows XML-based Web services to bring together disparate pieces of functionality—whether exiting or new, internal or external to an organization—into a coherent whole.

Web service core technologies include XML and SOAP. Once Web services receive requests from applications, Web services would retrieve data from different DBMS such as SQL server, Microsoft Access, and/or Oracle into data sets based on the requirements of applications. All data sets would be written in XML messages; in additions, SOAP would act as an XML envelope to wrap those XML-based data sets into SOAP messages. Then, these SOAP messages would be transmitted back to applications via HTTP. SOAP in Web service–based middleware provides a way to communicate between applications developed with different programming languages and running on different operating systems.

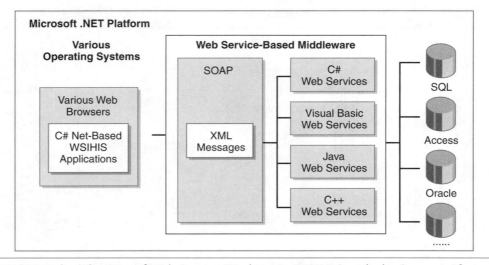

FIGURE 7.4   The Way of Web Service Working in WSIHIS with the Support of Microsoft .NET Technologies.

Additionally, the Microsoft .NET platform is another important part of the WSIHIS interoperability solution. First, it is language-neutral and best thought of as an open programming platform into which a variety of languages can be plugged. Second, how this is achieved is through translating all different programming languages into a common language called Intermediary Language (IL). Here, the source code is first translated into Microsoft Intermediate Language (MSIL). This IL code is language-neutral and is analogous to Java byte-code. The IL code then needs to be interpreted and translated into a native executable. The .NET framework includes the Common Language Runtime (CLR), analogous to the Java Runtime Environment (JRE), which achieves this goal. The CLR is Microsoft's intermediary between .NET developers' source code and the underlying hardware, and all .NET code ultimately runs within the CLR. Finally, Microsoft has indicated that the Microsoft .NET platform would also enable the system to run under different system platforms and Web browser platforms.

System Assessment on WSIHIS Interoperability

All results of this assessment have shown that WSIHIS could interoperate with data from different DBMS and different Web service–based applications developed in different programming languages. This section discusses how a Web service–based solution achieves the interoperability among HMIS applications.

The Web services exchange information in XML, a universal format for structured documents. To support XML document processing, a variety of specifications and standards have emerged, such as eXtensible Stylesheet Language (XSL), Document Object Model (DOM), Simple API for XML (SAX), and Resource Description Framework (RDF). Due to wide industrial support, the XML-formatted documents are much more searchable, integratable, reusable, and manageable. In fact, converting proprietary documents to XML is the most economical way to add intelligence to documents and to make them immediately consumable over the Internet. Figure 7.5 illustrates how easily an XML-formatted proprietary document is extracted from Hospital A's HMIS, transferred over the Internet, and consumed by different HMIS based in Hospitals B, C, and D.

In Figure 7.5, a Web service acts as a middleware among hospitals. If Hospitals B, C, and D need to get the data based in Hospital A, they would send their requests to the Web service over the Internet. All requests sent to the Web service would be wrapped in SOAP envelopes. These requests contain criteria and parameters for retrieving the data. Once the Web service gets the request, it would extract the data from the HMIS in Hospital A according to the criteria and parameters specified in the request. When the Web service obtains the required data, it would convert the data to an XML-based document. The XML-based document would then be wrapped in the SOAP envelope and sent to the other hospitals over the Internet. An XML-based document is in a standard-based format that can be readily parsed and consumed by other HMIS.

Applications in some legacy systems have been functioning reliably with the help of many years of maintenance efforts. These applications could still be useful for a certain period of time. As a result, it is important to enable these legacy systems to participate in new systems as

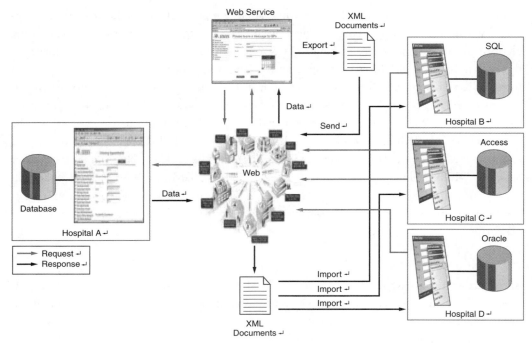

FIGURE 7.5   Web Service–Based Data Exchange between HMIS.

part of the clinical data and data-related activities to be performed. However, seamless system interoperability of legacy HMIS is a challenging task because these legacy systems were largely developed when there were no open standards. HMIS developers implemented these legacy systems through their proprietary technologies that are typically not interoperable with each other. In this sense, a Web service–based solution is critical to sharing information among the systems by providing a distributed computing environment for interoperating the healthcare-related services on the Internet using open standards and XML encoding. The use of standard XML protocols makes Web services platform-independent and language-independent. Built on the foundation of open standards, Web services eliminate the major interoperability issues. Based on the result of the system interoperability assessment, Figure 7.6 illustrates how the Web service–based solution addresses the WSIHIS interoperability between HMIS and legacy systems.

The Web service–based solution does offer a fundamentally different way to deliver business functions. It uses open standards to expose functions internally and externally to other systems. According to Figure 7.6, the Web service–based solution for system interoperability between WSIHIS and legacy systems consists of the following steps:

- Core functions of WSIHIS are based on different Web services, such as the appointment service, the patient ID validating service, the patient record search service, and the patient record update service. These Web Services could be developed in different programming languages. For example, for the purpose of system assessment, some of the Web services in WSIHIS were developed in C#, Visual Basic, C++, and Java.

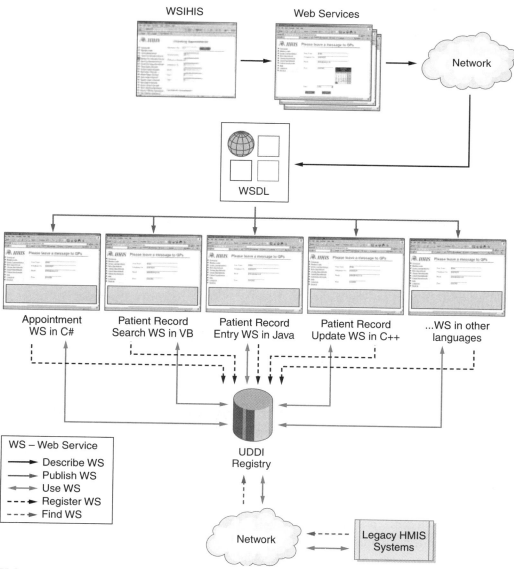

FIGURE 7.6 Web Service–Based System Interoperability between HMIS.

- Before exposing these Web services externally to other systems, WSDL is used to describe these services, specifying its location and publishing its operations (methods). WSDL provides a standard way to describe the Web service interfaces in enough detail to allow other systems to build a client application talking to the described Web service.
- Web service would then be registered with UDDI. UDDI offers Web service users a unified and systematic way to find service providers through a centralized registry of service. The registry of service is an automated online "phone directory" through which the

registered Web services advertise their business services. UDDI registry access is accomplished using a standard SOAP API for both querying and updating.

- Once these Web services are published and registered, legacy systems could start to use these services over the network.
- Legacy systems could find services via UDDI, which directs service consumers to relevant services according to the description of Web services.
- With respect to the previous step, applications or service consumers are able to invoke relevant Web services using SOAP transmitted via HTTP on the Internet.

Figure 7.6 shows how Web services enable legacy systems to participate in WSIHIS. Web services could also be applied in legacy HMIS systems. With minimal programming, a Web service, as an interface, can be layered on top of a legacy HMIS system to allow it to be accessed by other systems (e.g., WSIHIS) over the network. The Web service–based solution could provide HMIS with an open architecture, allowing both existing legacy HMIS and new systems to be rapidly and seamlessly integrated. It also allows developers to reuse the system's applications and yields loosely coupled open-system architecture. The legacy systems can continue to operate as stand-alone systems until the new HMIS become stable.

V. Conclusion

According to the standard system development life cycle (SDLC), a WSIHIS model has been designed and implemented based on a Microsoft .NET platform by using the C# programming language. To prove if Web services is an appropriate solution for the interoperability challenge, an assessment has been done concentrating on the system interoperability from several aspects. The major purpose of assessment attempts to ensure if WSIHIS could be run on different system platforms such as Linux system platforms, Windows system platforms, or other OS platforms integrated with some applications developed in different computer programming languages and different DBMS. The result drawn from the assessment satisfied the interoperability challenges, and there are reasons to believe a Web service–based solution implemented on the Microsoft .NET platform with use of the C# programming language would be suitable to overcome the system interoperability challenges for current HMIS.

Web service supports increased interoperability but also represent a significant increase in run-time cost for Web service solutions. Conversion to text format and parsing of XML documents is inherently more costly than the alternative mechanisms used to convert data to a common data representation for the network. The additional communications and processing costs are frequently perceived as a potential barrier to the use of Web services technologies. Hence, future research should try to find out a solution to overcome these shortcomings of Web services.

Notes

1. SAPHIRE: Intelligent Healthcare Monitoring Based on Semantic Interoperability Platform, http://www.ehealthnews.eu/content/view/282/27/.
2. S. Chu and B. Cesnik, "A Three-Tier Clinical Information Systems Design Model," *International Journal of Medical Informatics* 57, no. 2–3 (2000): 91–107.

3. L. G. Kun, "Telehealth and the Global Health Network in the 21st Century, From Homecare to Public Health Informatics," *Computer Methods and Programs in Biomedicine* 64, no. 3 (2001).

4. Department of Health and National Health Services, *Connecting for Health—A Public-Private Collaborative* (London: National Health Services, 2003).

5. G. K. Matsopoulos, V. Kouloulias, and P. Asvestas, "MITIS: A WWW-Based Medical System for Managing and Processing Gynecological–Obstetrical–Radiological Data," *Computer Methods and Programs in Biomedicine* 76, no. 1 (2004): 53–71.

6. M. Tsiknakis, D. G. Katehakis, and S. C. Orphanoudakis, "An Open, Component-Based Information Infrastructure for Integrated Health Information Networks," *International Journal of Medical Informatics* 68, no. 1–3 (2002): 3–26.

7. B. Varge and P. Ray, "Interoperability of Hospital Information Systems: A Case Study." In *Enterprise Networking and Computing in Healthcare Industry*, 5th International Workshop, 2003.

8. Matsopoulos et al. (2004).

9. Tsiknakis et al. (2002).

10. Varge and Ray (2003).

11. H. M. Deitel, P. J. Deitel, J. Listfield, and T. R. Nieto, *C# How to Program—Introducing .Net and Web Service* (London: Prentice-Hall, 2002).

12. T. M. Chester, "Cross-Platform Integration with XML and SOAP," *IT Professional* 2005. 9, no. 4 (2005): 67–70.

13. G. A. Duthie, *Microsoft ASP.Net Programming With Microsoft Visual C# .Net Step by Step* (Washington, DC: Microsoft Press, 2003).

14. M. W. C. Guah and W. L. Currie, "Logicality of ASP in Healthcare: The NHS Case Study." In *Proceedings of the 37th Annual Hawaii International Electrical and Electronics Engineers Conference*, 2004.

15. Matsopoulos et al. (2004).

16. S. Jablonski, R. Lay, and C. Meiler, "Data Logistics as Means of Integration in Healthcare Applications," *ACM Symposium on Applied Computing* 1 (2005): 236–241.

17. N. Maglaveras and I. Chouvarda, "The Citizen Health System (CHS): A Modular Medical Contact Center Providing Quality Telemedicine Services." *IEEE Transactions on Information Technology in Biomedicine* 9, no. 3 (2005).

18. G. Pronab and R. Pradeep, "Software Interoperability of Telemedicine Systems: A CSCW Perspective," *IEEE* 2000.

19. Ibid.

20. NpfIT, *Making IT Happen—Information about the National Programme for IT* (London, U.K.: Department of Health, 2005).

21. A. E. James and Y. H. Wilcox, "A Telematic System for Oncology Based Electronic Health Patient Records," *Information Technology in Biomedicine* 5, no. 1 (2001): 16–17.

22. M. Cross, "In Sickness or In Health?" *IEEE Review* 50, no. 10 (2004).

23. B. Albahari, P. Drayton, and B. Merrill, *C# Essential—A Comparitive Overview of C#* (Sebastopol, CA: O'Reilly, 2001).

24. National Health Services, "History of Connecting for Health," accessed December 2005 from http://www.connectingforhealth.nhs.uk/aboutus/history.

25. J. K. Zhang, W. Xu, and D. Ewins, "System Interoperability Study for Healthcare Information System with Web Services." In *Asia Pacific Association for Medical Informatics (APAMI) 2006—Towards Global Interoperability for Electronic Health Records* (Taipei, Taiwan: APAMI, 2006).

26. J. K. Zhang and W. Xu, "The Study of Web Service on the System Interoperability Concern in E-Healthcare System." In *Proceedings of World Conference on E-Learning in Corporate, Government, Healthcare, and Higher Education 2006.* (Chesapeake, VA: AACE, 2006).

27. National Health Services, "Electronic Transmission of Prescriptions (ETP) Programme," November 2005, accessed December 2005 from http://www.connectingforhealth.nhs.uk/newsroom/news-stories/news280205/.

28. Department of Health and National Program for IT, *Choose and Book Service Implementation Guide* (London: National Health Services, 2005).

29. A. G. Mathews and R. Butler, "A Vision for the Use of Proactive Mobile Computing Tools to Empower People with Chronic Conditions." In *Proceedings of the 18th IEEE Symposium on Computer-Based Medical Systems (CBMS'05)* (IEEE, 2005).

30. Department of Health and National Health Services, *NHS Connecting for Health Fact Sheet* (London: National Health Services, 2005).

31. A. Banerjee and A. Corera, *C# Web Services—Building Web Services With .NET Remoting and ASP.NET* (WROX, 2002).

32. A. Gokhale, B. Kumar, and A. Sahuguet, "Reinventing the Wheel? CORBA vs. Web Services." In *The Eleventh International World Wide Web Conference* (Honolulu, HI, 2002).

33. A. Umar, "The Emerging Role of the Web for Enterprise Applications and ASPs." In *Proceedings of the IEEE* (IEEE, 2004).

34. F. Curbera, M. Duftler, and R. Khalaf, *Unraveling the Web Services Web—An Introduction to SOAP, WSDL, and UDDI* (IEEE Internet Computing, 2002).

35. J. Sullivan, M. Uden, and K. P. Robinson, "Rehabilitation of the Trans-Femoral Amputee with an Osseointegrated Prosthesis: The United Kingdom Experience," *Prosthetics and Orthotics International*, 2003.

36. R. Sessions, *Java 2 Enterprise Edition versus The .Net Platform—Two Visions for eBusiness* (Texas: ObjectWatch, Inc., 2001).

37. C. Vawter and E. Roman, *J2EE vs. Microsoft .NET—A Comparison of Building XML-Based Web Services* (The Middleware Company, 2001).

38. J. K. Zhang and W. Xu, "Web Service-Based Healthcare Information System (WSHIS): A Case Study for System Interoperability Concern in Healthcare Field." In *International Conference on Biomedical &Pharmaceutical Engineering 2006* (Singapore: IEEE, 2006).

Chapter Questions

7–1. What are the major issues with existing HIMIS? Discuss why system interoperability is becoming a major concern for HMIS.

7–2. Discuss main components or protocols of Web services. Discuss how Web services could be fitted into or applied to HMIS.

7–3. Research potential advantages and disadvantages of Web services to HMIS. Discuss if there are any other effects or beneficial uses of Web services to HMIS besides as a solution for the HMIS interoperability issue.

7–4. Discuss how feasible the Web services solution is for HMIS.

7–5. What are the challenges with the Web services solution? How could these challenges be overcome for future HMIS implementations?

Health Management Information System Planning and Management

Health Management Strategic Information System Planning/ Information Requirements

Jon Blue and Joseph Tan

Editor's Note: HMIS strategic planning and information requirements are two of the early, but very critical, steps in the administration of HMIS for healthcare services organizations. This chapter lays the groundwork for the "hows" of all of HMIS initiatives (Part III), not just the "whys" (Part I), "whats" (Part II), and "whos" (Part IV). Beyond preparing students, practitioners, and administrators for aligning HMIS goals and objectives with corporate goals and objectives, and for deciding the best alternative means of developing that system which would fit well with organizational information requirements and culture as highlighted in this chapter, the next steps have to include HMIS analysis and development methodologies (Chapter 9), followed by practical advice on HMIS design, implementation, and evaluation through data stewardship (Chapter 10) and managing of pre-implementation, implementation, and post-implementation processes as well as IT service management (Chapter 11). Part III, therefore, bridges HMIS applications and technologies (Part II) on the one hand and HMIS standards, governance, policy, and international perspective (Part IV) on the other. Moreover, the cases in Part V cluster largely around HMIS planning and implementation in diverse organizational settings. Knowledge of this chapter thus provides readers with a solid base for initiating the HMIS planning and management process.

CHAPTER OUTLINE

Scenario: *Open Health Tools*

Scenario: Open Health Tools[1]

Open Health Tools (OHT), a collaborative health information technology (HIT) open-source site, continues to develop ways for healthcare services organizations to curtail electronic medical records (EMR) development costs and reduce time-to-market releases. Recently, the OHT has added code from the United Kingdom's National Health Service (NHS) and incorporated an academic outreach project to motivate students to embrace its programming tools. With support from major healthcare services organizations in the United States, Canada, the United Kingdom, and Australia; vendor giants, including IBM and Oracle; and health standards organizations HL7 and the International Health Terminology Standards Development Organization, OHT hopes that healthcare services organizations will use its open-source technology as the backbone for HMIS infrastructure.

Specifically, Open Health Tools is developing a free software platform that allows EHR data to be exchanged among various commercial products. In essence, OHT tools are the translator that permits various legacy databases to communicate with one another. This involves processes such as message and document interchanges, static model designers, simulators, adaptors, data transformers, and device access. The underlying frame is available under an open-source license so organizations can design and build applications without any payment required for the software.

OHT hopes to duplicate the success of the Eclipse, a popular nonprofit, open-source community whose projects are focused on developing an open platform for building, deploying, and managing software across its life cycle. Skip McGaughy, one of Eclipse's founders and OHT's executive director, envisions OHT to mimic a "satellite" of Eclipse.

"We're going to be using Eclipse technology," McGaughy claims, "but our governance is under the direction and control of the health and computer industry. We use the same development and intellectual property process, the same paradigms, and many of the same people. The Eclipse code has been downloaded and used by millions of programmers, so it's thoroughly tested and debugged. Programs using the Eclipse framework, through the use of plug-ins, are compatible."

As high-quality medical decisions are based on the reliability of health data, the need for reliable and accurate coding in healthcare services is essential. With increasing complexity of HMIS, it is argued that OHT's dynamic, open-source software tools have a unique advantage over other competitive commercial products. McGaughy further clarifies, "It's componentized, it's modular, and it's done in the open, so everyone understands what the requirements are, and there's a dialogue about the requirements."

McGaughy also maintains a perspective of HIT as a means to achieving the goal of improving health. "At the end of the day, what's really important is reducing costs, but also saving lives and improving care. And what is unique is the number of really good software developers who are joining this effort. So instead of just moving little bits on the screen, they can now save lives."

How do you feel about saving lives as a result of the willingness of the human spirits to join forces, to share, and to collaborate on HMIS software development—isn't this a noble cause? Yes, but it all begins with planning and strategizing, which are precisely the focus of this chapter.

I. Introduction

Information technology (IT) in health care changes rapidly and dictates the importance of information systems (IS) strategy planning. Subsequent to the planning, it is important that healthcare management be evaluated on meeting the specifics of the plan using predetermined criteria. Doing so will assist a healthcare services organization in meeting its goals. With the proliferation of managed healthcare organizations that affect nearly every healthcare organization, one would think that the task of strategic planning would be different. However, while the internal and external inputs and the requirements that are necessary to develop a healthcare organization strategic plan may differ, the process is exactly the same.

Healthcare senior management, when developing the overall strategy, provide the overall vision and mission for the organization. These executives expect that those individuals who comprise the health management information systems (HMIS) team not only share in the vision, but also develop achievable, measurable goals that are consistent with the strategy. The HMIS team also supports the objectives and carries out tactics in support of the mission. For example, a pharmacy department in a hospital may be responsible for reducing the number of prescription fulfillment errors by 8 percent in 18 months. The HMIS team may assist the pharmacy by suggesting the implementation of a mandatory technology of electronic prescribing (e-prescribing) and fulfillment that must be performed electronically. Among the benefits that will assist the pharmacy in reducing errors that occur due to doctors' or nurse practitioners' poor penmanship, other benefits will result.

Additionally, senior management may have goals for which the HMIS team is primarily responsible. If management's goal is to have the ability for all departments of the hospital to communicate electronically in four years, the HMIS team may be responsible for initiating, developing and/or securing, and rolling out the infrastructure and technologies needed to meet this goal. Such an implementation would include the telephony, systems, networking, software, hardware, and training.

In a supporting role, or as the primary responsible department in fulfilling the goals that cascade from the vision and mission, it is important that a health management strategic information system plan (HMSISP) be developed. With IS technology rapidly changing and the important role that IS services plays in nearly every healthcare department, the HMSISP will provide the systems structure and detail needed to assist a healthcare services organization to fulfill its overall vision and mission.

In this chapter, the roles of health management and how performance is normally evaluated in healthcare services organizations are reviewed. Also visited here are several techniques that can be used to acquire healthcare individuals' information needs that become a very important ingredient when developing an HMSISP. The HMSISP must tie directly into the health organization's mission and vision.

II. The Essence of Management

Management is a science as much as it is an art.[2] However, on a continuum of art and pure science, management leans toward "art" because managers must deal with people and their behavior and guide employees' activities. There is much discussion on how to maximize individual performance in different domains.[3,4]

Continued external pressures on health organizations and on their HMIS teams dictate that an HMSISP is necessary in order to avoid being reactive. For instance, U.S. politicians are pressuring healthcare services organizations by demanding legislation that mandates electronic health records (EHR). EHR would allow the records of patients to be standardized so their information is sharable across organizations. The movement toward the use of EHR has developed much further in countries other than the United States, where only 5 to 15 percent of practices use EHR.[5,6] EHR use by Israeli physicians is close to 100 percent; this level of use leads the world.[7] In the United Kingdom, as early as 1995, 80 percent of primary care physicians worked in facilities that were computerized, with more than 60 percent of these practitioners using EHR. Also in 1985, Danish general practitioner EHR use was 70 percent; use in Sweden was 60 percent and was 40 percent in the Netherlands.[8] There is very little support on EHR use adversely affecting physician and patient satisfaction.[9,10] Recent studies have also found EHR use to be perceived by patients and physicians as enhancing the overall quality of care.[11–13]

Another force pressuring HMIS teams in healthcare services organizations to innovate and reform is with the phase-in of the Health Insurance Portability and Accountability Act of 1996 (HIPAA). The mandated processes and procedures are in place to ensure that patients' information is secure and is only disclosed on a need-to-know basis. Noncompliance could result in the levy of fines by the Office of Civil Rights (OCR) of up to $25,000 a year for each violation. OCR is an office in the Department of Health and Human Services (HHS). Even with this threat of fines, the HIPAA Compliance Survey of 2006 indicates that full compliance only minimally improved over the previous three years.[14] Fortunately for many healthcare services organizations, there have not been any fines levied for the last several years, even though there have been more than 4,100 complaints. Nonetheless, if OCR begins to levy fines, a healthcare service organization needs to be ready. An HMSISP, with underlying objectives that detail activities to move an organization to full HIPAA compliance, will greatly assist in attenuating the risk of fines. To react most effectively and efficiently to events such as possible HIPAA violations, healthcare services organizations must strategically plan their HMIS to ensure that they can survive in the healthcare industry.

Considering that organization behavior is key to how management is applied, Longest[15] defines *management* as a process that has both interpersonal and technical aspects. Management specifies the goals for the healthcare services organization—and using technology, as well as human and physical resources or capital, accomplishes the objectives of the goals. Therefore, when used in a healthcare services organization context, the age-old process of health management is the art of planning, organizing, directing, and controlling (PODC). These activities are applied to both tangible and intangible resources such as people, facilities, equipment, information, and technology, such that the objectives that are resultant from the strategy, as prescribed, are met. The processes for combining and allocating these resources would be part of the intangible capital. Looking at this in context with healthcare services organizations, the entire process of managing resources and capital in a health organization needs to be done in the most efficient and effective way to provide the best services.

III. The PODC Model

The planning, organizing, directing, and controlling (PODC) model, as shown in Figure 8.1, has iterated often over the years. However, Henri Fayol[16] was the primary contributor. Fayol was one of the first to say that management is a science. He presented a specific body of knowledge and managerial activities: planning, organizing, directing, and controlling.

PODC is presented as an operationalized and rationally designed tool to assist in meeting organizational goals. We can still see Fayol's categorizations in today's publications such as Hellriegel, Jackson, and Slocum;[17] Lewis, Goodman, and Fandt;[18] Kinicki and Williams;[19] Rue and Byars;[20] Schermerhorn.[21] Several of these publications include areas of discussion other than PODC. Nonetheless, the *Fayol functions* are present and offer a solid base for these authors to build on.

As the PODC model is viewed, it is important to understand that in today's healthcare services organizations, there is not a hierarchical connection among the different functional levels

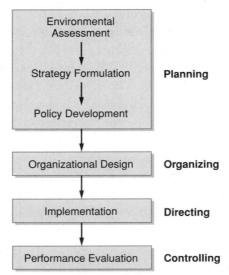

FIGURE 8.1   The Planning, Organizing, Directing, and Controlling (PODC) Model. *Source:* Reprinted from Henri Fayol (1949).

or activities. The functions continuously interplay with one another. Nor do these functions occur in any specific order; instead, they are practiced at all levels as are necessary throughout various times.

High-level strategic planning is initiated at the apex of healthcare services organizations. As stated, this often begins with the executive team formulating the vision and mission (at a minimum). The vision and organizational mission are broken down into goals, objectives, and tactics that are manageable, understandable, and measurable. Some senior management teams may go as far as formulating values, goals, and objectives. The executive team in these healthcare services organizations typically include, at minimum, the chief executive officer (CEO), chief financial officer (CFO), chief operating officer (COO), and chief medical officer (CMO). A chief information officer (CIO) is often also appointed and is becoming more commonplace in healthcare services organizations; it is possible, however, that at the executive level, the role of the CIO may be assigned to the COO or the CFO.

Strategy sessions are normally held at least annually, and it is during these meetings that the executive team sets the direction for the organization for years forward—normally at least three years. The mission statement sets the strategic focus of the business. As shown in Table 8.1, the mission and vision of healthcare services organizations vary, as well as the level of detail presented.

Senior executives of healthcare services organizations are consistently involved with building external relations, so they must ensure that the strategies they formulate are consistent with what is going on around them. This not only includes the community or segment of the population that their organizations serve, but also the laws and regulatory policies for which their organizations must comply. For instance, with a for-profit healthcare services organization, the

Table 8.1   Example Vision and Mission Statements

Organization	Vision	Mission
Penang Adventist Hospital*	A patient-centered teaching and learning tertiary healthcare facility with international quality standards bringing to the community acclaimed selected centers of excellence.	Penang Adventist Hospital is committed to demonstrating the love and healing ministry of Christ by providing comprehensive, competent, and excellent health care for all.
Blue Cross and Blue Shield of Louisiana**	To improve the lives of Louisianians by providing health guidance and affordable access to quality care.	To improve the lives of Louisianians by improving the quality, universality, affordability, and differentiation of the health guidance and health care they receive, and by improving the quality, universality, affordability, and differentiation of the services we ourselves provide directly on behalf of our membership. BCBSLA will, by every measure, enhance its role and its competitive standing, both in the state of Louisiana and beyond.
Brookhaven Memorial Hospital Medical Center***	Deliver leading-edge healthcare solutions through a focused and compassionate team in technologically advanced facilities. Achieving the capacity to invest in the future enables us to create recognized Centers of Excellence, provide a learning culture, and become the employees' and patients' provider of choice.	Deliver accessible, high-quality health services in a focused, caring environment, while providing health advocacy for the community and people we serve.

*Penang Adventist Hospital (2007). Vision, Mission & Values. Retrieved December 20, 2007, from http://www.pah.com.my/about_us/mission_and_values/index.asp

** Blue Cross Blue Shield of Louisiana (2007). Mission, Vision and Values. Retrieved December 20, 2007, from http://www.bcbsla.com/web/reddotcm/html/20_95.asp

*** Brookhaven Memorial Hospital Medical Center (2007). Mission, Vision and Core Values. Retrieved December 20, 2007, from http://www.brookhavenhospital.org/aboutus/missionvisionstatements.html

ultimate goal may simply be profit; thus, without a strategy for achieving cost-effective compliance with current legislations and regulatory requirements within a reasonable span of time, continuing the present operations of the organization may result in the increase of expenses, thereby leading to a loss.

Even though the executive team's main focus in strategic planning is to set the vision and mission, it may also be necessary for these managers to go beyond these initial steps and actually make specific decisions for the overall organization. Making these decisions prior to the plan rollout not only relieves other organization members of making some tough choices, but also provides leadership and dictates a clear organizational direction. The decisions could affect such things as the number of employees in the organization, the service level of the emergency room, or a sick leave policy. This increased level of direction does not occur often; executives primarily operate at a strategic level and do not dictate departmental strategies, objectives, and tactics. The executive role is to offer the vision, mission, values, and some goals. The majority of the divisional goals, objectives, and tactics are left for middle management and lower-level employees to develop that fit into the overall vision and mission. These goals, objectives, and tactics are subsequently reviewed and approved by the health organization's senior management team. The "big picture" is what executives should be focusing on primarily—they need to make sure that what is planned to occur will result in the organization meeting the mission and realizing the vision. An example of vision, mission, goals, objectives, and tactics of a hospital is shown in Exhibit 8.1.

Exhibit 8.1   Strategic Planning Focus

AREA A: The vision and mission are typically determined by the executive team.

Vision, Mission

The vision and mission statements, when articulated, clarify who the healthcare organization is. They will describe the organization.

Vision Statement

To be viewed internationally as a hospital that is based on comprehensive research activities and clinical excellence.

Mission Statement

To be considered by all our patients, and their families, as delivering excellent care and the utmost concern for their overall well-being.

AREA B: Senior Managers are typically evaluated on meeting goals.

Goals

Goals will allow a level of focus on how the vision and mission will be achieved.

Goals are usually provided in an outline or bulleted form. Each goal is specific and measurable and if all goals are met then the organization is successful and the vision and mission has been achieved. Both short-term goals (within 12 months) and long-term goals (3 to 5 years) should be presented.

Organization Goals

- Patient and family satisfaction will improve in 1 year.
- Within the next 6 months, 50% of our palliative care patients will have reported pain less than 5 (1–10 scale).
- Medical errors of commission and omission* will be reduced by 8 and 5 percent, respectively, in 18 months.
- Physicians will express satisfaction with the emergency care program after 2 years.
- Revenue will meet direct expenses within 3 years.

For each goal there is a series of objectives that need to be achieved in order to reach the goal.

[*Errors of commission would be errors such as prescribing a medication that has adverse side effects with another medication that the patient is taking. Errors of omission would be such errors as the failure to prescribe a medication to a patient that he or she would more than likely benefit from.]

(continues)

Exhibit 8.1   *(Continued)*

AREA C: Middle managers are typically evaluated on meeting objectives.

Objectives

The objectives delivered focus on how each individual goal will be achieved.

For example, for the goal:

> "Medical errors of commission and omission will be reduced by 8 and 5 percent, respectively, in 18 months"

four objectives might be:

- A mandatory electronic prescription system (EPS) will be introduced within 1 year that must be used by all clinicians when prescribing medications to patients.
- A wireless secure link between clinicians' personal digital assistants and the EPS will be available within 14 months.
- A bar-scanning mechanism that includes the patient, all hospital personnel who treat the patient, and the prescribed/administered service will be implemented within 1 year.
- The status of achieving this goal will be presented to the chief medical director monthly and to the chief executive officer quarterly.

AREA D: First-level managers and individual contributors are typically evaluated on meeting tactics.

Tactics

Tactics are described that will meet the objectives. There are usually several tactics that are needed to achieve each objective.

For each tactic include times and identify accountable individual(s).

Goal, Objectives, and Tactics

Goal: Medical errors of commission and omission will be reduced within 1 year by 8 and 5 percent, respectively, in 18 months.

Objective 1: A mandatory electronic prescription system (EPS) will be introduced within 1 year that must be used by all clinicians when prescribing medications to patients.

Tactic 1.1: Choose HMIS EPS project manager (PM) (1 month; owner: HMIS first-level manager).

Tactic 1.2: Engage consultant to assist in decisions and development needs (1.5 months; owner: HMIS team).

Tactic 1.3: Determine vendor (2 months; owner: HMIS EPS PM).

Tactic 1.4: Develop implementation and roll out plan (4 months; owner: HMIS EPS PM).

The middle managers are given the responsibility of communicating the strategy, mission, and goals. Some health organizations may develop tactics from the bottom up (meaning that individual employees suggest the tactics). Alternatively, tactics can be developed and mandated from the top. More likely, there could be a mix of the two methods. The difference depends on the organization and the objective. Mandates that have legal implications may need to come from, and be imposed by, the top level of the healthcare services organization. For instance, all 50 states require both laboratories and physicians to report to health departments the names of persons newly diagnosed with Centers for Disease Control–defined AIDS.[22] Executives may dictate this law's compliance by directing the human resources department to develop a rollout plan, delivering the plan, and developing employee noncompliance sanctions.

When providing strategic plans, healthcare executives, their management teams, and (possibly) hired organizational change consultants must ensure that the organization in its current form is capable of carrying out the vision. Additionally, the necessary resources must be available. For the plan to be realized, the current organizational structure may need to be scrutinized to determine if its current form facilities the team in meeting the objectives. If not, it is necessary for the executives to restructure the organization so that the mission can be realized. The restructuring effort may be as small as shifting employees among departments or as major as moving to an entirely different organizational structure. The healthcare services organizational structure determines the hierarchy within an organization: it determines who reports to whom.

Types of organizational structures include division structure, functional structure, and matrix structure. The *divisional structure* can take on three different forms: service, market, and geographic. In a service structure, employees are grouped by service in divisions that encompass such services as emergency, surgery, and dermatology. A market structure would divide services based on the market served such as pediatrics, adult health, and geriatrics. The last of the divisional structures is geographic. In this structure, employees are grouped based on specific geographic locations. This type of structure may occur in large healthcare services organizations that operate in many, or disperse, locations. In a *functional structure*, employees are grouped based on the functions of specific jobs within the organization. For instance, there may be a department of nursing (nursing function) and a customer service department (customer service function), each of which may be led by a director. A *matrix organization* groups employees by both division and function. This structure can combine the best of both separate structures. For instance, a nurse who works in the emergency room may report to both the emergency room manager and the manager of nursing.

Overall, the roles that managers are currently playing, and the roles that are necessary to best meet the strategy, must be reviewed. One way for this to happen is that senior management may direct an internal review of employee competencies. These are then matched with the required skills needed to accomplish the mission, and a gap analysis is conducted. Determining the fit and placement of individuals can be complex. Moreover, doing so is not a healthcare organization's core competency. Therefore, consultants are often enlisted to assist the healthcare organization.[23–25]

If it is determined that the current managers will not facilitate meeting the strategy, then a change in leadership may be necessary—or, at minimum, the executive management must ensure that the current leaders have, or are able to acquire, the required skills. What could occur, which would be counterproductive to achieving the organization goals, would be to force-fit the strategy into an organization that is not ready to carry out the activities that are needed to fulfill the executives' vision. Senior healthcare managers need to be forthright and determine if the current team—both health management and employees—is capable and able to do what it takes to achieve the mission. Based on this assessment, management has to decide if there is a need to redeploy the current personnel. In addition to assessing the organizational structure and employees, managers must provide the necessary resources to accomplish the vision, mission, goals, objectives, and tactics. The work systems and relationships must also be in place or established. Not having the resources, the work systems, or the relationships could jeopardize the realization of the vision.

Even if the executives paint a clear picture of where they would like to see the organization in the future, without employees' assistance in getting there, the vision will not be realized. Therefore, guidance from top and middle management is necessary. The managers must provide not only the day-to-day supervision, but they must work closely with their teams to determine the objectives and tactics needed to meet their specific team goals. Not only must a manager direct team members to do his or her part in implementing the strategy, the team leader must make sure that teamwork is optimized. Having the individual fulfill his or her part in meeting the objectives in order to realize the vision and the team working together to meet the organization's goals is paramount. As a part of control, to ensure that the goals are being met, measurable performance evaluations are necessary to assess how managers, individuals, and teams are meeting the overall objectives. What is most important is that the expectations of meeting the mission are cascaded throughout the organization in the form of performance objectives that are met prior to evaluation.

Senior managers' performance objectives are more in line with meeting the healthcare services organization goals, as shown in Area B of Exhibit 8.1. Middle managers are evaluated on how well their teams meet the organizational objectives, as shown in Area C of Exhibit 8.1. Individual contributors (nonmanagement) and frontline managers in the organization should be evaluated on how well they accomplish the tactics that contribute to meeting the objectives as shown in Area D of Exhibit 8.1.

The process of ongoing feedback among different levels of the organization occurs cyclically, and continuous feedback is exchanged among levels throughout the evaluation period. As is shown in Figure 8.2, the higher levels use environmental factors as input, among many other

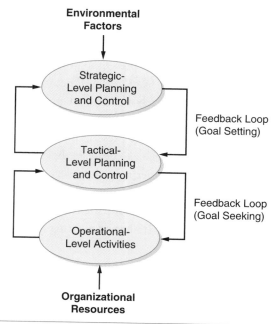

FIGURE 8.2   Levels of Feedback Loops for Organizational Thinking.

items. Organizational resources are infused into the operational levels of the organization. In addition, there is a feedback loop between the different levels of the organization. The feedback loop between the senior level and the middle levels of the organization is goal setting, and the interaction between middle management and the individual contributor level is goal seeking.

IV. HMSISP

In today's turbulent society, with globalization and an increased level of government intervention, developing an HMSISP has become quite necessary to remaining competitive. The process of developing an HMIS plan includes determining the computer-based applications that are needed to assist an organization in meeting business objectives.[26,27] Developing an HMSISP will facilitate an organization in identifying how they can use information systems to positively differentiate themselves from the competition. Such planning, followed by system acquisition and implementation, will hopefully create a competitive advantage.

The increased rate of change of environmental factors, the difficulty in predicting these changes, the scarcity of resources, and the degree of competition have been said to moderate the impact of strategic information systems planning.[28–31] Business executives indicate that they believe strategic information systems planning is challenging.[32] But even though developing an HMSISP may be difficult, healthcare professionals believe that doing so is necessary to remaining competitive.

While the overall higher-level strategic plan guides the entire health organization, the HMSISP must exist to assist the organization in fulfilling its objectives. There may be specific information systems objectives; however, most often, the HMSISP assists the realization of nonsystems objectives. Dunbar and Schmidt[33] have suggested that at least 35 percent of a healthcare service organization's strategic plan should tie in to the HMSISP.

A healthcare services organization's HMSISP that directs the implementation of an e-prescribing system is shown in Exhibit 8.2. Such a PDA e-prescribing focus would not only be helpful to the organization, but patients could benefit from it as well because of its appeal relative to another competing organization that would rely on manual prescription orders. In addition, healthcare services organizations that have implemented e-prescribing at varying levels can cut down on medication errors arising from illegible prescription scripts. In other words, this fulfills the HMIS objective of a hospital's pharmacy to decrease the error rate of prescription refills, as well as to shorten the time between the ordering and delivery of the medication. A PDA can also be used by providing doctors with a source of drug reference in aiding decisions on which drug and dosage should be prescribed for particular patients. As the cost of technology continues to decrease rapidly,[34] the impact that HMIS has on assisting in accomplishing the organization's strategic goals will also increase.

Figure 8.3, a diagram modeled from Tan,[35] is a partial presentation of a top-down hierarchical stages planning model. The model shown clarifies the planning activities and the order of the activities. Additionally, clarity is obtained on alternative techniques, methodologies, and the applicable strategies. This model is consistent with, and extends, the framework offered by Bowman, Davis, and Wetherbe.[36] Tan suggests that this model can be

Exhibit 8.2   PDA E-Prescribing Focus

It would be great if a clinician could:

- Print a copy of all patients for whom you prescribed a recently recalled drug.
- Easily look up drug interactions for a drug you are considering prescribing.
- Be able to create a script electronically that automatically determines the recommended dosage for a 30-lb., 3-year-old boy.
- Quickly determine the available dosages for a drug you want to prescribe to your hypertensive patient.

Such is possible today using a handheld prescribing device, such as a personal digital assistant (PDA) that is no larger than a prescription pad.

The handheld device comes on immediately, has a secure wireless connection to your computer, and can tell you your daily appointments. You can use your PDA to select a specific patient and immediately see her demographics and insurance plan. Drugs on the device are alphabetized and side effects are presented for each medication. The patient's health insurance information, as it pertains to the drug, is also displayed. Allergies and drug interactions for your patient are automatically determined from the patient's currently prescribed medications. To prescribe a medication, you choose the medication from a drop-down menu, select the correct dosage from another drop-down menu, digitally sign the medication, and then electronically send the script to the patient's pharmacy (or, optionally, securely send to your printer). At this point, the patient's EHR is automatically updated via a secure wireless connection.

used as a general framework that guides HMIS strategic planning, design, and development. An organization's ability to support the processes and business functions encountered in healthcare services delivery is determined by the information and technology architecture that is in place. He continues by suggesting that the organization's processes and business functions should determine the information that is needed to support an organization's business strategies.[37]

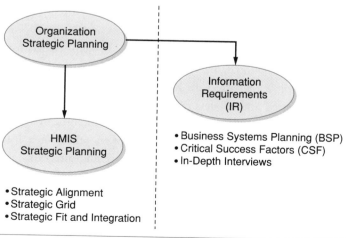

FIGURE 8.3   Partial Framework for HMIS Strategic Planning: A Top-Down Stages Planning Model.

It has been shown that alignment and fit of HMIS strategies to organizational strategies alone are not enough to ensure success. For success, in addition to plan alignment, many aspects (e.g., technology, structures, processes, skills) must be considered.[38] As important as these aspects are, the "people" element of implementing the HMIS must also be considered. Managers need to establish ways to minimize organizational resistance and business disruptions to ensure the best coexistence of the strategies.[39] If a clinic plans to implement a computerized physician order entry (CPOE) system, unless physicians are involved from the beginning, such a system is destined to fail. All HMIS users must be involved in the planning, the determination of needs, and the implementation—they must be a part of the solution.

While alignment among organizational strategies, HMIS strategies, and the delineations of HMIS goals is important, equally important is the determination of information requirements (IR). As can be seen in Figure 8.3, this is the next activity in HMIS strategic planning.

V. Information Requirements

Traditionally, information has been seen as a resource that needs to be managed by healthcare services organization executives—just like labor and capital. However, HMIS managers need to ensure that technology and information resources are used to meet the organization's IT needs. First, HMIS teams must investigate and prioritize the organization's information needs.

It is quite difficult to determine the information needs of different individuals and departments in healthcare services organizations. Prior to determining the appropriate HMIS that need to be implemented, it is necessary to identify the type of decisions that are made. With today's proliferation of managed care organizations, many decisions have already been determined. This is because, depending on the insurance company or organization (e.g., Blue Cross Blue Shield, Kaiser Permanente, Medicare), there may be limited choices available to the decision maker. Because managed care organizations have become more the norm than the exception, it is even more difficult for HMIS teams to identify the subset of choices that are applicable to different patients. These decisions can be broadly divided into strategic and day-to-day operational decisions. Executives make far more strategic decisions than others in the organization. Some healthcare employees primarily, if not totally, make operational decisions. The type of decision that needs to be made, whether strategic or operational, determines the information needs—and the needs differ.

Strategic decisions are those that affect the healthcare organization in the long term. The decisions are often unstructured and use less quantitative inputs than operational decisions.[40,41] These "soft" decisions are often difficult to make, and therefore, much of the information that is needed is not precise. Making strategic decisions often relies on a leader's experience. Decisions such as organizational restructuring and fund-raising directions are at the strategic end, whereas decisions such as daily budgeting, hiring, and training of personnel would be at the more operational end. While the ultimate decision is difficult, an HMIS could assist a decision maker in solving this unstructured problem, as well as semistructured, unprogrammed, and nonrepetitive problems.[42] Because strategic decisions are often "one-time decisions," the information needs are difficult to determine *a priori*. For instance, a healthcare executive may need to make a decision on the location of building a new outpatient clinic that will have the least social impact. For instance, one of the officers who reports to the leader may have provided the following list of locations to choose from: East Los Angeles, South Central Los Angeles, Compton, and North Hollywood. This decision is an unstructured strategic task because evaluating social impact is an unstructured problem. It is strategic in that it relates to a new clinic and could affect the entire organization.

Operational decisions happen more frequently, and the information that is needed for these short-term decisions is easier to predict than strategic decisions. As stated, those in lower levels of the organization often make the decisions. The type of department, as well as the type of healthcare services organization, often determines the type of decisions that need to be made. For example, an HMIS may be used to decide the etiology of a patient's pain in his leg. A simple binary decision can be developed that allows a physician to enter data, and the information systems (IS) could output possible causes, in probability order.

Information Sources

Many ways have been introduced that assist in gathering information needs in organizations. Methods such as in-depth interviews, brainstorming sessions, participant observation, document analysis, business systems planning, determining health service organization critical success factors, and ends–means analysis are a few among many.[43–45] Even though the techniques are abundant, it is still quite difficult to anticipate all of the information needs of a healthcare services organization. From a human behavioral point, many people cannot articulate the information they really need; at a minimum, it is difficult to predict all needs. This is specifically difficult as one elicits information needs from healthcare organization executives. As stated earlier, this is because the information needs of those at the higher end of the organizational apex are more closely tied to strategic, unique decisions.

Each of the different methods of gathering healthcare services organization information needs views IR differently. Often, HMIS teams use myriad ways in order to gather the most and the best data in different departments and at different levels. Business systems planning, critical success factor generation, and in-depth interviews are three of the ways that healthcare services teams use often to solicit IR.

Business Systems Planning

Initial work on business systems planning (BSP) began in the early 1970s by IBM and was introduced to support strategic information systems planning.[46] BSP was developed for use internally within IBM, but later it was offered as a planning method to customers. BSP focuses on data and processes. It is generic in its application, meaning that products, as well as HMIS services organizations, can benefit from its use. Healthcare services organizations use BSP when they want a new way to view the organization and determine the information needs in order to build HMIS. The process is very comprehensive; therefore, it is often time-consuming and expensive.

While there are other models used on occasion for planning (e.g., business process reengineering or enterprisewide architecture strategy [EWAS] methodology), all have been a rendition of BSP. The BSP defines the information architecture for an organization. The basic building blocks of the BSP are data classes and health services processes. The data classes are the categories of the necessary data to support the organization. Healthcare services processes are logically related activities and decisions that are required to manage the resources of the organization.

The steps to develop a BSP that are normally taken by HMIS management include the following:

1. The study is authorized.
2. The team is assembled.
3. The data classes and healthcare services processes are defined.
4. The information architecture is defined (from the data classes and healthcare services processes).
5. The as-is system (technically based system or not) is compared with the information architecture, and the needed HMIS are identified to fill the gap.
6. Healthcare services executives are interviewed to verify the architecture and to determine any problems.
7. Priorities are established on the major HMIS contained in the architecture.
8. The final BSP report is prepared and presented to the healthcare services management.

An example of the steps for developing a BSP for an e-prescribing system at a hospital is illustrated in Table 8.2.

Table 8.2 BSP Example for an E-Prescribing System

Step	Activity/E-Prescribing Example	
1	The study is authorized.	Senior management gives the directive to implement an e-prescribing system to replace the hospital's manual system.
2	The team is assembled.	The first-level HMIS manager assigns the project manager, consultant, and an HMIS employee to the team.
3	The data classes and health service processes are defined.	Table 8.3 shows a subset of the data classes/processes matrix for the e-prescribing system.
4	The information architecture is defined.	The flow of information and connections are determined, given the data classes/health service processes matrix from step 3.
5	The as-is system is compared with the information architecture, and the needed HMIS are identified to fill the gaps.	The current nonautomated system is compared with the information architecture from step 4, and the HMIS needed are chosen.
6	Health service executives are interviewed to verify the architecture and to determine any problems.	Interviews are conducted with senior management to ensure that the architecture developed in step 4 is correct and appropriate.
7	Priorities are established on the major HMIS contained in the architecture.	The HMIS from the architecture are prioritized, with the capabilities of each HMIS documented.
8	The final BSP report is prepared and presented to the health services management.	The e-prescribing HMIS BSP is completed and presented to the health organization executives for approval.

Table 8.3 Data Classes/Health Service Processes E-Prescribing System Matrix

	Data Classes								
	Patient Entry Event	Patient	Prescribing Physician	Assistant	Bar Code	Diagnosis	Patient Location	Prescription Document	Technology Resources
Component-Level Processes									
Create a new patient medication record	R*	C	R*	C	C	C	R*	C	
Update an existing patient's medication record	R	RUD	R	RUD	RUD	RUD	R	RUD	
Query the e-prescribing system for existing patient information	R	R	R	R	R	R	R	R	
Manage the component level e-prescribing system									CRUD
Department-Level Processes									
Provide departmentwide program management for e-prescribing system									CRUD

Legend: C: create, R: reference, U: update, D: delete
*Some data entities are created by processes that are out of the scope of this analysis.

In addition to the value that BSP adds to the health services, business process reengineering of the 1990s is based on the BSP concept. In addition, BSP identified the need to separate data and applications that use these data and supported the systems development database approach.

Critical Success Factors

Daniel[47] of McKinsey & Company was the first to introduce the term *success factors*. He suggests that companies need to identify and focus on the critical information needs that relate to corporate success factors in order to achieve control and management effectiveness. This focus on information needs is necessary because organizations are in times of continuous change and growth. Rockart[48] introduced the term *critical success factor (CSF)*, which identifies "for any business the limited number of areas in which results, if they are satisfactory, will ensure successful competitive performance for the organization." These areas are those that need to have continual and careful monitoring so that performance criteria are met and the existing areas of the organization are improved.

Bullen and Rockart[49] identify three main uses for conducting CSF planning: (1) determine an individual manager's information needs, (2) aid an organization in general corporate planning, and (3) aid an organization in its IS/IT planning. They present five prime CSF sources: the industry, competitive strategy and positioning, the environment, managerial position, and temporal factors. These authors suggest that the factors can further be classified by internal versus external (or monitoring versus building). The monitoring factors involve the review of existing situations such as performance management. Building factors are those that the organization needs to plan for or change for in the future. Johnson and Friesen[50] show how CSFs can be used in a versatile manner and how the approach can be applied to solve a wide range of quality, operational, and planning problems across many industries, including health care. As depicted in Figure 8.4, Tan[51] applied the Bullen-Rockart model to health care.

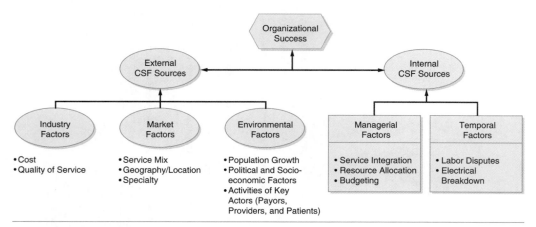

FIGURE 8.4 Bullen-Rockart's (1981) Five Prime Sources of Critical Success Factors Applied to Health Care.

In-Depth Interviews

Conducting in-depth interviews[52] can be quite productive in assessing healthcare services organization information needs. Unfortunately, while interviewing may appear to be simple, it is actually quite difficult; in order to ascertain the actual information needs of individuals, there are specific skills that an interviewer must use to be effective. There are five basis steps:

1. Select the interviewees.
2. Design the interview questions.
3. Prepare for the interview.
4. Conduct the interview.
5. Conduct a post-interview follow-up.

Interviewees are selected based on the type of information that is needed. Obtaining different perspectives from individuals at various levels of the healthcare services organization provides a more comprehensive picture of the health organization's information needs. This could include healthcare service middle managers and individual contributors, as well as executives in the organization. In addition, it is important to engage in discussions with individuals in different departments in the organization.

The design of interview questions varies. The HMIS team can perform interviews in a structured, unstructured, or semistructured format—each needing different types and numbers of "start" questions.

Structured interviews would be very specific and would focus on a specific problem area. The questions are scripted prior to the interview, and the recipe is closely followed. Using such a structure can possibly confine the application of the information needs. However, if a specific area is being studied, and the goal is to obtain only data about that specific area, this would be the most appropriate process to follow.

At the opposite end of the continuum are *unstructured interviews*. There is much less preparation in developing the questions prior to the interview. The interviewer acts more as a facilitator, allowing the participant to take the lead and only guiding the interview. Broad, roughly defined information is obtained from unstructured interviews. Using this type of process allows the interviewee to talk freely, with fewer boundaries than structured interviews. This method would be more appropriate when the HMIS teams want to understand needs in general. Using this method burdens the HMIS team in determining and prioritizing the many information needs that are uncovered.

The *semistructured interview* method falls between the other two processes. There is some question preparation prior to interviews; however, the interviewer is likely to follow up participant answers with additional probing questions to acquire additional detail. Semistructured interviews allow for a free-flowing, comfortable conversation with some direction in order to obtain the goal desired. An excerpt from a semistructured interview is shown in Exhibit 8.3.

The interviewer must prepare a general interview plan with a list of questions, anticipated answers, and follow-up questions. Having this plan keeps the interview on track and allows for an effective and efficient meeting. The interviewer needs to set priorities of what areas the

Exhibit 8.3   Semistructured Interview Focus

The following is an example of a portion of a semistructured interview of a physician about PDA use/nonuse:

Interviewer: OK, great. What is your familiarity with the use of PDAs in the healthcare environment? What do you know?

Interviewee: I have one, so probably most of what I know is my own experience. I bought a PDA I believe in 1998, so that gives me about 7, 8 years' experience. Originally, I just used it for keeping track of phone numbers, as a date book, and for memos. But I also have a program on it, which I've had for several years, probably at least 6 years, called Epocrates. I found it to be very helpful because it has a listing of medications and it's helped me 'cause it's updated, so I always feel like it's up-to-date, whereas a textbook wouldn't be; it gets out of date quickly. So, I found that to be helpful, too. And I do use that probably every day or a few times a day.

Interviewer: So, any time you need to look up a medication or something, you use your PDA? You usually go there first?

Interviewee: Now, we have other sources, too. We have the books here in the offices. That's more exhaustive. I do prefer that, but I'm much more likely to refer to the Epocrates in the PDA first. And we have drug references online. The *Physician's Resource* through the university medical center that's called *Up-To-Date*. And that is a medical database and it has information, different medical cases. And it also has a section on medications. So, I can type in a medication and get information on that as well.

Interviewer: Have you heard of other usages of the PDA for other applications of health care?

Interviewee: I know it's used for—and I have not used it so much for—equations, but I think in the hospital where they do calculations for drugs, they have to do special calculations for people with impaired kidney or liver functioning for certain drugs. Or if there's cancer or chemotherapy or things like that that involve a lot of calculations. Even for kids based on weight. I don't see kids here; they're all young adults or adults. So, I know there are other uses for it that way. There's like a body mass index they can get a calculation from. I just have a formula. I probably would get that if I could pick that up easily. There's a limit, I guess, as far as memory, too, so. There are a lot of other programs out there that I've heard about, but none of them seem like things that I need.

Interviewer: You say you brought a PDA in '98. Have you had the same PDA or have you upgraded or done anything different to it, or are you using the same one?

Interviewee: I think is the third one that I've had.

Interviewer: Same model or have you changed models?

Interviewee: Well, it's the model of where it's changed to. It's their standard model, so it's upgraded each time. So, I've sort of gone with like a standard or middle-of-the-road kind of model, not necessarily the absolute newest, because those are usually premium priced. So, middle-of-the-road model that I can get for about $200 or $250, something like that, or less.

Interviewer: So, you're using a PDA. Now, you talked a lot about within your profession. Personally, I think you said a little bit about names and addresses. So, do you use it in that aspect pretty much in—

Interviewee: I use it as my address book, basically, and phone book. So, I found that to be very helpful. Every time I get a new number, I try to enter it. So, my wife sometimes will ask me, do you have the number for so-and-so. And I can even be driving somewhere and I can pull it out and have it. You know each relative. My relatives, her relatives. I always have it.

Exhibit 8.3   *(Continued)*

Interviewer:	So, you keep it with you all the time.
Interviewee:	That's another thing I've found that I think it's most helpful if it's kept with one all the time. I know other folks say they have PDA, but it's in a drawer, they don't use it. They don't hot-sink it. So, when I got it, I try to make a point of having it with me all the time. I got a little Velcro strap to keep it from slipping out of my pocket. I just wrap that around. So, if I bend over from [inaudible], it doesn't slide.

Source: Modified from J. T. Blue, Dissertation, Virginia Commonwealth University, 2006.

information needs of the participant are mandatory, in the event that time becomes short during the interview. These priorities will ensure that the most important information needs are captured. Not only is a plan needed prior to the interview, the schedule, the reason for the interview, and the areas of discussion need to be detailed for the participant beforehand.

When the interview is conducted, the interviewer must appear to be professional and unbiased. To get different views from an interview, more than one interviewer may conduct the interview. This would attenuate the bias that could result from just one interviewer and increase the reliability of the results. Also, as much information as possible should be recorded. Actually, many interviews today are digitally recorded, transcribed, and loaded into a computer system for storage, management, and manipulation. However, some organizations have policies against recording and therefore the rules need to be reviewed prior to the interview. Of course, the interviewee needs to agree to the recording. Reviewing a recording after the interview allows the team to listen to the interview more than once in order to extract information needs and to delineate between facts and opinions.

Prior to concluding the meeting, the interviewers must make sure that all issues and terms are understood. If there are any questions, it is best to get answers before ending the session. The participant should also be given time to ask questions before concluding the session. Finally, in addition to ending on time, the interviewee should be thanked.

After the interview, the interviewers should prepare interview notes by summarizing key points. The consolidation of these notes becomes the interview report. After review of the report, the team can assess the gaps and determine possible additional questions that can be used in subsequent interviews.

VI. Conclusion

The work of today's senior HMIS managers is quite complex. Not only must they be viable members of the executive team that plans, organizes, develops, and controls the whole healthcare services organization, they are given the added responsibility of ensuring that the health management information systems are available to assist in meeting the overall health organization's vision and mission.

Potentially, taking advantage of HMIS technology can be used to counter competition in the healthcare field. With the decrease in the cost of IT overall, HMIS management is called on more and more to assist in meeting the corporate and department objectives. Why shouldn't HMIS be an integral part of the mission? While history has HMIS as an enabler that supports and assists in realizing a health organization's vision, in order to remain competitive there need to be more HMIS top-level strategies. Senior executives need to include specific HMIS strategies as part of the healthcare services organization mission. Doing so would allow the HMIS department's influence to move to a higher level and garner the deserved recognition as a CSF in healthcare services organizations.

Notes

1. C. Atoji, "Open Health Tools Hopes to Repeat Eclipse's Success," Digital HealthCare and Productivity, accessed June 6, 2008, from http://www.eclipse.org/org/.
2. B. B. Longest, *Management Practices for the Health Professional* (Norwalk, CT: Appleton & Lange, 1990).
3. G. Van der Vegt and V. D. Vliert, "Intragroup Interdependence and Effectiveness: Review and Proposed Directions for Theory and Practice," *Journal of Managerial Psychology* 14 (2001).
4. M. R. Edwards and M. W. Woolverton, "Appraising Work Team Performance: New Productivity Solutions for Agribusiness Management," *Agribusiness* 2 (2006): 43–53.
5. D. Bates, M. Ebell, E. Gotlieb, J. Zapp, and H. Mullins, "A Proposal for Electronic Medical Records in U.S. Primary Care," *Journal of the American Medical Informatics Association* 10 (2003): 1–10.
6. C. Aydin, J. Anderson, P. Rosen, V. Felitti, and H. Weng, "Computers in the Consulting Room: A Case Study of Clinical and Patient Perspectives," *Health Care Management Science* 1 (1998): 61–74.
7. I. Lejbkowicz, Y. Denekamp, S. Reis, and D. Goldberg, "Electronic Medical Record in Israel's Public Hospitals," *Israel Medical Journal* 6 (2004): 583–587.
8. A. B. Als, "The Desk-Top Computer as a Magic Box: Patterns of Behavior Connected with the Desk-Top Computer; GPs' and Patients' Perceptions," *Family Practice* 14 (1997): 17–23.
9. G. Garrison, M. Bernard, and N. Rasmussen, "21st-Century Health Care: The Effect on Computer Use by Physicians on Patient Satisfaction at a Family Medicine Clinic," *Family Practice* 34 (2002): 362–368.
10. G. Solomon and M. Dechter, "Are Patients Pleased with Computer Use in the Examination Room?" *Journal of Family Practice* 41 (1995): 241–244.
11. P. Marshall and H. Chin, *AMIA Annual Symposium*, Orlando, FL, 1998.
12. S. Ornstein and A. Bearden, "Patient Perspectives on Computer-Based Medical Records," *Journal of Family Practice* 38 (1994): 606–610.
13. A. Likourezos, D. Chalfin, and D. Murphy, "Physician and Nurse Satisfaction with an Electronic Medical Record System," *Journal of Emergency Medicine* 27 (2004): 419–424.
14. Phoenix Health Systems, in *HIPAA Survey*, ed. H. P. H. Systems, 2006, vol. 2007.
15. Longest (1990).
16. H. Fayol, *General and Industrial Administration* (London: Pitman, 1949).
17. D. Hellriegel, S. E. Jackson, and J. W. Slocum Jr., *Management: A Competency-Based Approach*, 9th ed. (Cincinnati, OH: South-Western, 2002).
18. P. S. Lewis, S. H. Goodman, and P. M. Fandt, *Management: Challenges in the 21st Century*, 3rd ed. (Cincinnati, OH: South-Western, 2001).
19. A. Kinicki and B. K. Williams, *Management: A Practical Introduction*, 2nd ed. (Boston: McGraw Hill/Irwin, 2006).

20. L. W. Rue and L. L. Byars, *Management: Skills and Applications*, 11th ed. (Boston: McGraw-Hill/Irwin, 2005).

21. J. R. Schermerhorn Jr., *Core Concepts of Management* (Hoboken, NJ: John Wiley & Sons, 2004).

22. A. Forbes, "Naming Names—Mandatory Name-Based HIV Reporting: Impact and Alternatives," *AIDS Policy and Law* 1 (1996): 1–4.

23. E. O. Olson and G. H. Eoyand, *Facilitating Organisation Change—Lessons from Complexity Science* (San Francisco: Jossey-Bass/Pfeiffer, 2001).

24. R. S. Kaplan and D. P. Norton, *The Strategy-Focused Organization, Strategy and Leadership* (Boston, MA: Harvard Business School Press, 2001).

25. L. Willcocks and G. Smith, "IT-Enabled Business Process Reengineering: Organizational and Human Resource Dimensions," *Journal of Strategic Information Systems* 4 (1995): 279–301.

26. B. H. Reich and I. Benbasat, "Factors That Influence the Social Dimension of Alignment Between Business and Information Technology Objectives," *MIS Quarterly* 24 (2000): 81–111.

27. A. L. Lederer and V. Sethi, "The Implementation of Strategic Information Systems Planning Methodologies," *MIS Quarterly* 12 (1988) 445–461.

28. H. E. Newkirk and A. L. Lederer, "Incremental and Comprehensive Strategic Information Systems Planning in an Uncertain Environment," *IEEE Transactions on Engineering Management* 53 (2006).

29. T. S. Teo and W. R. King, "Integration between Business Planning and Information Systems Planning: An Evolutionary-Contingency Perspective," *Journal of Management Information Systems* 14 (1997): 185–214.

30. R. Sabherwal and W. R. King, "Decision Processes for Developing Strategic Application for Information Systems: A Contingency Approach," *Decision Science* 23 (1992): 917–943.

31. D. Miller and P. H. Friesen, "Strategy-Making and Environment: The Third Link," *Strategic Management Journal* 4 (1983): 221–235.

32. J. C. Brancheau, B. D. Janz, and J. C. Wetherbe, "Key Issues in Information Systems Management: 1994–1995 SIM Delphi Results," *MIS Quarterly* 20 (1996): 225–242.

33. C. Dunbar and W. A. Schmidt, "Information Systems Must Represent 35 Percent of Total Strategic Plan," *Computers in Healthcare* 12 (1991): 22–24.

34. S. E. Kern and D. Jaron, "Healthcare Technology, Economics, and Policy: An Evolving Balance," *IEEE Engineering in Medicine and Biology Magazine* 22 (2003): 16–19.

35. J. K. H. Tan, *Health Management Information Systems: Methods and Practical Applications*, 2nd ed. (Gaithersburg, MD: Aspen Publishers, 2001).

36. B. Bowman, G. Davis, and J. C. Wetherbe, "Three Stage Model of MIS Planning," *Information and Management* 6 (1983): 11–25.

37. Tan (2001).

38. J. C. Henderson and J. B. Thomas, "Aligning Business and Information Technology Domains: Strategic Planning in Hospitals," *Hospital and Health Service Administration* 37 (1992): 71–87.

39. K.-K. Hong and Y.-G. Kim, "The Critical Success Factors for ERP Implementation: An Organizational Fit Perspective," *Information and Management* 40 (2002): 25–40.

40. S. Jarupathirun and F. M. Zahedi, "Dialectic Decision Support Systems: System Design and Empirical Evaluation," *Decision Support Systems* 42 (2007): 1553–1570.

41. H. Mintzberg, D. Raisinghani, and A. Theoret, "The Structure of 'Unstructured' Decision Processes," *Administrative Science Quarterly* 21 (1976): 246–275.

42. R. Bonczek, C. Holsapple, and A. Whinston, *Foundations of Decision Support Systems* (New York: Academic Press, 1981).

43. M. McDiarmid, S. Kendall, and M. Binns, "Evidence-Based Administrative Decision Making and the Ontario Hospital CEO: Information Needs, Seeking Behaviour, and Access to Sources," *Journal of the Canadian Health Libraries Association* 28 (2007): 63–72.
44. K. Holtzblatt and H. R. Beyer, "Requirements Gathering: The Human Factor," *Communications of the ACM* 38 (1995): 31–32.
45. R. L. Daft and R. H. Lengel, "Organizational Information Requirements, Media Richness and Structural Design," *Management Science* 32 (1986): 554–571.
46. J. A. Zachman, "Business Systems Planning and Business Information Control Study: A Comparison," *IBM Systems Journal* 21 (1982): 31–53.
47. D. R. Daniel, "Management Information Crisis," *Harvard Business Review* 111 (1961).
48. J. F. Rockart, "Chief Executives Define Their Own Data Needs," *Harvard Business Review* 57 (1979): 81–93.
49. C. V. Bullen and J. F. Rockart, ed. J. F. Rockart, A Primer on Critical Success Factors. Unpublished Sloan WP No. 1220-81. (Cambridge, MA: Center for Information Systems Research, Massachusetts Institute of Technology Sloan School of Management, 1981), p. 64.
50. J. A. Johnson and M. Friesen, *The Success Paradigm: Creating Organizational Effectiveness through Quality and Strategy* (New York: Quorum Books, 1995).
51. Tan (2001).
52. J. T. Blue, *Rebuilding Theories of Technology Acceptance: A Qualitive Case Study of Physician's Acceptance of Technology*. Unpublished Dissertation, Virginia Commonwealth University, 2006.

Chapter Questions

8–1. Describe the different organizational structures. Given your answer, how would the input be different if 98 percent of the patients are participants in a managed healthcare program?

8–2. Develop a matrix, and list the advantages and disadvantages of using each of the organization structures as presented in the chapter.

8–3. When would it be appropriate for executives in a healthcare organization to dictate tactics to an organization?

8–4. Using the objective "A bar-scanning mechanism that includes the patient, all hospital personnel that treat the patient, and the prescribed/administered service will be implemented within 1 year," develop four tactics for this objective as demonstrated in the strategic planning focus in Exhibit 8.1.

8–5. As presented in the chapter, the executives in a healthcare organization strategically plan and produce the vision and mission. What are some of the inputs that the senior management team would consider when developing the strategic plan?

8–6. Discuss how the different organizational structures, as presented in the chapter, would be applied in different types of healthcare organizations (private hospital, public hospital, clinic, urgent care facility, private doctor's office, etc.). Which structure do you think is most productive in the different healthcare organizations that you determine, and why?

8–7. What methods have you seen used in gathering information needs in organizations? How was the method used, and was it successful?

8–8. If you are the information systems manager at a community clinic and the clinic is planning to implement an EHR system (from a complete paper-based file system):
   a. List five semistructured interview questions that you would ask a physician.
   b. List five semistructured interview questions that you would ask a registered nurse.
   c. List five semistructured interview questions that you would ask a registration clerk.

Chapter Appendix: Glossary of Terms

accountability   The result of holding an individual responsible for delivering a set of goals, objectives, and/or tactics.

business process re-engineering   Analyzes and redesigns the workflow between and within business enterprises (emphasized by Michael Hammer and James Champy[1]).

business system planning (BSP)   Used by health service organizations to facilitate viewing the organization differently and determining the organization information needs in order to build health management information systems.

critical success factor (CSF)   "For any business the limited number of areas in which results, if they are satisfactory, will ensure successful competitive performance for the organization" (Rockart[2]).

data classes   Used in business system planning; the categories of the necessary data to support the organization for the application in question. Health service processes are logically related activities and decisions that are required to manage the resources of the organization.

e-prescribing   Using electronic systems to assist and enhance the communication of a prescription, helping the administration, choice, or supply of a medicine through supporting clinicians' decisions with a thorough audit trail for the entire medicine's use process.

EHR system   An electronic system that stores patient health information and data, provides for electronic order entry of processes, allows for the electronic view/review of information, and provides decision support.

electronic health record (EHR)   An electronic version of a patient's health record.

enterprisewide architecture strategy (EWAS)   Developed by John A. Zachman; a sophisticated framework that integrates the technical components within the larger enterprise architecture.

gap analysis   A technique in which the difference between the desired performance levels and the extrapolated results of the current performance levels is measured and examined. This measurement shows what resources are required and what needs to be done to achieve the mission of a healthcare organization's strategy.

goal   Adds focus to a healthcare organization's vision and mission. If the goal(s) is attained, the mission has been accomplished.

Health Insurance Portability and Accountability Act of 1996 (HIPAA)   U.S. law that provides standards for the interchange of patients' health, financial, and administration data—including privacy and security. The Act began to roll out in phases, with full compliance expected by 2004. Additionally, the law protects employees' health insurance when they lose or change jobs (U.S. Department of Health & Human Services[3]).

---

[1]Hammer, M., & Champy, J. (1993). *Reengineering the Corporation: A Manifesto for Business*. New York: Harper Business.

[2]Rockart, J. F. (1979). Chief executives define their own data needs. *Harvard Business Review, 57*(2), 81–93.

[3]U.S. Department of Health & Human Services HIPAA (2007). Office for Civil Rights—HIPAA. Retrieved December 20, 2007, from http://www.hhs.gov/ocr/hipaa/

health management information systems (HMIS)   A technologically based systems designed to operate in a healthcare environment.

health management strategic information systems plan (HMSISP)   A plan developed by the healthcare organization information systems team that lays out the requirements of systems for a healthcare organization that will assist in fulfilling an organization's strategy.

health service processes   Used in business system planning; logically related activities and decisions that are required to manage the resources of the organization.

managed healthcare   A system where non-medical administrators, like insurance companies, control and limit such things as medical procedures, medications, and the frequency of service.

mission statement   A concise description of a healthcare organization's fundamental purpose. A mission statement answers the question, "Why do we exist?"

objective   Provides focus on how a specific goal with be achieved.

planning, organizing, directing, and controlling (PODC) model   An operationalized and rationally designed tool to assist in meeting organizational goals (Fayol[4]).

strategy   According to Henry Mintzberg[5]:
- A "how"; a means of getting from here to there.
- A pattern in actions over time.
- Position; that is, it reflects decisions to offer particular products or services in particular markets.
- Perspective; that is, vision and direction.

tactic   A specific, measurable task that contributes to attaining a particular objective.

vision statement   Often referred to as a picture of the healthcare organization in the future. It should be the organization's inspiration and the framework for all strategic planning.

---

[4]Fayol, H. (1949). *General and Industrial Administration*. London: Pitman.

[5]Mintzberg, H. (1994). *The Rise and Fall of Strategic Planning*. New York: Simon & Schuster.

System Development:
Health Management Information System
Analysis and Developmental Methodologies

Joseph Tan

CHAPTER OUTLINE

Scenario: *Richmond Township*

Scenario: Richmond Township

The municipal government of Richmond Township, through the Richmond Economic Council, voted to fund a number of neighborhood sites to develop community health programs for surrounding residents. Each site was equipped first with a Macintosh computer and a small office run by a full-time program coordinator. The council requires that the site coordinators report to the community supervisor and the medical health officer (MHO) of the region for which the community was funded. Residents of these communities interact with their program coordinators as volunteers and as participants in community health awareness programs. The council also funds a team of evaluators, who are affiliated with certain university research groups, to provide technical assistance to the various community sites and to conduct independent reviews of the various community health demonstration programs.

Imagine yourself to be appointed as the site coordinator for one of these communities. Apart from setting up various community health programs and managing the daily chores of tracking levels of community participation in various programs, you must now try also to mobilize community support and delegate responsibilities to task forces for the different programs. Through the collaborative efforts of the community supervisor, the MHO, and, most importantly, the task forces (whose memberships mainly comprise volunteers drawn from various stakeholder groups in your community), you are able to initiate a number of healthy lifestyle programs. You are expected to report the latest developments on each of these programs during scheduled meetings and to perform your daily office routine efficiently and effectively.

Realizing the power of automation in achieving greater efficiency and effectiveness, you decide to get help from the evaluation team by asking for the design and implementation of Macintosh-based software that would track, on a real-time basis, the various pieces of information from each of the three programs currently being suggested: (1) the walking program, (2) the restaurant program, and (3) the worksite program. Because these are new programs and you are still uncertain about the response of the community at large to these planned activities, you find it difficult to give an accurate description of the process. To make matters worse, you would like to design the system yourself, even though you have only taken one introductory health management information systems (HMIS) course during your training as a health administrator. You therefore realize that you would need a great deal of technical assistance from the analyst, but it is your strong belief that if you do not champion the system design and software development efforts, you may not be using the resulting system after all. In this case, you may have to rely heavily on your current manual filing system, which is proving to be inadequate in helping you carry out your various responsibilities.

In your first interaction with the analyst from the evaluation team, who is assigned to assist you with the technical details involved in designing and developing the community health information systems (CHIS) to satisfy the need for moving these programs forward, both of you arrive at a rich picture following a general analysis of the situation for which the CHIS is to be used. This rich picture is shown in Figure 9.1. You and the analyst then proceed to design the main menu and the organization of several possible screen layouts. Figure 9.2 shows the structure

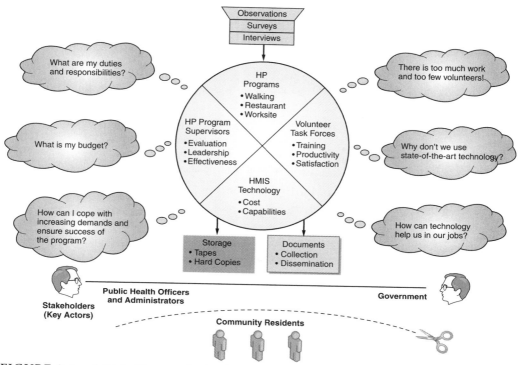

FIGURE 9.1 A Rich Picture of a Multicommunity Health Promotion Project.

of the main menu with its interface to the various subsystem menus for your community site, which is designated as Site A by the evaluation team.

While helping you think about how you could specify your information requirements and how these requirements might be translated into a well-structured data model, your analyst comes up with a rough entity-relationship (E-R) model. This E-R model is depicted in Figure 9.3. You then proceed with the analyst to design the user interface for the "main and new

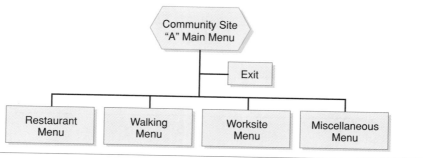

FIGURE 9.2 Main Menu Subsystem for Multicommunity Health Promotion Project Community Site A.

Health Promotion Supervisor
Health Promotion Program
Participant
Events
One-to-One Relationship
One-to-Many Relationship
Many-to-One Relationship
Many-to-Many Relationship

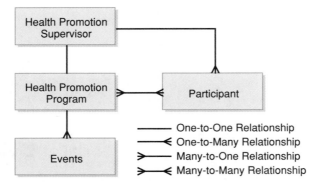

FIGURE 9.3 An Example of an Entity-Relationship Diagram for the Multicommunity Health Promotion Project.

event" screen as well as the "new participant" screen for your community. The resulting screen displays are shown in Figures 9.4 and 9.5.

In designing these interfaces, you feel that the earlier step of trying to list the information you wanted has helped you and your analyst greatly in determining what data elements should be appearing in the respective data entry screens (views). The process has also helped clarify the data elements to be captured in the CHIS. You now realize that it is possible to generate reports

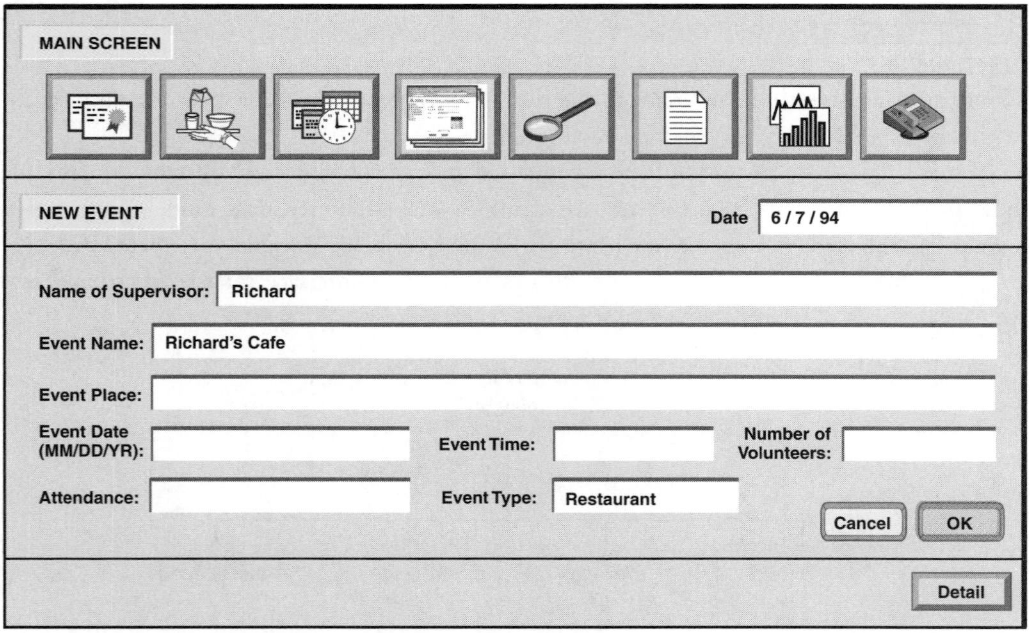

MAIN SCREEN
NEW EVENT
Date
6 / 7 / 94
Name of Supervisor:
Richard
Event Name:
Richard's Cafe
Event Place:
Event Date (MM/DD/YR):
Event Time:
Number of Volunteers:
Attendance:
Event Type:
Restaurant
Cancel
OK
Detail

FIGURE 9.4 The Main and New Event Screens for Community Site A. *Source:* Courtesy of Microsoft Corporation, Redmond, Washington.

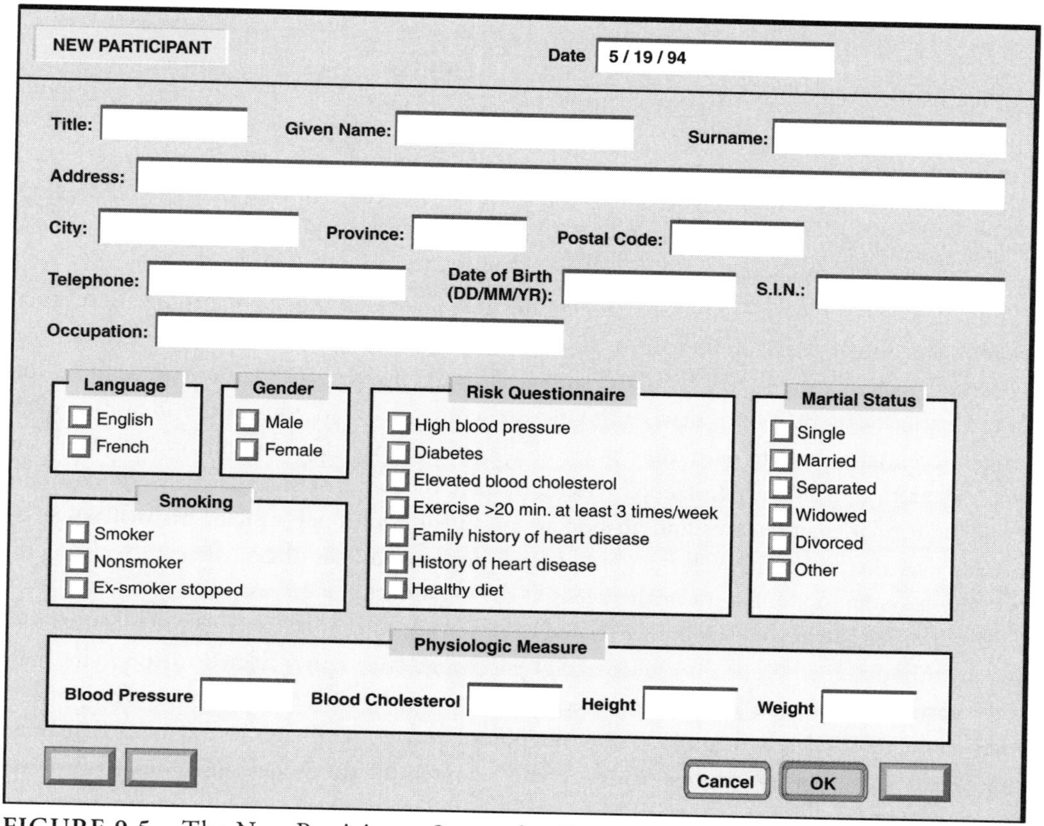

FIGURE 9.5 The New Participant Screen for Community Site A. *Source:* Courtesy of Microsoft Corporation, Redmond, Washington.

by combining and statistically manipulating the different data elements that are entered into the CHIS. Think about the kind of aggregate information you may want from the data that will be captured in the CHIS to help you structure your reports on the latest developments of the different programs.

At this point, you are informed by members of one of the task forces that two of the participating volunteers would be able to spare some additional time to help you with questions, work with other residents, and update information on CHIS whenever necessary if only you are able and willing to train them. Essentially, this would mean that the CHIS must be developed to be used by these volunteers, who may have even less knowledge of computerized systems than you do. Your analyst also informs you that you have the choice of customizing an off-the-shelf application to fit your needs or pursuing self-developed CHIS. Contemplate how you would go about making an informed choice about this and what additional information you might want in order to manage the process of this CHIS analysis and project development. Remember also that you only have a very limited budget and time line to complete the CHIS project.

I. Introduction

In this chapter, we discuss a variety of approaches used to deal with the challenges of initiating and coordinating HMIS analysis and developmental efforts. Each of the different classes of methodologies to be covered may be based on a philosophical view, which can range from a complete focus on the humanistic side to the technical aspects of HMIS analysis and development. For example, many traditional methodologies emphasized *systems analysis (SA)*, whereas others focused on *systems design (SD)* phases within the larger systems development life cycle (SDLC). The SDLC represents essentially an iterative process in project managing an information system project development from its beginning to end: it first encompasses the analysis phase in which existing system(s) is (are) studied so as to uncover gaps that have to be filled; followed typically by designing new and/or needed components to address the identified challenges; eventually resulting in the "physical" programming, the training of staff, and the implementation of a newly developed system. In turn, the new system apparently also raises the need for regular maintenance and ad hoc attention for additional refinements or changes as needed over the years. This will then put us back into the analysis phase, when the existing information system no longer meets the needs of the organization it serves.

Briefly, then, SA involves activities related to reviewing current information architecture and the organizational environment, whereas SD encompasses activities related to specifying new information architecture and systems requirements. Most traditional systems development methodologies (SDM) will employ a combination of SA and SD phases in a sequential manner, that is, SD to follow SA process. More recently, contemporary models, including computer-aided software engineering (CASE) tools and Multiview, attempt to take a contingency approach, thereby providing a framework for managing SA and SD phases, contingent on changes in the organizational environment.

Beyond SA and SD phases is systems implementation. *Systems implementation* involves the selection and inauguration of new system architecture and applications, which is the subject of an entire chapter of its own. A key phenomena in the evolution of SDM, however, is open-source software (OSS), which focuses on the adoption of working "prototypes" that contain shareable codes to be used freely or modified freely as a result of end-user computing (EUC) or development process. We will therefore also discuss the OSS approach and conclude the chapter with some thoughts and recommendations on EUC.

II. HMIS Analysis and Development Methodologies

Early computer applications were typically designed without adequate analysis and planning. As HMIS evolved, the need for a "systematic" approach became increasingly necessary. Consequently, numerous approaches to managing the SDLC have emerged.

Systems development methodologies (SDM) are systematic approaches to HMIS planning, analysis, and design.[1] A methodology is a collection of procedures, techniques, tools, and documentation aids to help HMIS developers in their efforts to implement a new information architecture and system. It therefore provides a framework (consisting of phases and subphases) that guides the developers in their choice of appropriate techniques at each stage of a project. A technique is a way of performing a particular activity in the system development process. Widely used techniques include rich pictures, E-R modeling, normalization, data flow diagrams (DFDs), decision trees, decision tables, structured English, action diagrams, and the entity life cycle, several of which have already been discussed and illustrated throughout this text. We focus the discussion here on two major techniques often applied with surprising effective results in HMIS analysis to assist communications between the analyst and the layperson, who will eventually become the end-user of the system: rich picture and DFD.

A rich picture[2] as shown in Figure 9.1 at the beginning of this chapter, for example, is simply a convenient tool for documenting themes or issues for an ill-defined problem situation, specifically for soft and fuzzy issues to be discussed among different laypeople when doing an HMIS analysis. This innovative diagramming tool does not subscribe to any standards (or a particular convention). It uses the language and terminology of the environment and shows how those who developed the picture perceive various pieces of a problem situation as relating to each other. The aim here is to record the problem situation as a whole, that is, in a holistic fashion without limiting it to the agenda or biases of key actors and decision makers. Figure 9.1 illustrates the various parties who share the information pool and some of the tasks and concerns encountered in the community health promotion project (CHPP) discussed in the chapter-opening scenario. Based on the information provided in this picture and a further investigation of other available health services programs in Richmond Township, the first step in the HMIS analysis process is to ask the various CHPP stakeholders to provide a sense of where and how the different proposed health promotion programs and services can be situated and fitted appropriately into the larger picture of the present healthcare services delivery system of Richmond Township. In other words, the CHPP rich picture provides a starting point for discussions on how various HMIS components and systems thinking can be combined to lead to resolving CHPP challenges and generating an acceptable HMIS to support the CHPP program.

As for the DFD, it is a network representation of a system, which itself may exhibit varying degrees of automation. Essentially, DFDs are top-down hierarchical diagrams, which can provide successive levels of details and are particularly useful in documenting data flows and processes in a system. Like other information flow diagrams such as node diagrams, block diagrams, data flow graphs, or even bubble charts, DFDs provide a standardized approach to systems documentation and aid in the development of future system designs. DFDs are useful for documenting the logical design of an information system by graphically showing how data flow to, from, and within an HMIS, as well as the various processes that transform the data into meaningful and useful information. The main purpose of DFDs is to break down a system into manageable levels of detail that can be visualized—first at a very general (context) level and then gradually in greater detail, in a process termed *leveling*. For example, a walk-in clinic serving the medical needs of the community could review its overall services by sequencing the steps a patient takes to access any or all of its services. The staff's corresponding actions and flow of information can then be listed and categorized to clarify the center's operations. Thus, a large complex information process is first depicted as a context diagram. Each subprocess can also be subdivided into successive levels of "detailed" DFDs, with corresponding subsystem details. This ability to expand and contract levels of details as needed, depending on the particular requirements at that moment, is what makes a DFD such a valuable and flexible information flow documentation technique.

In formalizing a DFD, the basic schema of inputs, processes, and outputs becomes essential. To operationalize this relation for HMIS solutions, two different aspects—variables and processes—can be utilized. *Variables* here refer to the input and output data. A variable must be defined specifically before any formal analysis of the system can take place. Examples include patients who are admitted daily and drugs that are prescribed weekly. In contrast, the *processes* are defined by algorithmic relations or other computations and are the mechanisms for making changes to the variables over time. In essence, a DFD is a network representation of a system, which itself may exhibit varying degrees of automation. As shown in Figure 9.6, DFDs are constructed by using four basic symbols: arrows, rounded boxes, open boxes (rectangles with three sides), and rectangular boxes.

Arrows represent the movement of data (with directions) between processes, data sources (sinks), and data stores (files). Arrows are therefore used to denote data flows. Each data flow arrow should be labeled to indicate the type of data involved, for example, "admission notification (phone)" and "chart package," as shown in Figure 9.7.

In DFDs, rounded boxes represent the operational transformation of input data to output data. Labeling of these processes typically involves verb clauses such as "Prepare patient chart package" and "Review and implement physician's orders for work requests," as shown in the example. Open boxes are used to represent data stores, that is, repositories of data used in the system. Examples of data stores are files, databases, microfiches, and binders of paper reports. In Figure 9.7, "patient charts" represent data stores.

Data sources or external entities, represented by rectangles, are the entities that lie outside the system. Patients, laboratories, wards, customers, banks, and even employees may be regarded as external entities. These data sources (or sinks) help define the boundary of the system. In our case, the emergency room, the pharmacy, and the dietetics department are examples of data sources.

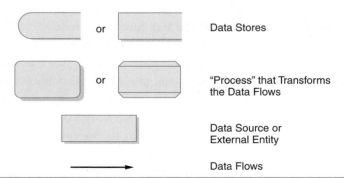

FIGURE 9.6 Conventional Data Flow Diagram Symbols.

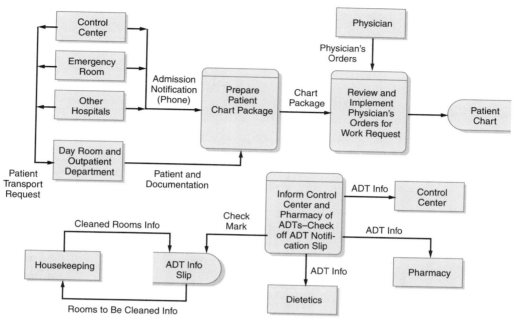

ADT = Admission Discharge Transfer

FIGURE 9.7   Surgical Interdepartmental Data Flows at a University Hospital.

To illustrate the use of DFDs, we examine an actual application in the health service field. Figure 9.7 illustrates the flows of data involved in a surgical department at a university hospital. As noted, DFDs are used to provide both overall and detailed views of an HMIS. What takes place within a process box in one DFD can be "exploded" in greater detail by another DFD. For instance, the process "Review and implement physician's orders for work requests" in Figure 9.7 is expanded in the DFD shown in Figure 9.8. In other words, these two figures are "leveled" in terms of context and details. Figure 9.8 breaks down a process (from Figure 9.7) into its subprocesses.

In summary, an accurate picture of various subsystem interactions involved in a typical surgical procedure at a local hospital is given by these two figures, yet each has its own special functions. The context DFD facilitates higher-level decision-making activities like strategic planning, whereas the more detailed DFD is more suitable for aiding operational and tactical decision making.

Additionally, each technique employed within an SDM may involve using one or more tools. Examples of tools include database management systems (DBMS), query facility, data dictionaries, fourth-generation languages (4GL), methodology workbenches, project management tools, and expert systems. The phases and subphases of an SDM also help the developers plan, manage, control, and evaluate their HMIS projects. As an example to illustrate SDM concepts, imagine running a general business election meeting. To do this, you can follow an

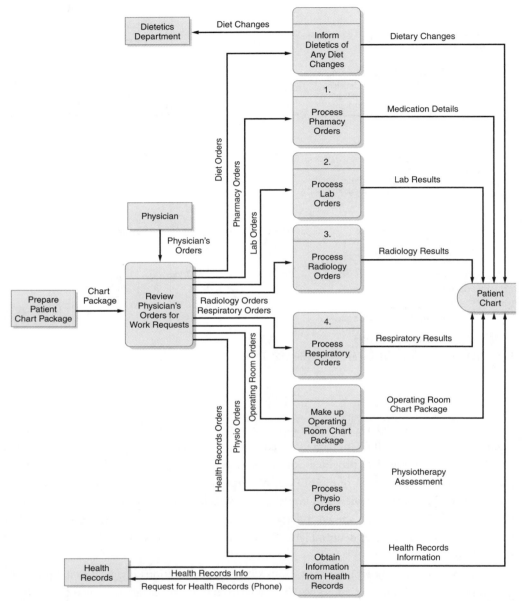

FIGURE 9.8 The Process of "Review and Implement Physician's Orders for Work Request" in Detail.

agenda (methodology) to guide the progress of the meeting. One technique used in making decisions during the meeting may be "voting," which might entail the use of a certain "tool," such as the use of a ballot card for each member to ensure equitable representation based on the principle of "one member, one vote."

Making use of a methodology lessens the risk of wasting resources during the course of systems analysis and development. Holloway[3] notes that use of an SDM increases the productivity of the development staff by providing a standard framework (to avoid reinventing the wheel for each HMIS project), the right tools (to assist successful completion of each stage of development task), effective review procedures (to identify errors and inconsistencies early), and a productivity aid (to reduce the amount of development documentation). A good SDM not only allows healthcare management to review the progress of an HMIS project, but also permits the developer to accurately identify the user needs. Effective SDM make HMIS project planning easier by allowing both designers and users to plan, correct, and re-plan the project as it progresses.

More generally, the benefits of employing well-tested SDM include user satisfaction, the meeting of management needs, timely development, the avoidance of systems implementation deficiencies, and the appropriate provision of maintenance and support activities. The methodologies described in this chapter can be evaluated on these criteria or standards.

III. SDLC-Based Methodologies

During the late 1970s, the Waterfall model was proposed as a formal approach to systems development. It was a first-generation SDM, embodying the systems development life cycle (SDLC) concept, a highly regarded concept among healthcare services systems analysts as a way to provide much more control over SA and SD processes than was previously possible. This model consists of six hierarchical steps.

1. Feasibility study.
2. Systems investigation.
3. Systems analysis (SA).
4. Systems design (SD).
5. Systems implementation (SI).
6. Systems maintenance, evaluation, and review.

Essentially, the SDLC dictates that whenever a systems review indicates that the current system is no longer adequate, a new feasibility study is then initiated for the new system, as shown in Figure 9.9.

The Waterfall model was a landmark achievement and included all the attributes expected of a methodology—a philosophy (systemic approach that leads to reduced costs and gains in productivity), a series of steps (from the feasibility study to system maintenance), a series of techniques (e.g., ways to evaluate the costs and benefits solutions), and a series of tools. Although this conventional methodology was a definite improvement, it was frequently criticized; for example, it failed to meet the needs and expectations of end-users because they were not involved in the systems analysis and development process. Incomplete systems and large application backlogs resulted from the lack of emphasis on front-end planning. Ignoring the SA process gave rise to inflexible and overly ambitious SD. Revisions were also not easily accommodated during the SD process. This traditional methodology involved a heavy maintenance workload and was laden with problems of documentation.

The next-generation SDM integrated basic techniques and tools to create more complete specifications for the systems designer. Table 9.1 summarizes three of these methodologies: accurately

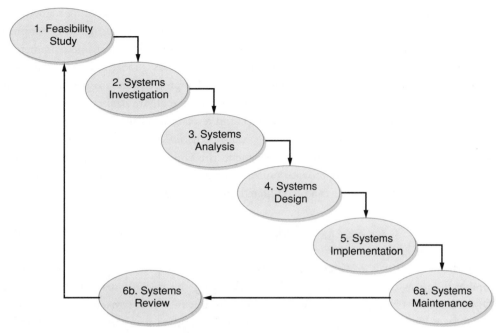

FIGURE 9.9   The Waterfall Model.

defined systems (ADS), business information analysis and integration technique (BIAIT), and business systems planning (BSP). Many of these early methodologies, which are classified as SDLC-based methodologies, focus on the planning involved in developing HMIS that will meet the objectives of the health organization. They are outlined only briefly in this discussion.

ADS comprise an integrated systems representation of systems inputs, outputs, processes, procedures, and files.[4] The analysis package also includes cross-referencing structures, which

Table 9.1   Traditional Methodologies Based on SDLC (Second-Generation Development Models)

Methods	Major Concepts
Accurately defined systems (ADS)	Represents system inputs, outputs, processes, procedures, and files; also includes cross-referencing structures to ensure consistencies.
Business information analysis and integration technique (BIAIT)	Creates a grid based on seven close-ended binary questions to aid analysts in systems planning and future analysis.
Business systems planning (BSP)	Similar to SDLC model except that it has a two-level design stage theme and a new emphasis on strategic planning.

ensure consistency across the sets of documents produced. Some aspects of ADS may now be automated to assist in the development process.

BIAIT addresses top management requirements by using a set of seven close-ended binary questions to generate a model that aids the analyst in determining an organization's information requirements.[5] The resulting profile is a grid (matrix) of possible responses classifying existing "order-supplier" relations and identifying the data owners and users. This matrix is then used for effective systems planning and future analysis.

A BSP addresses the requirements of top management by aligning systems planning with the organization's strategic plan. Three principles are observed in BSP: the need for an organizationwide perspective, top-down analysis but bottom-up design and implementation, and the need for independence of the business plan from computer applications (i.e., changes in the business plan may take place without effecting changes in the application systems).

Except for greater emphasis on strategic planning in the analysis stage and the subdivision of the design stage into general and detailed design phases, the phases in these second-generation SDM are fundamentally similar to the Waterfall model. The lack of attention to data structuring in SDLC-based methodologies has slowed progress in software design and given rise to the need for greater structural detailing in SDM. This brings a whole new perspective to systems development and gives rise to structured programming techniques and structured methodologies, the third-generation SDM.

IV. Structured Methodologies

The structured methodologies represent a new level of SA and SD approaches that address multiple structural issues.[6] Among the structured SDM that have earned wide acceptance and popularity are systems analysis and design technique (SADT), structured analysis and structured designs (SA/SD), and structured systems analysis and design methodology (SSADM). Table 9.2 summarizes these models.

SADT was proprietary, but a public version has since been released.[7,8] In addition to depicting data flows between functions, SADT diagrams portray the control under which each function operates and the mechanisms responsible for the function implementation. This is

Table 9.2 Structured Methodologies (Third-Generation Systems Development Models)

Methods	Major Concepts
System analysis and design technique (SADT)	Both data and process oriented; provides analytical detail at all levels and is easy for nontechnical personnel to use.
Structured analysis/structured design (SA/SD)	Supports analysis and design stages; uses transformational and transactional analysis; generates hierarchical structure charts for defining the various functions.
Structured system analysis and design methodology (SSADM)	Supports both analysis and design stages; used by the British government.

analogous to information structural diagrams (ISD), an example of which is shown in Figure 9.10. Here, a block represents an object with attributes, and a line with arrows shows the relationship between objects and the inheritance properties. The ISD therefore outlines how the objects within a class are related to each other. In Figure 9.10, ISD is used to show patient–physician interactions in a hospital setting. Even more comprehensive than ISD, the SADT diagramming technique is supported by function descriptions and a complete data dictionary package. A data dictionary is a catalog of data types that includes their names, structure, and usage. A function that reports on cross-references between the components of a data or business model is provided. SADT therefore combines basic elements of traditional approaches with structured methods. Olle et al.[9] describe SADT as both a data-oriented and a process-oriented methodology, while Colter[10] claims that it provides analytical detail at both high and low levels and is reasonably usable for nontechnical personnel. However, SADT has been criticized as focusing primarily on the SA stage; other competing structured methodologies such as SA/SD and SSADM have since been developed to provide more comprehensive support for the different SDLC stages.

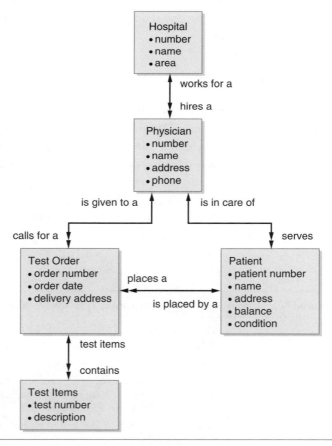

FIGURE 9.10 Example of an Information Structure Diagram.

Unlike SADT, the SA/SD methodology clearly supports both the SA and SD stages.[11] Two techniques often used to transition from SA to SD include transformational analysis and transactional analysis. Essentially, these are design strategies for deriving modular structures from different parts of the DFD. It is claimed that continuous applications of these strategies will ultimately result in the generation of hierarchical structure charts[12] for defining the various functions to be performed by the separate modules. SA/SD is also closely related to certain other structured methodologies, such as structured analysis, design, and implementation of information systems (STRADIS); structured analysis and system specification (SASS); and Yourdon and Constantine's.[13] Olle et al.[14] summarize the various perspectives of these methodologies as process oriented, data oriented, or behavior oriented.

SSADM is a powerful methodology sponsored by the British government and has been successfully promoted as a standard in all central government computer projects in Great Britain since 1983.[15] SSADM extends soft system methodology (SSM), which used rich pictures. Like SA/SD, SSADM strongly supports the SA and SD stages of the SDLC model. As noted in Tan, the major stages in SSADM include analysis of the current system, specification of the required system, user selection of service levels, detailed data design, detailed procedure design, and physical design control.[16]

Despite their popularity, both SDLC-based and structured methodologies require the user to know precisely what information will be required in the system weeks, months, or even years in advance. Yet users often find it difficult to specify what they want; even if they can, their wants often may not match their real needs. This is evidenced by the number of revisions that systems go through after implementation before users get to tell all the information they really need. Prototyping, a fourth-generation SDM, which is discussed next, deals with this problem.

V. Prototyping

Over the past few decades, much controversy has been generated around prototyping. This debate concerns how prototyping may best be applied to achieve the productivity gains in software development claimed by vendors. Table 9.3 summarizes two opposing views of prototyping emerging from this debate: the evolutionary approach versus the revolutionary approach.[17]

Table 9.3   Prototyping (Fourth-Generation System Development Models)

Methods	Major Concepts
Revolutionary approach	Applies programming tools and techniques in a new and revolutionary way; argues against traditional methodological mind-sets.
Evolutionary approach	Merges prototyping techniques and produces an evolution of traditional and structured programming.

Advocates of the "evolutionary" approach want to see prototype techniques incorporated into the "proven" SDLC and structured methodologies, which in essence will produce a merging of traditional (structured) and new (4GL) programming approaches. They argue that prototyping using 4GL does not encourage a structured approach, which may result in considerable difficulties in interfacing newly developed applications with existing SDLC-based applications. They also argue that prototyping using 4GL provides only marginal benefits because this new approach primarily affects the coding phase of the application development. Thus, it appears reasonable to incorporate prototyping using 4GL into classical SDLC and structured models in order to achieve fine-tuning of the development process in the same way that structured methodologies were incorporated to fine-tune earlier SDLC-based approaches. McNurlin and Sprague[18] believe that many developers will likely prefer this "safer" approach when adopting new methods of 4GL programming.

In contrast, advocates of "revolutionary" prototyping argue that the only way productivity gains in software development can be realized is by applying them in new and innovative ways. Here, the rationale is that the traditional methodological mind-set (e.g., the emphasis on precise specifications of application systems before they are built, the abstraction of a static set of user requirements, and the concern about code details and exactness) prevents the effective use and application of prototyping tools and techniques. Rather, these tools and techniques are meant for people who can adapt to an environment supportive of a creative trial-and-error process—for example, nontraditional programmers who will use 4GL to support interactive editing and updating until the "right" system is developed. The framework of the applications is of major concern, and details should be ignored until later. Earlier methodologies address the problem of analyzing and designing a system "right"; however, there is also the problem of designing the "right system." The revolutionary approach addresses this problem.

VI. Contemporary Models

The proliferation of HMIS development methodologies over the years has caused some confusion as to which methodology is best. Many argue that no single approach is superior, but each methodology has its strengths and weaknesses. Tools and techniques that are appropriate for one set of circumstances may not be appropriate for others. Choosing an appropriate methodology will therefore depend on the context, the organization, the users, and the analysts who are developing the HMIS. The best compromise is therefore to choose an approach in which the choice of techniques and tools can be made within a loose methodological framework. This gave rise to contemporary models emphasizing a flexible systems approach.

Contemporary models synthesize many earlier approaches and include the automation of techniques and tools. The CASE method, which automates different parts of software or systems development, is one such option. Multiview is another. Both of these approaches support flexibility in SA and SD processes. Finally, a more recent development in SDM has been open-source software (OSS), which appears to provide a promising approach to rapid and inexpensive HMIS design and development for healthcare services organizations.

Computer-Assisted Software Engineering (CASE) Tools

CASE tools can assist with any or all aspects of the SA and SD processes. The CASE tool customer usually wants a tool that will help organize, structure, and simplify the development process. The goal is to develop better software more quickly. It has been shown that close to 80 percent of the problems in a given application system stem from SA and SD stages.[19] Hence, automating the SA and SD functions, rather than only those of physical development, should make development effort more efficient and productive.

The CASE concept includes tools for building systems, platforms for integrating tools, methods for developing applications, and techniques for managing the SA and SD processes. CASE encourages an environment for interactive development and automation of core and repetitive HMIS developmental tasks. It has been called "a philosophy of application development which embraces a systems approach,"[20] in which better connections between end-users (health professionals) and HMIS developers are supported. Traditional approaches focus on technical aspects of applications and the best way to solve a given problem; the CASE approach looks at the broader health organizational context and searches to identify the right problems to solve, as well as how to solve those problems.

In the past, CASE tools have provided some functions to automate different aspects of systems development, but not all of them, because one truly integrated tool set covers the entire SDLC process. In this sense, an individual CASE tool automates one small, specific part of the development process. There are several categories of tools. For example, diagramming tools pictorially depict systems specifications. Screen and report painters create systems specifications and may be used for basic prototyping. Dictionaries are information management tools that facilitate storing, reporting, and querying of technical and project management information. Specification tools detect incomplete, syntactically incorrect, and inconsistent system specifications. Code generators can generate executable codes from the pictorial system specifications. Finally, documentation generators can produce technical and user documentation that is necessary in using structured approaches. As summarized in Table 9.4, Brathwaite describes three types of CASE tools, including SDM tools, systems development support (SDS) tools, and programmer/project productivity (PP) tools.[21]

Table 9.4 Three Types of CASE Tools

Tools	Concepts
System development methodology tools	Combine to minimize effort and maximize coordination; enforce methodology rules and provide expertise to users.
System development support tools	Support systems development tools and techniques at any stage in the life cycle; do not necessarily enforce a methodology.
Programmer/project productivity tools	Provide support for software programmers and designers at the back end of the development life cycle.

SDM tools combine to minimize effort and maximize coordination. These tools give support for an SDM at any (or all) of the stages of the SDLC process. They can include any of the tools appropriate to the methodology being used, while enforcing methodological rules and providing expertise to the users. SDS tools provide support for SA and SD techniques used at any stages of the SDLC process, but they do not necessarily enforce a methodology. PP tools provide support for programmers/designers of software mostly at the back end of the development life cycle. Examples include project management and documentation tools. Project management is discussed later.

Alternatively, CASE tools may also be classified according to a different taxonomy: CASE toolkits, workbenches, frameworks, and methodology companions. *CASE toolkits* are integrated tools that automate only one part of the SDLC process. *CASE workbenches* provide integrated tools to automate the entire SDLC. CASE tools that are integrated and linked with non-CASE systems developmental tools are known as *CASE frameworks*. IBM's application development/ cycle (AD/Cycle) is one proprietary example of an open platform or CASE framework within which any CASE tool can participate. AD/Cycle can support HMIS application developers with everything CASE has to offer to date and has the ability to adapt and incorporate future technologies. *CASE methodology companions* sustain a specific methodology by automating the entire SDLC process.

It can be difficult to decide which of the many CASE tools available is most appropriate for a given situation or environment. Brathwaite[22] proposes using a series of simple questions such as:

- What are the future direction and functionality of the tools?
- Does the tool's manufacturer have a philosophy of "open architecture"?
- Does the tool interface with other CASE tools being considered?
- Does the tool provide a detailed means of prototyping?
- Does the CASE design provide analysis support for design documentation?
- Does the tool enhance project management?

Although CASE has been in existence for many years, it is still poorly interfaced with users (humans). For many years, technical aspects of SDM predominated over human aspects. Only recently has there been a shift to a more humanistic perspective. This shift has resulted in the emergence of new systems development methodologies, which are even more contemporary, such as Multiview.

Multiview, which is discussed next, brings together what appear to be the most flexible (as the name suggests) of alternative methodologies to create synergy in a merged methodology.

Multiview

Multiview is a comprehensive methodology and is described in considerable detail by Wood-Harper et al.[23] The authors saw it as a blending of the previous methodological approaches but especially emphasized the influence of SSM and effective technical and human implementation of computer-based systems (ETHICS),[24] both of which strive to incorporate the human aspects of systems development. Indeed, Multiview is based on the systems paradigm and emphasizes the relationship between the organization and its environment. In this aspect, the ultimate objective of Multiview is to amalgamate the human and technical subsystems for the enhancement of HMIS development as a whole.

Multiview is a nonprescriptive methodology that strives to be flexible. As a result, it continues to evolve as an SDM. *Action research*, in which knowledge gained from real applications in the field is incorporated, continually refines the Multiview methodology. The methodology was originally designed to aid development of IS/IT for small-business and small-scale HMIS projects, but it is no longer limited to this scope.[25]

The methodology contains five major steps:

1. Analysis of human activity.
2. Analysis of information (information modeling).
3. Analysis and design of sociotechnical aspects.
4. Design of human–computer interface.
5. Design of technical aspects.

Figure 9.11 illustrates the Multiview framework and the relationships among the five stages, whereas Table 9.5 summarizes activities entailed within each of the five components of the Multiview framework.

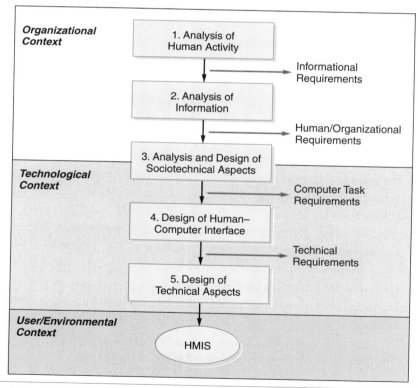

FIGURE 9.11   A Layered Multiview Framework for HMIS Design and Development.

Table 9.5   The Stages of the Multiview Framework

Stage	Major Concept
1. Analysis of human activity	Identifies problems within organization and suggests HMIS solutions to solve problems.
2. Analysis of information	Uses information modeling techniques to analyze the problems of stage 1.
3. Analysis and design of sociotechnical aspects	Balances the social objectives with the technical objectives, and ranks and chooses among these alternatives.
4. Design of human–computer interface	Gathers user input to create the technical design of the HMIS.
5. Design of technical aspects	Formulates the technical specifications of the HMIS.

Stage 1: Analysis of Human Activity

The objective of stage 1 is to identify the purpose and problem related to HMIS within the context of the organization. This stage attempts to answer the question of how the HMIS is supposed to further the aims of the organization. Rich pictures are frequently used to accomplish this stage for connecting the analysts to the users' view of the problem situation. Its ultimate objective is to identify problems and avenues to relieve these problems via HMIS design and development.

The first stage of Multiview provides the information necessary to conceptualize the human activities within the health service organization and helps to understand what HMIS can do for the organization. It also provides the inputs for the subsequent stages.

Stage 2: Analysis of Information

The objective of stage 2 is to analyze the information on data flow and data relationships collected in stage 1. This stage attempts to answer the question of what information processing functions the HMIS is to perform. There are two primary steps: (1) the development of a functional model and (2) the development of an entity model. The functional model begins by identifying the main functions of the system. This model is then progressively broken down into subsystems until they can no longer be subdivided (usually four to five levels). This may be accomplished by using a DFD.

The development of an entity model serves a slightly different function. The entity model defines all entities within the system. An entity is anything that is relevant to records keeping; for example, in a bed allocation system, care providers, patients, and hospital beds are entities perceived to be useful for generating information about the system. It is also important to describe the relationship between entities and any other relevant attributes for designing an effective HMIS database.

Stage 3: Analysis and Design of Sociotechnical Aspects

The objective of stage 3 is to produce a design that incorporates the needs of individual users, as identified in the preceding stages, while balancing them with the technical objectives of the system.

The sociotechnical analysis follows a logical sequence of events that begins with the identification of separate objectives for both the social and technical aspects and then goes on to develop alternatives that blend the objectives. Alternatives are ranked according to their ability to meet both sets of objectives, and a final selection is made of the best sociotechnical option. Unlike other stages, this stage addresses the question of how the HMIS can be incorporated into the working lives of the people in the organization.

Stage 4: Design of Human–Computer Interface

The objective of stage 4 is to define the technical aspects of the system, including, for example, whether it will be command driven, have a main menu and submenus, or use a point-and-click (mouse) interface. The users are major contributors to these decisions, but this stage relies heavily on the systems analyst to guide the process and detail the final technical requirements. Equally important is the ability to incorporate the multiplicity of hardware and software already in existence within the overall HMIS design. Users should express their concerns to the analyst, who must in turn find the most appropriate human–computer interface to address these concerns. This stage attempts to answer the question of how individuals (i.e., users) can best relate to the HMIS in terms of operating and using the system.

Stage 5: Design of Technical Components

The objective of stage 5 is to formulate the technical requirements of the system. At this point in the development, the human needs should already be integrated into the HMIS design. Therefore, this stage is only technical because the analyst concentrates on detailing the full specifications of the HMIS design for efficient operations. This stage attempts to answer the question of what technical specifications are required for the HMIS to satisfy the needs identified in the four preceding stages.

Altogether, the Multiview methodology is characterized by several underlying assumptions. First, it provides a framework for resolving a problem. Multiview is not intended as a development prescription; rather, it offers guidelines within which to assemble a set of tools and techniques for developing an HMIS. More importantly, it is situation dependent, and the people who employ Multiview must be knowledgeable about the methodology as well as the problem situation, the users, and the organization. The practical approach produces knowledge for subsequent applications within similar contexts (i.e., action research). Finally, it strives to integrate the human and technical subsystems, whereas past practices tended to focus on just one domain while ignoring the other.

Open-Source Software

The lack of standards and the absence of systems interoperability have continued to challenge the successful deployment and adoption of new HMIS practices and emerging systems development models in healthcare services organizations. Many applications have also failed to keep pace with the changing and growing needs of new forms of consolidated or complemented healthcare services organizations. Lately, considerable attention among healthcare practitioners and researchers has been given to open-source software (OSS).

With OSS, any programmers can adopt, modify, use, and reconstruct the rich libraries of source codes available from well-tested products (such as Massachusetts General's COSTAR and the Veterans Administration's VISTA software) without incurring licensing fees, provided the newly developed and modified software is also made available for others wanting to adopt these derivative products just the same way as the original source codes were made freely available to them. With OSS, HMIS designers therefore have great opportunities to innovate and help proliferate a range of key products that would resolve many of the major challenges facing the healthcare system constraints by growing demands but limited IT resources. The Regenstrief Institute, for example, has also contributed in the same manner by channeling all of their future HMIS development efforts to the OSS model. Apparently, the OSS trend is here to stay, encouraged by the rapidity to which many useful HMIS products can be generated through a collaborative exchange among governmental agencies, university researchers, and nonprofit and public institutions.

Key advantages of OSS adoption include, but are not limited to, promoting interoperability, reducing overall HMIS costs, supporting efficiencies of software development processes, decreasing backlogs with complex HMIS product design and development, and increasing the diffusion of OSS products. Additionally, these OSS products will also become more reliable and secure, enabling standards and scalability as well as minimizing vendor lock-in.[26] Specific reasons for these advantages are that source codes can be examined and tested for security flaws and/or bugs before it is applied; software developers' time can be put to better use for attacking new and interesting challenges, rather than focusing on previously solved problems; and maintenance of these source codes can now be openly contracted, even if the original software developers are no longer available because the bulk of the codes and software components used in OSS products already exist.

Conversely, some other researchers have noted that it is the vendors who have mostly fueled OSS adoption in hospitals and that it is the lack of in-house development and/or the "perceived lack of security, quality, and accountability of OSS products" that are slowing down OSS adoption.[27(p. 16)] Moreover, OSS applications are seen to also be more general-purpose oriented than domain specific. Altogether, the contemporary models appear to emphasize integrating both the technical and human aspects of systems development and trending toward end-user computing (EUC), which is highlighted as we move to conclude this chapter.

VII. Conclusion

The need to balance the human and technical aspects in the evolution of SDM was fueled by the predominance of the technical components and the subsequent user dissatisfaction. The shift to a more humanistic perspective and the infiltration of the microcomputer at the worksite have led to the emergence of EUC.[28] EUC is not personal computing; personal computing is a subcategory of EUC. An *end-user* is anyone who uses information generated by a computer. Hence, EUC is any direct use of the computer by an individual whose primary interest is something other than just that use. Stated simply, EUC is the capability of users to have direct control of their own computing needs.

When EUC began, most projects were simple applications. Today, EUC spans the whole organization and has a significant effect on HMIS functioning of the entire healthcare services organization. The literature on EUC agrees on two primary guidelines for the successful inclusion of EUC within the organizational HMIS planning process:

1. *HMIS policies and procedures for the use of system quality control.* To maximize the benefits of EUC, an organization should have strategies for promoting, managing, and controlling the evolution of EUC.[29]
2. *HMIS support services.* The development of end-user applications or OSS products does not obviate the need for guidance and assistance with difficult and challenging problems, especially those of a technical nature.

In this light, HMIS service management and the development of an HMIS support center in a healthcare services organization is almost a given in order to achieve successful HMIS implementations.

For today's health services organizations, it is crucial to incorporate an SDM as a key instrument in the effective and efficient development of HMIS. These systems development methodologies have evolved from rigid, step-by-step formulas for success to contemporary models, such as CASE, Multiview, and OSS model. In the end, the problem of choosing among alternative SDM approaches is one of recognizing the broader environmental, organizational, and technological contexts in which the need for health information systems design and development is embedded.

Notes

1. J. Rowley, *The Basics of Systems Analysis and Design for Information Managers* (London: Clive Bingley, 1990).
2. D. Avison and G. Fitzgerald, *Information Systems Development—Methodology, Techniques and Tools* (Boston: Blackwell Scientific Publications, 1988).
3. S. Holloway, *Methodology Handbook for Information Managers* (Aldershot, U.K.: Gower Technical, 1989).
4. J. Cougar et al., Eds., *Advanced System Development/Feasibility Techniques* (New York: John Wiley & Sons, 1982).
5. D. Burnstine, *BIAIT: An Emerging Management Discipline* (New York: BIAIT International, 1980). Read this reference for a detailed discussion of the seven questions used in the BIAIT method.
6. M. Colter, "A Comparative Examination of Systems Analysis Techniques," *MIS Quarterly* 8, no. 1 (1984): 51–66.
7. D. Ross and K. Schoman, "Structured Analysis for Requirements Definition," *IEEE Transactions on Software Engineering* SE-3, no. 1 (1977): 6–15.
8. D. Ross, "Structured Analysis (SA): A Language for Communicating Ideas," *IEEE Transactions on Software Engineering* SE-3, no. 1 (1977): 16–34.
9. T. Olle et al., *Information Systems Methodologies: A Framework for Understanding* (Reading, MA: Addison-Wesley, 1988).
10. Colter (1984).
11. T. DeMarco, *Structured Analysis and System Specification* (Englewood Cliffs, NJ: Prentice Hall, 1979).

12. C. Floyd, *Information Systems Design Methodologies: Improving the Practice* (Amsterdam: North-Holland, 1986).

13. E. Yourdon and L. Constantine, *Structured Design* (Englewood Cliffs, NJ: Prentice Hall, 1979).

14. T. W. Olle et al., Eds., *Information System Design Methodologies: A Comparative Review* (Amsterdam: North-Holland, 1982).

15. E. Downs et al., *Structured Systems Analysis and Design Method: Application and Context* (Englewood Cliffs, NJ: Prentice Hall, 1988).

16. J. K. H. Tan, "Health Care Information Systems: An Organized Delivery System Perspective." In L. F. Wolper, Ed., *Health Care Administration: Planning, Implementing, and Managing Organized Delivery Systems*, 3rd ed. (Gaithersburg, MD: Aspen Publishers, 1995).

17. J. K. H. Tan and J. Hanna, "Integrating Health Care: Knitting Patient Care with Technology through Networking," *Health Care Management Review* 19, no. 2 (1994): 72–80.

18. B. McNurlin and R. Sprague, *Information Systems Management in Practice*, 2nd ed. (Englewood Cliffs, NJ: Prentice Hall, 1989).

19. L. Towner, *CASE Concepts and Implementation* (New York: McGraw-Hill, 1989): 2. This is a technical book that is part of an IBM series.

20. S. Montgomery, *AD/Cycle: IBM's Framework for Application Development and CASE* (New York: IBM, 1991): 9.

21. K. Brathwaite, *Applications Development Using CASE Tools* (New York: Academic Press, 1990): 108.

22. Ibid.

23. A. Wood-Harper et al., *Information Systems Definition: The Multiview Approach* (Oxford, U.K.: Blackwell Scientific Publications, 1985).

24. E. Mumford and M. Weir, *Computer Systems in Work Design: The ETHICS Method* (London: Associated Business Press, 1979).

25. D. Avison and A. Wood-Harper, "Information Systems Development Research: An Exploration of Ideas in Practice," *Computer Journal* 34, no. 2 (1991): 98–112.

26. W. Raghupathi and W. Gao, "An Eclipse-Based Development Approach to Health Information Technology," *International Journal of Electronic Healthcare*, forthcoming.

27. G. Munoz-Carnejo, C. B. Seaman, and A. G. Koru, "An Empirical Investigation into the Adoption of Open Source Software in Hospitals," *International Journal of Healthcare Information Systems & Informatics* 3, no. 3 (July–Sept 2008): 16–37.

28. R. Panko, *End User Computing: Management, Applications and Technology* (New York: John Wiley & Sons, 1988).

29. G. B. Davis and M. H. Olson, *Management Information Systems: Conceptual Foundations, Structure and Development*, 2nd ed. (New York: McGraw-Hill, 1985).

Chapter Questions

9–1. Define the following, and describe a health-related example that incorporates these terms:
  a. Methodology.
  b. Technique.
  c. Tool.
  d. Phases and subphases.

9–2. Discuss the SDLC, and explain why this concept is critical for understanding HMIS development.

9–3. Provide a list of the second-, third-, and fourth-generation methodologies as well as the flexible and integrated methodologies (i.e., contemporary models) discussed in the chapter, and devise taxonomies to contrast and compare the main features, advantages, and disadvantages of these alternative system development methodologies.

9–4. Why use CASE tools? Discuss how CASE supports various aspects of systems development and the challenges with CASE applications.

9–5. List at least three tools or techniques that can be used within the Multiview framework to aid in the development of an information system. Identify at what stage each tool/technique is most appropriate, which inputs are required, and the intended outputs.

9–6. Define open-source software (OSS), and distinguish the advantages of an OSS approach from other methods of software development. Describe an example of an OSS "success" story in the healthcare services industry.

Data Stewardship:
Foundation for Health Management Information System Design, Implementation, and Evaluation

Bryan Bennett

Editor's Note: In this chapter, the author takes on the perspective of data quality and data stewardship and relates and integrates these two major concepts to bear on the significance of designing, implementing, and evaluating the right health management information systems (HMIS) for the right people at the right time. The organization of the chapter is straightforward. After the opening scenario, the introduction (Section I) touches on the need for high-quality data in HMIS design, implementation, and evaluation. Next, the concepts of the change continuums, namely, *technology, people*, and *processes*, are introduced (Section II). The author perceives these three major HMIS components as the bases for transforming healthcare services organizations and driving high-quality versus poor-quality HMIS design, implementation, and evaluation. Without a focus on data quality and an understanding of how these various HMIS components need to be aligned, many challenges with HMIS design, implementation, and evaluation remain unresolved. Section III then discusses how the four major aspects of data stewardship—data quality, data management, data security, and business intelligence—can affect HMIS design, implementation, and evaluation. Section IV outlines the HMIS implementation and post-implementation process, followed by a discussion that moves back to the case scenario and applies it to achieve a broader understanding of the HMIS design, implementation, and evaluation topic.

CHAPTER OUTLINE

Scenario: *The Metropolitan Medical Group*

Scenario: *The Metropolitan Medical Group*

Four internal medicine physicians formed the Metropolitan Medical Group as a general medicine medical practice. The practice has grown from a single office to five offices in the local area and now includes a gynecological practice, outsourced laboratory services, X-ray and mammography screening, and nutrition counseling. See Figure 10.1 for a diagram depicting the current network infrastructure of Metropolitan Medical Group.

The practice also owns several of the buildings in which it has offices and rents unused office space to other noncompetitive medical practices. Each office has a separate network, with the billing function as the only function networked among the offices.

Dr. Mark Jones, one of the practice founders, has been attending several seminars and reading articles about the benefits of an integrated health management information system (HMIS) that could network all five offices and the administrative function. Functions that could be included in this integrated HMIS include a patient database, patient billing, provider billing, referral database, and treatment codes database.

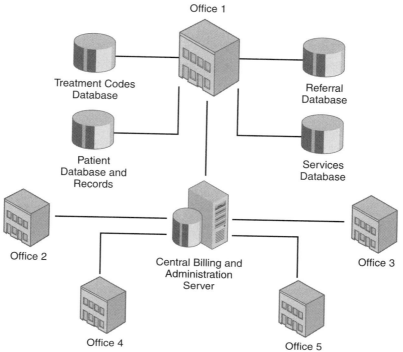

FIGURE 10.1   Current Network Diagram. (All offices have individual databases like Office 1.)

I. Introduction

When HMIS initiatives are based largely on inaccurate or poor-quality data, it is similar to building a house on sand: the foundation will keep shifting until the house finally collapses.

Unlike many other industrial manufacturing and/or production services sectors, where the ultimate products may just be satisfying growing demands for material goods or the accumulation of capital assets by humankind, the importance of accurate, reliable, and timely data is even more critical in healthcare services management because these services are much more concerned with resulting outcomes that will significantly affect the health and well-being of humankind compared with all other production or service processes.

Accordingly, high-quality data may be considered as the number-one priority when designing, implementing, and evaluating HMIS. There are many hidden risks associated with poor data quality that could cost the healthcare services organization a sizable amount of money and/or lost opportunities, including but not limited to the following:

- Poor customer service and strained physician–patient relations as patients requiring special care are not being easily identified and/or served adequately by staff manning the front offices.
- Revenue losses from utilizing incorrect billing codes or billing the incorrect health insurance provider for the service and/or treatment performed by the respective caregiver.

- Patchy partnership or referral information, which could eventually lead to misunderstanding of the value of a relationship with partners and physician referrals made and received.
- Lost opportunities from new and/or ongoing services and treatments that should have been added or eliminated.
- Higher capital expenditures as equipment purchases are made before the revenue stream is in place to support a reasonable return on investment.

Applying these various risks characterizations to the chapter-opening scenario, the following episodes could be an outgrowth:

> Mrs. Smith is a middle-aged woman who has been a patient of Dr. Jones for the past 12 years. Two years ago, she developed an illness that requires her to see the doctor every two months for follow-up tests and monitoring. Mrs. Smith is normally a nice person, but she hates waiting in drafty waiting rooms for a long time. When the doctor is running late, she gets very cranky and takes it out on the front desk staff. When she does see the doctor, she is not very cooperative, has her tests done, and leaves.
>
> Additionally, the front desk clerk forgot to verify her insurance provider information and missed the fact that she has recently changed jobs and her corresponding insuring care providers. Dr. Jones also recognized that he requested the same tests for Mrs. Smith that were also requested for two other patients that morning and had referred her to the same specialist he referred someone else to yesterday. He began to wonder if Metropolitan Medical Group should add these laboratory services and/or a new specialty to their group practice.
>
> Unbeknownst to Dr. Jones is the fact that one of the tests has been requested several times a day by him and his practice partners, while the other is requested only three times a month. Moreover, the referral he made for Mrs. Smith was to a physician that a doctor at one of their other facilities has had repeated complaints about (regarding that physician's recurring tardiness).

II. The Change Continuums

Besides the requirement for quality data, management of healthcare services organizations must factor in several other considerations prior to making a decision to design, implement, and/or evaluate HMIS.

In practice, many of these factors stem typically from one of three basic continuums: technology, processes, and people. We now illustrate where the applications of each of these continuums are key to transforming the healthcare services organizations in achieving successful HMIS design, implementation, and evaluation.

Technology

In healthcare services organizations, patient data are the basis for many health administrative and clinical decisions. The patient data warehouse that is built with the accumulated data it contained should therefore be completely synchronized with the data in the services/treatment database and the patient billing, health organization billing, referral, and finance databases. Not only will this help the healthcare services organization better align corporate goals and objectives with HMIS goals and objectives, but management of the healthcare services organization will then have a greater appreciation of the impact an individual patient can and will have on the entire operation.

Nonetheless, accurate billing is a challenge faced by many healthcare services organizations. In spite of their attempts to maintain accurate patient and healthcare organization billing records, the human factor can easily negate all of the technology and precautions that have been implemented throughout the years. With the massive amount of data generated and collected from each patient interaction on a day-to-day basis for populating their electronic medical records and new changes to business processes and procedures over time, it is imperative that an organization design, implement, and evaluate HMIS policies and procedures to keep the different systems properly updated.

Moreover, there may also be redundant processes that could be eliminated to improve the efficiency of technology use and data processing. This brings us to the next level of consideration, processes.

Processes

Without an accurate and repeatable entry and update process, the organization risks updating the wrong record, incorrectly updating the correct record, or not updating any record at all.

A system has to be structured and defined to ensure that the flow of data is well organized and properly tracked so as to take into account all of the necessary follow-up actions in order for a cycle of transaction updates to fully be completed. Thus, understanding the flow of information across the different units of the healthcare services organization from the point a patient enters the system to the point a patient is being served and/or discharged is paramount. Any of these actions, or inactions, put the organization at risk both financially and legally.

People

People are always a factor in any HMIS design, implementation, or evaluation attempt. Past studies and experience have, for example, indicated that more than 75 percent of the bad-quality data is likely caused by employee data-entry errors. This is a major obstacle that can only be overcome through improved human resources training, reengineering of business processes, and/or instituting technological checks and balances that will automatically reject or accept entries, or entry types, based on predefined criteria.

III. Data Stewardship

Having high-quality data is not just about the accuracy of each patient record. It also involves controlling access to the data, managing data updates, and validating the data. Taken together, this process is commonly referred to as *data stewardship*, which goes beyond just the physical managing of the data. It is a process with the goal of delivering the right information, to the right person, at the right time. By doing so, it will enable the healthcare services organization to make the right decision.

Data stewardship has four major components, each of which must be addressed within the context of HMIS design, implementation, and evaluation.

- *Quality.* This component is concerned with providing current, accurate, and consistent information whenever and wherever the data are accessed.
- *Management.* This is the physical aspect of handling or managing data from the point the data are collected to the point the data are used and archived. This component not only includes the hardware and software technology, but also the processes, as well as both the people and the machine involved in managing the data.
- *Security.* This component has to do with controlling access to the data to ensure that not only are data available and retrievable to those who are supposed to access the data but the release of data is also securely guarded from those who are not supposed to have access to the data.
- *Business Intelligence.* This component has to do with utilizing the data to yield better, more complete, and more usable information. This is what some have called "putting the information back into information technology."

We now take a closer look at each of these components and highlight their potential impacts on HMIS design, implementation, and evaluation for healthcare services organizations.

Data Quality Implications

The implications for data quality on HMIS design, implementation, and evaluation are multifaceted. For the data to be accurate and consistent, rules for standardizing data, transforming it, or mapping it to existing data are essential. This is often complicated by healthcare services organizations having and maintaining legacy systems that also have accommodating processes and designs, which allow for errors or poor-quality data to be entered.

Indeed, many of these problems often begin at the initial data-entry stage. For example, patient information can be entered by a wide variety of individuals, including physicians, nurses, and other clinicians such as laboratory assistants and pharmacists. As a result, without the adoption of shared standards throughout the healthcare services industry or within the different units of the healthcare services organization itself, a patient's name can even be entered multiple ways, multiple times—for instance, Robert Stevens, Robert Stephens, Rob Stephens, and Bob Stevens may all be referring to the same person.

Having processes in place that allow for selecting the specific patient from a list of current patients will help minimize future data-quality issues. Use of a master patient index (MPI) also helps differentiate and uniquely identify a particular patient from among all the other patients whose data are also stored in the same database. In the current age of information technology explosion, it appears safe to assume that most, if not all, healthcare services organizations would already have some kind of standard adoption practices and a proper data verification process in place.

Data quality can also be affected by the HMIS design and structure. This is most prevalent when several systems or databases are permitted to be in use simultaneously. One system may use a single address field for street address and unit number, while another may use multiple fields for this same data. Additionally, one system may use standardized state abbreviations from a drop-down menu, while another may allow free-flowing entry of two or three characters for the state. Along this line of reasoning, the adoption of consistent and shared coding standards across all organizational units is one approach to reducing and eventually eliminating the possible proliferation of data redundancies and data update anomalies throughout the different databases and systems.

Data Management Implications

In the context of HMIS design, implementation, and evaluation, there are generally two types of data that need to be managed: the master data and transactional data.

The master data are the most commonly used data across the organization, such as patient data, provider data, and billing code data, among others. These are generally static data that are extracted from the transactional data derived from various sources. These data are cleansed, deduced, standardized, matched, transformed, and loaded into the master data warehouse.

The transactional data are the actual invoices and receipts and are stored in a separate data warehouse after similar standards are applied. These data are mainly created for analytical and tactical purposes, whereas the master data are used for providing the "single version of the truth" about the patients, providers, suppliers, and other relevant third parties.

Between these two data warehouses, a complete 360-degree enriched view of the patient or provider is often possible and delivered.

Data Security Implications

Data security is probably the most important aspect of HMIS design, implementation, and evaluation. No matter how complete the data may be, or how high their quality, if at the end of the day, an employee of the healthcare services organization can walk out the door with the data undetected, or if the wrong employee has access to the confidential and personal data of certain patients and uses these data improperly, everything the organization has done to protect the privacy and preserve the integrity of the data will be opened for federal investigations under the Health Insurance Portability and Accountability Act (HIPAA).

The primary concerns with data security, therefore, have to be releasing private and personal health information and permitting authorized individuals to access only the data they need for their normal business activities. Protecting against viruses, spyware, and intrusion attacks is also becoming more of an issue lately.

In terms of data security, another issue most organizations fail to truly and completely prepare for is disaster recovery so as to ensure business continuity. Such a disaster need not come from a terrorist attack—it can be as simple as the computer room being flooded after a harsh storm. How can a practice open the office the next day? What happened to the patient records? These are very real situations that need to be envisioned and procedures for recovery properly documented before they occur. Backing up the system on a weekly basis and taking the tapes home is not an acceptable solution. What happens to all the patient and provider billing transactions that occurred since the system was backed up? Some sort of incremental daily backup mechanism should be in place.

Fortunately, several organizations are now offering secure online backup services. These services have several advantages, including:

- The backups can be programmed to occur automatically.
- The data are maintained in a secure off-site location.
- Downtime is shortened in the case where the data are needed, because there is no need for time to be wasted in traveling to the off-site storage location to retrieve the backup tapes.

To ascertain that proper data security and business continuity protocols are in place, a yearly security assessment of the HMIS privacy and security procedures and policies by a qualified organization is highly recommended.

Business Intelligence Implications

An effective data stewardship function in the context of HMIS design, implementation, and evaluation eventually leads to better business intelligence (BI) for the healthcare services organization. It will enable an organization to better monitor and track the state of the business by providing the user with actionable information, which can lead to better and more intelligent decisions.

Dr. Jones, in our chapter-opening scenario, would know how many of each test his practice performs with the application of a good BI tool. In many cases, the information is just a click away, making it very timely because it is typically accessed in real time or near real time.

Still, there has been some confusion about what BI is and what it can or cannot do, especially among healthcare management students. Some of the myths are addressed here:

- *"It only involves technology!"* BI involves changes in technology, processes, and people. No amount of technology will fix human input errors without some corresponding checks and balances. No amount of technology will fix an organization's multiple definitions of key elements such as treatment codes. These inconsistencies can and do cause many organizations to spend more time reconciling one report to another versus acting effectively on the information.
- *"I need a PhD to be able to use it!"* With advancing technologies in this day and age, many end-users are finding complex software easy to manipulate and use. Indeed, many off-the-shelf BI tools currently available include functionality such as natural query language, which allows the user to query the data in the form of almost English-like regular sentences

versus a structured query statement. Some of the tools also include an iconic drag-and-drop interface, which allows a user to just drag the elements needed for the query to a workspace.

- *"It's for customer data only!"* BI is for creating information from any kind of data. Whether the information is about customers, vendors, pharmaceuticals companies, financial and/or legal compliance, or customer service, BI will help the entire enterprise because it presents the single version of the truth about the entire operation.

- *"It's all about dashboards and pretty pictures!"* The dashboard visually displays important information on a single screen. It can quickly convey to the user actionable information to monitor the state of the business, which is useful in consolidating relevant data from several sources and presenting it visually for immediate absorption. They are great in monitoring and communicating information, which helps in the organizational strategic and high-level decision-making process.

- *"It's too costly!"* Even though the software may be a bit costly, especially if the wrong-sized solution is purchased for the situation, it is important to match the right tool to the size of the organization, number of data elements, and business needs. The most important investment should be up-front in determining the organization's needs, data profiling, and process mapping, as well as determining the initial state of business intelligence required. This process is unlikely to be as costly as the cost of missed opportunities, over-purchased assets, or mismatched future treatment demand.

- *"I can wait until later!"* BI can be a competitive advantage for a healthcare services organization if its concept and uses can be better understood. In other words, BI helps management and employees alike to better understand their own organization and how it is currently being positioned to compete in the larger marketplace vis-à-vis their competitors. Surely, if BI is properly utilized, it can help identify opportunities, such as cost savings, efficiencies, or process changes that will improve the positioning of the healthcare services organization.

IV. Implementation Process

At this point, we move the discussion to HMIS implementation, which involves five essential steps: (1) assessing the available resources, (2) assessing data and data inventory, (3) profiling data and determining the valid values for each attribute, (4) reviewing processes, and (5) reviewing personnel responsibilities.

Step 1: Assessing the Available Resources

The first step in HMIS implementation is to determine if the organization is prepared and has the necessary internal resources and skill sets required to perform the work for a project of the magnitude envisaged. If it is found that internal personnel resources are lacking, augment the staff with some external personnel for the project. Referrals from trusted friends and colleagues would be the safest route for identifying external consultants to hire.

In addition to the proper staffing levels and skills, other factors to be considered include the technology that is needed—hardware and software—as well as additional staff training that may be needed once the HMIS are implemented. As previously discussed under the change continuums, technology is only a part of the change process. The right people must be in place to perform the right tasks.

Regardless of how the project is to be staffed, it is essential to set clear and attainable goals at the outset. The key stakeholders should agree upon the desired outcomes, such as when the product is expected to be completed. They also have to be very specific. For example, stakeholders cannot just say "this is not what I wanted"; instead, they have to indicate which aspect of the product is not acceptable, such as "the screen shots are not easy to read because of the color used" or the "information regarding patient name should be longer to accommodate someone having a 10-character surname." To keep the project on track, a project plan with identifiable milestones is recommended. The project should then be managed to the plan such that at any given time, the status can quickly be assessed.

Step 2: Assessing Data and Data Inventory

Like any asset, the data need to be inventoried as the next step. The organization needs to determine what data it has, what the sources of these data are (e.g., internal departments versus external suppliers or vendors), who handles the data in the healthcare services organization, and what the final state of these data will be after any manipulation.

A data inventory should be accompanied by a data assessment to determine where the weaknesses in the healthcare services organization are that could affect achieving the full potential from the data.

Step 3: Profiling Data and Determining the Valid Values for Each Attribute

One of the more difficult tasks to perform is profiling the data and correcting any inaccuracies. The purpose is to eliminate duplicate records, standardize addresses, verify use of valid billing codes, and more.

In this step, fields that must only contain numeric characters are identified and the data in those fields verified, such as billing rates. Fields that are of a fixed length are also identified and verified, such as state, billing code, or zip code. This step is difficult because there is only so much that technology can do for you. Many times, it requires direct human intervention to make specific decisions on whether certain records should be combined, remain separate, or altered.

Step 4: Reviewing Processes

Each process that takes place in the healthcare services facility should be documented. This serves not only as a good starting point for the healthcare services organization's current state, but also helps identify weaknesses that could affect the HMIS design, implementation, and evaluation. Some of the processes that should be diagrammed include:

- Patient receiving and processing.
- Cash receipts.
- Cash disbursements, including accounts payable and payroll.

- Provider billing.
- Medical and office supplies inventory management.

Figure 10.2 provides a flowchart depicting an example of an accounts payable process for the Metropolitan Medical Group as discussed in the chapter-opening scenario. Typically, flowcharts

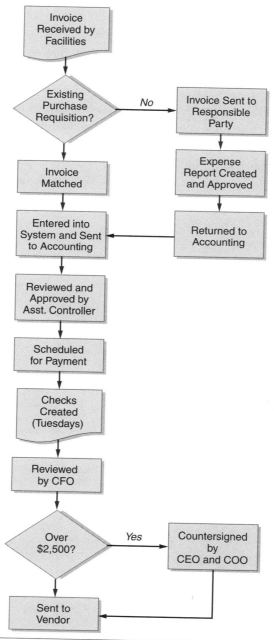

FIGURE 10.2 Metropolitan Medical Group Accounts Payable Process.

are constructed so that the general direction is from left to right and top to bottom; otherwise, a snakelike layout makes the flow of the process difficult to follow. The criteria for the decisions indicated by the diamond-shaped symbol need to be shown in all instances, even by referring to supporting documents, where the detailed criteria are spelled out. For instance, "Over $2,500" could have been replaced by "Approval" decisions, which may have to be judged acceptable or unacceptable for each instance as set out in a separate but detailed reference document.

Step 5: Reviewing Personnel Responsibilities

The last step is reviewing personnel responsibilities. With documented processes, the organization can identify who is receiving, manipulating, or entering data into the system. These *touch-points* are usually where most of the errors occur. Some areas to examine closely include personnel who are critically involved in multiple processes. For a small practice, that may be unavoidable; however, in larger practices, a clear separation of duties with oversight is possible.

Additionally, a person's workflow may be constantly interrupted by his or her responsibilities. This is a concern because of the loss of concentration that is involved, which can lead to input errors. Once these risk areas are identified, changes in the tasks and/or staffing levels can be made. Figure 10.3 provides a diagram of the new network configuration, detailing the different

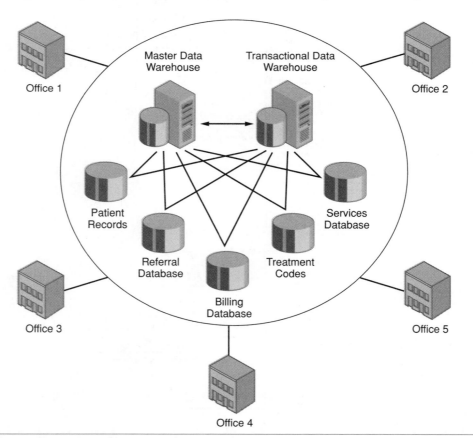

FIGURE 10.3   New Network Diagram.

databases providing sources of data that are linked to the two major data warehouses (master data warehouse and transaction data warehouse) that could now be shared and accessible in an integrated HMIS environment among the five offices. Such a network could then replace the earlier network configuration shown in Figure 10.1.

Post-Implementation Review

Unfortunately, the work is not over even when the project is completed. Many of the same implementation processes that were just completed must be performed on a regular basis to maintain the quality of the data and integrity of the system. Otherwise, the HMIS will be back to its pre-implementation stage before too long.

These reviews should take place as post-implementation reviews a couple of times a year, more intensely during the time period immediately following implementation. Some of these reviews may also have to be performed after significant changes in billing codes, when new physicians or services are added to the practice, or when new administrative staff are hired. The only way to make sure the entire office is operating to its fullest is to make sure everyone is performing their tasks as they should.

Notes

1. B. Bennett, "Data Centricity Leads to Customer Centricity," *DM News*, June 26, 2006.
2. B. Bennett, "Six Myths about Business Intelligence," *Biz Insights*, Fourth Quarter 2006.
3. "Seven Steps to Flawless Business Intelligence," Cognos White Paper, September 2005.
4. R. Gonzales, "Dashboards Can Help You Align Operations with Business Goals," *BI Report*, September 2006.
5. W. Laurent, "The Case for Data Stewardship," *DM Review*, February 2005.

Chapter Questions

10–1. Identify critical success factors for the system integration of the two practices discussed in the MMG mini-case that follows.

10–2. What are some of the project management implications for the integration of the practices?

10–3. List some the master data and transactional data elements that should be captured and managed. What is the difference between these types of data elements?

10–4. How would you secure access to the data and what personnel implications do you foresee? How do you ensure that the proper records are updated in a timely manner?

10–5. The combined practice wants to implement wireless notepads for the physicians and staff to make changes directly to a patient's records. What data integrity and security issues do you foresee?

10–6. What key performance indicators should the management of the practice monitor?

10–7. How can the information system be utilized to bring the receivables and payables balances and aging into sync?

10–8. What is the importance of having end-user involvement in the implementation of the combined HMIS? How do you go about getting them engaged in the process?

10–9. After the system integration, how will you maintain data integrity throughout the system?

Mini-Case: The Metropolitan Medical Group (MMG)

The Metropolitan Medical Group (MMG) merged with the Oak Grove Medical Group (OGMG). The Oak Grove Medical Group has four offices and owns the medical office building where their imaging and radiology lab and physical therapy and diagnostic laboratory centers are located.

Although the size of staffs in both practices is about the same, OGMG has a very different financial structure. Not only are their receivables a lot higher, but the aging of their receivables is much older. This has caused them to miss payments to their vendors, resulting in a higher accounts payable balance. Further analysis revealed that some of the doctors from remote offices have referred patients for laboratory tests and to specialists outside the practice when these same tests or specialists are available internally at other offices.

The room that houses the network servers is not climate controlled, secure, or backed up off-site.

Managing Health Management Information System Projects:
System Implementation and Information Technology Services Management

Joseph Tan

Scenario: *Louisiana Rural Health Information Exchange*[1]

Louisiana Rural Health Information Exchange (LARHIX) is a pilot project championed by Louisiana Senate President Don Hines and Representative Francis Thompson as a means of servicing the state's rural residents with better healthcare delivery, the need for which was made even more evident following Hurricane Katrina. The initiative aims at demonstrating the possibility of, and potential benefits of, exchanging patient information electronically between Delhi Hospital, a small hospital in rural Delhi, Louisiana, and a major health sciences center such as the Louisiana State University (LSU) Health Sciences Center in Shreveport. According to Michael Carroll, Delhi Hospital's CEO and administrator, success of the LARHIX project will permit patients in underserved rural areas, especially those suffering from chronic ailments and mental diseases, to be treated regularly by physicians situated in a major health sciences center. "We treated hundreds of people . . . (at LSU) . . . that didn't have any medical records at all after the hurricane," McCarroll noted. "We were starting from scratch and at that point, we realized that we needed portable, transferrable medical records in order to avoid this kind of situation in the future."

Interestingly, the project started with a physician at the LSU Health Sciences Center in Shreveport showing how he could remotely instruct a Delhi clinician to perform a simulated, but complete, evaluation of a surrogate patient—checking and collecting vital statistics on the patient. Flat-screen 50-inch monitors, advanced cameras, and other equipment were used in each examination room located at the two sites to transmit a live telecast of the remote physician–patient interactive session.

In addition to EHR solutions, LARHIX utilizes Fusion, a clinical portal from Carefx (Scottsdale, Arizona) to aggregate patient information from the various sources. Brenna Guice, Delhi Hospital's information systems (IS) head, notes that real-time Delhi patient care to be delivered by LSU physicians will begin only when laboratory IS, pharmacy IS, and radiology IS are all implemented and integrated into the health information exchange (HIE) system. Other vendors participating in the project included Chicago-based Initiate Systems, which offered the software for the HIE's enterprise master person index (MPI) numbers, and EHR vendor

Dairyland Healthcare Solutions—even though the requirements for LARHIX are independent of any HIE and EHR vendor products, so long as these software solutions are interoperable with those of other hospitals.

While Delhi was among the first of seven facilities to be piloted in the LARHIX initiative, the longer-term vision is actually an extended project inclusive of all 44 members of the Louisiana Rural Hospital Coalition following an approved five-year proposed funding. According to a representative in charge of rolling out the five-year project: "Not all facilities will need a brand new system, and some may only need an upgrade. The ultimate goal is, at the end of that five-year period, to have everyone on a state-of-the-art system that can communicate with the hospital in Shreveport."

Imagine you have lost everything following Katrina, except for your identity papers, the prescriptions you were taking just before Katrina, and a disk drive containing some of your personal health records, which you happened to have downloaded from your personal computer with other important information prior to Katrina. How do you perceive something like the LARHIX project could be of any help to you as you go about reconstructing your life and your personal health information? Why might it be important to keep good records of your personal health information, and what kind of a system would you trust your family physician to implement for the safekeeping of your personal health records?

I. Introduction

Systems implementation (SI) in healthcare services organizations entails a process whose success is dependent on the fulfillment of a number of key activities. These may include strategic planning, a thorough preliminary systems analysis, broad and detailed systems design specifications, user training and education, and hardware–software vendor selection. Health information systems analysts and professionals are among the best people overseeing such projects due to the project management skills that are needed to ensure a well-managed project that is completed on time and within budget.

In practice, certain critical factors can influence the success of health management information systems (HMIS) implementation. For example, two broad areas have played key roles: (1) the application of well-tested guidelines and standard protocols and (2) the enforcement of ethical and legal concerns. Our focus here is on the HMIS implementation process; some of these factors and challenges are addressed in the chapter on standards, which is also accompanied by a policy brief included in Part IV of this text. Figure 11.1 shows that once HMIS planning is fine-tuned to address success factors for HMIS implementation on the one hand, and organizational planning and management considerations on the other, the actual steps including specific activities for HMIS implementation can be specified, directed, monitored, and controlled by project planning and management directives.

This chapter highlights the steps necessary to achieve HMIS implementation success within a healthcare services organizational setting. It draws from previous parts of the book, in particular Chapters 8 through 10, to show how HMIS implementation is no more than an outgrowth

FIGURE 11.1   The Implementation Process.

of strategic planning, systems development, and data stewardship. Even so, with the growing complexity of HMIS applications and the increased investments placed on HMIS projects, all (or most) healthcare services organizations today require that success be a prime criterion in any HMIS implementation effort. We begin with a look at the critical success factors (CSFs) underscoring HMIS implementation.

II. Critical Success Factors for Systems Implementation

Many critical factors have been found to affect the success of HMIS implementation in healthcare services organizations. Top management should focus undue attention on these CSFs before any major HMIS implementation exercise is undertaken. Generally, management should position the organization for HMIS technology adoption. More particularly, management must pay special attention to those factors that are likely barriers or constraints to the implementation process. Minor issues that do not warrant top management consideration can be delegated to middle managers, who can oversee these issues or control them with inputs from top management on an ad hoc basis during the actual implementation. However, there may be times when minor issues are truly major issues in disguise, and if so, these should then be flagged for top management intervention.

   In general, the CSFs for HMIS implementation fall into one of three broad categories: user characteristics, systems design characteristics, and organizational characteristics. Figure 11.2 shows specific examples of factors from each of the three categories that contribute to successful or unsuccessful HMIS implementation.

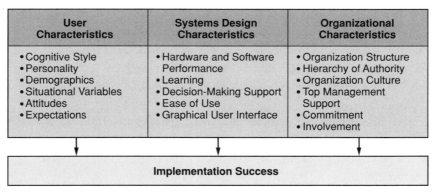

User Characteristics	Systems Design Characteristics	Organizational Characteristics
• Cognitive Style • Personality • Demographics • Situational Variables • Attitudes • Expectations	• Hardware and Software Performance • Learning • Decision-Making Support • Ease of Use • Graphical User Interface	• Organization Structure • Hierarchy of Authority • Organization Culture • Top Management Support • Commitment • Involvement

Implementation Success

FIGURE 11.2   Characteristics of Implementation Success Factors.

User Characteristics

Among the factors believed to influence HMIS success, user characteristics (i.e., the "people problem") are by far the most extensively studied.[2,3] Examples include individual differences such as learning style, cognitive behavior, user attitudes, and user expectations of what the HMIS can do for them.

HMIS implementation often carries with it great expectations. It is not unusual, for instance, to find that many end-users who have little or no direct involvement with system development become disappointed with the final results of HMIS implementation because the end-product does not match their expectations. Indeed, the argument that HMIS applications are a "mirage" is familiar.[4] Clearly, the HMIS solutions are not a panacea, in and of themselves, but the HMIS, if developed properly, will certainly help managers make better choices as well as speed up processes that were previously handled manually. Adopting an attitude that HMIS applications are the ends and not the means sets up impossible goals and expectations that can only result in unfulfilled expectations. Consequently, this is another reason to involve personnel from across all organizational units in HMIS planning and implementation right from the beginning. In so doing, we can generate positive attitudes and feelings among end-users, with realistic expectations that can only enhance successful HMIS implementation. Further, the adoption of a comprehensive user education program can serve to increase the likelihood of meeting operational objectives sought in initial HMIS planning.

Among various personal reactions to HMIS, resistance is the most destructive behavior related to HMIS implementation. Dickson and Simmons noted five factors relating to resistance.[5] First, the greater operating efficiency of HMIS often implies a change in departmental or divisional boundaries and a high potential to eliminate duplicating functions. This can create a sense of fear of job loss among operational and clerical workers. Second, HMIS can affect the informal organizational structure as much as the formal one by creating behavioral disturbances such as doing away with informal interactions. Third, whether individuals will react favorably to HMIS implementation depends on their overall personalities (e.g., younger, inexperienced workers are less likely to resist than older, more experienced ones) and cultural background (e.g., the replacement of interpersonal contacts with human–computer interface). Fourth, the presence of peer pressure and previous experiences with HMIS implementation can also influence the organizational climate for success. Finally, the management techniques used to implement HMIS (e.g., the use of project planning and scheduling methodologies) directly affect user perception of the system.

The recognition of potential dysfunctional user behaviors is a first step toward successful HMIS implementation. User orientation, training, education, and participation are ways to minimize the behavioral problems that may follow the introduction of HMIS in healthcare services organizations.

Systems Design Characteristics

Aside from user characteristics, systems design characteristics also play an important role in determining the eventual HMIS acceptability. Examples here include hardware–software performance, the characteristics of information and decision-making support provided to the user, and systems interface characteristics, such as the availability or incorporation of easy-to-use and easy-to-learn features into the HMIS.

The essential ingredients of any computer-based HMIS are the hardware, software, firmware, and middleware. Common sense dictates that configuration of wares be applicable to the organizational performance and strategies. For an organization's information needs to be satisfied from a systems design perspective, they need to be articulated and documented during the early planning stages and acted upon using tailored implementation techniques. Further, the reliability of hardware, software, and middleware is critical to HMIS performance. It is important to acknowledge, for example, that most information needs demand a certain amount of flexibility, notwithstanding the needs for completeness, accuracy, validity, reliability, frequency, and currency (timeliness) of information to be supplied to the user.[6] Flexibility necessitates an ability to cope with growth and variability in an ever-changing healthcare services environment.

Systems interface is a subject that could fill an entire chapter of its own and has been briefly discussed earlier in one of the *Technology Briefs*. To relate this topic to HMIS implementation, examples are provided. First, HMIS should be designed in the way end-users such as nurses organize themselves. For example, many nurses organize their thoughts about patients by using patient room numbers as a constant frame of reference.[7] Inevitably, when a dietetics system in a hospital uses the alphabet as an organizing scheme, the systems interface becomes inadequate to support the nurses in performing their routines. This has happened in real life, where a group of nurses and clerks who were exposed to the system complained about the time it took to enter diet orders and changes into the HMIS. They became less efficient and increasingly anxious, frustrated, and dissatisfied with the system. The result was to abandon the system unless software would be redesigned to follow through with the patient room number organizing scheme.

Second, HMIS interface design should incorporate favorable factors, such as the proper use of graphics and color.[8] One patient registration system used bright primary colors that were "hard on the eyes" and thus distracting during prolonged use. The system also produced graphics that were difficult to read and interpret. The system was almost abandoned until it was discovered that both the graphics and colors were changeable.

Third, the design of HMIS should consider the users' previous knowledge. For instance, in a long-term care facility, nurses who, for years, had used large desktop screens to register new patient information have found the smaller screen-size bedside monitoring and tracking system extremely cumbersome for entering this information. In that case, the incorporation of a coded identification bracelet placed around the wrists of the patients along with an automated remote scanning device resolved the problem. Nurses quickly embraced the new bedside tracking system in place of the old desktop system.

These cases illustrate the significance of human–computer interface in HMIS implementation success.

Organizational Characteristics

Organizational characteristics can also influence HMIS implementation success. Examples of variables include organizational structure and power, organizational culture, and other managerial factors, such as top management support, commitment, and involvement.

One of the key areas affecting implementation success is the influence of top management. Exercising sound project control, resolving issues in a timely manner, allocating resources accurately, and avoiding short-lived changes in critical areas are all serious management considerations.[9] The strategic alignment of corporate HMIS planning and the application of proper project planning and scheduling can together serve to prevent costly delays in HMIS implementation. Such an alignment also ensures that the organization is not forced into a reactive as opposed to a proactive role.[10] Here, a proactive strategy anticipates industry trends and instills innovative processes for competitive advantages and operational efficiencies, whereas a reactive strategy takes into account current industry trends and chooses to adopt a known process developed elsewhere.

Key strategies to achieve successful HMIS implementation include a realistic situational assessment, accurate identification of necessary resources, and development of an action plan.[11] It is therefore critical to encourage top management involvement in many areas, and there should be a CIO or another knowledgeable senior member of the management team taking charge of HMIS implementation.

HMIS implementation in healthcare services organizations is no different than in business organizations. The degree of commitment and involvement of all end-users and especially the support, commitment, and involvement of top management affect long-term success. All users need to invest their energy in HMIS planning and implementation in order to create a system that is going to be accepted and adopted. Top managers in particular must provide support and act as role models to their subordinates. Potential heavy users, such as middle managers, physicians, nurses, and support staff, also need to be committed and involved in the HMIS implementation process in order to improve the likelihood of its long-term success.[12,13] In short, HMIS success requires inputs that come directly from all users, not just systems professionals.

III. Strategic Planning and Management Issues

Our analysis of CSFs for HMIS implementation reveals a number of critical considerations involved in HMIS planning and management. Often, careful attention to these details in the early planning stages can facilitate the creation of strategies that will enhance HMIS success.

Figure 11.3 shows the various types of planning and management issues that will influence the process and the strategy chosen to optimize HMIS implementation for healthcare services organizations. The key issues to be addressed are staffing issues, organizational project management, reengineering considerations, end-user involvement, and vendor involvement, as well as other additional considerations.

Staffing Issues

HMIS staffing issues can be addressed by first simply asking the question: "Do we have the adequate human resources and HMIS expertise to carry out a successful implementation project?" The answer to this question was articulated in previous discussions, which essentially advocate the use of an internal audit of the current HMIS staffing situation.

For new organizations, HMIS development is relatively straightforward; that is, all individuals with the needed skills are simply to be recruited externally. However, once beyond that, it is a more complicated process. It becomes necessary to identify potential knowledge gaps in HMIS staff that need to be filled. The following are more specific questions that need to be answered.

- Are the current staff members already working at capacity?
- What level of knowledge and skills does the current staff have, and how does this affect recruitment and training?
- How many new staff members will be needed, and when will they be needed?

The answers to these questions enable the planning of staffing strategies to be layered into an HMIS implementation plan. It is critical that these considerations be addressed so that arrangements can be made well in advance to hire the necessary staff or to plan for the needed training.

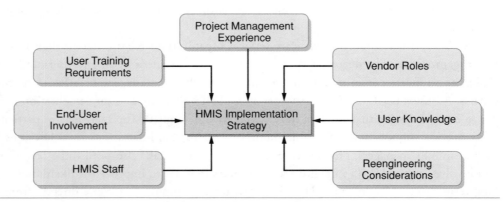

FIGURE 11.3   Planning and Management Issues.

For instance, carrying through with an implementation schedule requires data on the availability of staff members with HMIS expertise for certain periods. Conversely, the training of staff members and the scheduling of recruitment depends on the overall implementation schedule. Clearly, a lack of needed expertise among existing personnel can slow the process of HMIS implementation, often leading to increased pressure and frustration among the existing staff members and possibly resulting in missed opportunities associated with on-time and "seamless" project completion. A projection of future staffing needs is also warranted if the project has a long-term focus.

Although the staffing issues can be resolved at the systems implementation stage, management of healthcare services organizations must establish clear reward policies to encourage the retention of experienced staff members. Gray documented that the demand for new systems personnel of all types grows at a rate of 15 percent per year, whereas the turnover of information systems personnel averages about 20 percent per year.[14] Reducing this high turnover rate can immediately improve productivity and reduce operation costs.

To reward good technical HMIS personnel, health organizations can use a *dual career path* or a *professional stage model*.[15–18] In the former, a pathway of promotions in the technical level is created to parallel the managerial path in rank and salary. For example, a technical staff member would be promoted from programmer to systems analyst, then to systems specialist, and finally to senior analyst and technical specialist. In the latter, the path for promotions can be from apprentice to colleague to mentor to project sponsor.[19] Both models provide significant incentives for the return of experienced staff members past the initial stage of HMIS implementation, thereby sowing the seed for long-term success.

After examining various staffing issues at the system level, an important issue at the individual level—user knowledge—must be briefly examined. HMIS implementation in health organizations requires an assessment of in-house systems and expert knowledge. This assessment should take into account future user needs. Together with staffing needs assessments, management can ascertain the educational requirements of the organization. By doing so, the organization also avoids heavily diverting its resources to educating and training users during and after the online implementation. Thus, educational planning—including general training for managers, technical training for HMIS professionals, and specific end-user training to satisfy the needs of various user groups—helps ensure a smooth and timely HMIS implementation.[20]

Numerous difficulties, both expected and unexpected, associated with the initial three months of online operations can be prevented through proper orientation and HMIS staffing and training. In certain cases, this responsibility can even be off-loaded to software vendors. This approach may be particularly desirable for "turnkey" systems prepackaged and serviced by a single vendor. However, the costs in the long run can be significant.

Alternatively, if the organizational structure is capable of supporting this role with an internal training department and knowledgeable personnel, it may be more cost-effective to provide the staff education in-house. If in-house training is to be conducted, the training personnel should be able to distinguish between two levels of training—holistic training and technical training. *Holistic* (or *ideological*) *training* here refers to training modules focused on the systems, and not the operational, perspective. Systems goals and benefits, systems constraints and limitations, organizational effects, and functional implications are sample topics for this level of training. In short, holistic training intends to bring the entire system into view and to analyze its relationship with its surrounding elements (the macro view). This kind of training should be directed primarily to managerial staff, who need to view HMIS in its entirety, and secondarily to operational staff, who are more concerned with the day-to-day operations (the micro view).

Technical (or *operational*) *training* is aimed at familiarizing the appropriate personnel with the operational aspects of HMIS that pertain to their tasks. This level of training may encapsulate such topics as completing forms, report abstracting, data-coding standards, data validation, standard data input or update procedures, and introduction of routine tasks. This kind of training is directed primarily to technical or operational staff, who are concerned with daily use of HMIS, and secondarily to managerial staff, who also need to know the procedures of their subordinates.

In any event, it should be recognized that the use of a team approach in-house does have the added benefit of increasing user acceptance and reducing resistance in the long run. Regardless of how a healthcare services organization is planning to conduct the needed staff training, the quality of the training should be stressed, because well-managed training for HMIS operations has the potential to reduce anxiety and potential user resistance and to promote an organizational climate toward HMIS implementation success.

Organizational Project Management

The style of project management is extremely dependent on the organizational culture and on the depth of experienced personnel who are available to manage such a process. In many instances, experienced project managers with both technical and application knowledge are difficult to find. Consequently, outside consultants are often used. However, time is needed to educate these consultants on specific situational and historical characteristics, both internally and externally, that can at times be significant enough to make outside consultation counterproductive. As within the healthcare services organization, there is often a trade-off. Although team or committee management of the implementation process provides the benefits of internal knowledge, user acceptance, and overall effectiveness of implementation,[21] the need for a fresh look from an external, unbiased perspective should not be overlooked.

Although it is difficult to make specific recommendations with respect to HMIS implementation, certain techniques are useful in project management. Here, a brief examination is given to some of the commonly used techniques for project scheduling and program coding. To ensure that the system implementation is completed by a certain date, a detailed and realistic schedule needs to be prepared and followed at the initial and subsequent planning stages. At the same time, the schedule should be flexible enough to accommodate some unexpected delays. Moreover, a detailed timetable for implementation is often essential to inspire management confidence in the installation plan. Here, two techniques to assist project scheduling are discussed—the critical path method (CPM) and Gantt charts.

When using the CPM, the duration of all the tasks involved and the sequence (indicated by arrows) of all tasks need to be compiled in a network representation, as shown in Figure 11.4.

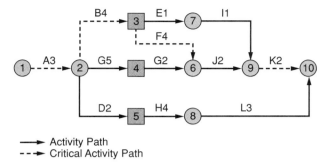

— Activity Path
- - - Critical Activity Path

FIGURE 11.4   A System Implementation Schedule in a Network Representation for the Critical Path Determination.

Note: Letter–numbered pairs represent the name of the path and the amount of time (in days) it takes to travel it. For example, "A3" indicates that path A takes 3 days.

In the figure, the numbers in circles represent different stages of implementation, the letters represent different tasks involved, and the numbers beside the letters represent the number of days needed to complete the task.

After translating the implementation schedule into a network representation, the critical path of the network can then be determined. The critical path is the sequence of activities that will take the longest period to complete. The time needed to complete all the activities on this critical path is the minimum period required to complete the entire project. Figure 11.5 lists all the possible paths (activities in sequence) and the time needed to complete each. In this example, the path through activities A-B-F-J-K is the longest, requiring 15 days for completion. This is therefore the critical path of the project. In other words, the project cannot be completed in less than 15 days unless certain tasks are started early or shortened.

Another way of representing the details in Figures 11.4 and 11.5 is to use Gantt charts, which represent project tasks with bar charts. They are often easier to construct and understand than CPM but may capture and generate less information. Figure 11.6 shows a Gantt chart for the same project described. It is worth mentioning that the exact start and end dates of certain noncritical tasks can be moved without causing delay to the overall schedule. For instance,

Path	Days Required
A → B → E → I → K	11
A → B → F → J → K	(15)
A → C → G → J → K	14
A → D → H → L	12

FIGURE 11.5   Possible Paths through the Critical Path Network in Figure 11.4.

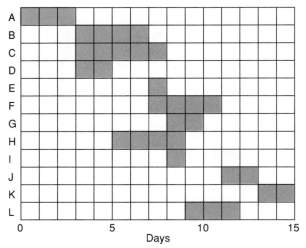

FIGURE 11.6   A Gannt Chart Representation of the System Implementation Schedule in Figure 11.4.

if every other task in Figure 11.5 commences and finishes on time, task L can be postponed for a day without delaying the final completion date.

Program coding, or simply *programming*, refers to the process of writing instructions that the computer system can execute directly. This is usually a very labor-intensive task, and as a result, coordination among programmers needs to be emphasized. Here, two useful coordination techniques—data dictionaries and walkthroughs—are introduced.

Data dictionaries, containing definitions and proper uses of entities that are in alphabetical order, can be computerized or manually compiled. Data dictionaries should also have the identities of database programs used; the names of all the data fields found in the database, along with the names of the programmers that use them; and descriptions of the data and the personnel responsible for the data. Just like regular dictionaries, data dictionaries are useful in program coding coordination, because they allow the names of data elements to be cross-referenced, help programmers locate blocks of codes that are reusable in new applications rapidly, and ensure that all codes are consistent with the overall application.

Another very useful tool in program coding is conducting a *walkthrough* (or *review*). A walkthrough can take place at various stages of program design and development. It is essentially peer evaluation and testing of a programmer's work, with the primary objective of soliciting constructive feedback. In other words, walkthroughs act as control points in programming, making sure that what is programmed is in line with specific goals and objectives and other operational constraints. It is not in any way directed personally at the programmer.

Reengineering Considerations

Often when new HMIS applications are implemented, work flows and processes may also change drastically because of the inherent differences of daily operations with the computerization.

Even without the changes as a result of computerization, users may still find changes to daily operations as their tasks at work gradually change from time to time. Whereas adequate training initially helps better prepare end-users for some of these changes, end-user involvement in the reengineering process can greatly enhance satisfaction with computerization. This again relates to the importance of the "people aspect" in HMIS.

To gain maximum benefit from HMIS implementation, all operations must be redesigned periodically to accommodate environmental changes and maximize operational benefits, while still maintaining the necessary controls in the process. If the delivery systems are not reengineered to meet new organizational needs, the increase in efficiency brought about by the HMIS implementation may be offset by the unmet demands in the environment.

Often, it is inefficient simply to automate old systems processes, because computerization lends itself to a new workflow, thus demanding extra personnel and resources. A good example of this is the attempt to automate patient charts to mimic paper-based systems currently in place. This document is primarily a legal document on paper, but once captured in HMIS, it can become a much more versatile tool. Very often, healthcare services organizations are reluctant to rely totally on HMIS and therefore opt to keep the paper copy for backup. Therefore, health professionals are required to continue filling out these forms manually, which essentially is a duplication of effort, thus creating an unnecessary workload.

To decide how HMIS operations (or parts thereof) are to be reengineered, it is useful to solicit inputs from the staff already acquainted with existing procedures. Team or committee forums on system-supported group decision settings are excellent means to decide what should or should not be modified. This leads us to the topic of end-user involvement.

End-User Involvement

In healthcare services organizations, HMIS planning and development are recognized to be slow compared with the rapid pace of change in the business world. However, lessons learned in the business sector have been found especially useful; one such lesson is the empowerment of end-users through their involvement in systems planning and design.

HMIS planning and development require active (not passive) end-user involvement throughout the entire process in order for implementation to be truly successful. It has been recognized that unless HMIS staff, physicians, and nurses are involved in systems planning and ongoing evaluation, HMIS success will be short-lived.[22] In fact, in the healthcare services system, which consists of a much broader group of individuals representing many technical and professional groups, it seems wise to extend this to users of all the different modules or areas of HMIS. For this to materialize, adequate time and resources need to be allotted, and critical committees and internal and external liaisons have to be established such that all aspects of HMIS can be optimized while generating organizationwide user acceptance.

Specific considerations with respect to acceptance of end-users include the effect of the change on the need satisfaction of the affected personnel, the position of those affected, and the leadership style of those managing the change. Furthermore, direct involvement of application program vendors, which is the next topic of discussion, is often of critical importance.

Vendor Involvement

The traditional view that vendors specialize only in sales of equipment or computer software is fast giving way to the realities of the vendors of today. Although the primary function of computer systems vendors is and will continue to be the actual equipment sale, there is rapidly increasing emphasis on the sale of "services" beyond the realm of equipment maintenance. In other words, vendors can be—and in fact very often are—involved in some degree of systems development and implementation, including HMIS implementation. IBM is a prime example of such a vendor.

The options with respect to the roles of vendors vary between two extremes. Here the term *vendor* usually refers only to software vendors because they dictate much of the implementation. However, the hardware vendor is also important when considering outsourcing HMIS services. On the one hand, there can be complete turnkey implementation by the software vendor (turnkey systems are prepackaged, ready-to-go application programs that are often products supplied by a single vendor). On the other hand, there is the option of exercising complete in-house organizational control. Between these extremes lies the most used option, a blend of vendor and organizational responsibilities, with each performing in areas of specialty to tailor the process to the needs of the HMIS implementation.

Depending on the strengths of the organization and the vendor, areas of responsibility that can be shared include analyst support, project management, user training, hardware and facilities planning, software modification, interface development, conversion assistance, procedure development, and implementation audits. The means through which vendors can be involved vary from one organization to another. In some cases, a single vendor acts as the sole handling agent for all technical problems and even some user training; in others, several vendors may have to cooperate to deal with systems problems.

Nevertheless, there are generally six steps through which a healthcare services organization can solicit and apply useful inputs from vendors.

1. Initial conceptualization.
2. Strategic planning.
3. Feasibility study.
4. Request for proposals.
5. Proposal evaluation and selection.
6. Physical implementation.

These, as well as post-implementation upkeep issues, are outlined later in the chapter.

Additional Considerations

A few other considerations that are not often described in the literature can help ensure smooth HMIS implementation. The first of these is related to the concept of quality. Several methodologies can be adapted to address quality in the healthcare services delivery industry. The methodology continuum consists of quality control, quality assurance, continuous quality improvement, total quality management, Six Sigma, and reengineering. Depending on the organization's information status, implementation may be facilitated by the inclusion of any one of these principles.

Another consideration that needs to be taken into account pertains to the manner in which healthcare services organizations have been changing the way they measure performance. Many organizations are progressing from an efficiency and throughput approach to an effectiveness and outcome measurement approach. Experiencing the economic pressure perceived by many businesses, healthcare services organizations are also increasingly being pressured to link the utilization of various healthcare resources to their level of outcome and demand and, in many cases, to justify the utilization with the outcome produced.

Although almost all organizations are run differently with respect to performance measurements, management styles can directly affect HMIS implementation. For example, the structure of management within organizations—such as departmental organization, program management, matrix design, hierarchical design, and circular design—can influence HMIS implementation. In keeping with the changing priorities in the healthcare services delivery system, there has been a demonstrated need for more highly integrated and interoperable HMIS.[23] Thus, it is critical to keep these considerations in mind when making decisions regarding any HMIS implementation project.

It is also crucial to keep in mind that leadership roles exhibited by the CEO and the CIO can affect the success of HMIS implementation. Information technology, therefore, needs to be integrated from the cultural perspective of an organization. For this to occur, both the CEO and CIO must leverage HMIS in achieving the goals and objectives of the organization and communicate this effectively within the organization.

In particular, Austin has called attention to several areas that should be addressed when monitoring and evaluating HMIS implementation: productivity, user utility, value chain, competitive performance, business alignment, investment targeting, and management vision.[24] Although it is recognized that these criteria suit profit-oriented organizations, several seem equally applicable to nonprofit healthcare services organizations.

IV. Systems Implementation

Regardless of the strategies utilized in HMIS implementation, there are several steps most healthcare services organizations should take in order to optimize internal and external processes in a manner that ensures an efficient and effective outcome. In general, these steps fall into two broad stages: pre-implementation preparation and post-implementation upkeep, each of which is now discussed in greater detail.

Pre-Implementation Preparation

The stage of pre-implementation preparation begins with the initial HMIS conceptualization and ends with the initial online operation of the system. The major steps included are initial conceptualization, strategic planning, feasibility study, request for proposal, proposal evaluation and selection, and physical implementation.

Initial conceptualization can take place in a variety of ways. For instance, the CEO of a long-term care facility may be impressed by another healthcare services organization's HMIS in the same community or regional area; the board of directors of a health facility may have discussed HMIS in their 10-year plan; staff members of a health maintenance organization (HMO) may complain about their aging islands of technological applications. In short, the initial conceptualization represents a genuine wish to consolidate and improve the information flows, data storage, and information exchange capabilities in a healthcare services organization.

As stated previously, incorporating organizational *strategic planning* into HMIS strategic plans is a desirable milestone in any HMIS implementation. HMIS development must be based on a strategic information plan that is aligned with the organization's mission, vision, goals, and objectives. Adopting a strategic approach helps focus measurable goals and objectives for IS/IT implementation that best suit internal and external information needs. Only in this way can the necessary factors and considerations (such as outcome measurement, future technological change, networking, and process reengineering) be included.

Once strategic information planning is completed, a *feasibility study* can be carried out. In general, this study aims to determine the extent to which the implementation and the HMIS upkeeps are feasible. It includes results from various meetings with the board, middle management, and even staff members who are likely to be affected (user involvement) to solicit their input. It also incorporates financial (how much is available) and physical (whether the facility is too crowded for extra equipment) feasibility research. Moreover, the feasibility study can also make recommendations on the schedule of implementation, its speed, and other issues of concern. In many healthcare services organizations, the reports for the feasibility study need to be approved or endorsed by the board of trustees. In these cases, the feasibility study report also acts as project proposals subject to extensive inquiries. The study reports should always be produced professionally and should be subjected to peer review.

Following the feasibility study, the detailed goals and objectives for the HMIS project can be outlined on the basis of an internal and external needs assessment. Needs assessment makes it possible to formulate a *request for proposal* (RFP) for the various hardware and/or software vendors to submit bids. The RFP can include details on the organization, its information needs, and the specifics of the organization's goals and objectives that the system is expected to fulfill. When vendor replies are received, it is then possible to correlate proposals on the basis of such internal objectives as budget and infrastructure compatibility issues in terms of existing hardware and software. This leads to the next stage of proposal evaluation and selection, which is followed by physical implementation. Separate discussion sections are dedicated to each of these important steps.

Proposal Evaluation and Selection

As soon as all the proposals have been submitted, it is time to evaluate them to make a selection. In the *proposal evaluation and selection* process, two methods commonly used are benchmark tests and the vendor rating system. In a benchmark test, the healthcare services organization provides the vendors with a set of mock data. This set of data then acts as inputs in a prototype of the proposed system. The prototype system then simulates the performance of the real system using this list of computations. The actual performance of the prototypes is then compared with the prespecified standards for evaluation.

Benchmark testing attempts to create an environment that is as close to the real clinical setting as possible. As the prototypes are being tested, it is not uncommon to find that the real, constructed system may, in fact, perform at a lower level due to the heavy load of information to be processed in real life. Nevertheless, benchmark testing gives the organization a "concrete" feel for what the system would look like and how it would function (to some extent) in the clinical setting. In comparison, the *vendor rating system* is simply one in which the vendors are quantitatively scored as to how well their proposed systems perform against a list of weighted criteria. Commonly used criteria include user friendliness, data management, graphical and reporting capabilities, forecasting and statistical analysis capabilities, modeling, hardware and operating system considerations, vendor support, and cost factors.

The importance of the "people" aspect to the success of HMIS implementation cannot be overemphasized. As a direct consequence, user friendliness should be a prime concern when evaluating system proposals from vendors. User friendliness can be manifested in a variety of ways. The consistency of language command, the use of natural language and touch screens, automatic grammar checker and spelling correction, and the availability of the "Help" and "Undo" commands are examples of user-friendly hardware and software features. Moreover, menus and prompts, novice and expert modes, spreadsheet display of data and results, as well as what-you-see-is-what-you-get features also contribute to the user friendliness of the system.

Designed as advanced "data-processing" facilities, HMIS should have adequate data management tools to handle the massive volumes of data to be processed in the day-to-day operation of a healthcare services organization. Such features as a common database manager, data security measures (log-in password, etc.), simultaneous access (without significant trade-off in performance), data selection, data dictionaries, and data validation should be supported and included. The primary HMIS function is to produce timely and accurate information for making intelligent healthcare decisions. Accordingly, HMIS should have the capability to generate standard and custom reports; to generate basic graphical plots and three-dimensional charts; to allow multicolor support and the integration of graphical and text files; and to allow compatibility and interoperability with existing graphics devices, the legacy systems, the Internet, new organizational IS/IT applications, or other electronic devices.

An important theme emphasized throughout this latest edition of our HMIS text is systems integration and interoperability. The selection of HMIS should take this matter into consideration. In practice, this can be viewed in terms of hardware and operating system considerations. Compatibility with various operating systems (icon-based versus command-based), microcomputer support, compatibility with workstation requirements, and printer and plotter support, as well as server and network compatibility, should also be considered when selecting HMIS. Even so, the interoperability most likely is a matter of software or middleware capabilities. As noted in previous chapters, Web services and open-source systems provide interoperable solutions to many islands of HMIS and legacy systems.

Finally, vendor involvement can positively influence HMIS implementation. In selecting HMIS, the amount of vendor support can definitely be a valid selection criterion. Vendor support can be provided in a variety of ways: consultation, training, active research and development, maintenance of local branch offices, technical support personnel, and continuing enhancements. Also, the financial stability and credibility of the vendor should be confirmed before reaching a final decision.

Probably the most important factor for all health organizations is the cost. In evaluating HMIS proposals, it would be very helpful to bear in mind how the costs are calculated and which items are or are not included. A modular pricing approach combined with some form of "packaged offer" is one of the more common approaches. In this case, the management should pay particular attention to the initial license fees, license renewal fees, maintenance arrangements, documentation, and resource utilization, as well as to hidden conversion costs. Certainly, the cost of training and staffing has to be estimated by the management itself.

Figure 11.7 presents a sample evaluation sheet used in a vendor rating system. Note that although these criteria are generally applicable to all healthcare services organizations, specific criteria are more important to each organization by virtue of its unique environment. These should be specified separately and weighted accordingly.

VENDOR RATING

Vendor: Proposed System:

Criteria	Weight	Score	Weighted Score	Criteria	Weight	Score	Weighted Score
User Friendliness • Language Command • Help Command • Undo Function • Others: _____				**Data Management** • Common Database Manager • Security • Simultaneous Access • Others: _____			
Reports and Graphs • Report Format • Basic Graphs • Graph Previews • Others: _____				**Forecasts and Statistics** • Linear Regression • Multiple Regression • Curve Fitting • Others: _____			
Modeling • Mathematical Functions • User-Defined Functions • Procedural Logic • Others: _____				**Hardware and Operating System** • Hardware Compatibility • Operating System Compatibility • Workstation Compatibility • Others: _____			
Vendor Support • Consultation • Training • Technical Support • Others: _____				**Cost Factors** • Total Budget • Leveraged Payment • Maintenance Cost • Others: _____			

Total Score:

Additional Comments:

Evaluated By: _____   Signed: _____   Date: _____

FIGURE 11.7   Sample Evaluation Sheet for HMIS Proposal.

Physical Implementation

Once the vendors are chosen, a contract is signed, thereby beginning the *physical implementation* stage—the stage when the most "action" takes place. This stage actually consists of several steps, including recruitment of personnel, training of staff, acquisition of equipment, installation of equipment, uploading of initial data, system testing, documentation, and on-line implementation.

All these steps are performed in a logical progression (some carried out simultaneously), depending on the needs of the organization and how these are reflected in decisions based on the described factors and considerations. The keys to a smooth implementation process are effective planning and project management. Some variations may be necessary, depending on the differences in each organization, but some common steps (including some earlier steps) in initial HMIS implementation are shown in Figure 11.8.

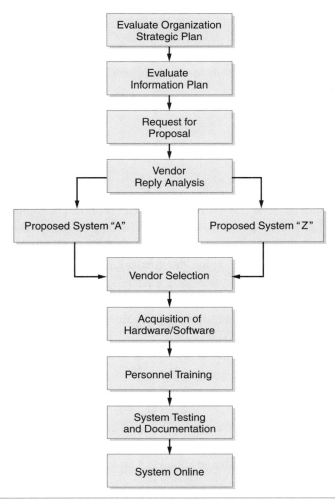

FIGURE 11.8   Common Steps of Initial Implementation of an HMIS.

Among these steps, the recruitment of HMIS personnel and training of existing staff members have already been discussed. The modes of acquisition and installation of the equipment are highly dependent on the characteristics of each health organization, as well as on the contract between the vendor and the management. In addition, whether the equipment is acquired over some period or at the same time ultimately depends on the payment scheme agreed upon by the vendors and the management.

The uploading of initial data and systems testing are sometimes conducted simultaneously. The initial sets of data are used to test whether the system is functioning at the desired level. If there are any significant discrepancies between the predesignated level of performance and the actual level, the system may have to be modified. Accordingly, there should be ample time allotted to these two steps.

Very often, documentation can proceed simultaneously with systems testing because the structural layout of the system is already fixed. Any additional modifications along the way can then be documented as updates or memos. Ideally, there should be at least one copy of the master documentation with details on how to operate the system at the technical level and on how to manage the system at the tactical and strategic levels. The distributing copies as well as the master copy should be updated periodically, incorporating the ad hoc updates or memos.

Online implementation involves four common approaches:

1. Parallel approach.
2. Phased approach.
3. Pilot approach.
4. Cutover approach.

In the *parallel approach*, systems activities are duplicated; the old system and the new system are both operated simultaneously for a time so that their results can be compared. In the *phased approach*, different functional parts of the new system become operative one after another. This approach is relatively safe and less expensive than the parallel approach because the systems are not duplicated. The *pilot approach* requires the installation of the new system in sites that are representative of the complete system (e.g., in a small geographical area). This means that certain locations or departments are to serve as "alpha" pilot test sites first, followed by other "beta" pilot sites or departments until all sites operate under the new system. The *cutover approach* is also called the "cold turkey" or "burned bridges" approach. Essentially, this approach requires the organization to "flip the switch" to the new system all at once. If the results are not satisfactory, the system can be revised and activated again.

Figure 11.9 gives a diagrammatic representation of the four common approaches to online implementation. As to which approach is most suitable, it depends directly on the specific environment of each health service organization. For instance, the general level of HMIS knowledge in the staff, the availability of resources for systems implementation, and the amount of data handled per day will and should all affect the choice of online implementation approach.

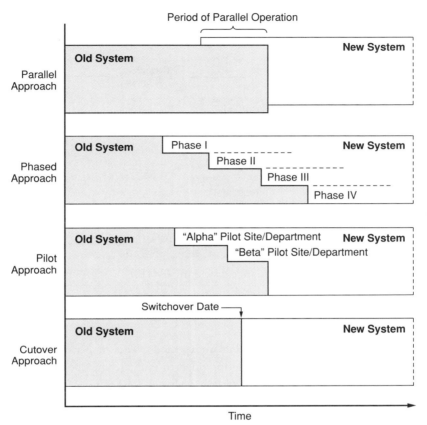

FIGURE 11.9   Common Approaches to Online Implementation.

Post-Implementation Upkeep

Although full, online HMIS implementation is a prominent milestone, it is definitely not the end of the story. Once the HMIS become operational, ongoing maintenance kicks in—good maintenance is essential to achieve implementation success in the long run.

In general, ongoing upkeep is required because of problems within the system and changes in the environment. Problems within the system may be errors that have not been discovered by previous tests or may develop primarily because of an unexpectedly heavy workload. Changes in the environment include those in related systems, such as in inventory order systems, and those in the organization of human resources. In many cases, simply because of the length of time it takes to develop HMIS, there are some deviations between the initial planning and final production; these deviations also contribute to the need for close post-implementation monitoring.

Regardless of why the system needs to be maintained and modified, the maintenance cycle depicted in Figure 11.10 captures the major steps involved.

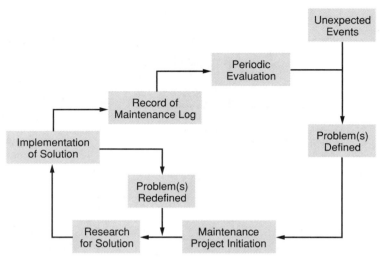

FIGURE 11.10 A Sample Maintenance Cycle for HMIS.

Problems are usually discovered in either unexpected events or periodic systems evaluations. Post-audits (or post-evaluations) are intended to evaluate the operational characteristics of the system, thereby acting as control points throughout the operation of the system. Once the problem is defined, a maintenance project can be initiated. Very often, because of creativity and the uncertainty involved, this type of project is relatively unstructured, characterized by numerous attempts to search for the ultimate "ideal" solution. Here, the concepts of *IT services management*, which are highlighted in the next section, are very useful. After a feasible solution is found, it is then implemented and tested. If the problem is still not completely solved, it may need to be redefined. Attempts to search for an acceptable solution are then resumed. If the problem is solved, the project can be completed by making notations on maintenance logs and by producing the appropriate documentation for circulation.

It is also worth noting that documentation does not just take place at the end of the maintenance cycle. Rather, it occurs throughout the entire cycle in the form of documentation of problems, written requests for change, and memos on possible sources of problems and solutions. The documentation at the end of the cycle therefore emphasizes the incorporation of all these forms and memos into a mini-report that can be used for future reference or for incorporation into the system manual.

Figure 11.11 recaptures the main steps of the overall schema of HMIS implementation. Throughout the entire implementation process (both pre-implementation preparation and post-implementation upkeep), active involvement of both the users and the managers cannot be overemphasized, for reasons described earlier.

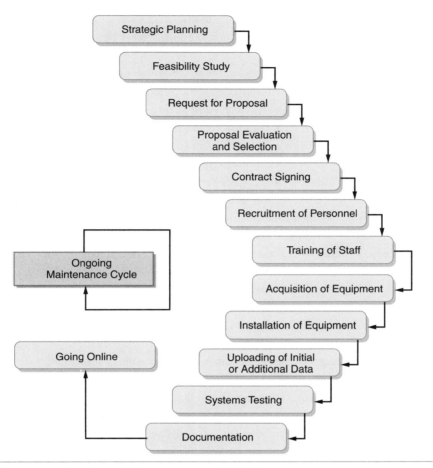

FIGURE 11.11   The Overall Schema of an HMIS Implementation.

V. IT Services Management Concepts

After examining the various steps of HMIS implementation, we now turn to an emerging field relating to the upkeep of HMIS products after these have been implemented: IT services management concepts.

At present, a growing number of governmental bodies in the United Kingdom and non-profit organizations around the world have been formed to assist in the establishment of best practices in IT services management based on core principles of ITIL® standards and guidelines. ITIL, a registered community trademark of the Office of Government Commerce (OGC) that stands for IT Infrastructure Library, is essentially a set of publications that together offers a framework of "best practices" management guidance for all aspects of IT services.

Major categories include guidance for planning to implement service management, the business perspective, IT infrastructure management, application management, service delivery, service support, and security management.

In this text, concepts of HMIS strategic *planning and implementation* have been covered primarily from a general organizational and management perspective, but not specifically along the IT service management perspective, which emphasizes a continuous service quality improvement process. Nonetheless, key processes underpinning IT services planning, implementation, and management are akin to those of HMIS planning, implementation, and review—beginning with a vision; assessing the external marketplace and scouting the environments to surmise the best and most appropriate strategies that should be considered to improve expected outcomes; providing strong leadership support and directions to subordinates whenever possible and practical to do so; striking a balance among the different roles played by human resources, technology, and culture within the boundaries of an organization; setting goals; deciding on measurable targets; conducting process improvement cycles; and achieving goals based on specific predetermined measures and metrics.

The *business perspective* essentially conveys the message of the need for aligning IT goals and objectives with the broader corporate goals and objectives. To achieve a well-knitted alignment, the processes emphasized by ITIL include: (1) building long-term business relationships and recognizing the value chain as part of the business partnership management; (2) enhancing supplier relationships, including supply chain management; (3) reviewing, planning, and developing IT applications as these applications relate to the business goals and objectives; and (4) providing liaison, education, and communication on IT services so as to influence, gain support, and achieve changes through IT services for greater business competitive advantage. Many of these concepts have also been covered throughout parts of this new edition of the text.

In the domain of *IT infrastructure management*, IT managers are challenged to managing appropriately the people, products, processes, and partners (4 *P*s) associated with IT services throughout the different HMIS life cycle stages. The key steps include, but are not limited to, feasibility analysis, systems requirements, design specifications, software development, testing, implementation, operation, review, and retirement. All aspects of infrastructure management and administration, design and planning, technical support, and operational deployment are covered. The IT infrastructure manager coordinates among the different players to ensure that all necessary support processes are in place to aid service efficiencies and the effective use of IT services throughout daily operations, during periods of change management, and when in crisis management situations. Various aspects of these concepts relating to HMIS planning and management have been discussed and illustrated in earlier sections of this and the previous few chapters.

In the domain of *application management*, it is important to relate service management concepts to application development and management in that all deployed applications should be designed for services. In this sense, all applications have to be more flexible, scalable, interoperationable, available, reliable, maintainable, manageable, usable, and in compliance with design specifications and organizational requirements. Service management is concerned with the activities relating to the release, delivery, support, and optimization of the application. Again, a critical theme emphasized throughout this text has been the interoperability of HMIS applications and the management of systems that do not support interoperability.

In the domain of *service delivery*, various forward-looking delivery aspects of IT servicing are covered, including availability management, capacity management, financial management for IT services, IT service continuity management, and service-level management. Availability ensures that IT services are reliable, available, secure, serviceable, and able to be maintained. It is the key to quality servicing in IT service management. Capacity management ensures that employee requests for capacity to meet business needs and goals are given priority consideration at all times. Financial management sees IT servicing run as a business within the larger corporate business operation. In other words, employees and technicians are both cost-conscious about IT services and will minimize future expenditures by trying to take care of problems in the best way possible to the extent that these problems can be eliminated once and for all. IT service continuity management entails setting in place a recovery plan for crisis situations management and ensuring that a certain level of servicing be made available within an agreed-upon work schedule to minimize any unnecessary work disruption. Finally, service-level management (SLM) refers to the satisfactory delivery of services on a daily operational level based on the service-level agreement (SLA) acceptable to the organization.

In the domain of *service support*, daily maintenance and support services are covered, including (1) incident management, where incident reports are filed with the support personnel manning the computer help line or help desk; (2) problem management, where a proactive approach is taken to reduce the adverse impacts from the same problem or persistent incidents; (3) change management, where a more centralized approach is taken at a higher level to control persistent problems; (4) release management, in which new releases are being considered due to major changes so as to reduce work discontinuity and improve business processes; and (5) configuration management, where IT assets such as the centralized or enterprisewide databases are being managed for the successful running of the enterprise.

In the domain of *security management*, the IT services management must institute a security policy to ensure all personnel are aware of the significance of protecting IT assets and information resources and conduct risk analyses from time to time throughout the life cycle of the IT servicing, including planning and implementation, operation, evaluation, and auditing. Topics on regulatory policies related to the release and protection of health information and HMIS resources have also been covered separately in the *Policy Brief* accompanying Chapter 12 of this text.

VI. Conclusion

In summary, successful HMIS implementation and the continual evolution of HMIS as the information backbone of healthcare services organizations are the ultimate objectives of the healthcare services delivery field. Among the various steps along the path from initial conceptualization to physical implementation to operation, the stage wherein HMIS acceptance resides in the spotlight of organizationwide attention seems to be the post-implementation stage. This is when the employees of the organization are truly milking HMIS to perform key task activities and achieving the goals of the corporation. But it is also here that IT services management concepts play a most critical role to determine if HMIS will be of value to assist the healthcare services organization attain the goals of high-quality healthcare services delivery.

This chapter has discussed various concerns to be addressed in HMIS implementation and some general steps involved. It is, however, not expected that managers of all healthcare services organizations follow the same steps and address the same concerns in an identical fashion. Rather, it is hoped that the chapter has provided the "essentials" for healthcare managers and planners as well as health administration students interested in HMIS implementation or expansion to oversee new projects in HMIS such as an integration of new systems with legacy systems. With the lessons learned, the students will then be able to adapt this global knowledge to schemes suitable to the special environment of each healthcare services organization.

Notes

1. Maureen McKinney, "Louisiana Rural Health Information Exchange Counts First Success," May 20, 2008, http://www.digitalhcp.com/2008/05/20/larhix-pilot.html.
2. J. E. Toole and M. E. Caine, "Laying a Foundation for the Future Information Systems," *Topics in Health Care Financing* 14, no. 2 (1988): 17–27.
3. R. W. Zmud, "Individual Differences and MIS Success: A Review of the Empirical Literature," *Management Science* 25, no. 10 (1979): 966–979.
4. J. Dearden, "MIS Is a Mirage," *Harvard Business Review* 50, no. 1 (1972): 90–99.
5. G. Dickson and J. Simmons, "The Behavioral Side of MIS: Five Factors Relating to Resistance," *Business Horizons* 13, no. 4 (1970): 59–71.
6. K. Kropf, *San Bernadino County Medical Center Implementation of a Hospital Information System* (New York: New York University, 1990): 7–8.
7. M. Staggers, "Human Factors: The Missing Element in Computer Technology," *Computers in Nursing* 9, no. 2 (1991): 47–49.
8. J. K. H. Tan, "Graphics-Based Health Decision Support Systems: Conjugating Theoretical Perspectives to Guide the Design of Graphics and Redundant Codes in HDSS Interfaces." In *Health Decision Support Systems*, J. K. H. Tan with S. Sheps, Eds. (Gaithersburg, MD: Aspen Publishers, 1998).
9. R. Lemon and J. Crudele, "System Integration: Tying It All Together," *Healthcare Financial Management* 41, no. 6 (1987): 46–54.
10. H. Austin, "Assessing the Performance of Information Technology," *Computers in Health Care* 9, no. 11 (1988): 56–58.
11. Ibid.
12. R. J. Feldman, "System Evaluation and Implementation Strategies." In *Information Systems for Ambulatory Care*, T. A. Matson and M. D. McDougall, Eds. (Chicago: American Hospital Publishing, 1990): 67–78.
13. H. W. Ryan, "User-Driven Systems Development: Defining a New Role for IS," *Information Systems Management* (Summer 1993): 66–68.
14. S. Gray, "DP Salary Survey," *Datamation* 28, no. 11 (1982): 114–128.
15. J. Couger and R. Zawacki, "What Motivates DP Professionals," *Datamation* 24, no. 9 (1978): 116–123.
16. K. Bartol and D. Martin, "Managing Information Systems Personnel: A Review of the Literature and Managerial Implications," *MIS Quarterly*, Special Issue (1982): 49–70.
17. J. Couger and M. A. Colter, *Motivation of the Maintenance Programmer* (Colorado Springs, CO: CYSCS, 1983).

18. J. Baroudi, "The Impact of Role Variables on Information Systems Personnel Work Attitudes and Intentions," *MIS Quarterly* 9, no. 4 (1985): 341–356.

19. K. C. Laudon and J. P. Laudon, *Management Information Systems: A Contemporary Perspective* (New York: Macmillan Publishing, 1988): 698.

20. C. J. Austin and S. B. Boxerman, *Information Systems for Health Service Administration*, 5th ed. (Ann Arbor, MI: AUPHA Press/Health Administration Press, 1998).

21. Feldman (1990).

22. Ryan (1993).

23. Lemon and Crudele (1987).

24. Austin (1988).

25. D. M. Robinson, "Patient Access to Health Records: New Legal Developments and Implementations," *Healthcare Communication and Computing Canada* (4th Quarter 1992): 54–60.

26. D. M. Robinson, "Health Information Confidentiality: Balancing Extremes," *Healthcare Communication and Computing Canada* (3rd Quarter 1991): 8–9.

Chapter Questions

11–1. What are some of the critical success factors in HMIS implementation?

11–2. Why is careful planning so important to HMIS implementation?

11–3. With respect to HMIS staffing, what are some of the major concerns for HMIS planners?

11–4. Describe some useful tools in HMIS implementation project management.

11–5. Why is end-user involvement important in HMIS implementation? How can end-users be more involved in the process?

11–6. What are the key concepts underlying IT services management? Why are these various concepts important, and how do these relate to the HMIS post-implementation stage?

Health Management Information System Standards, Policy, Governance, and Future

Health Management Information System Standards:
Standards Adoption in Healthcare Information Technologies

*Sanjay P. Sood, Sandhya Keeroo, Victor W. A. Mbarika,
Nupur Prakash, and Joseph Tan*

Editor's Note: Part IV (Chapters 12, 13, and 14) acquaints readers with HMIS standards, governance, policy, and future. Part IV begins with Chapter 12 on HMIS standards—a topic of increasing significance for HMIS students, practitioners, and researchers. Major standards relating to data-coding standards (vocabulary), data-schema standards (structure and content), data-exchange standards (messaging), and Web standards that work toward a common language for sharing health information electronically among care providers are covered. This chapter also links to earlier parts of the text relating to HMIS foundational concepts about use of data for managerial decision making and for online health data searches (Part I); HMIS technology and applications on databases, community health networks, and data integration via Web services (Part II); and HMIS planning, data stewardship, and systems management (Part III).

CHAPTER OUTLINE

Scenario: *HHS to Form Standards, Operability Group to Spur Health IT Adoption*

Scenario: HHS to Form Standards, Operability Group to Spur Health IT Adoption[1]

Mike Leavitt, who served as U.S. Department of Health and Human Services (HHS) Secretary during President George W. Bush's second term, championed the creation and development of a national collaboration in terms of standards adoption in order to aid rapid health information exchange and the diffusion of health information technologies (IT) among U.S. healthcare facilities. Such a vision was to lead the way for achieving interoperable medical information systems and to further motivate patients and healthcare providers such as nurses, doctors, hospitals, insurance companies, and employers to agree on standards for electronic health records (EHR).

An EHR is essentially a digital database of a patient's medical history and clinical information. Such patient data could include patient demographics, vital signs, immunizations, diagnosed medical conditions, lab test results, and ordered prescriptions. "The use of electronic health records and other information technology will transform our health care system by reducing medical errors, minimizing paperwork hassles, lowering costs and improving quality of care," Leavitt claimed.

"Once the market has structure, patients, providers, medical professionals, and vendors will innovate, create efficiencies, and improve care," Leavitt touted. "The national strategy for achieving interoperability of digital health information is for federal agencies—[which] pay for more than one-third of all health care in the country—to work with private-sector healthcare providers and employers in developing and adopting an architecture, standards, and certification process."

To this end, HHS has elected to consult with the American Health Information Community (AHIC) on various key issues and questions such as how to protect the privacy and security of patient health information; what health IT capabilities are needed to yield the most immediate results and benefits to healthcare consumers, including matters relating to drug safety, laboratory testing, and dissemination of such test results; and bioterrorism surveillance, as well as thoughts about instituting a standard-setting and harmonization process so that patient health records may be shared digitally among interoperable systems, while preserving the confidentiality and security of such transactions. Recommendations made by AHIC will also include a separate product certification process.

Taking the leadership role, not only will HHS fund creative proposals for data standardization processes, for a means to work toward nationwide Internet-based health information exchange architecture, and for the planning and development of policies relating to patient privacy and security, but HHS will also ensure that both Medicaid and Medicare programs adopt standards and data-sharing processes for Internet-based applications. It is envisaged that the initial public–private collaboration championed by HHS will eventually turn into a private-sector health information community initiative to set additional needed standards, certify new health IT, and provide long-term governance to transform the U.S. healthcare system.

Imagine having traveled to a foreign country and fallen ill while abroad. How could you ensure that your personal health records could be accessible to you? Do you think this information is at all useful to the foreign doctor trying to treat you? What if you do not have access to your personal health records but know that your family doctor is willing to share your data with the foreign doctor—what needs to be in place for the foreign doctor to have online access to your personal health records? Also, would the coding of these records be meaningful to the foreign doctors?

I. Introduction

The origins of healthcare management information systems may be traced back to hospital database systems. The first articles on information management in medicine appeared in the 1950s; the number of publications in this domain rapidly increased between the 1960s and 1970s as *medical informatics* (MI) became identified as an emerging field and a new specialty.[2] Before that time, other terminologies and acronyms were also used, and some are being used even to this day—examples include *medical computer science*; *medical information science*; *computers in medicine*; and other more specialized terms, such as *nursing informatics*, *dental informatics*, and *bioinformatics*.[3]

Medical informatics, as the buzzing interdisciplinary–multidisciplinary topic of the 1960s, is today honored for being recognized as a maturing scientific discipline that has evolved in its own right over the past century. While there still is no consensus on a universally accepted definition for such a field as medical informatics, crossing all boundaries, the discipline is dynamically evolving with its very own language of communication. Accordingly, different authors have taken on diverse perspectives to suggest an overwhelming number of definitions for MI as it evolves; attempts have also been made to differentiate among the various subfields within the broader MI field. Still, MI confronts considerable idiosyncrasies to find a common ground to claim its so-called identity. Yet, the continuous diffusion of this field into other healthcare and IT-related disciplines such as health informatics, healthcare technology management, and bioinformatics has spawned a movement for multiple subspecialties and subfields to emerge, each of which may have some overlapping concepts, theories, methods, and applications drawn differently from well-established reference disciplines within the broader IT and systems movements, influenced by the booming evolution of computing and information management technologies.

Turning now to the field of health management information systems (HMIS), information systems (IS) in healthcare, or healthcare information technology (HIT), the evolutionary roots and history of the various HMIS-related fields appear to parallel those of the history and evolution of MI concepts, except for the differing emphasis of the two emerging disciplines. For example, the long-standing challenge of MI in etching an identity to establishing itself is well known among health informaticians based on the many attempts to define its scope of coverage—just as the paralleled efforts of many healthcare administration and information systems academics, health records specialists and practitioners, and healthcare IT pioneers and researchers in establishing an identity and defining the boundaries of the HMIS field over the last several decades are known as well. Currently, these two broad disciplines are still facing the need to overcome the ostensibly intransigent problems of increasingly unmanageable health records and the explosion of biomedical knowledge and clinical information about patients, coupled with the need to merge myriad uncontrolled movements of administrative, financial, and clinical test reports generated from physician referrals and patients changing health insurers or seeking alternate opinions from different care providers. Apparently, while the field of MI is more concerned with clinical-based data accumulation and diagnostic, therapeutic, and prognostic decision making, the field of HMIS emphasizes the integration of administrative, financial, and clinical data sets. Herein lies the key difference between the two broad disciplines.

Yet, despite the many similarities and/or differences among all health IT–related disciplines, especially the broader MI and HMIS disciplines, the need to improve the accuracy, reliability, consistency, and sharing of medical process and knowledge; the need to automate clinical guidelines and streamline administrative workflow; the need to enhance administrative and managerial directives, as well as physician decision making and research; and the need to permit electronic data interchange among care providers and to achieve higher-quality health care have all given rise to the need for adopting standards. Among the key benefits of standards adoption would be empowering the medical sector to share patient information, encouraging the merging of medical discoveries and MI developments, and optimizing the applications of the new medical technologies. Hence, interface solutions in the form of standards are critical to bringing together the contributions of multiple caregivers; to combining the contributions from diverse health IT–related research; and to satisfying the unique needs of the health and medical field, especially in areas where data integrity and reliability, relevancy, responsiveness of knowledge, and security are of utmost importance.

II. HMIS Standards

Today, we are already seeing major standards being applied across many hospital-based information systems developed as a result of growing MI expertise and HMIS know-how such as electronic health records (EHR), clinical decision support systems (CDSS), computerized physician order entry (CPOE), radiological information systems (RIS), laboratory information systems (LIS), and pharmacy information systems (PIS). Without these HMIS standards, the medical field would have been at a standstill in terms of rapid IT adoption and diffusion, which explains why, in the past decades, nurses and physicians were particularly resistant to new technologies and why it took years for many routine hospital activities such as nurse scheduling, prescription orders, and physician workflow to be computerized.

The intensive information-generating and health-providing "industry" epitomized by hospitals and health maintenance organizations (HMOs) has been notoriously slow in exploiting and making optimum use of the new technologies and computing practices, thereby still lagging behind in this competitive century of today. Several reasons underpin the slow automation of medical records. For instance, the widespread use of narrative text and lack of standard vocabulary, shared medical terminology, and relevant taxonomic code schemes in the field have worsened the situation. Imagine a diabetic patient who would unknowingly be ordered multiple and seemingly different, but redundant, test procedures while moving from one doctor to another when, in effect, the same intended treatment is needed just because of the different terminologies used in the patient's prescriptions. Additionally, the lack of political spirit and fragmented markets, with scarce income streams to support new systems development and with sluggish adoption of technically feasible medical standards, further fuel the problem. This also accounts for the often cumbersome, slow, expensive, and sometimes unreliable technology adoption by healthcare organizations.

But the laudable effort on the part of concerned standards development organizations (SDOs) in quest of bridging the gap between the medical field and IT cannot be ignored. Well-established and influential SDOs, like HL7, the Institute of Electrical and Electronics Engineers (IEEE), the American National Standards Institute (ANSI), and many others such as the World Wide Web Consortium (W3C)—all of whose efforts have significant implications for the medical information systems and healthcare informatics community—are engaged in developing and promoting the adoption and diffusion of pertinent gold standards to ease the exchange of complex medical information, among other types and forms of information. Although these burgeoning standards exist in niche areas, significant effort still needs to be made so that nations and government agencies around the world are willing to trust and adopt a good number of the more established standards and embrace new ones such as Logical Observation Identifiers

Names and Codes (LOINC), Systematized Nomenclature of Medicine (SNOMED), Medical Information Bus (MIB), American Society for Testing and Materials (ASTM), Healthcare Informatics Standards Board (HISB), and Comité Européen de Normalisation (European Committee for Standardisation; CEN).

Indeed, many of these standards, if adopted and shared by government and healthcare services organizations around the world, would automatically lead to higher-quality healthcare services for both individuals and the population at large. Not only would the appropriate and proper sharing of health information and medical knowledge improve healthcare service efficiencies, but it would make healthcare services more cost-effective as well as more readily available when people of one country travel to another country. Consequently, the potential benefits and implications of key standards adoption for international data interchange standards would soon become apparent. The following is part of an ever-expanding list of direct beneficiaries of HMIS standards adoption:

- Individuals.
- Independent healthcare providers.
- HMIS suppliers, consultant companies, and developers.
- University-affiliated teaching hospitals and major healthcare centers and research bodies.
- Major corporations such as those in the medical devices and pharmaceutical industrial sectors.
- Healthcare maintenance organizations, nongovernment organizations, nonprofit healthcare organizations, and third-party payors.
- Governments and/or funding agencies.

In the next few sections, we highlight some of the more established and widely accepted standards, such as international data-coding standards, HL7, DICOM, and Web standards.

III. HIPAA to Spur Data Standards Adoption

The migration from traditional paper-based health data processing to electronic data collection, storage, and dissemination of pertinent health information points to the need for standardizing procedures and guidelines in protecting against authorized access of patients' private and personal information. In this sense, the Health Insurance Portability and Accountability Act (HIPAA) was enacted on August 21, 1996, by the U.S. Congress to accelerate the development of data standards to improve the privacy, confidentiality, integrity, and security aspects of personal health information and to simplify the movement of individual patients' protected health information (PHI) between healthcare professionals and other covered entities that require the information, such as insurance companies.[4]

Because HIPAA is separately discussed in the accompanying *Policy Brief*, our focus here is primarily on the resulting influence of HIPAA on data standards adoption—in particular, data-coding standards or terminology–vocabulary standards. Many health professionals have realized that the lack of comprehensive data standards is key to inhibiting the sharing of medical information electronically. For example, an influential 1993 report by the U.S. General Accounting

Office[5] highlighted the need for data standards and grouped these needs into three broad categories: vocabulary standards, structure and content standards, and messaging standards. These taxonomies correspond neatly to our categories of data-coding, data-schema, and data-exchange standards.

Data-coding standards (vocabulary) aim at defining common medical terms and specifying how medical data are to be coded within the records. For example, the ICD-9-CM is a standard numeric coding system adopted by many U.S. health provider organizations to ensure that similar diagnoses and procedures are similarly coded.[6] Using standard codes (i.e., the same abbreviation to represent similar conditions and treatments) allows not only achievement of data reliability, integrity, comparability, and consistency, but also helps with the easy retrieval of needed data. The following standards are among the key terminology–vocabulary standards that any HMIS students should be familiar with when it comes to classifying and separating healthcare data sets:

ICD: International Classification of Disease

- MS-DRG: Medicare Severity Diagnosis-Related Groups
- CPT: Current Procedural Terminology
- LOINC: Logical Observation Identifiers Names and Codes
- SNOMED: Systematized Nomenclature of Medicine Reference Terminology
- CCC: Clinical Care Classification
- ICPC: International Classification of Primary Care

ICD, developed under the auspices of the World Health Organization (WHO), refers to an internationally recognized standard classification of diseases in the form of standardized diagnostic codes with ICD-10-CM (ICD 10th Revision, Clinical Modification, June 2003) representing a progression of ICD-9-CM coding standards' capability to cover an expanded vocabulary and new requirements generated by the 1996 HIPAA. MS-DRG, which is based on Medicare Severity DRG derived from ICD-9-CM, is a classification system primarily used by healthcare services organizations such as the Centers for Medicare and Medicaid Services (CMS) for inpatient prospective payment services and billing. In addition, MS-DRG coding can be used for utilization review such as aiding in the planning of hospital inpatient discharge services by providing the hospital wards with critical information pertaining to the most prevalent groupings of inpatient services and/or average length of stays. CPT, published by the American Medical Association (AMA), provides standard procedure codes for professional reimbursement and billing. The CPT code book, maintained by the CPT Editorial Panel, is structured according to specialty, body system, or service provided. LOINC is a classification system used for identifying laboratory results and clinical observations. Therefore, two major sections of LOINC are Lab LOINC and Clinical LOINC. SNOMED, developed and maintained by the College of American Pathologists (CAP), is a coding scheme meant to integrate the data accumulated from multi-provider care processes by mapping with ICD, LOINC, and various other data classification standards. CCC, previously known as Home Health Care Classification (HHCC), offers a taxonomic framework for documenting holistically hospital-based patient care process along two interrelated dimensions: (1) CCC of Nursing Diagnoses and Outcomes and (2) CCC of Nursing Interventions and Actions. ICPC-2, developed by the International Classification Committee of the World Organization of National Colleges, Academies, and Academic Association of General Practitioners/Family Physicians (WONCA), is a coding taxonomy that maps to ICD-10 for primary care services. A severity of illness checklist and functional status assessment charts are included in ICPC-2.

Not surprisingly, new versions of codes have continued to evolve, including ABC codes and numerous others (e.g., CRM or Galen Common Reference Model, LOINC, UMLS, NDC, and NANDA).[7,8] Table 12.1 summarizes a sampling of the more popular codes.

Data-exchange standards (messaging) use a standardized interconnecting system protocol to predictably transmit electronic data, that is, standardizing the order and sequence of data during transmission between two points across a network or subnetwork. Open-systems interconnection (OSI) is an open architecture having seven layers, each demanding a different level of functionality for data exchange to materialize among different systems. These OSI levels include physical, data link, network, transport, session, presentation, and application as described

Table 12.1   A Summary of Coding Systems Representing Healthcare Concepts

Standard	Description
Read codes	Detailed set of codes used to explain patient care and treatment information.
LOINC	Standard codes and classifications for identifying laboratory and clinical terms.
ICD-10 codes	New diagnostic codes developed by the World Health Organization (WHO), not yet used in North America.
IFC	International Classification on Functioning, Disability, and Health; a taxonomy to describe bodily functions and structure, domains of activity and participation, and environmental factors interacting with these components.
CPT4 codes	Procedure codes developed by the American Medical Association for professional billing and reimbursement for outpatient and ambulatory care.
HCPCS	Healthcare Common Procedure Coding System; provides codes used for reporting physician services for Medicare patients.
APC	Ambulatory Payment Classification system; refers to outpatient reimbursement based on groupings of CPT/HCPCS–coded procedures.
CDT-2005	Code on Dental Terminology; a dental procedural and nomenclature standard.
NANDA	North American Nursing Diagnosis Association code; set of nursing diagnoses.
National Library of Medicine (NLM) Unified Medical Language System (UMLS)	A cross-referenced collection of codes and related information sources.
APA DSM-IV	Diagnostic codes organized by the American Psychiatric Association (APA).
ECRI	Codes used to identify medical equipment.
Others	Diagnosis-related group (DRG) databases, SNOMED, IUPAC Codes, Arden Syntax, etc.

in Table 12.2. Other standards for system networking include IBM's SNA (system network architecture), DEC's DNA (DEC network architecture), TCP/IP (transmission control protocol/Internet protocol), and MUMPS. Table 12.2, extracted from Bourke,[9] provides brief summaries of these layers and accompanying functions and a comparison of various standards that can be used in the respective layers.

Data-schema standards (structure and content) involve defining essential data elements in the database, such as a minimum data set (MDS), and specifying the structure, domains, rules, and relationships among these data elements to be maintained within the records to facilitate data retrieval. In the manual system, the data entry was serial and not random at the functional level. Computerization allows the data representation to become functionally complex. Here, the data comes with different type, categorization, and transaction identities assigned at each functional level. This led to the development of widely used data schema, such as hierarchical, network, and relational data models, which were detailed in one of the *Technology Briefs* earlier in this text. Complex data object models have also evolved, which allow users to view data at a high conceptual level.

Coupled with HIPAA, all of these data standards will serve to minimize potential misuse of patient information and limit access to medical records by so-called covered entities, including physicians, clearinghouses, healthcare providers, hospital administrators, clinical researchers, and other employees. Because of the potential for serious harm through discrimination, loss of insurance, unemployability, or stigmatization, HIPAA regulations provide federal protection for this health information.[10] With respect to security and confidentiality of electronic health

Table 12.2   Layers of Open-Systems Interconnection (OSI) and Other Standard Protocols

OSI Layers	Description	IBM	DEC	TCP/IP
Physical	Immediate network characteristics	Twinax (AS 400)	Twisted pair/MMJ	Twisted pair coaxial
Data link	Node-to-node transfer of data via access to immediate subnet	Bisync SDLC	DDCMP	Arcnet Starian Asynch
Network	Routing across subnets to deliver data packets	SNA	DNA/LAT	TCP/IP and others
Transport	Data integrity, packaging data for transmission	SNA	DNA/LAT	TCP/IP and others; NetBios
Session	Dialogue management between two end systems	SNA	DNA	TCP/IP and others; NetBios
Presentation	Data encoding	SNA	DNA	NetBios
Application	User interface, e-mail, remote database access, file transfer, document exchange, transaction	Various IBM standards	Various DEC standards	Windows SMTP (TCP) FTP; others

Source: Adapted with permission from M. K. Bourke, *Strategy and Architecture of Health Care Information Systems*, © 1994, Springer-Verlag.

information, HIPAA legislation makes adequate as well as excessive provisions to cover certain exigencies in cases where legislation was not passed. For example, the HIPAA further enhances the healthcare information and communications technology (HICT) agenda. In HIPAA's Administrative Simplification provisions, the National Committee on Vital and Health Statistics (NCVHS) was named to advise the Secretary of the Department of Health and Human Services (HHS) on those dimensions that related to confidentiality and security, identifiers, and standards for computer-based patient records.[11] Furthermore, HIPAA revised and reformulated the NCVHS from a venerable committee into the nation's health information policy advisory committee.

IV. HL7: Health Level Seven

Health Level Seven (HL7), as accredited by ANSI, is a system development organization whose aim is to promote interoperability for the interchange of healthcare data. "Level Seven" refers to the highest level of the International Organization for Standardization (ISO) communications model for open-systems interconnection (OSI)—the application level.[12] HL7 was built on existing production protocols, predominantly those of ASTM Standard 1238. It operates as a nonprofit volunteer-, vendor-, and provider-supported organization to encourage information scientists and various experts in the healthcare field to endeavor toward the development of standards for the management, processing, integration, and exchange of electronic healthcare information.

The Vocabulary Problem

The chief aim of HL7 is to address the *vocabulary problem*, which has paralyzed HMIS developers, implementers, and users of computer-based applications in medicine. The vocabulary problem is best characterized by the failure among communities of healthcare information end-users to find a common denominator for representing healthcare knowledge and discoveries. Despite many years of countless efforts invested by medical terminology developers and informatics specialists, the vocabulary problem remained until the emergence of HL7. HL7 provided a common interface among the various healthcare user communities in terms of the nomenclature of health-related knowledge—its growing popularity hinges on its promise to realize the semantic interoperability of the HL7 Message Development Framework (MDF), which aims at easing the exchange and use of clinical information among disparate systems as well as enhancing clinical research and promoting population health management.

HL7 is responsible for driving the development of specifications for messaging standards that will enable disparate healthcare applications to exchange key sets of clinical and administrative data. It is not specifically a programming language meant for handling HMIS software development. Current core clinical standards available through HL7 include order entry, scheduling, medical records management, imaging, patient administration, observation (laboratory results, radiographic reports, examination findings, and so on), and patient financial messages.[13] Being a message standard protocol, HL7 handles clinical information communication such as diagnostic results, scheduling information, clinical trials data, and master file records.

HL7 serves the purpose of data sharing among disparate vendors or sources of electronic data interchange within the healthcare organizational environment. HL7 acts as a means to reduce, if not eliminate, the level of interface programming and program maintenance. It, therefore, ensures timely data exchange with minimal deficit of clinical knowledge.

HL7 Development

In 1987, the first version (HL7 version 1.0) was published and was responsible for the scope and format of the HL7 standard. The following year, version 2.0, which serviced a number of data-interchange demonstration projects, appeared. In 1990, HL7 version 2.1 was broadly adopted on a global scale, followed by the development of HL7 version 2.2 in 1994. In 1996, ANSI adopted HL7 as the first healthcare data interchange American National Standard. In 1997, with HL7 progressively expanding its scope through the provision of standards for further data exchange related to patient administration (such as admission, discharge, and transfer), billing, order entry, clinical observation data, medical information management, and messages supporting communication for problem-oriented records, HL7 version 2.3 appeared.

In 1999, a complete revision of HL7, which was based on the common Reference Information Model (RIM), was undertaken and appeared as HL7 version 3. All the data content for HL7 messages would now originate from the HL7 RIM, serving as a coherent and mutual information model. More recently, Health Level 7 has also been developing standards for the representation of clinical documents such as discharge summaries and progress notes.[14] Bakken et al.[15] discussed the development of two sets of principles to provide guidance to terminology stakeholders: (1) principles for HL7-compliant terminologies and (2) principles for HL7-sanctioned terminology integration efforts. To help healthcare services organizations achieve HL7 compliance, the key activities undertaken by HL7 organizations today include the completion of a survey of terminology developers, the development of a process for HL7 registration of terminologies, and the maintenance of vocabulary domain specification tables.

A summary description of HL7 strategies includes the following:

1. HL7 will maintain the meaning and/or semantics of nomenclature of health-related knowledge and will promote the development of relevant and compatible standards that would support the efficient transfer and sharing of healthcare knowledge and information between computers.
2. It will evolve a formal methodology to support the creation of HL7 standards from the HL7 RIM.
3. It will disseminate information on the benefits of healthcare information standardization to academic institutions, healthcare management organizations, healthcare services providers, policy makers, and the public at large.
4. It will encourage the adoption and diffusion of HL7 standards worldwide through the efforts of HL7 international affiliate organizations, which will be formed to participate in developing and localizing HL7 standards.

5. It will bring together domain experts from academic institutions, healthcare services provider organizations, and healthcare management organizations to collaborate and develop standards for HL7 inclusion in various specialty areas.

6. HL7 will join with other SDOs and national and international sanctioning bodies such as ANSI and ISO to promote the mutual exchange and use of compatible and other healthcare information standards.

7. HL7 will ensure that current propagated standards fulfill the diverse requirements of the present era and will initiate effort to meet the emergent requirements.

8. HL7 will institute membership policies to ensure that all requirements are met uniformly and equitably with quality and consistency.

HL7 Adoption

The relentless efforts put forward by HL7 have paid off in that countries such as Argentina, Australia, Canada, China, the Czech Republic, Finland, Germany, India, Japan, Korea, Lithuania, The Netherlands, New Zealand, the Republic of South Africa, Switzerland, Taiwan, Turkey, and the United Kingdom have now become part of HL7 initiatives. Presently, HL7 is also being used by about 2,000 leading hospitals in countries like Japan, Germany, Sweden, and Holland. In the United States alone, HL7 standards have been influential—more than 150 U.S. healthcare institutions, U.S. Centers for Disease Control and Prevention (CDC), large referral laboratories and eminent universities have adopted these standards. Moreover, countries like New Zealand and Australia have already adopted HL7 as their national standards. Today, HL7 is known to be the most widely implemented healthcare data-messaging standard and boasts more than 500 organizational members along with more than 2,000 individual members, including top healthcare executives, health information system vendors, and pharmaceutical representatives and computer manufacturers.

V. DICOM: Digital Imaging and Communication in Medicine

Originally, the joint committee of the American College of Radiology and the National Electronic Manufacturers Association (ACR/NEMA) oversaw the development of Digital Imaging and Communication in Medicine (DICOM) standards. DICOM, which has emerged to fulfill the need for transferring digital images of various formats as well as related information between devices (irrespective of the device manufacturer), is a nonproprietary data interchange protocol.[16]

The comprehensive specification of DICOM includes the detailed engineering information used as a blueprint for information structures and procedures. These engineering details will enhance the network connectivity among the community of vendors' products, thereby enabling exchange of various formats of medical information within and outside the healthcare services organizations through the far-fetched abilities of telemedicine and other technologies.

The DICOM standards documentation comprises the following modules:[17]

- PS 3.1: Introduction and Overview
- PS 3.2: Conformance

- PS 3.3: Information Object Definitions
- PS 3.4: Service Class Specifications
- PS 3.5: Data Structure and Encoding
- PS 3.6: Data Dictionary
- PS 3.7: Message Exchange
- PS 3.8: Network Communication Support for Message Exchange
- PS 3.9: Retired
- PS 3.10: Media Storage and File Format for Data Interchange
- PS 3.11: Media Storage Application Profiles
- PS 3.12: Media Formats and Physical Media for Data Interchange
- PS 3.13: Retired
- PS 3.14: Grayscale Standard Display Function
- PS 3.15: Security Profiles
- PS 3.16: Content Mapping Resource

The DICOM Standards Committee comprises several working groups; the description and objectives of each group are beyond the scope of this chapter, but readers can get more details about WG 1 through WG 21, and WG 22 through WG 26 from Klein[18] and the DICOM Standards Committee website.[19] There are five general application areas covered by the DICOM standards:[20]

- Network image management.
- Network image interpretation management.
- Network print management.
- Imaging procedure management.
- Off-line storage media management.

In 1985, DICOM version 1.0 was developed by ACR/NEMA. It has since undergone two consecutive revisions. Consequently, a revised version 2.0 emerged in 1988, which included version 1.0 but with additional information on new commands to uniquely identify any information object from the hierarchy scheme and to add data elements for precise description of an image. Today, DICOM version 3.0 is recognized as the improved and most recent version.

Purpose of DICOM

The DICOM message standard, in collaboration with other standard groups, vies for the compatibility with other MI and HMIS standards. The aim is to enhance the form and flow of digital information between medical imaging systems across the different healthcare services delivery environments globally. With its growing success, DICOM intends to bring together all the medical societies, universities, governmental and nongovernmental agencies, and nonprofit as well as for-profit organizations to join or participate in the DICOM Standards Committee. Awareness and knowledge of the DICOM standards will create ample room for its adoption and diffusion as well as its further extension.

The DICOM standards are used, or will soon be used, by virtually every medical profession that utilizes images within the healthcare industry, such as cardiology, dentistry, endoscopy, mammography, ophthalmology, orthopedics, pathology, pediatrics, radiation therapy, radiology, and surgery. The DICOM standards are even used in veterinary medical imaging applications. There is an escalating interest regarding the efficient management of digitizing medical images for easy transfer between electronic devices. These standards are structured to support the formatting and exchanging of complex medical imaging applications in all the major medical disciplines noted earlier. Tele-radiology has emerged as the bridge to close the gap between the general physicians and the referral specialists, including radiologists, cardiologists, orthodontists, ophthalmologists, pathologists, radiation therapists, pediatricians, surgeons, and other medical specialists who are used to reading radiological images to support the continuing care of their patients. Today, these encoding and communications protocols have largely moved into electronic storage, exchange, pre-fetching, real-time retrieval, and return of diagnostic and therapeutic images and image- and non-image-related information in emergencies and other high-stress medical environments.

The DICOM standards aim to bridge the gap through interoperability while enhancing the workflow efficiency between medical imaging equipment and other medical image–intensive departments on a global scale. By so doing, DICOM standards will enhance communication among image acquisition, waveform, picture archiving, and information system components. During the 1990s, laudable effort was done to achieve filmless radiology. The strides of DICOM standards were recognized in achieving this goal. The flexible nature of DICOM standards enables users to create an image management system. Designing a system around DICOM can prevent a department from being "trapped" by a single vendor and limited to a proprietary family of products; still, naive implementation of DICOM standards does not guarantee this flexibility.[21]

The DICOM standards allow proper organization of "information objects" by aggregating images having similar attributes. It further provides free-text and coded-data entry as well as fields for structured encoding. This increases the direct benefits of information retrieval through precise encoding. With the compatibility provided by DICOM standards, it is anticipated that use of image management systems would soon become a "plug-and-play" channel suitable for handling by any non–technically oriented physician. The DICOM standards also minimize duplicate data entry at the modality console due to the work lists received by the imaging modality. Additional facilities like query, storage, retrieval, print, and other functionalities are also supported by the DICOM standards. These cooperative standards promote network connectivity through interoperability of multi-vendor devices by specifying levels of conformance. DICOM standards maintain nomenclature of a multipart document to support the evolving standards by the addition of new features. DICOM standards will accommodate explicit hierarchy of information objects ranging from images, graphics, texts, reports, waveforms, and printings. Service classes are used to uniquely identify information objects from the hierarchy as part of the DICOM standards. A lexicon having the nomenclature in groups defines the hierarchy of information objects, while each data element defining the individual object consists of a data tag, a data-length specification, and the data value.

Adoption of DICOM Standards

One of the reasons DICOM standards have been popularly accepted and adopted across a wide variety of clinical imaging contexts is that these standards specify a conformance statement that improves the communication of software specifications for imaging equipment.[22] Being a part of cooperative standards, DICOM connects every major diagnostic medical imaging vendor for cooperating individual testing. The participation of the vendor's professional societies around the world will also support and further result in the enhancement of these standards.

With such a long listing of well-tested benefits provided by DICOM, concerned organizations such as imaging vendors, physician users, SDOs, and those of general interest would not need to hesitate in embracing DICOM standards. In an effort to improve healthcare imaging, these standards have long been used and adopted by highly reputed academic institutions such as Harvard Medical School and other major medical establishments. The radiology department at Massachusetts General Hospital (MGH), for example, adopted DICOM standards years ahead of others for all of its tele-radiological programs.

VI. Web Standards

In 1994, Tim Berners-Lee founded the World Wide Web Consortium (W3C)—a consortium formed to ensure compatibility and agreement among industry members in the adoption of new Web standards. W3C's mission is "To lead the World Wide Web to its full potential by developing protocols and guidelines that ensure long-term growth for the Web."[23]

The World Wide Web (WWW) differs from the Internet in that it essentially is a set of software protocols that resides on the network or the Internet and that allows easy access of information for the end-user. W3C establishes the agreed-upon Web standards. Web standards basically encompass many formal standards and other technical specifications that define and describe various aspects of the WWW. Among the more popular conceptualization of Web standards is that these standards are linked to the trend of endorsing a set of established best practices for building websites and a philosophy of Web design and development that includes those methods.

Many interdependent standards and specifications exist, which can directly or indirectly affect the development and administration of websites and Web services. Some of these standards govern aspects of the Internet—and not just the WWW. More particularly, strong advocates of "Web standards" tend to focus on the higher-level standards that most directly affect the accessibility and usability of websites. Examples include standards to ensure compatibility and interoperability between a server computer and its client computers, standards that entail integrating the variety of different hardware–software configurations that accumulate the Web-based data on a routine basis, or standards that must support easy access and sharing of Web-based patient information virtually among multiple end-users. For example, prior to the creation of the W3C, incompatible versions of HTML were offered by different vendors with emphasis chiefly on increasing market share over the needs of interoperability, thereby increasing the potential for data inconsistency among Web pages.

Web standards, when translated, can be separated generally into two different categories, namely, a "table-free site," and a site "using valid code." However, Web standards themselves involve broader aspects. A website built to comply with Web standards should adhere to commonly accepted standards such as Hypertext Markup Language (HTML), XHTML and

Modularization, Extensible Markup Language (XML), Cascading Style Sheets (CSS), Document Object Model (DOM), and others (e.g., MathML) while utilizing valid code practices, accessible code, semantically correct code, and user-friendly URLs (universal resource locators). In the broader sense, Web standards, therefore, comprise the following generally accepted specifications:

- *Hypertext Markup Language (HTML).* HTML 4.0 is widely used on the Web for adding structure to text documents; Web browsers interpret these documents, representing the structure in media-specific ways to the user.
- *XHTML and Modularization.* XHTML 1.0 is a reformulation of HTML as an XML application; XHTML 1.1 is an upgrade.
- *Extensible Markup Language (XML).* XML 1.0 is a markup language that allows you to define your own elements.
- *CSS: Cascading Style Sheets.* CSS is a mechanism for changing the appearance of HTML or XML elements by assigning styles to element types, self-defined classes of elements, or individual instances.
- *Document Object Model Level 1 (DOM 1),* DOM allows the full power and interactivity of a scripting language such as ECMA Script, the standardized version of JavaScript, to be exerted on a Web page.
- *MathML: Document Markup for Mathematics.* MathML is an XML enabling application for sharing mathematical documentation through standardized notations adoption for conveying both the structure and content of Web-based mathematical information.

Complying with Web standards can give Web pages greater visibility in Web search engines such as Yahoo! and Google. The structural information present in standards-compliant documents makes it easy for search engines to access and evaluate the information in those documents. Websites get indexed more accurately due to the use of Web standards, making it easier for server-side as well as client-side software to understand the structure and content of the document.

Web standards are adopted so that old browsers will still understand the basic structure of a document. Writing Web pages in accordance with the standards shortens site development time and makes pages easier to maintain. Debugging and troubleshooting become easier as the code follows a standard of Web page development. This all ties in with the W3C mission statement to help ensure positive long-term growth for the Web.

VII. Conclusion

Both MI and HMIS disciplines are undergoing a state of rapid metamorphosis and promising new initiatives that will have significant effects on the practice of medicine. Together with fields like medicine, health sciences, systems sciences, information technology, education, and computer and electrical engineering, these disciplines have fueled myriad gold standards. Despite the overwhelming array of benefits presented by the gold standards of these disciplines, their adoption has either been too sluggish or not universal. Why? Systems developers generally indicate that, while they would like to make use of standards, they cannot find one that meets their needs. What are those needs? The answers to this question are less clear. The simple answer is, "It doesn't have exactly what I want." In the quest of decreasing the health disparities and despite the hopeful aims of these standards, the knowledge gap has limited the acceptance of some. A major challenge is, apparently, adopting those standards that will become gold standards.

During the past century, the medical field has experienced thrilling changes like new drugs, new devices, and new techniques. These mega-changes are being constantly adopted, but the real metamorphosis will be seen when the concepts of MI and HMIS help build real-world solutions for the administrative, clinical, and relevant systems that would enhance seamless interoperability and multilateral communication between the business units of the enterprise, whereby a cohesive information model can be maintained to promote the strategic goals of the enterprise. If we want to enjoy the benefits of information management technologies, we must embrace and even streamline many of these standards for the welfare of the planet. Heterogeneity of clinical knowledge and the continuing diversity that preclude effectiveness have plagued users, developers, and implementers of computer-based applications in medicine. International standards in healthcare information systems have provided the pivotal backbone to integrating clinical knowledge discovery. Standards such as ICD-9, HL7, and DICOM have been so overwhelmingly accepted that when strengthened by an enforceable law like HIPAA, these standards promise to satisfy the demanding capabilities of the electronic and digital needs in medicine.

Notes

1. M. Mosquera, GCN Staff, http://www.gcn.com/online/vol1_no1/35995-1.html?topic=e_gov#, accessed July 30, 2008.
2. M. F. Collen, "Origins of Medical Informatics," *Western Journal of Medicine* 145 (1986): 778–785.
3. http://www.ii.metu.edu.tr/~ion535/demo/lecture_notes/week1/week1-3.html#1-2, accessed April 8, 2006.
4. W. D. Pace, E. W. Staton, and S. Holcomb, "Practice-Based Research Network Studies in the Age of HIPAA," *Annals of Family Medicine* 3, suppl 1 (2005): S38–S45. DOI: 10.1370/afm.301.
5. "Standards for Automated Medical Records," General Accounting Office report GAO/IMTEC-93–17, April 30, 1993.
6. The ICD-9-CM is a standardized system of codes describing diagnoses developed and maintained by the World Health Organization (WHO).
7. Physicians' Current Procedural Terminology (CPT) is a coding system established in 1966 by the American Medical Association to provide a uniform language to accurately describe medical, surgical, and diagnostic services. Each procedure or service is identified with a five-digit code.
8. Detailed descriptions of ICD-10 codes and many other coding schemes can be found in various websites or from links to the Duke University Medical Center site (www.mcis.duke.edu).
9. M. K. Bourke, *Strategy and Architecture of Health Care Information Systems* (New York: Springer-Verlag, 1994).
10. J. K. O'Herrin, N. Fost, and K. A. Kudsk, "Health Insurance Portability Accountability Act (HIPAA) Regulations Effect on Medical Record Research," *Annals of Surgery* 239 (2004): 772–778.

11. E. S. Berner, D. E. Detmer, and D. Simborg, "Will the Wave Finally Break? A Brief View of the Adoption of Electronic Medical Records in the United States," *Journal of the American Medical Information Association* 12 (2005): 3–7, DOI 10.1197/jamia.M1664.

12. http://www.hl7.org/about/, accessed March 18, 2007.

13. Ibid.

14. R. H. Dolin et al., "The HL7 Clinical Document Architecture," *Journal of the American Medical Information Association* 8 (2001): 552–569.

15. S. Bakken, K. E. Campbell, J. J. Cimino, S. M. Huff, and W. Hammond, "Toward Vocabulary Domain Specifications for Health Level 7-Coded Data Elements," *Journal of the American Medical Information Association* 7, no. 4 (2000): 333–342.

16. A. T. Ramos, "Information Object Definition–Based Unified Modeling Language Representation of DICOM Structured Reporting. A Case Study of Transcoding DICOM to XML," *Journal of the American Medical Information Association* 9 (2002): 63–71.

17. "Digital Imaging and Communications in Medicine (DICOM), Part 1: Introduction and Overview," PS 3.1-2004, http://medical.nema.org/dicom/2004/04_01PU.PDF, accessed December 5, 2006.

18. G. O. Klein, "Review Paper: Standardization of Health Informatics—Results and Challenges," *Yearbook of Medical Informatics* (2002): 103–114.

19. Dicom Standards Committee, http://www.nema.org/prod/med/upload/DICOM%20STANDARDS%20COMMITTEE-3.pdf, accessed December 2, 2006.

20. W. D. Bidgood, S. C. Hori, F. W. Prior, and D. E. V. Syckle, "Understanding and Using DICOM, the Data Interchange Standard for Biomedical Imaging," *Journal of the American Medical Information Association* 4 (1997): 199–212.

21. Ibid.

22. Ibid.

23. W3C, http://www.w3.org/consortium, accessed December, 2008.

Chapter Questions

12–1. Define the following terms:
  a. Medicine.
  b. Medical informatics.
  c. Standards.
  d. HIPAA.
  [Hint: All these terms come from the list of Medical Subject Headings (MeSH) maintained by the U.S. National Library of Medicine. It is updated annually and keeps record of the nomenclature of the world's medical literature index; see http://www.nlm.nih.gov/cgi/mesh/2007/MB_cgi.]

12–2. What are data standards? Discuss the usefulness of these standards to implementing HMIS. [Think, for example, what the purpose of a unique patient identifier (PID) would be and who should be authorized to access and share this information to whom.]

12–3. How should one go about adopting a major HMIS standard, for example, HL7 or DICOM?

12–4. The Complete Reference observes:

> *The economic justification for [standardized] codes vanished years ago. Computers are now fast enough and cheap enough to accommodate the humans, and work in human languages with words that humans understand. It is high time that they did so. Yet, without really thinking through the justifications,*

developers and designers continue to use codes willy-nilly, as if it were still 1969. . . . There is an immediate additional benefit: key entry errors drop to zero because the users get immediate feedback, in English, of the business information they are entering. Digits aren't transposed, codes aren't remembered, and in financial applications, money rarely is lost in suspense accounts due to entry errors, with very significant savings.

As a student of health information systems, can you justify the continuing use of standardized codes for referencing medical data?

HIPAA, Privacy, and Security Issues for Healthcare Services Organizations

Joseph Tan and Fay Cobb Payton

Introduction

Health management information systems (HMIS) relate to the accumulation of paper-based and electronic data applicable to health administrative and clinical decision making that will assist an organization to achieve its predetermined goals and specific objectives. It is, therefore, in the best interest of every member of a healthcare organization to be responsible for the critical task of securing and protecting the quality, management, privacy, and confidentiality of health information kept within the HMIS of the healthcare organization.

The Fourth Amendment to the U.S. Constitution essentially guarantees every American resident his or her basic rights to privacy and freedom. Everyone employed by a healthcare services organization, but especially those who are asked to handle sensitive personal health information, such as patient health records, has the responsibility of protecting the privacy, confidentiality, and security of these records or any other means of identification. Congress has, furthermore, enacted laws to help prevent private information from being inappropriately released or handled and to ensure that the personal information of Americans is kept confidential. With the growing use of electronic information exchanges, and the resultant spike in identity theft and other electronically based misdeeds, it is no wonder that the public is becoming increasingly apprehensive about providing personal data. In this policy brief, our focus is on the Health Insurance Portability and Accountability Act (HIPAA), the Privacy Rule, confidentiality, and security issues related to health information handling and information resources management.

HIPAA

Specifically tailored for the healthcare services industry, the HIPAA rulings, along with other security measures, have been instituted to protect the freedom, security, privacy, and confidentiality of individuals. Such measures arise amid the patients' increased sharing of personal health-related information with authorized agencies and care providers. In the United States, therefore, every citizen has the basic right to the protection and safeguarding of his or her health information and for those managing and handling these data to take an ethical responsibility to uphold the laws within our ever-changing, innovative technological environment.

In 1996, Congress passed Public Law 104-191, otherwise known as HIPAA.[1] HIPAA required the U.S. Department of Health and Human Services (HHS) to establish, with far-reaching implications and consequences, new guidelines, key principles, and national standards for handling electronic healthcare transactions. Everyone working within the U.S. healthcare system must strictly adhere to these principles, guidelines, and standards. Covered entities include, but are not limited to, individual caregivers such as doctors, nurses, and pharmacists; healthcare facilities such as hospitals, clinics, and nursing homes; and groups and organizations such as private physician organizations (PPOs), private health insurance companies, and health maintenance organizations (HMOs). Even government programs, such as Medicaid and Medicare, must follow the HIPAA-imposed guidelines. HIPAA, therefore, covers the majority, or even the entirety, of the U.S. healthcare system, including private, public, and government healthcare facilities, as well as practicing health professionals.

What information, precisely, is HIPAA protecting? This federal mandate covers the protection of any information in an individual's personal records, including diagnosis and treatment reports, progress notes, recommendations, and even conversations with personal caregivers. It also safeguards the information that is processed into computer systems used by care providers for billing, medication, clinical evaluation reports, radiological images and reports, laboratory test results, and any information collected by individuals or organizations that has a health semantic.[2] Therefore, HIPAA essentially protects *all* personal health information, stored in any medium, located in any U.S.-based organization, regardless of whether this information was obtained directly from an individual or through third parties. Owing to the vast amount of information being collected daily on patients by their healthcare insurers, these organizations must be particularly conscious of HIPAA's requirements for the protection of this collected information. HIPAA law simply states that all persons who have access to health information must comply with the regulations, including the protection of anything, whether written or spoken, that deals with a particular patient's current medical condition and his or her past or ongoing treatments.

Privacy and Confidentiality

HMIS pose a threat to all health information stored electronically if the healthcare organization, as the custodian, does not act responsibly in securing the information gathered from its trusting patients. One critical success factor toward maintaining health information security, privacy, and confidentiality, therefore, is simply to educate those who use and handle HMIS on a daily basis about how to protect a patient's health information. The HIPAA not only establishes national standards and guidelines to protect access to, and use of, a patient's health information, but also gives the patient specific rights. Under HIPAA, each individual patient has the right to obtain a copy of his or her own medical records and the right to review the content of these records. If, at any time, a patient feels that there are errors found on these records or that the individual rights under HIPAA have been violated, he or she has the right to have corrections and/or notes appended to these records, as well as the right to file a complaint with the healthcare provider organization, and, at an even higher level, with the U.S. government.

HIPAA regulations also state how healthcare providers and insurance companies are to comply with the law.[3] HIPAA grants patients the right to receive notice when their health information is being used or shared. Specifically, patient consent is always a basic requirement for health information releases, except when such uses are only for certain marketing purposes, in which case aggregated information is largely derived from statistical summaries of patient health records. Moreover, if a patient's information has been used, the patient has the right to receive a report on when and why this information was used. Reports stating why someone's records have been shared are important because these provide the documentation on who, when, and why someone, or an organization, has attempted to access a certain patient's medical history. In essence, HIPAA protects any private information regarding the health status of the patients, and the care they have received from U.S. health organizations. Also, for a higher level of protection, the patient may also exercise the right to request communications from somewhere other than his or her home, as long as it is within reason.

Healthcare services organizations that want to take further steps to protect personal private health and medical information will also find that HIPAA offers guidelines on education—specifically, with operations that involve health information within the HIPAA legal framework. Basically, HIPAA requires organizations to respect and safeguard the privacy and confidentiality of collected personal health-related information. This is accomplished by demanding that organizations educate the direct handlers and users[4] of such information about the process an information release request must follow—for example, to whom or which organization, or for what purposes (such as personal safekeeping, marketing, specialist referrals, and/or research) the information can or cannot be shared and/or other steps that organizations can take to keep an individual's health information private.

In fact, after Congress passed HIPAA in 1996, the HHS introduced the "Privacy Rule" to further refine and clarify HIPAA's articulated view of privacy. In July 2001, and again in August 2002, HHS released a series of guidelines to clarify questions pertaining to the original Privacy Rule, describe policies and key elements of the final modified Privacy Rule's requirements, and provide further modifications that would lead to the Final Rule.[5] Within the HIPAA privacy framework, HHS also incorporated appropriate safeguards for personal health information. Certain aspects of the modified rule acknowledge marketing capabilities and the privacy of an individual's health information. Other areas deal with clarifying consent and notice, uses of disclosure, and authorization specifications. The modifications define issues with incidental use, parents and minors, and research. Designed to give patients more control over their own health information, the Privacy Rule sets boundaries on health records and limits on how these records can be used and viewed. It also determines who can view the records and when; for example, a person's health information may not be disclosed to a third party unless consent has previously been given, and if so, the information should be released within 30 days upon request.

Generally speaking, the Privacy Rule comprises five key principles: (1) consumer control, (2) the setting of boundaries, (3) accountability, (4) public responsibility, and (5) security. *Consumer control*, which was highlighted earlier, provides individuals with the right to control the release of their information. For example, patients now have to sign a specific authorization before a covered entity can release their health information to a life insurer, bank, marketing company, or any other entity for any use not pertaining to healthcare services. Herein lies the crux of the *boundaries* concept; that is, healthcare information should be used for healthcare purposes, such as treatment and payment options, unless there is an exceptional reason for not doing so. *Accountability*, the next principle, infers that all covered entities must be held responsible for their actions; for example, each healthcare organization is accountable for guaranteeing its patients the secure storage of their health information, so that it is not released without the patient's specific written consent. *Public responsibility* implies that there are certain exceptions when dealing with the support of national priorities. These exceptions may include emergency circumstances, identification of a deceased person or cause of death, catering to public health needs, or activities related to national defense and security. Anything that will affect the public and national *security* must be handled promptly, with a certain amount of exception to the Privacy Rule.

To comply with HIPAA standards regarding privacy,[6] affected individuals and organizations can enact several changes. The use of privacy screens such as standard blur, double axis, and blackout on computers is one example. Recognizing information privacy and protecting it when an employee of the healthcare organization is entering identifiable health information into a computer is important. What these privacy screens do, essentially, is to block the screen so it cannot be viewed by anyone outside a 25° angle from the screen. In this sense, nobody, except the person entering the information, will be able to discern what is being entered. Another means of privacy control is the use of encryption, which is also an excellent choice for security and access control. Encryption takes the text and scrambles the letters into many different combinations, so that without the "key" to decipher the encrypted text, the information remains locked. A popular form of encryption is 256-bit encryption, which amounts to precisely 2^{256} possible combinations. This would render it physically impossible to figure out the encrypted message, simply due to the gargantuan number of possible combinations.

Finally, the emergence, in recent years, of wireless Internet services and mobile wearable devices has introduced a new dimension to safeguarding and protecting individuals' private healthcare information. In August 2007, the standards for electronic transactions, which cover the rules and regulations for sending and receiving an individual's private health and medical records, were released.[7] Previous legacy HMIS render interoperability among systems a challenging issue, but the lack of such data-sharing capabilities also provided an easier and better privacy control environment. The implementation of Web services, as well as other advancing data interchange technologies today, will raise further concerns over the privacy and security of personal health data, because they are being shared among automated intelligence and applications. HIPAA addresses what strategies are appropriate for staying in compliance with the federal law. To insure HIPAA compliance, HHS issued seven regulatory steps that healthcare services organizations must follow:

1. *Encryption of private health data* will prevent intruders from locating transmissions across cyber space and makes recoding the transmission more difficult.
2. *Authentication* will help the organization identify who is, or is not, allowed to access specific documents and records.
3. *Access control* will minimize the inappropriate retrieval of critical information stored in HMIS.
4. *Integrity control* will protect the validity and reliability of HMIS-accessible data.
5. *Alarms* will provide warnings and alerts about attempted or intended intrusions into stored private data.
6. *Audit controls* will allow for meaningful tracing of inappropriate acts of information access and retrieval.
7. *Event reporting* will ensure that any breach of HIPAA standards and regulations is swiftly reported, and resulting damages controlled within a short span of time.

Security

Security is essential to every aspect of life. For healthcare services, patients must feel safe when providing their caregivers and/or healthcare services organizations with sensitive and personal information. This is essential to the construction of a trusting relationship between the patients and their caregivers.

The security law, which is the final component of HIPAA, was put into place in February 2003. Security deals with the protection of identifiable health information against both inadvertent disclosure and deliberate misuse. Two types of security breaches result in the imposition of penalties. One is the failure of a covered entity to comply with HIPAA standards. Here, the penalty can be up to $100 per violation and up to $25,000 per year. The other type, where the imposed penalties are steeper, is for any intentional misuse of someone's health information—whether it was done for commercial advantage, personal gain, or malicious harm. These penalties can range from a fine of $50,000 and 1 year in prison to $250,000 and 10 years in prison.

The final security law established standards and regulations for healthcare providers on the required procedures toward ensuring administrative safeguards. For ensuring the security of information, for example, the access points to the information are crucial. Passwords and log-ins are often used as the first line of defense in HMIS. Physical, as well as technical, safeguards must also be in place. These safeguards protect the healthcare services organizations from security violations and the maintenance of an individual's private health and medical records. The final security law also specifies the type of security policies and procedures that the organization must follow. If a person feels that a complaint about the security of his or her identifiable health information should be filed, he or she can first approach the care provider or the insurer. If that is not responded to in a satisfactory manner, request for enforcement must then be submitted in writing within 180 days of the occurrence. This complaint should then be sent to the Office for Civil Rights (OCR) within the Department of Health and Human Services.

Security, confidentiality, and privacy of clinical, financial, and management health data (whether computerized or not) are, therefore, major concerns for healthcare services organizations. As such, the development and enforcement of stringent HMIS policies and procedures must strike a balance between restrictive user access and data sharing. The management and retention of patient records and the security of health networks are particularly important. Nowadays, owing to the massive storage capacity of computers relative to physical storage, it may be easier for healthcare services organizations to electronically store and share massive amounts of health information across organizational units, but it is also easier for thieves and computer hackers to steal large amounts of information in incredibly short periods of time. As malicious attacks on HMIS are expected to be on the rise, it is crucial for healthcare services organizations to endure the cost of installing the best security mechanisms so that the sensitive healthcare information under their custodianship is well protected.

Aside from computer hackers, another common security threat is that of computer viruses, which are program codes used to clog the capacity of an organization's system and eventually alter and/or destroy data in the server database, thereby ruining the entire system. Viruses spread popularly through spam e-mails; in light of this, security procedures to protect against viruses from organizational networks may include:

- Scanning incoming e-mails and installed software with an anti-virus program.
- Updating anti-virus, firewall, and anti-spam programs on a regular, even daily, basis.
- Using and enforcing effective security codes and changing passwords for network users.
- Periodically running anti-virus software on network servers, workstations, and nodes.

There are also firewalls that regulate access to organizational computer systems, which, through the usage of ports and IP addresses, admit based on a certain determined level of trust. The most significant danger that has been introduced along with wireless technology into an organization's HMIS is the ability for thieves to bypass physical security measures that had been counted on in the past by healthcare professionals.

In the end, each of us must take an active role in keeping our personal information safe; for example, we must safeguard the personal information that is stored on our home computers, because it can also be at risk. As noted, one of the ways to address the security issue is to implement controls at various levels: systems control, procedural control, and facility control as shown in Figure PB1.1.

Procedural controls are an important aspect of systems security. These controls specify how the information services of the healthcare services organizations should be operated, such that

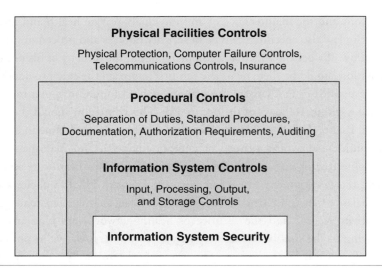

FIGURE TB5.1   Levels of Security Controls.

maximum security can be achieved, along with high accuracy and integrity of the HMIS functions and operations. There are three major means of achieving procedural controls:

1. Separation of duties.
2. Standardizing procedures and documentation.
3. Authorization requirements.

To prevent the possibility that a single group will gain unrestricted access to related HMIS functions, systems development, computer operations, and control of health data and program files should each be assigned to a separate group. Development of standard procedures, through manual and software help displays, promotes uniformity and minimizes errors and fraud. In addition, to further enhance system uniformity and minimize potential destruction, there should be a formal review and authorization on any major system development projects, program changes, or system conversion by the chief information officer (CIO), the departmental head, or a supervisor, all of whom are expected to have reached a certain level of security clearance.

Procedures for effective health data backup include preparing for disaster recovery through regular copying or duplication of programs, files, and databases; adequate logging of transactions to reconstruct any lost data; detection of missing or incomplete records; and institution of other backup operational procedures for use during system failures—such as having an alternative manual or computerized system ready and functional in the shortest possible time. Fault-tolerant procedures, which are designed specifically for fault treatment, error detection, and recovery, provide a high degree of system stability and reliability.[8] Policies governing the process, as well as the frequency of the procedures, are also crucial in protecting the integrity of health data. Whereas duplicated data can be secured and stored in a location separate from the central site, for instance, procedures must exist during any downtime experienced at the primary site, whether scheduled or unscheduled, so that systems can continue operating. In addition, highly sensitive files should be backed up on disks and the disks secured to prevent unauthorized access.

Because computer hardware and software undergo replacement in most healthcare services organizations from time to time, security measures to protect these investments are essential. Such essential measures include the location of workstations, servers, printers, and other accessories in lockable, secure areas when not in use. Name tags, organizational labels, access codes, and physical cable-lock systems are examples of inexpensive ways through which newly acquired hardware and software can be protected.

All sensitive health information should be maintained in designated areas and subjected to strict security control. Such information should only be used in areas that are considered private and inaccessible to unauthorized personnel. For example, terminals should shut down automatically when not in use, and mechanisms should be in place to disconnect terminals after a specific number of invalid attempts to access the system. Written policies should delineate who can access what information and for what purpose; for instance, researchers may only access a specific population's health information for the purpose of research and education. Oftentimes, this means that de-identification is critical to safeguard patients within the specific population used for research and education objectives. Health records personnel must be trained experts in aspects of confidentiality, record access, and storage and should become excellent resources in policy development and implementation.

HIPAA clearly states that no information shall be released without written consent from the data owner (patient), unless otherwise legislated, such as in emergencies or unusual situations. Thus, policies and procedures are essential to guiding health professionals and health records personnel in safeguarding confidential information for both normal and emergency or unusual circumstances. Examples of unusual circumstances where access to a patient's record may be requested include review by a coroner in preparation for an inquest; litigation against the hospital or physician; and potential for litigation because of serious misadventure, alleged malpractice, or complication.

Attention on security and confidentiality regarding electronic health records (EHR) add another layer of complexity. On the one hand, concern about the confidentiality of patient records typically underlie the positive attitude that many patients maintain toward EHR. Ornstein and Bearden interviewed 16 patients of eight different physicians from a medical university.[9] One strategy to ease the concern they found was to have patients kept informed about their records and uses. Borst[10] noted that most patients thought computer-based medical records were unsafe, particularly due to their vulnerability to blackmail. Inevitably, insurance companies and future employers can use these records to make decisions on who to (or not to) insure and/or hire. The potential does exist for discrimination against cases of mental illness, people with HIV infection, or other ill-fated problems. On the other hand, technologies have been developed and are available to ensure the security of EHR. These include Internet security software such as firewalls, intrusion-detection programs, digital certificates, and authentication and authorization software. For example, Andreae[11] discussed how public key cryptography could be used to reliably enhance authentication and authorization of data transfer, thereby eliminating access to confidential information on networks. Unfortunately, nearly 60 percent of all cyber crime goes undetected or unreported, so nobody really knows the extent of cyber-attacks today. However, the same legal requirements that apply to paper records still apply to computer-based records. Waller and Fulton[12] argued that "insiders" (i.e., employees who use the computers on a daily basis) pose the greatest threat to security, given that they are the "closest" to accessing the data.

Retention of records is another major issue of concern because patient records and other information may be needed for legal defense. The retention period should be at least as long as the limitation period during which the organization can face a targeted lawsuit. Thus, these retention periods may vary depending on the type of facility and the governing legislation. The courts have also extended limitation periods depending on the patients involved. Destruction of health information is also controlled by legislation; therefore, written institutional policies must specify the methods of destruction to be used, such as shredding or burning. Routine destruction methods of daily paper accumulation that contains health data and periodic destruction methods of inactive or outdated recorded health data should also be specified, with particular attention to the designation of personnel who will witness or attest to the destruction in writing. Methods of erasing health information that has been recorded or stored by electronic means should also be specified. The point is that issues related to confidentiality, security, and privacy should not impede patient care.

All employees and health data users should also be asked to sign a pledge of confidentiality that incorporates computerized health information within its scope. How to report breaches in security should be included in the policies as well, along with a statement of disciplinary measures for violation of computerized data security. It may be important to note that the acceptance of the electronic signature as a legal signature for admissibility as evidence in court is still not clearly established. Principles of documentation, in the context of computerized health information, should meet legal and professional standards. Appropriate orientation programs, ongoing educational seminars, and attendance at conferences are essential to ensure that managers, health record professionals, and other hospital staff are fully aware of the policies and procedures governing information access, security measures, and confidentiality expectations.

Finally, essential aspects of HMIS security are the use of audit controls and the enforcement of original policies and procedures, with regard to systems and information access. For example, users should only have authorized access to data files that are necessary for completing their assigned work, and breaching of policies must be swiftly and professionally handled to ensure confidence in data integrity and protection of confidentiality. In this business, it should be noted that the biggest concern is the loss of public trust and image. Imagine how patients would feel about giving away their personal information to an organization incapable of and unable to safeguard this information.

Conclusion

In conclusion, the Health Insurance Portability and Accountability Act is a major accomplishment of the U.S. Congress in signifying to the general public that an interest is being taken to protect their personal private health and medical records. If the information was not carefully protected, then the trust between the patients and their caregivers would be jeopardized. The federal government can now assure individuals that healthcare services organizations responsible for transmitting and storing their personal information have to adhere to legally enforceable standards and regulations. Individuals now have more control over their health records and can obtain a copy for their own medical records at any time. They are allowed to file a complaint if, in the healthcare services organization's HMIS, there is a violation of the HIPAA ruling pertaining to the safekeeping of their personal information. Healthcare services organizations now also have a set of guidelines and procedures that they must follow when handling private medical records. These organizations have to hire workers who have knowledge of HIPAA requirements. They have to make sure that the organization respects the law and does not receive a fine from the federal government for not obeying regulations. Failure to follow all procedures and rules can result in a significant penalty against the organization.

HMIS encompasses each aspect of life. Just as the sun is an information system, the same goes for each of us as a human being. Our bodies are information systems that contain everything we will ever need for survival, even in our increasingly complex environment. Our heart is equipped with the necessary software and hardware to pump blood through our complex system of veins; our brains are wired with information useful for transmitting and exchanging signals with all the other parts of our body so that our organs can keep functioning correctly and so we can have the proper use of each of our limbs. We, just as with any other information systems, need protection. Therefore, our bodies have built-in "anti-virus software" that is intended to protect us from certain attacks, such as the common cold. But if our defensive system breaks down, we can always go to a physician for advice on how to enhance that protection against viruses, which our bodies may not always be naturally able to fight. Because the information contained in our bodies is important to our survival, it is also similar to the information that is significant for our continued well-being. Information such as our name, date of birth, and social security number is just as important as our vitals. If our vitals are low, we need the proper care to bring them back to normal. To safeguard our personal information, guidelines and standards must be used to maintain a healthy personal life. With advancing technologies, ensuring the privacy of personal information will have to improve and adapt, just as medication must do for any and all illnesses.

Notes

1. "Status of HIPAA," Online Image, *LRG Healthcare*, http://www.lrgh.org/default.aspx, accessed December 5, 2007.
2. "What, Who, How, When, Penalties," Online Image, *IT Defense Magazine*, http://www.itdefensemag.com/7_06/images/hipaa.gif, accessed December 5, 2007.
3. "HIPAA Compliance Lifecycle," Online Image, HIPAA *Learning Module, Health Care Education and Training*, http://www.hcet.org/graphics/hipaa/cycle.gif, accessed December 5, 2007.
4. J. B. Earp and F. C. Payton, "Information Privacy in the Service Sector: An Exploratory Study of Health Care and Banking Professionals," *Journal of Organizational Computing and Electronic Commerce* 16, no. 2 (2006): 105–122.

5. U.S. Department of Human and Health Services, "Medical Privacy—National Standards to Protect the Privacy of Personal Health Information," April 2007, http://www.hhs.gov/ocr/hipaa/, accessed September 29, 2007.

6. U.S. Department of Health and Human Services, Office for Civil Rights, "Standards for Privacy of Individually Identifiable Health Information," December 4, 2002, http://www.hhs.gov/ocr/hipaa/finalmaster.html, accessed December 5, 2007.

7. U.S. Department of Health and Human Services, "Standards for Electronic Transactions and Code Sets," *HIPAAdvisory*, August 17, 2000, http://www.hipaadvisory.com/regs/finaltrans/summary.htm, accessed December 5, 2007.

8. T. Anderson and P. Lee, *Fault Tolerance: Principles and Practice* (Englewood Cliffs, NJ: Prentice Hall, 1981).

9. S. Ornstein and A. Bearden, "Patient Perspectives on Computer-Based Medical Records," *Yearbook of Medical Informatics* (1995): 247–251.

10. F. Borst, "Synopsis: Computer-Based Patient Records," *Yearbook of Medical Informatics* (1995).

11. M. Andreae, "Confidentiality in Medical Telecommunication," *Lancet* 347 (1996): 487–488.

12. A. Waller and D. Fulton, "The Electronic Chart: Keeping It Confidential and Secure," *Journal of Health and Hospital Law* 26, no. 4 (1993): 104.

Health Management Information System Governance, Policy, and International Perspectives: HMIS Globalization through E-Health

Anantachai Panjamapirom and Philip F. Musa

Editor's Note: The readers should be informed of the choice for including this chapter near the final part of this health management information systems (HMIS) text. Apparently, the application of e-health extends the use of information and communications technologies (ICT) in healthcare as much as HMIS in healthcare services organizations. Accordingly, *HMIS* used in the context of this text is a broad term encompassing all healthcare information systems and technologies applied in a healthcare services organizational context, whereas *e-health* is used specifically in the context of this chapter as an umbrella term encompassing all ICT and related applications in a global healthcare services context. Hence, there is true parallelism in terms of the need for ICT governance, policies, and sharing of innovations among developed, developing, and underdeveloped countries both for HMIS and for e-health. As the editor, I have therefore inserted the term "HMIS" where appropriate to sound the underlying message of the similar challenges facing designers and administrators of healthcare systems—whether deployed as a system for healthcare providers (health informatics), healthcare services organizations (HMIS), or entire populations (e-health). The placement of this chapter near the end of this text represents an attempt to move the readers toward an international perspective of HMIS and to see how the much more organizationally focused discussions in earlier chapters now have the opportunity for embracing a wider and higher perspective to be applied along a global scale. Readers who are interested in this perspective can consult J. Tan (Ed.), *E-Health Information Systems: Introduction to Students and Professionals* (San Francisco: Jossey-Bass, May 2005), a book entirely devoted to the subject of e-health.

CHAPTER OUTLINE

Scenario: *TriZetto and TeleDoc Alliance*

Scenario: *TriZetto and TeleDoc Alliance*[1]

With the increasing expense of providing healthcare for employees, companies are looking for value-based solutions to complement their existing medical coverage. In response to this trend, the TriZetto Group and TelaDoc Medical Services have recently announced a distribution alliance to provide TriZetto's customers with telephone access to TelaDoc's national network of licensed primary care physicians (PCPs). This consumer-centric approach gives patients with noncritical health issues access to care 24 hours a day, 7 days a week, 365 days a year.

Michael Gorton, chief executive officer of TelaDoc, is quick to praise this telephone-based healthcare approach, called *tele-health*. "Telehealth emerges as a high-value, mainstream model, and TriZetto's extensive client base allows TelaDoc to bring this valuable service to the largest population of consumers served by an industry leader with best-practice access, convenience, and savings."

The service is simple and straightforward. Once a TriZetto customer is enrolled in TelaDoc, plan members can call to request a consultation. TelaDoc guarantees a return call from a doctor within three hours, upon which the doctor will provide a brief consultation and may offer follow-up advice. In addition, the physician has the ability to prescribe short-term, over-the-counter medications if appropriate.

"TelaDoc services improve access to care and can deliver significant savings to self-insured organizations," notes Jeff Gary, executive vice president of TelaDoc. "Employers value TelaDoc for its role in sustaining a healthy, productive workplace and providing access to care for individuals who travel and cannot connect with their regular doctor."

Now, imagine that such a service is acceptable and available to everyone throughout the world. How would it affect future healthcare services delivery?

I. Introduction

> *As the world shrinks and nations become increasingly more interconnected, no one nation can afford to turn inward and focus solely on health status, health professions education, or health system development and enhancement simply for the sake of its own citizenry.*
> —Roger J. Bulger, David Hawkins, and John Wyn Owen[2]

Globalization is a comprehensive phenomenon exhibited throughout the long history of the growth of population and the advancement of civilization. Although it may be traced as far back as the 14th century,[3] the phenomenon of the global exchange of ideas, goods, and services has gained much popularity since the close of the 1980s.[4] The antecedents of globalization substantiate an understanding of the current circumstances, whereas the results and their implications are the agents that stimulate changes and future development. Globalization encompasses an array of interactive factors that greatly affect the world in different ways. The term generally has an application on at least six major diverse discourses: economic, technological, environmental, political, social, and cultural contexts.[5,6] It is the intertwined connection among these facets that has transformed the world into its new millennial era.

The world has recognized extensive advantages of globalization. The most common benefits revolve around economics. Economists assert that globalization can lead to free trade, greater competition, economies of scale, more efficient approaches for resource allocation, and increase in economic prosperity, which in turn result in poverty reduction.[7–9] Through the globalized system, nations and their citizens are engaged in exchanging information, embodying cross-cultural diffusion, and creating unprecedented global cultures. As a result of the economic and social globalization, nations have formed relationships in which agreements must take place. Therefore, international political organizations such as the United Nations (UN)[10] and the World Trade Organization (WTO) provide rules and regulations that are utilized to manage the rights of, and relationships among, nations.

To date, many international initiatives have been established to address global degradations in our environment through air and water pollution, as well as global warming.[11,12] Such integral efforts have informed us that globalization is an imperative process to which we must pay close attention. As the achievement of any process requires the right tool, globalization cannot occur without technological advancements. Technology acts as both the catalyst and the enabler of globalization. While the introduction of logistics and information technologies allow the world population to connect and access resources around the globe, the need for more effective and efficient means have prompted constant creation of innovative technologies.

Paradoxically, some people have argued that globalization has given rise to some detrimental effects such as inequality and vulnerability.[13] However, empirical studies have shown that developing countries that have open policies for globalization exhibit lower poverty rates than those that are using inward-oriented policies.[14] Moreover, the World Bank[15] reported that the openness to international integration is a vital factor that contributes to less inequality among countries. Evidence also shows that even though the effect of gross domestic policy (GDP) volatility on developing countries was greater than that of developed countries, the overall volatility on both GDP and export growth for developing countries significantly decreased during the 1990s, except for the East Asia region due to the 1997–1998 financial crisis.[16] Accordingly, these negative effects should not be perceived as adverse consequences of globalization, but rather a result of the unorganized involvement of nations in the global network.

One suggestion is that ideas from globalization in the major contexts can be adapted to the healthcare services industry. If properly implemented, this industry can wholly benefit from globalization. The healthcare services industry can take advantage of the current advancements in information and communications technologies (ICT). A number of empirical studies show that ICT play a prominent part in the solution to various predicaments confronting the global healthcare environment such as an upward spiral of medical costs, unacceptably low quality of care in many countries, increasing medical errors, and administrative inefficiencies.[17]

As a background, calls for the globalization of health care started to gain momentum in the mid-1990s when ICT came to be employed as a new channel to deliver care to patients in remote locations. Since then, various terms such as tele-care, telemedicine, tele-health, and e-health have been used interchangeably. While the ultimate goal of these nomenclatures is to build an integrated, globalized healthcare system that will create values to all populations of the world, they have certain differences in their characteristics and scope. The differences will be explained shortly. To this point, various organizations in both public and private sectors at local and federal levels have remained independent in their efforts toward the same goal. The synergy through the integrated healthcare system[18] would permit developed, developing, and underdeveloped countries to contribute both tangible (i.e., human resources, money, and technology) and intangible (i.e., infrastructural shifts, knowledge, and skills) assets that would otherwise be limited.

We utilize two economic applications—the production possibilities frontier and positive externalities—to analyze the economic perspectives of ICT deployment in health care. This chapter also investigates the barriers to e-health adoption. Using the e-health strategic framework developed by the World Bank[19] and the World Health Organization (WHO), the current status of telemedicine and e-health adoption in developed, developing, and underdeveloped countries is explored. Moreover, we propose methods by which developed and developing countries can contribute to this supreme healthcare management information systems (HMIS) globalization initiative.

II. Tele-Care, Telemedicine, Tele-Health, and E-Health

Numerous definitions have been proposed for various terminologies that are used to identify ICT deployment in health care. However, no one definition has been universally accepted. Even though many of these terms share common and overlapping characteristics, each one conveys a different semantic and covers a different scope or boundary.

Barlow, Bayer, and Curry[20,p.397] define *tele-care* as "a set of services bringing care directly to the end-user" at a remote location via ICT deployment. Among the most commonly cited definitions of *telemedicine* is that given by Dr. Salah H. Mandil, WHO Director of Health Informatics and Telematics, as "the practice of medical care using audio, visual, and data communications: this includes medical care delivery, consultation, diagnosis, treatment, education, and the transfer of medical data."[21,p.4] As referenced by the American College of Nurse Practitioners, *tele-health* refers to "the removal of time and distance barriers for the delivery of health care services or related health care activities. Some of the technologies used in tele-health include telephones, computers, interactive video transmissions, direct links to health care instruments, transmission of images, and teleconferencing by telephone or video."[22] To enhance the understanding of these interrelated terms and bring them into harmony, we borrow from the works of Norris,[23] as presented in Table 13.1.

As shown in Table 13.1, the definitions reveal similar aspects, yet each focuses on different users and recipients of the services. While *tele-care* is central to medical services provided to patients, *telemedicine* involves services benefiting both patients and physicians. In addition, *tele-health* serves patients, physicians, and administrators. Readers who are interested in an in-depth treatment of how these various terminologies relate to each other may also refer to Tan.[24] For completeness of this review, we elaborate on the prevailing view of telemedicine in the next section.

Table 13.1   Definitions of Tele-Care, Telemedicine, and Tele-Health

Term	Definition
tele-care	"the use of information and communication technologies to transfer medical information for the delivery of clinical services to patients in their place of domicile" (p. 4)
telemedicine	"the use of information and communication technologies to transfer medical information for the delivery of clinical and educational services" (p. 4)
tele-health	"the use of information and communication technologies to transfer medical information for the delivery of clinical, administrative, and educational services" (p. 4)

Source: Adapted from Norris, 2002, p. 4. This table is created with permission from Dr. Norris.

III. Types of Telemedicine

Norris[25] identifies four major current categories of telemedicine; the categorization is not meant to provide an exhaustive list of services provided through telemedicine. Whether or not the scope of telemedicine can be expanded depends heavily on the innovative progression of ICT.

Tele-Consultation

This type of telemedicine can occur in the context of real-time provider–provider or provider–patient interactions. Telephone and videoconferencing are the basic ICT used to deliver these services. The more advanced technologies used for *tele-consultation* are mobile health technologies[26,27] and a combination of "a high-speed network, a medical image database, a super-high-definition imaging system, and an IP-based video conferencing system."[28] The main application is tele-radiology in which X-ray files are transmitted 24/7 to obtain result interpretations and consultations around the world. Some other applications include tele-ophthalmology, tele-dermatology, and tele-oncology. Illustrated by their names, these applications represent the utilization of telemedicine in a particular branch of medicine such as ophthalmology, dermatology, and retinology. For example, *tele-opthalmology* refers to the use of ICT to facilitate the provision of care to patients with visual pathway diseases.[29] Some applications of tele-opthalmology are ophthalmic imaging and visual rehabilitation consultations.[30] Basically, tele-opthalmology is the practice of telemedicine of eye care. *Tele-dermatology* is the use of ICT to assist dermatologists and other related health professions to provide care to patients with skin diseases.[31] *Tele-oncology* is used to facilitate the delivery of cancer care covering the entire episode of care ranging from diagnosis to supportive care and follow-up services.[32]

Tele-Education

Knowledge is power. Being able to access and retrieve information and knowledge anywhere, anytime is another service of telemedicine. The most common use of *tele-education* is continuing medical education (CME) in which physicians are not required to participate in live conferences or workshops, but can learn and gain the most up-to-date information or practice guidelines about particular diseases through accessing the Internet. In the United States, the Accreditation Council for Continuing Medical Education (ACCME) is the accrediting body of continuing medical education, ensuring the quality and reliability of information utilized by physicians to maintain their competence and incorporate new knowledge.[33] Therefore, physicians can rely on ACCME-accredited programs that are offered online. Tele-education benefits not only practitioners, but also consumers. Patients are able to access information regarding their symptoms and diseases from multiple legitimate websites, which are provided by highly reputed healthcare services organizations such as world-renowned academic health centers and governmental health-related institutions. The indirect advantage for the patients is that they can have some control over their own health and participate in the shared medical decision making and practice.[34,35] Moreover, this application can act as a new conveyor of medical education, adding value to conventional text-based classrooms. The academics can also benefit from the availability of online publishing and literature searching, as well as collaboration, which will enhance the diffusion of knowledge. The quality of publications can be ascertained among the peer-reviewed journals, popular publications, and authoritative academic databases.

Tele-Monitoring

This type of telemedicine is important; through its use, patients can be consistently monitored even after they are discharged. They can communicate with their physicians concerning their current status, and the ongoing treatment scheme can be modified accordingly. Patients are able to recover in their place of residence rather than being institutionalized in hospitals or other healthcare delivery settings. *Tele-monitoring* can play an important role in life-threatening and time-sensitive conditions such as those arising from a heart attack. One of the tele-monitoring applications is tele-cardiology. *Tele-cardiology* can be used to facilitate disease management among patients with coronary artery disease and chronic heart failure.[36] The patients can self-monitor electrocardiogram (EKG), body weight, and/or blood pressure at home and consult the results with physicians or nurse practitioners. Researchers have found that tele-cardiology is effective in improving patient compliance, increasing the quality of life, and potentially reducing costs.[37]

Tele-Surgery

This is a relatively new concept compared with the others just mentioned. There are two types of *tele-surgery*: tele-mentoring, where specialists provide assistance to the surgeons from a remote location, and tele-presence surgery, where surgeons utilize robotic arms to carry out surgical procedures from a distance. International evidence has confirmed the benefits of both types of tele-surgery. Anvari[38] observed the utilization of tele-mentoring and tele-robotic surgery and reported that knowledge from these practices can be translated rapidly and effectively. He also predicted that these services would eventually transform the surgical world because more advanced HMIS can be deployed. A group of Japanese surgeons and researchers also reported the safety and efficacy of tele-robotic surgery in patients with mucosal or submucosal lesions.[39]

E-Health

Apart from the aforementioned nomenclatures, *e-health* is the recent buzzword that combines everything related to the use of ICT and computers in medical practice and health care. Similar to telemedicine, there are many definitions of e-health. In fact, a review of the literature yields more than 50 unique definitions of e-health.[40] Eysenbach[41] provides a broad definition of this new concept:

> *E-health* is an emerging field in the intersection of medical informatics, public health and business, referring to health services and information delivered or enhanced through the Internet and related technologies. In a broader sense, the term characterizes not only a technical development, but also a state of mind, a way of thinking, an attitude, and a commitment for networked, global thinking, to improve health care locally, regionally, and worldwide by using information and communication technology.

The WHO is currently focusing on e-health as a central theme that connects ICT and health care. Thus, it simply defines e-health as "the use of information and communication technologies (ICT) for health."[42,p.1] The WHO categorizes the application of e-health into three broad areas. These areas are related to the types of telemedicine identified earlier. The categorization also places an emphasis on the services provided to patients and practitioners.

1. *Public services.* These services provide information to people via the Internet.
2. *Knowledge services.* These services are comparable to tele-education in that they aim at conveying medical information, knowledge, and education to the healthcare professionals who are in training and practice.
3. *Provider services.* These services focus on the utilization of e-health applications to deliver healthcare services to others.

For conciseness, we now present these four major terms in the same diagram, as illustrated in Figure 13.1. As shown, *tele-care* is a subset of *telemedicine*, and *telemedicine* is a smaller level of *tele-health*. *E-health* is an umbrella term that embraces the entire medical-related interventions being delivered and connected through ICT. For this reason, the term *e-health* will be used throughout this chapter, as it is the most encompassing term in the globalization of health care.

IV. The Economic Perspectives of ICT and E-Health

Through the innovative advancement of ICT, the world is getting smaller, yet more dynamic. While individuals are connected around the globe by means of information technology (IT) networks, healthcare services organizations have adopted HMIS for both strategic and support purposes. As a consequence, HMIS has become an integral part of the healthcare services industry. With a rapid increase in IT adoption rates, the tremendous advantages of IT have been extensively recognized. Atkinson and McKay[43,p.1] stated that "[t]he integration of IT into virtually all aspects of the economy and society is creating a digitally enabled economy." In effect, IT provides social and economic benefits to the adopters and society as a whole. Therefore, this

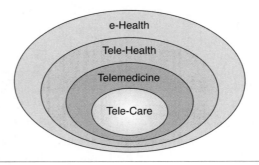

FIGURE 13.1   Tele-Care, Telemedicine, Tele-Health, and E-Health in Perspective.

notion reflects the beneficial implications of the integration of ICT into health care and offers increasingly robust opportunities for globalized e-health.

However, as society strives to attain maximum utilization from limited resources, at least two concerns arise among economists: efficiency and equity.[44] Economists are concerned with production efficiency because it identifies "whether the [products or] services (for a given level of quality) are produced at the lowest cost."[45,p.405] To reach such a goal, products and services must be produced in the most effective way. The other issue is how limited resources can be equitably distributed to the population. As previously discussed, the World Bank found that there is less inequality among nations participating in globalization. Therefore, nations adopting healthcare globalization should permit their citizens to have equal opportunities to access better medical care. Research also supports the notion that telemedicine provides social efficiency.[46] Two theoretical tools—production possibilities frontier and positive externalities—are employed to demonstrate the economic benefits of HMIS or ICT in health care.

Before these two theoretical tools are discussed, we make an assumption to differentiate two periods of e-health adoption. The periods may be illustrated using the rate of adoption theory and an S-curve.[47] The theory states that the adoption of innovation is slow at the initial stage, is followed by a rapid growth, moves into the stabilization, and eventually declines. As illustrated in Figure 13.2, the first period starts from the initial adoption to point A, and the second period is from point A forward.

We argue that both quality and quantity of care increase in the first period, while the second period experiences an increase in quality and a decrease in quantity. These arguments are discussed later.

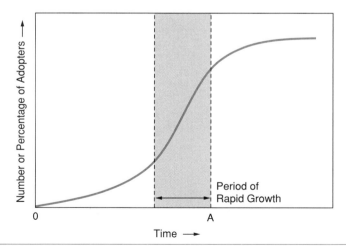

FIGURE 13.2 Rogers's S-Curve Representing Rate of Adoption of an Innovation over Time. *Source:* Adapted from Rogers, 2003. The S-curve diagram has been adapted from Rogers' (1962) written work. E. M. Rogers, *Diffusion of innovation* (New York: Free Press, 1962).

Production Possibility Frontier

Under the assumption that the society only produces two goods and all factors related to production are completely utilized, the production possibility frontier (PPF) model or curve represents all efficient combinations of outputs.[48] The PPF model also illustrates the concepts of "trade-off" and "opportunity costs." In this particular circumstance, we use a PPF curve to explain the trade-off between quality and quantity of care provided to people in the society. As depicted in Figure 13.3, the *x*- and *y*-axes represent the quantity and quality of healthcare services delivered in society.

The assumption is that at point *A*, e-health globalization does not exist. The global healthcare system provides *A(QL)* amount of quality to *A(QN)* people. Once the benefits of ICT are realized, and ICT is brought into the system, the PPF curve is shifted upward and outward. At the new PPF curve, the system can increase the quality of care to *B(QL)* and increase the number of people receiving care to *B(QN)*. This phenomenon takes place in the first period because the production of quality and quantity of medical services provided without ICT are limited. But once the ICT is introduced and its adoption starts to take off, the society as a whole will benefit from the efficiency that ICT brings to the healthcare system. This trend will continue until the society moves into the second period, in which the utilization of ICT in healthcare becomes a commodity and adoption is leveled off.

Thus, with ICT adoption and diffusion, we have the scenario in the second period, where the quality of care continues to increase to *C(QL)*, but the quantity provided will decrease to *C(QN)* because at this point e-health has become an ordinary practice in the global healthcare system from which the majority of citizens in nations can benefit. Because the majority of people

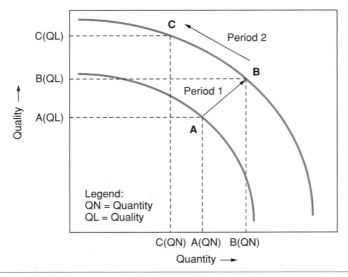

FIGURE 13.3 Production Possibility Frontier between Quality and Quantity in Health Care Delivery System at the First and Second Periods.

have had access to better healthcare services, they are likely to be healthy. Healthy people in turn require less care, and thus lead to the reduction in the amount of medical services produced. This process should be perceived as a cycle. Whenever the new application of ICT is employed in health care, people would continue to gain benefits from it. The notion of positive externality can also be used to substantiate our call for globalization of health care through e-health implementation.

Positive Externality

Goods or services with positive externalities provide benefit to members of society who are not directly involved in the production, transaction, and consumption of the goods or services.[49] Presented in Figure 13.4, the supply curve S is treated as a social marginal cost, which is also equivalent to private marginal cost, and the demand curve D1 represents an individual benefit.[50] Point A represents the free market (i.e., actual equilibrium), where private marginal cost equals private marginal benefit. When a good with positive externalities is present in the market, which results in the socially optimal level or point B (i.e., ideal equilibrium), the problem becomes that there is a discrepancy between the demand curve D1 at the free market and the social marginal benefit curve, which is D2. While we want the society to have Q(2) of e-health and its benefits, the demand at the free market is only D1. For that reason, a public and/or

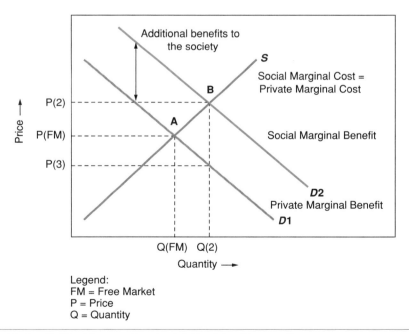

FIGURE 13.4   E-Health as a Good with Positive Externality.

Note: This figure illustrates the increase in social benefit when a good with positive externality is present in the market. *Source:* Adapted from B. Sen, "Externalities," University of Alabama at Birmingham, September 13, 2005. This diagram is created with permission from Dr. Sen.

international policy regarding the price and supply of goods or services with positive externalities is among one of the top priorities of nations and related international organizations.

E-health is considered to be a service with positive externalities that will bring values to the society. The positive externalities of e-health can be derived from two major sources: ICT and health care. Atkinson[51] provided the case that the necessary applications of ICT utilized in e-health, such as broadband telecommunications, lead to positive externalities. An obvious example of how e-health produces positive externalities in healthcare services settings is the increase in preventive care and reduction in infectious disease.[52] If individuals receive care for their infectious disease at the early stage of the contagion, they reduce the risk of infection for other members of the society. In essence, these individuals do not only produce a positive externality by getting care of their conditions, but also avoid a negative externality that could have occurred. Some other benefits to the society include, but are not limited to, the increase in productivity of healthy people and the federal budget savings from fewer needs in healthcare services that can be utilized in other social programs such as education and transportation. While the benefits are initially accrued at the individual level, the positive consequences of these benefits will lead to the socially optimal level. At point A, e-health (a good with positive externality) gets undertraded, and the society would like to reach the ideal level at point B. However, the problem at point B is that an investment in e-health costs $P(2)$, while the market is only willing to pay $P(3)$. The amount that healthcare delivery organizations, or even the government of developing and undeveloped nations, are willing to pay for e-health infrastructures might be limited due to scarce resources. In this situation, international organizations such as the World Bank and WHO have to take action in order to provide the global society with the optimal benefit level.

V. Factors Influencing the Adoption of E-Health

To study adoption of innovation, researchers have extensively utilized four different theoretical paradigms from which they draw antecedent factors. These frameworks include the technology adoption model, the theory of planned behavior, the diffusion of innovation theory, and the technology-organization-environment framework. Based on these models, a number of technological and nontechnological antecedents influencing the adoption of e-health are discussed.

Technology Acceptance Model

Developed by Davis,[53] the technology acceptance model (TAM) has become one of the most influential theoretical foundations used in studying an acceptance of new technology at an individual level. Two main constructs included in this model—perceived usefulness (PU) and perceived ease-of-use (PEOU)—are related to the perception of users toward the new technology.[54,55] This model is used to study the acceptance of telemedicine technology among physicians in Hong Kong and is found to have a reasonable prediction.[56] TAM has also been modified based on studies in developing countries that identified accessibility as a factor that played a major role in ultimate adoption of technology.[57] In another related study, TAM was extended to study sustainable adoption of technologies for human development in developing countries.[58] Some studies in the healthcare context included additional factors to the original TAM and still found PU and/or PEOU to be strong determinants of intention to use Internet-based health applications or telemedicine.[59,60] Over the past several years, numerous studies have shown that TAM is a valid and parsimonious theoretical framework for examining adoption of technological innovation.[61,62]

Theory of Planned Behavior

Extended from the psychological theory of reasoned action (TRA) by Ajzen and Fishbein,[63] the theory of planned behavior (TPB)[64–66] suggests that an individual's intentions to adopt and use technology can be explained by three factors:

1. *Attitudes toward behavior*, or an individual's perceptions toward his or her performance of particular behavior (i.e., adopting technology).
2. *Subjective norms*, or an individual's perceptions about particular behavior that are influenced by social normative pressures (i.e., significant others' beliefs on whether an individual should or should not adopt technology).
3. *Perceived behavioral control*, or an individual's perceptions about ease or difficulty of performing a particular behavior (i.e., adoption of technology can be influenced by his or her efforts).

Utilizing a theory comparison approach, Chau and Hu[67] employed both TAM and TPB in examining physicians' intentions to accept telemedicine technology. Their findings suggest that TPB may be less applicable than TAM in a study of ICT innovation acceptance.

Diffusion of Innovation Theory

Initially introduced in 1962, Rogers's diffusion of innovation theory (DOIT) has become a seminal theory employed among researchers in studying adoption of innovation.[68] Unlike TAM and TPB, DOIT focuses on the attributes of innovation as predictors of adoption and may be applied at an organizational level. To lend itself more readily to be adopted, an innovation must contain five attributes: relative advantage, compatibility, complexity, trialability, and observability. Menachemi, Burke, and Ayers[69] provide an informative analysis of how these attributes can affect adoption of telemedicine among physicians, patients, hospital administrators, and payors.

Apart from these attributes, Rogers also emphasizes several other important factors that play a major role in adoption of innovation. Rogers asserts that a *communication channel* is an important means through which messages are passed along from one individual to another. He further explains that even though *mass media* are a great means to rapidly communicate with the public and potential adopters, *interpersonal communication* or word-of-mouth is more effective in persuading people to espouse an innovation. The interpersonal communication channel is even more powerful if individuals share similar socioeconomic status and educational level.[70] In addition, because potential adopters are a member of the *society, social norms, behaviors, structures*, and *systems* are inevitable factors that researchers must take into considerations when studying adoption of innovation.

Technology-Organization-Environment Model

Tornatzky and Fleischer[71] developed the technology-organization-environment (TOE) model, a comprehensive framework, to study adoption of technological innovation at an organizational level. They argue that technological, organizational, and environmental aspects of an organization influence its adoption and implementation of innovative technology.

The *technological* facet refers to the availability of technologies that an organization can access internally and externally. These include existing technologies currently available in-house and other technologies that an organization can acquire in the market. The *organizational* facet describes the characteristics of an organization, such as firm size, type of organization structure, complexity of managerial structure, and the amount of slack resources. The *environmental* aspect encompasses many factors regarding the industry structure, competition, suppliers, and politics and regulations.

One of the advantages of this model is that it more closely reflects the nature of an organization's operation. While researchers utilized this model as a theoretical framework to conduct studies of adoption of innovation in other industries,[72–74] it has not been employed for such studies in the healthcare services industry.

VI. Barriers to E-Health Adoption

Researchers have classified different types of barriers to the diffusion and adoption of e-health.[75] This discussion focuses on four major issues: financial, technological, social/cultural, and legal. The awareness and comprehension of these barriers are important because they prevent the society from achieving the ultimate goal of healthcare globalization through initiatives such as e-health.

Financial Barriers

Even though HMIS development costs have significantly dropped over the past decade, some nations still find it difficult to acquire the necessary infrastructure. Some developing countries argue that an investment in HMIS is not prudent or possible when their citizens still lack basic necessities such as water, food, housing, and basic education. Lam[76] stated that the limited resources, different needs, and healthcare settings in developing countries should serve as an urgent need for us to search for new treatment methods that are more effective and efficient than existing practices utilized in developed countries. Even for developed nations that have the means, the cost of fully implementing e-health and telemedicine in all locales and regions is considered a major undertaking.

Another financial barrier is rooted in the cost-effectiveness analysis. Researchers have attempted to conduct cost-effectiveness analysis of telemedicine, but they are confronting some uncertainties such as the rapid change of HMIS and the costs of implementing such systems, joint costs among different ICT used in health care, and multiple uses of HMIS.[77,78]

However, recent research studies have found that widespread utilization of telemedicine can contribute to a considerable reduction in costs. Spaulding[79] and his research team reported that the cost of tele-consultation dropped from $7,328 when only one tele-consultation was performed to below $150 when 200 tele-consultations were achieved. As a result, the true financial benefits of telemedicine or HMIS can be realized when there is an economy of scale. Thus, e-health makes complete sense if it is globalized.

Technological Barriers

Whenever technologies, especially HMIS, become the center of discussion, we must deal with the problems of infrastructure, standardization, compatibility, reliability, capacity, availability, assistance, and maintenance. E-health and telemedicine cannot be accomplished unless a telecommunications infrastructure is sufficiently available to handle the transmission of tele-medical data and information. Even though standardization and compatibility are critical issues for HMIS implementation, assistance and maintenance are inevitable for ongoing operations. The initial investment in HMIS infrastructure is more problematic in underdeveloped and developing countries than developed countries. The strategies used to overcome this barrier are covered in a later section.

Social and Cultural Barriers

Obviously, there are social and cultural differences among nations around the world. As neither ICT nor HMIS are artifacts, it is almost impossible to ensure that a specific e-health application would be acceptable similarly across various societies and cultures. Therefore, most such applications would normally need to be modified to fit local contexts. This requires that healthcare processes that affect interactions among global, regional, and local levels be understood.[80] Moreover, countries take different approaches in handling and managing healthcare planning and policies. Lack of political will is another important issue. Whether an e-health system will be fully implemented depends on the commitment among various groups in the society, especially the political group and the government that leads the country. These fragmented systems only obstruct the growth and successful development of global e-health.

Legal Barriers

Legal conundrums are the top concern among physicians, healthcare managers, and policy makers. An overwhelming list of key issues includes "confidentiality and security, patients' right of access, data protection, duty of care, standards of care, malpractice, suitability and failure of equipment, physician licensure and accreditation, physician reimbursement, intellectual property rights," and income taxes.[81,p.37] These obstacles add another critical facet to the complexity of e-health at a global level.

Altogether, these various barriers imply a high need for an establishment of a central entity that will act as a strong advocate of global e-health, organize the collaborative efforts among nations of the world, and provide a practical strategic framework. The framework can then be utilized as a map and a compass that would guide all nations of the world to the same destination of healthcare globalization. Because e-health processes involve various stakeholders, we now present some of the key constituents with a major stake in e-health.

VII. Stakeholder Analysis

E-health is a systemwide integrated process innovation; thus, the level of success in its widespread adoption must be accelerated by various stakeholders and is dependent upon multiple factors. The power of e-health to affect healthcare services delivery systems at the global level not only is beneficial to humanity, but also contributes to the complexity of its adoption. Therefore, the involvement of major stakeholders and their perspectives concerning this process innovation must be addressed.

This section illustrates an extensive, but not exhaustive, list of important stakeholders involved in the process of planning, adoption, and implementation of e-health. No single group of stakeholders is more important than another. Each and every stakeholder plays an important and unique role in the process of adoption.

International Organizations

Because e-health is a worldwide paradigm shift in healthcare delivery systems, the major international entities such as WHO, the World Bank, and the United Nations take on key roles in setting the strategic directions; acting as central collaborating organizations; providing both monetary and nonmonetary resources; and enacting international policies regarding the adoption, implementation, and utilization of e-health. WHO has built a strategic framework that nations could employ as a guideline in adopting and implementing e-health.[82] Details of the WHO strategic framework are presented in a later section.

Government

At the national level, the government of each country is an influential body that can support and expedite the development of e-health policies and its standards, as well as the adoption and implementation of e-health among other relevant stakeholders. A number of countries, such as the United States, Canada, and the United Kingdom, are placing e-health at the top priority of their national agendas. The political will shared among the members of the government leadership is inevitable to the success of this systemwide process innovation. However, even though the government is playing a highly supportive role, the federal government of various countries, including both developed and developing countries, is confronting the most fragile issue of minimal available funding. Nevertheless, some countries, such as Canada and Ireland are heavily investing in e-health.[83,84]

Physicians/Clinical Providers

Physicians and other clinical providers, such as nurses, form another group of vital stakeholders of the e-health system because they are the direct users of the system and are arguably assumed to have a share in taking the responsibility for such an investment. Physicians and nurses must be directly involved in the design process of any e-health platform simply because this system will eventually replace their routine activities. Moreover, they have to contribute the medical knowledge to be incorporated into the system. One of the major barriers among the care providers is the lack of time,[85] which might prevent them from participating in the various steps of e-health adoption and implementation. Moreover, the alteration of routine practices might lead to the decrease in productivity and efficiency for both administrative and clinical staff—at least for a time.

Hospitals

Hospitals have a comprehensive awareness of e-health and have been a leading entity in its investment. Hospitals are a major provider of healthcare services, are most ready in terms of facility and infrastructure, and thus are assumed to acquire ICT needed for e-health. As with other stakeholders, limited funding and increasing IT costs are the major concerns for all hospitals. Moreover, most hospitals, especially those with for-profit status, are reluctant to share information that could benefit competitors. However, if fully implemented, e-health could help reduce the asymmetric pattern of information distribution among all hospitals, as well as between the hospitals/providers and consumers/patients. In effect, if the hospitals and providers have access to the same types and amounts of information and are not concerned too much about using unrevealed information to create competitive advantages, they may turn their attention, time, and effort to focus on improving quality of care and saving lives.

Patients

As the world moves farther into the information age, patients and/or health consumers have better awareness of information regarding diagnosis, symptoms, and available treatment alternatives. They tend to support the concept and completion of e-health. However, a large percentage of population of the world is living in underserved areas that bar them from necessary infrastructure, as well as the knowledge and information about e-health. Although patients are more likely to support this innovation, they are still addressing some imperative concerns. The most critical concern is privacy protection because with this system, patients' individual information and personal health records are transmitted electronically and can be accessed by multiple people, ranging from bill collectors to physicians associated with various types of healthcare services organizations. In some countries such as the United States, where the majority of the population relies on the provision of private or employer-sponsored health insurance, consumers are also concerned that insurance companies will use their information to limit benefits, increase premiums, or possibly eliminate their insurance coverage policy. Under employer-sponsored health plans, employees are afraid that their employers will terminate employment upon having knowledge of their adverse health status.

Application Vendors

This group takes a completely supportive role in the e-health system because it has a direct benefit from developing an e-health platform. However, the competition among vendors is a major concern. There are many components related to the applications of e-health (in most geographic markets), so it is unlikely that any one vendor will have a dominant market share. However, the first mover will be able to take advantage of initial occupant of a market segment.

As many entities are trying to set a standard for e-health, vendors are uncertain about what will happen to their existing or in-development platforms and products. Also, many approaching policies on e-health standards and products in different countries are threatening the stability of many vendors. Because of the fact that different medical services providers might have different needs in their system and might require some customization, vendors cannot take advantage of fixed cost allocation for mass production.

Third-Party Payors

Third-party payors include different entities such as insurance companies, government agencies, and employers. These groups have important stakes in the development of e-health. First, when patients do not directly pay for their medical services, the third-party payors are the source of reimbursement of payment for medical bills charged to the patients by hospitals and physicians. Thus, they indirectly act as the provider of funding of any programs in which hospitals or physician practices want to invest. Second, third-party payors play a vital role in the successful implementation of e-health because they are involved in the daily transaction of an innumerable amount of health information. The data they collect can benefit both providers and patients in numerous ways, such as elimination of repeated diagnostic orders, prevention of prescription errors, and improvement of overall quality. However, similar to hospitals, insurers are concerned about availability of information to competitors, which could be manipulated against their competitive advantages.

Even so, while government agencies are inclined to publicly support e-health, some private insurance companies are still suspicious about the financial and time benefits.[86] The principal goal of insurance companies is to keep the "medical loss ratio" as low as possible. The medical loss ratio is "the percentage of the insurer's premiums paid out in medical claims" and is used by Wall Street for judging their performance.[87,p.1250] Therefore, the lower the medical loss ratio, the higher the profits insurance companies will make. Whether or not e-health can really reduce the amount paid out in medical claims is uncertain and requires further evidence-based studies or more business cases. Regarding the time savings for medical claim processing, insurers argue that slow adjudication is caused by the presumption that every claim is subject to errors and misrepresentation and thus requires scrutiny for potential frauds and abuses. However, insurance companies should benefit a great deal from using the administrative portion of e-health to track frauds and abuses.

VIII. WHO's Strategic Framework for E-Health Development

Based on the World Bank's logical framework on e-strategies, the WHO has developed the e-health development model,[88] which is illustrated in Figure 13.5. The model encompasses three tiers and constructs a solid foundation for enacting policies and actions toward the provision of e-health systems. Specifically, it is a guideline for strategic planning and implementation, as well as monitoring and control. It also offers assistance to nations in terms of preparation for the aforementioned challenges.

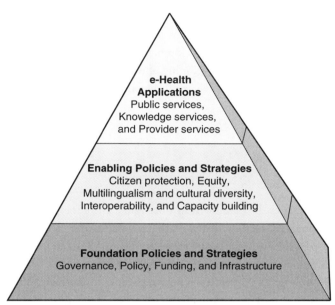

FIGURE 13.5   Framework for Strategic-Health Development. *Source:* Adapted from WHO, 2007, p. 15.

The bottom tier in Figure 13.5 is the basis for e-health implementation in nations. The national commitment to this innovation is vital to further development at the top two tiers. Established at a national level, a governing entity must include multiple stakeholders, delineate the vision, and bestow leadership and directions. It is also responsible for creating e-health policies and funding approaches and mechanisms for infrastructure development that supports e-health systems.

The second tier defines enabling actions that link foundation policies and strategies to the e-health applications. This level addresses the barriers and quests for strategic solutions that are appropriate and practical. The enabling actions involve citizen protection, equity promotion, multilingual capabilities, groundwork for cultural diversity, assurance of interoperability among e-health systems, and enhancement of HMIS and ICT capacity and capabilities among healthcare professionals and students.

The top tier is the linkage between the e-health systems and the citizens of the nations. It is the e-health services that are delivered to consumers and providers. The success of e-health applications relies heavily on the strong foundation and proper execution in policies and strategies determined in the first two tiers.

In 2005–2006, the WHO utilized this model as a background framework to conduct a global survey to examine the current status of e-health across various countries. WHO emphasizes the components in all three tiers. The participating countries are divided into income groups defined by the World Bank[89]: high, upper-middle, lower-middle, and low. The results indicated a projected relative growth of 35 percent in national e-health policy by 2008, which would result in a total of about 85 percent of the countries. This number exhibits a promising trend of e-health development around the world. The overall prediction is that as e-health applications become more widespread, countries in the lower-middle- and low-income groups would remain less progressed in e-health development than those in the high- and upper-middle-income counterparts, suggesting that developing and undeveloped countries would need additional guidance and support from WHO and other international entities in both public and private sectors.

IX. Flow of Resources between Developed and Developing Countries

This section briefly discusses the possible flow of tangible and intangible resources between developed and developing countries. Although the results of the WHO global survey imply higher needs among developing and undeveloped countries, they can—at the same time—contribute to the development of healthcare globalization. While the developed countries have advantages in supplying tangible resources such as capital for investment, they can in turn gain knowledge, which is the most powerful intangible asset, from developing and undeveloped countries.

World Bank focuses on development through knowledge. It identifies the importance of knowledge in the process of transforming limited resources into things that meet our needs. Knowledge-sharing through ICT is the highlight of e-health that is expected by both international organizations and countries. Through continuous knowledge-sharing, the healthcare system will gain inner coherence because scientific medicine is enforced by accountability and legitimacy.[90]

Researchers in developed countries can learn and benefit from the studies conducted in developing and undeveloped countries. Many empirical studies related to telemedicine as well as HMIS have been conducted in developing parts of the world, and the results from these studies can lead to more care and research and may introduce alternative treatments to some existing diseases.[91,92] Along with a rapid increase in international travel, the emergence of serious infectious diseases, such as human immunodeficiency virus (HIV) and the recent international outbreaks of severe acute respiratory syndrome (SARS), has prompted countries around the world to prepare for these global threats. We believe that e-health globalization would provide some much-needed intervention in these circumstances and countless other scenarios.

The use of directly observed therapy, short-term (DOTS) for treating tuberculosis is a good example to show that developed countries can learn and adopt the practices from developing countries. This particular treatment for tuberculosis was found to be effective in Africa and Asia in the early 1950s and has since become the standard method of treatment, but the U.S. Centers for Disease Control and Prevention (CDC) first recommended it for tuberculosis patients only in 1993.[93] Even though developing countries might lack sophisticated technology and hefty research and development funds, they do have some natural resources and can conduct efficient but innovative research that can produce a lot of knowledge that could be shared with the rest of the world. Research experience can also be transferred among various contexts across the world.

X. Conclusion

E-health has widely opened more channels for distributing medical information and knowledge across international boundaries. We suggest that the production possibility frontier (PPF) economic tool theoretically demonstrates that e-health can improve the wellness of the world population and increase efficiency and effectiveness in the healthcare delivery system. The implication of external, positive effects of e-health calls for urgent political support and investment from private sectors. To help accelerate the adoption of e-health development, international entities such as the WHO and World Bank should take action in restricting or controlling the price of ICT, co-fund research and major international efforts in HMIS implementations, and/or encourage developing and undeveloped countries to adopt and invest in e-Health by providing some levels of subsidies and transferred expertise.

The international agenda should increase the emphasis on social values while maintaining the focus on the economic value of trade. Through this combination, policies and actions can aim toward maximizing the economic values without imposing negative consequences on citizens of the world. Several theories that help with the understanding of the factors that influence e-health adoption were presented, as well as some of the barriers to e-health adoption. We also presented a discussion on key stakeholders in e-health, because understanding each stakeholder's perspective and role enhances the implementation and adoption process. The strategic framework set forth by WHO can serve as a strong foundation for the healthcare globalization through e-health. Furthermore, the current status of e-health development in developed and developing countries shows a positive trend. The collaboration among countries and international entities is imperative in the process of design, implementation, and evaluation of e-health endeavors.

While developed countries have the ability to provide tangible supports to this global health and wellness initiative, developing countries are also able to contribute in terms of natural resources and knowledge sharing. Research has shown that developed countries can attain benefits from innovative research studies conducted in developing countries. Through mutual exchange, the world can achieve the ultimate goal of an integrated, globalized healthcare system.

Notes

1. "TriZetto & TelaDoc Team to Help Benefits Administrators Expand Member Access to Physicians," *Business Wire*, http://findarticles.com/p/articles/mi_m0EIN/is_2008_May_19/ai_n25433162, accessed May 19, 2008.

2. R. J. Bulger, D. Hawkins, and J. W. Owen, "Forward." In D. E. Holmes (Ed.). *Reflections of Globalization of Health: Consequences of the 3rd Trilateral Conference* (Washington, DC: Association of Academic Health Centers, 1999): v–vi.

3. D. Ludden, "A Quick Guide to the World History of Globalization" (2007), http://www.sas.upenn.edu/~dludden/global1.htm, accessed August 9, 2007.

4. F. W. Riggs, "Globalization: Key Concepts" (July 29, 2000), http://www2.hawaii.edu/~fredr/glocon.htm, accessed August 9, 2007.

5. P. Raskin, T. Banuri, G. Gallopín, P. Gutman, A. Hammond, R. Kates, and R. Swart, *The Great Transition: The Promise and the Lure of the Times Ahead* (Boston: Stockholm Environment Institute, 2002).

6. International Monetary Fund, "Globalization: Threat or Opportunity?" (April 12, 2000), http://www.imf.org/external/np/exr/ib/2000/041200.htm, accessed August 9, 2007.

7. T. Levitt, "The Globalization of Markets," *Harvard Business Review* 61, no. 3 (1983): 92–102.

8. P. Masson, "Globalization: Facts and Figures" (2001), International Monetary Fund website, http://www.imf.org/external/pubs/ft/pdp/2001/pdp04.pdf, accessed August 9, 2007.

9. J. D. Sachs, *The End of Poverty: Economic Possibilities for Our Time* (New York: Penguin Press, 2005).

10. United Nations, "Definition of Developed and Developing Countries" (2007), http://unstats.un.org/unsd/cdb/cdb_dict_xrxx.asp?def_code=491, accessed December 22, 2007.

11. World Health Organization, "Global Environmental Change" (2007a), World Health Organization website, http://www.who.int/globalchange/en/, accessed August 9, 2007.

12. J. A. Charles, "The Environmental Benefits of Globalization: Rising Global Affluence Is a Good Thing for Environmental Sustainability" (July 14, 2004), http://www.globalenvision.org/library/1/645/, accessed August 9, 2007.

13. World Bank, "Poverty in an Age of Globalization" (2000), World Bank website, http://www1.worldbank.org/economicpolicy/globalization/documents/povertyglobalization.pdf, accessed August 9, 2007.

14. Sachs (2005).

15. World Bank. (2000).

16. Ibid.

17. J. Walker, E. Pan, D. Johnston, J. Adler-Milstein, D. W. Bates, and B. Middleton, B. "The Value of Health Care Information Exchange and Interoperability," *Health Affairs*, Suppl. Web Exclusives (January–June 2005): W5-10–W5-18.

18. J. Tan (Ed.) *E-Health Information Systems: Introduction to Students and Professionals* (San Francisco: Jossey-Bass, 2005).

19. World Bank, *World Development Report 1998/99: Knowledge for Development* [electronic version] (Oxford, UK: Oxford University Press, 1999).

20. J. Barlow, S. Bayer, and R. Curry, "Implementing Complex Innovations in Fluid Multi-Stakeholder Environments: Experiences of 'Telecare.'" *Technovation* 26, no. 3 (2006): 396–406.

21. N. Al-Shorbaji, "Health Informatics and Telematics with Reference to the Work of WHO/EMRO" (2000, p. 4), World Health Organization website, http://www.emro.who.int/publications/IT.pdf, accessed July 11, 2007.

22. American College of Nurse Practitioners, "What Is Telehealth?" (2007), http://www.acnpweb.org/i4a/pages/Index.cfm?pageID=3470, accessed August 10, 2007.

23. A. C. Norris, *Essentials of Telemedicine and Telecare* (West Sussex, UK; New York: John Wiley & Sons, Ltd., 2002).

24. Tan (2005).

25. Norris (2002).

26. P. Olla and J. Tan, "The M-Health Reference Model: An Organizing Framework for Conceptualizing Mobile Health Systems," *International Journal of Health Information Systems & Informatics* 1, no. 2 (April–June 2006): 1–19.

27. P. Olla, "Mobile Health Technology of the Future: Creation of an M-Health Taxonomy Based on Proximity," *International Journal of Healthcare Technology and Management* 8, no. 3/4 (2007): 370–387.

28. T. Yamaguchi, T. Sakano, T. Fujii, Y. Ando, and M. Kitamura, "Design of Medical Teleconsultation Support System Using Super-High-Definition Imaging System," *Systems and Computers in Japan* 33, no. 8 (2002): 9–18.

29. M. Kifle, V. Mbarika, and P. Datta, P. (2006). "Telemedicine in Sub-Saharan Africa: The Case of Teleopthalmology and Eye Care in Ethiopia," *Journal of the American Society for Information Science and Technology* 57, no. 10 (2006): 1383–1393.

30. Ibid.

31. A. J. Watson, H. Bergman, and J. C. Kvedar, J.C. (2007). "Teledermatology" (2007), http://www.emedicine.com/derm/topic527.htm, accessed December 22, 2007.

32. R. S. Weinstein et al., "The Innovative Bundling of Teleradiology, Telepathology, and Teleoncology Services," *IBM Systems Journal* 46, no. 1 (2007): 69–84.

33. Accreditation Council for Continuing Medical Education, "About Us" (2007), http://www.accme.org/index.cfm/fa/about.home/About.cfm, accessed December 22, 2007.

34. R. M. Kaplan, "Shared Medical Decision-Making: A New Paradigm for Behavioral Medicine—1997 Presidential Address," *The Society of Behavioral Medicine* 21 (1999): 3–11.

35. R. M. Kaplan and D. L. Frosch, "Decision Making in Medicine and Health Care," *Annual Review of Clinical Psychology* 1 (2005): 525–556.

36. A. Roth, H. Korb, R. Gadot, and E. Kalter, "Telecardiology for Patients with Acute or Chronic Cardiac Complaints: The 'SHL' Experience in Israel and Germany," *International Journal of Medical Informatics* 75, no. 9 (2006): 643–645.

37. F. Giallauria et al., "Efficacy of Telecardiology in Improving the Results of Cardiac Rehabilitation after Acute Myocardial Infarction," *Monaldi Archives for Chest Disease* 66, no. 1 (2006): 8–12. Abstract retrieved August 10, 2007, from PubMed database.

38. M. Anvari, "Telesurgery: Remote Knowledge Translation in Clinical Surgery," *World Journal of Surgery* 31, no. 8 (2007): 1545–1550.

39. Y. Hirano, N. Ishikawa, K. Omura, N. Inaki, C. Hiranuma, R. Waseda, and G. Watanabe (2007), "Robotic Intragastric Surgery: A New Surgical Approach for the Gastric Lesion" [electronic version], *Surgical Endoscopy* (online publication ahead of print).

40. H. Oh, C. Rizo, M. Enkin, and A. Jadad, "What Is eHealth (3): A Systematic Review of Published Definitions" [electronic version], *Journal of Medical Internet Research* 7, no. 1 (2005): e1.

41. G. Eysenbach, "What Is E-Health?" [electronic version], *Journal of Medical Internet Research* 3, no. 2 (2001): e20.

42. World Health Organization, "Global Observatory for eHealth" (2007b), World Health Organization website, http://www.who.int/ehealth/resources/bf_full.pdf, accessed July 11, 2007.

43. R. D. Atkinson and A. S. McKay, "Digital Prosperity: Understanding the Economic Benefits of the Information Technology Revolution" (2007), Information Technology & Innovation Foundation website, http://www.itif.org/files/digital_prosperity.pdf, accessed July 11, 2007.

44. P. J. Feldstein, *Health Policy Issues: An Economic Perspective*, 3rd ed. (Chicago: Health Administration Press, 2003).

45. Ibid.

46. V. Stolyar, A. Selkov, O. Atkov, and E. Chueva, "Social Efficiency of Modern Telemedicine" (April 21, 2004). Paper presented at the Med-e-Tel 2004 Conference. Abstract retrieved August 10, 2007, from http://www.medetel.lu/index.php?rub=educational_program&page=parallel_sessions_2004.

47. E. M. Rogers, *Diffusion of Innovations*, 5th ed. (New York: Free Press, 2003).

48. S. Folland, A. C. Goodman, and M. Stano, *The Economics of Health and Health Care*, 4th ed. (Upper Saddle River, NJ: Pearson Education, 2004).

49. B. McPake, C. Normand, and L. Kumaranayake, *Health Economics: An International Perspective* (New York: Routledge, 2002).

50. B. Sen, "Externalities" (Birmingham: University of Alabama at Birmingham, September 13, 2005).

51. R. D. Atkinson, "The Case for a National Broadband Policy" (2007), http://www.itif.org/files/CaseForNationalBroadbandPolicy.pdf, accessed September 28, 2007.

52. L. Androuchko and I. Nakajima, "Developing Countries and E-Health Services" (2004), http://ieeexplore.ieee.org/iel5/9246/29313/01324524.pdf, accessed September 28, 2007.

53. F. D. Davis, "Perceived Usefulness, Perceived Ease of Use, and User Acceptance of Information Technology," *MIS Quarterly* 13, no. 3 (1989): 319–340.
54. F. D. Davis, R. P. Bagozzi, and P. R. Warshaw, "User Acceptance of Computer Technology: A Comparison of Two Theoretical Models," *Management Science* 35 (1989): 982–1003.
55. R. P. Bagozzi, F. D. Davis, and P. R. Warshaw, "Development and Test of a Theory of Technological Learning and Usage," *Human Relations* 45, no. 7 (1992): 660–686.
56. P. J. Hu, P. Y. K. Chau, O. R. L. Sheng, and K. Y. Tam, "Examining the Technology Acceptance Model Using Physician Acceptance of Telemedicine Technology," *Journal of Management Information Systems* 16, no. 2 (1999): 91–112.
57. P. F. Musa, "Making a Case for Modifying the Technology Acceptance Model to Account for Limited Accessibility in Developing Countries," *Journal of Information Technology for Development* 12, no. 3 (2006): 213–224.
58. P. F. Musa, P. Meso, and V. Mbarika, "Toward Sustainable Adoption of Technologies for Human Development in Sub-Saharan Africa: Precursors, Diagnostics, and Prescriptions," *Communications of the Association for Information Systems* 15, no. 33 (2005): 592–608.
59. W. G. Chismar and S. Wiley-Patton, "Does the Extended Technology Acceptance Model Apply to Physicians," *Proceedings of the 36th Annual Hawaii International Conference on System Sciences (HICSS'03)*, (January 2002), p. 160a, http://csdl2.computer.org/comp/proceedings/hicss/2003/1874/06/187460160a.pdf, accessed November 17, 2007.
60. D. Vieru, "A Model for Telemedicine Adoption: A Survey of Physicians in the Provinces of Quebec and Nova Scotia," M.Sc. dissertation, Concordia University, Canada (2001). Retrieved November 18, 2007, from ProQuest Digital Dissertations database (Publication No. AAT MQ59291).
61. V. Venkatesh, M. G. Morris, G. B. Davis, and F. D. Davis, "User Acceptance of Information Technology: Toward a Unified View," *MIS Quarterly* 27, no. 3 (2003): 425–478.
62. V. Venkatesh and F. D. Davis, "A Theoretical Extension of the Technology Acceptance Model: Four Longitudinal Studies," *Management Science* 46, no. 2 (2000): 186–204.
63. I. Ajzen and M. Fishbein, *Understanding Attitudes and Predicting Social Behavior* (Englewood Cliffs, NJ: Prentice-Hall, 1980).
64. I. Ajzen, I. (1985). "From Intention to Actions: A Theory of Planned Behavior." In J. Kuhl and J. Bechmann (Eds.), *Action Control: From Cognition to Behavior* (New York: Springer, 1985): 11–39.
65. M. Fishbein and I. Ajzen, *Belief, Attitude, Intention, and Behavior: An Introduction to Theory and Research* (Reading, MA: Addison-Wesley, 1975).
66. I. Ajzen, "The Theory of Planned Behavior," *Organizational Behavior and Human Decision Processes* 50 (1991): 179–211.
67. P. Y. K. Chau and P. J. Hu, "Investigating Healthcare Professionals' Decisions to Accept Telemedicine Technology: An Empirical Test of Competing Theories," *Information and Management* 39 (2002): 297–311.
68. Rogers (2003).
69. N. Menachemi, D. E. Burke, and D. J. Ayers, "Factors Affecting the Adoption of Telemedicine—A Multiple Adopter Perspective," *Journal of Medical Systems* 28, no. 6 (2004): 617–632.
70. Rogers (2003).
71. L. G. Tornatzky and M. Fleischer, *The Process of Technology Innovation* (Lexington, MA: Lexington Books, 1990).
72. K. Zhu, K. L. Kraemer, S. Xu, and J. Dedrick, "Information Technology Payoff in E-Business Environments: An International Perspective on Value Creation of E-Business in the Financial Services Industry," *Journal of Management Information Systems* 21, no. 1 (2004): 17–54.

73. K. Zhu, K. L. Kraemer, and S. Xu, "A Cross-Country Study of Electronic Business Adoption Using the Technology-Organization-Environment Framework," *ICIS 2002: 23rd Annual International Conference on Information Systems* (December 2002): 337–348. Retrieved November 17, 2007, from http://www.crito.uci.edu/publications/pdf/CrossCountryStudy.pdf.

74. K. K. Y. Kuan, and P. Y. K. Chau, "A Perception-Based Model for EDI Adoption in Small Businesses Using a Technology-Organization-Environment Framework," *Information & Management* 38, no. 8 (2001): 507–512.

75. H. Tanriverdi and C. S. Iacona, "Diffusion of Telemedicine: A Knowledge Barrier Perspective," *Telemedicine Journal* 5, no. 3 (1999): 223–244.

76. C. L. K. Lam, "Knowledge Can Flow from Developing to Developed Countries," *British Medical Journal* 312 (2000): 830.

77. J. E. Sisk and J. H. Sanders, "A Proposed Framework for Economic Evaluation of Telemedicine," *Telemedicine Journal* 4, no. 1 (1998): 31–37.

78. M. Beach, P. Miller and I. Goodall, "Evaluating Telemedicine in an Accident and Emergency Setting," *Computer Methods and Programs in Biomedicine* 64, no. 3 (2001): 215–223.

79. R. J. Spaulding (2007). "Cost Analysis: Does Telemedicine Cost More, Less, or about the Same as Traditional Methods of Consulting with Patients?" http://www2.kumc.edu/telemedicine/research/costanalysis.htm, accessed August 9, 2007.

80. Musa (2006).

81. Norris (2002): 37.

82. WHO (2007b).

83. E-Health-Media, "Ireland to Invest Euros 500m in E-Health" (August 8, 2007), http://ehealtheurope.net/News/2935/ireland_to_invest_euros_500m_in_e-health, accessed November 18, 2007.

84. Canada Ministry of Health, "$150M Investment in E-Health to Improve Patient Care" (May 2006), http://www2.news.gov.bc.ca/news_releases_2005-2009/2006HEALTH 0028-000518.htm, accessed November 17, 2007.

85. A. M. Audet, M. M. Doty, J. Peugh, J. Shamasdin, K. Zapert, and S. Schoenbaum, "Information Technologies: When Will They Make It into Physicians' Black Bags?" *Medscape General Medicine* 6, no. 4 (2004): 2.

86. J. D. Kleinke, "Vaporware.com: The Failed Promise of the Health Care Internet," *Health Affairs* 19, no. 6 (2000): 57–71.

87. J. D. Kleinke, "Dot-gov: Market Failure and the Creation of a National Health Information Technology System," *Health Affairs* 24, no. 5 (2005): 1246–1262.

88. World Bank, "What Is Stakeholder Analysis?" (2007), the World Bank website, http://www1.worldbank.org/publicsector/anticorrupt/PoliticalEconomy/PDFVersion.pdf, accessed December 22, 2007.

89. Ibid.

90. G. Miscione, "Telemedicine in the Upper Amazon: Interplay with Local Health Care Practices," *MIS Quarterly* 31, no. 2 (2007): 403–425.

91. M. Mitka, "Developing Countries Find Telemedicine Forges Links to More Care and Research," *Journal of the American Medical Association* 280, no. 15 (1998): 1295–1296.

92. I. Nakajima and S. Chida, "Telehealth in the Pacific: Current Status and Analysis Report (1999–2000)," *Journal of Medical Systems* 24, no. 6 (2000): 321–331.

93. D. I. Morse, "Directly Observed Therapy for Tuberculosis—Spend Now or Pay Later," *British Medical Journal* 312 (1996): 719–720.

Chapter Questions

1. Define *tele-care*, *telemedicine*, *tele-health*, and *e-health*. Discuss the similarities and differences among these terms.
2. Name four major types of telemedicine and provide some applications of each.
3. Discuss the production possibility frontier (PPF) and positive externality economic perspectives and their implications on e-health.
4. Identify the factors that can influence the adoption of e-health among healthcare organizations and providers.
5. Discuss at least four barriers to e-health adoption.
6. Discuss the importance of the process of stakeholder analysis, and identify the major stakeholders in globalized e-health.
7. Discuss the relevance of each tier in the WHO (World Health Organization) framework for strategic e-health development presented in this chapter.

Mini-Case: M&P Cardiovascular Center Inc.

M&P Cardiovascular Center Inc. (MPCC) is a U.S.-based large specialty hospital, providing numerous services related to diagnosis, treatment, and prevention of heart and cardiovascular system diseases. It is currently operating in 20 states with its headquarters in San Francisco, California. Throughout its 95 state-of-the-art facilities, MPCC has served more than 200,000 diverse patients in both rural and urban areas. Medical staff at MPCC has employed some forms of e-health applications (e.g., tele-surgery and tele-consultation) to perform diagnosis and treatment procedures for patients across the facilities. The illustration of real-time surgery provides educational activities to other medical staff. Through the current e-health system, administrative staff members are also able to share critical and secured information without wasting time to travel to the meetings and going through various possible hassles.

MPCC also has a nonprofit research branch that conducts a number of studies related to cardiovascular diseases. Its goal is to provide up-to-date knowledge regarding the state of cardiovascular diseases, as well as diagnosis regimens and treatment alternatives. The opportunity to expand internationally will allow its research fellows and medical staff to establish a reciprocal relationship with their peers in other countries and to have access to patient cases, information, and knowledge about cardiovascular diseases in different parts of the world. Therefore, researchers and medical staff will be able to enrich and broaden their horizon and experience. Moreover, MPCC provides the public with an online healthcare portal or a content-based website that offers rich information about cardiovascular diseases, their symptoms, diagnosis procedures, and treatment alternatives. The "24/7 online doctors" feature allows patients to communicate with and to receive advice from medical staff at any time.

The management team has explored an opportunity to partner with hospitals, other cardiovascular centers, and/or laboratory facilities in some countries such as India, Thailand, and Mexico. To scrutinize the circumstances, possibilities, threats, and opportunities, MPCC has put together a team of internal staff and external consultants that will be responsible for creating a strategic plan for this project. The major component of this project is the development of an e-health system that can be beneficial to MPCC, its partners, and especially prospective patients. The team starts off with the WHO e-health development model presented in the chapter. Even though this model focuses on the development of e-health system at the national level, it is also applicable the organizational level.

MPCC must perform an environmental analysis to examine the social/cultural, legal, and technological issues in each country. These factors are critical to the successful partnership and the development of an interorganizational e-health system. A thorough investigation into the policies and regulations regarding e-health and telecommunications in the various countries, as well as the availability of ICT infrastructure, must be addressed at the initial phase. The internal analysis of slack resources (i.e., both monetary and nonmonetary) is of significance to the level of investment in the new system. MPCC has an advantage in creating the interorganizational e-health system because its operation in the United States has already utilized major e-health applications on a daily basis. This will help facilitate the establishment of and transition between the new and existing systems. MPCC also plans to conduct a cost-effectiveness analysis to demonstrate the economic value of an integrated e-health system.

Mini-Case Questions

1. Other than the information discussed in the case, what other necessary components should the company encompass in its strategic planning process for developing an e-health system with its partners? What kind of data or information does the team need to analyze the situation both externally and internally? From what sources can such data and information be obtained?

2. Given that security is an important element in e-health applications, how would you ensure that MPCC's database is secured and meets all required laws and standards across the countries in which MPCC partners are located?

3. MPCC has already heavily invested in e-health applications for its operations in the United States. However, the world of information communications and technologies is rapidly changing, and the new applications are constantly presented in the market. You as a team member must balance state-of-the-art technology, the core operations of the company, and limited budgets. Would you recommend the company keep the existing system and expand on it, or replace the existing system with a new one altogether in both domestic sites and offshore facilities? Provide rationales to support your argument.

4. What role do you see the patients of both MPCC and its partners play in this partnership opportunity? Should they be involved in the planning process? If so, how?

Chapter Appendix: Glossary of Terms

barriers to e-health adoption The barricades that prevent individuals and institutions from adopting the practice of e-health. Four major barriers include financial, technological, social/cultural, and legal issues.

developed countries and developing countries According to the United Nations, there is no central convention that is used to designate developed or developing countries (United

Nations, 2007). Different international institutions such as the United Nations, the World Bank, and the International Monetary fund have their own systems for the identification of country categories. However, in common practice, economic status is a guideline for considering a placement of a country into different categories.

e-health   The use of information and communication technologies (ICT) for health (World Health Organization, 2007b, p. 1).

e-health adoption   The adoption of e-health practices among health professions and their organizations.

globalization   A comprehensive phenomenon that has exhibited a long-range history of the growth of population and the advancement of civilization.

health care   The prevention, treatment, and management of illness and the preservation of mental and physical well-being through the services offered by the medical and allied health professions (Health Care, no date).

positive externalities   Goods or services with positive externalities provide benefit to members of society who are not directly involved in the production, transaction, and consumption of the goods or services (McPake, Normand, and Kumaranayake, 2002).

production possibility frontiers   A curve illustrating the trade-offs between two categories of goods (Folland, Goodman, and Stano, 2004, p. 21).

stakeholder analysis   A methodology used to facilitate institutional and policy reform processes by accounting for and often incorporating the needs of those who have a "stake" or an interest in the reforms under consideration (World Bank, 2007).

tele-care   The use of information and communication technologies to transfer medical information for the delivery of clinical services to patients in their place of domicile (Norris, 2002, p. 4).

tele-health   The use of information and communication technologies to transfer medical information for the delivery of clinical, administrative, and educational services (Norris, 2002, p. 4).

telemedicine   The use of information and communication technologies to transfer medical information for the delivery of clinical and educational services (Norris, 2002, p. 4).

Health Management Information System Innovation:
Managing Innovation Diffusion in Healthcare Services Organizations

Tugrul U. Daim, Nuri Basoglu, and Joseph Tan

Editor's Note: The readers should understand why a discussion on innovation diffusion constitutes the final chapter of this health management information systems (HMIS) text. Apparently, the benefits of HMIS should extend beyond just individuals, even beyond healthcare provider groups and healthcare services organizations. It is everyone's business that HMIS diffuse and raise the quality of healthcare services delivered to each and every one of us. As with the management of any innovation, HMIS innovation diffusion management is definitely not going to be an easy, static process. Instead, it is a very dynamic and adaptive one, depending on how the healthcare services delivery system changes vis-à-vis the organizational changes affected by movements in the larger political, technological, social, and cultural environments in which any HMIS innovation is to be deployed. This chapter touches on the barriers to HMIS implementation and innovation diffusion and provides key theoretical concepts for HMIS innovation management.

CHAPTER OUTLINE

Scenario: *MedeFile International*

Scenario: *MedeFile International*[1]

MedeFile International, a publicly traded personal health records (PHR) vendor, recently launched a month-long advertising campaign to encourage greater adoption of its PHR offerings. Although the commercials were aired on cable channels CNBC, CNN, MSNBC, Fox News Channel, and Bloomberg Television, CEO Milton Hauser admits the commercials were primarily targeted to human resources managers and group purchasers. Currently, he believes that it is far more efficient to reach out to this demographic than directly to patients.

MedeFile sets itself apart from other data-aggregation platforms like Google Health and Microsoft Health Vault by claiming to offer the only PHR program that collects data from both electronic and paper records. Hauser explains, "The average person's medical record is like a puzzle, with pieces scattered all over the place. What we do is put the pieces of the puzzle together."

Not only can MedeFile import data from electronic medical records, pharmacy records, and test results, the company also scans paper records into files that can be viewed online by doctors and hospitals. The service is subscription-based and retails for $249 per year. In addition to collecting PHR data, the service also includes reminders for customers to take their medications and see their doctors for managing chronic diseases.

Imagine having all of your personal health records, regardless of whether they were previously kept as paper-based records or electronic ones, stored on MedeFile. Do you agree with CEO Milton Hauser that this is an "innovation" whose time may have come?

I. Introduction

A recent NSF symposium (www.picmet.org) focused on technology management that is relevant to, and may have significant impact on, the healthcare services sector. A critical takeaway from this symposium was that healthcare services organizations can benefit from the merger of nano-, bio-, and information technologies. Yet the current service architecture of organizations in this sector is not supportive and conducive to the diffusion of such innovations.

In this final chapter of the text, we focus on the barriers inhibiting the diffusion of healthcare management information systems (HMIS) innovations and attempt to view the healthcare services delivery system from a complex adaptive system behavioral perspective. As a first step to gathering evidence on how best to manage HMIS innovation diffusion, we have engaged a panel of experts to confirm part of our initial findings and propose a tentative list of interesting propositions to test—with additional data collection—the general beliefs on potential impacts of HMIS innovation diffusion in healthcare services organizations.

Figure 14.1 is the complaint push model, an overly simplified characterization of the current service model in healthcare services organizations for many developed and developing countries, including the United States.

Figure 14.2, a data pull model, is what we perceive and project to be the future service architecture that healthcare services organizations would be expected to, or can, move into as information and communications technologies (ICT) in health care diffuse and merge with other emerging technologies. However, the path toward achieving the ultimate goal of widespread HMIS diffusion is likely to be a long one, whether near term or long term, which would therefore requires us to further understand the current barriers and challenges underpinning the success of this structure.

Over the past 30 years, almost every industrial sector in the world economy has made a transformation in collecting, managing, and transmitting information with the results of increased

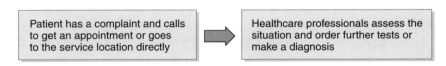

FIGURE 14.1   Current Service Model in Healthcare Services Organizations (Complaint Push Model).

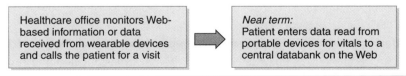

FIGURE 14.2   Future Service Model in Healthcare Services Organizations (Data Pull Model).

productivity and efficiency. Yet today's healthcare industry, representing one of the fastest-growing services industries in the world economy, has lagged behind most other industrial sectors with respect to managing the HMIS and ICT diffusion. The difficulties that the healthcare services industry faces today may possibly include, but not be limited to, high expenditures, inconsistent quality and gaps in the care process, lack of standards policies and procedures, fear of risk taking due to putting human life in danger, and the accessibility of quality patient health information—which creates a huge challenge for the policy makers and healthcare managers. These problems also affect the U.S. economy in a negative way, requiring national attention and a comprehensive technology management and diffusion infrastructure.

Technology, especially HMIS technology, is an important means for achieving healthcare services effectiveness. Therefore, the absence of the technology component in healthcare can have a major impact on the quality of the care services being delivered. Healthcare services have to make more use of technologies to improve routine operational efficiencies, enhance clinical effectiveness, and increase the productivity of caregivers. Past studies and research in this area emphasize the importance and the need for widespread adoption of HMIS solutions to overcome the indicated problems.

Nonetheless, it is noteworthy to point out that the healthcare services industry has a unique structure, and the diffusion of innovations depends on a very different dynamic compared with some other services industries such as banking and transportation. The dynamics in healthcare services are formed from the factors that affect the HMIS diffusion process. In other words, it is critical to identify key factors underpinning innovation diffusion and build a model to perform empirical testing before we can have any certainty of what would be an effective strategy to implement innovative HMIS solutions within the healthcare services organizational context.

In the next section, we identify the critical components affecting diffusion of healthcare information technologies. The effects of such a diffusion are then discussed, following an overview of the theory on complex adaptive systems, which is the foundation for understanding managing changes in healthcare services organizations, especially changes pertaining to HMIS innovation diffusion. A comprehensive literature review as well as expert interviews were conducted to gather the data presented here. Interviews were done with a panel of healthcare experts in the Portland, Oregon, metropolitan area.

II. Background

Within the healthcare services organization context, healthcare services delivery is often performed in a complex and multifaceted environment in which technology and its management have been a critical challenge for decades.[2,3]

In this context, healthcare technology may be conceptualized broadly. Specific to this discussion, healthcare technology can be related to the "devices, drugs, medical and surgical procedures and the knowledge associated with these to prevent, diagnose and treat diseases. It can be also associated with the organizational and supportive systems within which care is provided."[4] Management of healthcare technology therefore involves not only the planning and integration of specific and/or a broad range of technology, but the monitoring, surveillance, evaluation, and assessment of that technology, along with the need for user training during the technology implementation phase. Put simply, the healthcare organization managers have to deal with a wide scope of activities in technology management, which requires the involvement of staff from many disciplines, including those from the medical, technical, clinical, financial, and administrative areas.[5,6]

In addition, for an effective integration of any HMIS technology within the healthcare services organizational context, a collective responsibility—including the government, policy makers, planners, managers, and staff members from the care facility at all levels who will be the primary users of the technology—is required.[7] Nowadays, greater numbers of technology-related systems (such as online consultation systems for remote patient care, image-annotation and reasoning systems to support the assessment procedure of medical screening, medical imaging database management systems to store medical images, textual metafiles containing descriptions of clinical features and their diagnostic results, and others) are being integrated into healthcare services organizations.[8] With the introduction of health databases and automated data warehouses, a large amount of routinely extracted data from multiple sources can now be more fully integrated and mined, thereby making available a new type of knowledge, which could be further exploited. Physicians, aided by intelligent clinical decision support systems, can then better provide care for their patients and make their practices more efficient and effective by drawing on timely clinical reminders and alerts based on previously captured expert knowledge of specific diseases.

A summary of selective past studies on some of the key healthcare technologies contributing to HMIS innovations today as applied in a healthcare services organizational context and their corresponding benefits is presented in Table 14.1. Effective management of such healthcare technology can contribute to the improved efficiency in the healthcare services sector, resulting in enhanced security and better health outcomes and more sustainable healthcare services.[9] Additionally, health technology utilization also improves access, quality, and cost efficiency of public healthcare services, especially in developing countries.[10] Within this context, information systems, communications systems, data management systems, and hospital operational management systems have been the main interest areas in the healthcare services industry.[11] Policy formulation, planning, standardization, training, implementation, and maintenance issues have also been widely discussed in these studies.

Among key benefits that can be gained from the acceptance and diffusion of medical and healthcare information and decision support technologies are:

- Shorter length of inpatient stays.
- Faster communications of test results.
- Improved management of chronic diseases.
- More accurate and complete medical documentations.
- Improved accuracy in capturing charges associated with diagnostic and procedure codes.
- Improved communications and information exchanges among care providers to enable them to respond more quickly to patients' needs.

Table 14.1   Discussed Technologies in the Healthcare Sector

Technology	Benefits	Healthcare Sector	Researchers
Wireless local area network (WLAN)-based mobile computing system; wearable monitoring devices	Increase the quality of patient care, improve a hospital's overall operation, and reduce costs.	Information/decision support	Chau and Turner[12]; McCormick[13]
Clinical reminder systems	Provide just-in-time reminders to clinicians at the point of care, consistent with the latest evidence-based medicine guidelines	Information/decision support	Zheng et al.[14]
Clinical decision support systems	Assist with diagnosing a patient's condition, drug dosage; procedures administering reminders to patients	Information/decision support	Wong and Legnini[15]
Computerized patient records and electronic medical record systems	Digitize patient information for decision support	Information/decision support	Anderson[16]
Telemedicine	Use IT to deliver healthcare services from one location to another	Clinical technology, information/decision support	Sheng and Hu[17]

Despite these advantages, the findings reported in the literature repeatedly indicate the significant level of user resistance to technological systems, thereby creating a barrier to healthcare technology diffusion within the context of healthcare services organizations. More specifically, a large proportion of users tend to demonstrate a consistently low or decreasing level of usage over time.[18] Because innovation diffusion in healthcare services is not always adopted most quickly,[19–21] it is important to look at the diffusion process of innovations and discuss the challenges to then understand the technological dynamics within the healthcare industry. The reasons could vary from user resistance such as insufficient computer literacy, diminished professional autonomy, lack of awareness of long-term benefits of HMIS use, and lack of desire to change conventional behaviors to overcome organizational barriers.[22]

Even though researchers in numerous past studies and peer-reviewed articles have advocated the need to focus more on healthcare technology management through the application of theoretical models, scientific methods, and best practices, the field of technology management (in particular, that of healthcare technology management) has, unfortunately, not enjoyed a cumulative tradition, unlike other, more single-discipline-based knowledge domains within the larger healthcare services research framework.[23] This has, in turn, created a huge gap in the knowledge base of our understanding on how best to manage healthcare technology diffusion for an information-intensive U.S. healthcare delivery system that has now grown to be increasingly complex, inefficient, and highly fragmented.[24]

Table 14.2 summarizes innovations in the healthcare services industry that have been widely noted in the extant literature and the barriers that makes their diffusion more difficult to be implemented.

For effective innovation diffusion, it is not sufficient to focus on the assessments of system characteristics. It is also important to understand the barriers for the innovations as outlined in Table 14.2. Innovations should not create information overload and distract the user from the normal operation. Even if an innovation is rejected at first, it is important to reengineer it according to the feedback from the user and have it ready for implementation.

There is growing interest among researchers on various aspects of the innovation diffusion in healthcare services organizations. Within this context, HMIS, a technology enabler, are becoming more prevalent both with individual healthcare workers and in organizations. The information-intensive dependent characteristic of healthcare services also makes HMIS diffusion a very important topic to explore and realize. Equally important is the fact that HMIS adoption in health care provides a powerful tool to transform the practice of medical care.[25] In a study by the U.S. Government Accountability Office, it has been purported that cost reductions in the healthcare services delivery organizations associated with medication errors, communication and documentation of clinical care and test results, staffing and paper storage, and operational information processing could be achieved by the effective deployment of information technology (IT).[26] Studies by the Institute of Medicine also emphasized the importance of widespread adoption of IT solutions to improve patient safety and clinical effectiveness.[27]

Table 14.2   Barriers for Innovation Diffusion in the Healthcare Sector

Technology	Description	Barriers
E-health (telemedicine, tele-health)	Uses information and communication technologies in support of healthcare services, health surveillance, health literature, health education, knowledge, and research	Requires an extensive understanding and reworking of the fundamental organizational service processes; interoperability; start-up costs; legal issues; economic interests; privacy standards; language barrier
Wearable monitoring devices	Display and document physiological information obtained at regular intervals over time from sensors attached to the patient or other input devices	Battery life; privacy and security; invisibility and social acceptance; usability; language barriers; fragmented data standards
RFID (radio-frequency identification)	Uses radio waves to automatically identify people or objects	Cost; infrastructure; wireless network; security; global standards; RF impact
Semantic Web	World Wide Web of connected data, radically different than today's Web of discrete data	Technology barrier; business barriers

A recent study found that medication errors can be easily prevented through computerized systems in hospitals.[28] Moreover, the large annual increases in healthcare expenditures stress the urgency and need for healthcare productivity improvement and the more effective use of HMIS before escalating costs of healthcare services become a threat to the U.S. economy. Health IT will allow comprehensive management of medical information and its secure exchange between healthcare consumers and providers.

Briefly, Glaser[29] notes that broad use of health IT will:

- Improve healthcare quality.
- Prevent medical errors.
- Reduce healthcare costs.
- Increase administrative efficiencies.
- Decrease paperwork.
- Expand access to affordable care.

As well, interoperable HMIS will not only improve individual patient care, but will also bring about many public health benefits—for example, early detection of infectious disease outbreaks around the country, improved tracking of chronic disease management, and the evaluation of healthcare services based on comparative valuation enabled by the collection of disaggregate pricing and quality information.

Aside from the administrative and financial aspects of information technology automation that exist in today's healthcare industry, there is still the need to expand HMIS applications to the clinical side, which is often neglected in healthcare services organizations.[30] It is therefore important to migrate the IT infrastructure in the healthcare services organizations to one that can support the patient care functions (pharmacy, digital radiology, order entry), the safety and quality control functions (infection control, data warehousing), and the administrative and business functions (admitting, discharge, transfer, scheduling, billing). The challenges in HMIS implementation and how HMIS innovation diffusion processes can be managed require the students to adopt a new perspective of healthcare services organizations—the complex adaptive systems perspective[31]—which is discussed next.

III. Complex Adaptive Systems

As with the management of any innovation, HMIS innovation diffusion management is definitely not going to be a static process. Instead, it is a dynamic one depending on how the healthcare services delivery system changes vis-à-vis the organizational changes affected by movements in the larger political, technological, social, and cultural environments in which any HMIS innovation is to be deployed. However, prior to jumping into the details of the complex adaptive systems conceptualization, it is important to begin with the traditional healthcare systems perspective as dictated by the classical systems theoretic view, more specifically, the general systems theory (GST).

General Systems Theory

GST has been around for decades.[32] One popular view is given by combining the analysis of individual parts of the system with the study of the interactions among its parts. The theory begins from the empirical observation that in every system, the whole is greater than the sum of its parts.

A system may be thought of simply as a set of interrelated elements, each having its own identity and differentiated from external events, objects, or other such subsystems in its environment. A system combines all objects and their attributes within its boundaries and defines the relationships among these objects. A closed system is self-contained and, unlike an open system, does not interact with its environment. Open systems are often referred to as *intelligent systems* because they can be influenced drastically by external factors. *Complex systems* are those systems that result when closed and open systems are combined.

Despite numerous efforts aimed at rationalizing one or more key aspects of the changing healthcare services industry sector in both the United States and Canada, these attempts have occurred in a rather piecemeal fashion. Although each of these rationalizations may provide some explanation to particular changing trends, few can provide a broad, comprehensive framework upon which a holistic understanding of the healthcare services industry may be based. Gillies et al.[33] argue that achieving clinical integration of services is key to enhancing system and HMIS performance in healthcare services organizations. The idea of clinical integration outlines the coordination of patient care services within the functional activities and operating parameters of an integrated, complex healthcare services delivery system. With the dramatic advances in capabilities and a decrease in the cost of information technology, it is not difficult to envision the possibility of integrating existing systems at multiple delivery sites. However, past attempts of HMIS implementation efforts among major teaching hospitals and today's multi-provider health organizations across the United States and Canada have met with disappointments due to the lack of understanding of how to deal with changes, in particular, the management of HMIS innovation diffusion. This amounts also to the need for an understanding of chaos theory and complex systems behaviors, in particular, those of complex adaptive systems.

Complex Adaptive Systems

Essentially, a *complex adaptive system* may be conceived as one that typically comprises a *large number of interacting parts*, is *interactively complex*, and is *self-organizing*.[34] Multi-provider health maintenance organizations (HMOs) and today's integrated delivery systems (IDS) are examples of complex adaptive systems (CAS) in the U.S. and Canadian healthcare services delivery systems. These systems involve the intricate network of complex relationships that constitutes most social systems, often making it difficult to describe simple causal relationships among individual components of the system. This phenomenon of system complexity aptly captures the statement that the whole (system) is greater than the sum of its parts. Moreover, causal relationships are subjected to the definer's perspective. The same phenomenon may be viewed in terms of different systems and environments by different observers. In addition, complex systems are also defined by their hierarchical and/or nested structure of subsystems, each having some meaningful functions while interacting to produce the overall system. Large systems in today's healthcare services organizations can be divided into multiple subsystems, and these in turn can be subjected to further subdivision in a complex, nested arrangement.

Tan et al. further note that at any one time, CAS may be at one of the following three different stages on a continuum: static, edge of chaos, and chaos. In the *static* stage, the system experiences a period of order; if it fails to respond to changes in its environment, it can eventually expect to self-destruct. At the *edge of chaos*, systems are constantly battling between static and chaos. They fluctuate randomly into static or chaos as feedback loops in these systems return them to one stage or the other in a seemingly random fashion. Yet, this is the one place where CAS can be spontaneous, adaptive, and alive. When systems get too far into the *chaos* stage, these systems become unmanageable and their "ability to find a niche in the fitness landscape disappears in a flurry of uncontrollable, dizzying oscillations."[35] Innovation diffusion is no less than moving the organization into a chaos stage, and managing that chaos requires substantial managerial expertise and skills.

Handling Complexity in Healthcare Services Organizations

When functioning as complex adaptive systems, many hospitals, multi-provider HMOs, and integrated delivery systems cannot be entirely controlled. However, understanding a few principles can help guide survival of the CAS as well as its progress:

1. Major CAS changes may be achieved with small-scale initial perturbation.
2. System performance may be improved with appropriate feedback.
3. In the static stage, standardization with flexibility maintains care quality.
4. At the edge of chaos stage, shortened response time with backup redundancy improves effectiveness.
5. In the chaos stage, intelligent and trustworthy leadership are essential.

Healthcare services organizations today are too complex and difficult to control, and the same may be said about HMIS innovation diffusion. Unpredictable consequences may result with relentless management-driven changes. Hence, incremental structural and process changes (particularly as starting conditions), which test their intended effects on a small scale whenever possible, are advised. Management should be prepared for unexpected behaviors at various levels within the system.

Appropriate feedback, which is direct, specific, and generally constructive, can be effective to guide performance improvement. Inconsistent feedback, especially through a third party following a long silence, or implemented without early warning signs, is unlikely to be effective. Feedback loops should operate at all levels and times.

In the static stage, standardization should be encouraged for repetitive processes and should be instituted intelligently with input from frontline workers. In high-performing systems, frontline personnel typically have great freedom of action when dealing with unexpected situations.[36] In complex healthcare services delivery systems, for example, physicians will always have to act with a high degree of autonomy. For HMIS applications to be accepted, used, and diffused among physicians and nurses, standardized diagnostic or treatment protocols should never limit these professionals when confronting the unusual or unexpected situation.

At the edge of chaos, increased operational efficiencies and reduced clinical errors will result if appropriate HMIS technologies are readily accessible and if relevant and high-quality health information can be made available more promptly. Shortened response times here will improve the ability of the system to self-organize. As well, some form of redundancy can only curtail the failure rate given that human errors are inevitable. A small failure rate may, in fact, be preferable to the administrative burden associated with reducing it to zero. Thus, most high-performing systems are designed to "absorb" errors and/or mitigate their consequences, rather than eliminate all errors.

In chaos, intelligent and trustworthy leadership is essential. When everyone is attempting to avoid responsibilities, someone must take charge to identify common goals and build compromised consensus among dissenters. Leadership in today's healthcare services organizations may have "hierarchical" features, but it still is quite different from what is traditionally considered hierarchical leadership. High-performing systems create mutual trust and respect between management and its subordinates. These systems will evolve a culture in which service excellence, continuous learning, and quality improvement become the norm rather than performance metrics that have to be forced.

IV. Practice

Key barriers to challenge HMIS implementation include:

  a. Limited financing sources
  b. Lack of training and technical expertise
  c. Cultural resistance from end-users
  d. Lack of standards, interoperability, and HMIS immaturity
  e. Lack of academic research and published reports
  f. Traditional mind-set and averse to high risks
  g. Other less tangible benefits that may not be apparent

To provide our thoughts on the challenges that can be encountered in HMIS implementation for healthcare services organizations, we discuss various factors that have been extracted from our expert panel based on results of our interviews within a healthcare services organizational setting. These findings were also corroborated by the extant literature.

First, the *financial* aspect of HMIS implementation has been identified as one of the biggest challenges that may postpone an effective innovation diffusion.[37] The financial aspect is only a general identification of the several financial metrics involved in the diffusion of the innovations; in order to have a better understanding of this barrier, the financial metrics have to be disaggregated and analyzed in depth. Start-up costs (as well as the return on investment) are one of the most important barriers to HMIS implementation. Lack of incentives and investments—especially from the government—are also challenging for the healthcare services industry.[38]

The indirect benefits of HMIS are typically not integrated fully into the direct fiscal metrics. A good strategy to overcome the high HMIS cost barrier is to measure the system's impact on the hospital efficiency and display the cost savings and hospital benefits so that the investors can build the relationship between the investment and the outcome. In addition, incentives from the government and HMOs or other insurance companies could also help healthcare providers implement HMIS to streamline the workflow. These incentives can be in the form of grants or loans to decrease the cost or reimbursement to hospitals that have met a certain standard of HMIS usage.[39]

The lack of *skills* or *knowledge* to develop, design, implement, and use a specific and appropriate HMIS application is another major barrier identified in the literature on innovation adoption.[40] Clinicians and system users are often neglected in the development and design phase of the systems. Related to this, few people are trained to work at the intersection of biomedicine and IT. Systems developers usually have less knowledge about the medical needs that will be satisfied by the HMIS. Nonetheless, there is a growing shortage of qualified HMIS professionals. Alpay[41] also pointed out that the challenge in effective HMIS implementation has been in the area of education and training for these systems and identified the biggest gap as the need for IT training in the context of a technologically evolving healthcare sector. In particular, Keen and Malby,[42] as well as Carlile and Sefton,[43] have identified the lack of appropriate skills and unwillingness to enhance one's practice skills and status with HMIS use in the workplace to be a major challenge in healthcare services organizations, especially for physicians and nurses. Lack of access to the structured knowledge and criteria regarding the system capabilities and implementation processes has also been purported as another major concern.

Resistance from the HMIS users such as physicians, nurses, and other clinicians can also have a great impact on the innovation diffusion process. In general, cultural resistance to computational algorithms and low computer literacy levels among physicians are identified as critical barriers in the diffusion of innovation in healthcare IT. Most physicians may associate HMIS as an interruption, having a negative impact on the workflow, and thus prefer using the traditional paper-based systems. To overcome this challenge, user training, while not offering a complete solution, can help alleviate the concern. With a very tight schedule to see patients, most physicians will find it hard to adapt fully to a hospital-run training program. Moreover, physician motivation for such training is typically low. Thus, strong leadership from the hospital management, the chief medical officer, and the head nurse is needed if there is any hope of overcoming end-user resistance—especially for physicians and nurses. These hospital leaders must believe in the benefits offered by HMIS innovation and show full support and commitment to the implementation process. A clear communication channel has to be formed between the hospital leaders and the staff in describing these benefits with a clear understanding of how the entire process will then contribute to the overall mission and vision of the hospital. Lastly, user involvement in the HMIS vendor selection and evaluation is key to successful implementation. This enables the user to share the concerns with the vendors up-front and do the necessary changes prior to the very costly HMIS implementation.

The lack of *standardization*, *interoperability*, and *immaturity* of HMIS and the need for *compliance* with national standards for privacy, security, data storage and exchange, legal issues, and the threat of data confidentiality are other barriers discussed widely in the literature and in the other chapters of this text. Many systems are limited to exchanging information in only one location; these systems are simply not compatible for information sharing across institutional boundaries. Not evaluating expectations of the user and the absence of feedback could also negatively affect the decision of a physician.[44] Different vendors may offer isolated HMIS solutions to support individual systems such as cardiology care, intensive care, or home care, thereby increasing the islands of systems used within the organization enterprise. Accordingly, today's healthcare services industry clearly needs a more comprehensive and integrated platform to manage HMIS solutions. Many hospital-based HMIS products have also been identified as not meeting the demands of hospitals, and extensive modifications are needed to fit the workflow of the specific healthcare facility to these products. To this end, the selection of the vendor, the vendor's commitment to the product, and the vendor–client relationship are all key elements to take into consideration if the HMIS diffusion process is to be managed properly.

The lack of published reports citing the HMIS benefits and the support from academic *research* and practitioner *development* are also described as barriers in the literature. The unique structure of the healthcare industry is also among the challenges faced when trying to achieve successful HMIS implementation. Health care is highly information dependent, relying on accurate patient-specific data and expert clinical knowledge. To implement HMIS successfully, the implementer has to deal with extremely complex requirements, multiple users, different data types, and complicated workflows and information needs.

Finally, the *risks and challenges* in HMIS implementation can be highly stressful—many implementation failures have been documented throughout history. Indeed, not many HMIS projects have been completed on time, within budget, and according to specifications and user requirements as scoped during the planning stages. Moreover, management of the healthcare services organizations could also be a barrier to effective HMIS diffusion when they struggle with their organizations' use of, and commitment to, IT. The traditional mind-set and organizational culture are also seen as major barriers for HMIS diffusion. Healthcare leaders need to be transparent in their dealings with physicians, other managers, and administrative staff and be cognizant of their perspectives, clearly identifying with them on what could be the major issues preventing them from adapting to change. Dialogues and active end-user involvement will increase the effectiveness of the HMIS adoption and diffusion process.

Physicians, nurses, clinicians, and all of the administrative staff must be included in the decision process for implementing HMIS. HMIS innovation requires special sets of skills, specialized knowledge, and the use of technology to accomplish the ultimate goals and objectives of the business. In other words, there must be strategic alignment between corporate goals and objectives vis-à-vis HMIS goals and objectives. This IT fit will affect both the usefulness and ease of use the user perceives from IT.[45,46] *Perceived usefulness* incudes the relative advantage, subjective norms, compatibility, and feedback, whereas *perceived ease of use* includes usability, perceived behavioral control, and support. The perceptions determine the HMIS adoption decision.

We summarize the major HMIS barriers in Table 14.3 and provide further cross-references to research that has been released to date.

Table 14.3   Barriers for HMIS Adoption and Diffusion—Mitigation Approach

Researchers	Barriers Identified for Effective HMIS Use and Diffusion	Type	Mitigation Approach
Wong and Legnini[47]	Depersonalization of health care and barriers to the traditional rapport between clinicians and patients	End-user	Increase the perceived benefit from the system
Poon et al.[48]	Cultural resistance to algorithms and management systems among physicians	End-user	Expanding medical education to include clinically related IT, making the systems user-friendly and integrating them into the daily work flow; informal communication networks, physicians networks
Glaser[49]	Lack of training, lack of access to the structured knowledge and criteria regarding the system capabilities and implementation processes	Organizational and end-user	On-site or off-site training to be provided to the end-user
Paul[50]	Clinicians and system users not involved in the process of design and selection	Organizational and technical	Involvement of the end-user in the HMIS design phase
Shortliffe[51]	Indirect HMIS benefits not integrated in the direct fiscal metrics	Organizational and technical	Integrating HMIS in the financial models
Bower[52]	Compliance with national standards for privacy, security, data storage and exchange, legal issues, threat for data confidentiality	Technical and end-user	Certification process for HMIS; well-designed systems with suitable attention to authentication and authorization
Alpay[53]	Few people trained to work at the intersection of biomedicine and IT	Organizational and end-user	Special trainings for healthcare systems
Tan[54]	Standards—noncompliance	Organizational, technical, and end-user	Integration of HMIS development and standardization
Glaser[55]	Start-up cost	Organizational and technical	Not relying on governmental sources only, but trying to create alternative resources
Anderson[56]	Lack of published reports citing the HMIS benefits	Organizational and technical	Documentation
Poon et al.[57]	Unique characteristics of health care (content and complexity)	Organizational, technical, and end-user	Utilizing the systems for the unique structure of health care

(continues)

Table 14.3 *(Continued)*

Researchers	Barriers Identified for Effective HMIS Use and Diffusion	Type	Mitigation Approach
Tan et al.[58]	Industry's organizational structure—being local and small	Organizational	Involving investors in today's complex healthcare industry
Dixon[59]	Lack of incentives and investments	Organizational	Implementing right incentives to use the systems
Tan[60]	The lack of interoperability and standardization among systems	Technical	Working together with the state and federal governments to establish a common framework for healthcare organizations
Anderson[61]	The lack of clinical leadership	Organizational and end-user	Training the CIOs of the healthcare organizations to create effective leadership
Glaser[62]	Vendor's inability to satisfactorily deliver products and services	Technical	Rating process for vendors according to their proven product and service quality
Glaser[63]	Return on investment	Organizational	Direct fiscal measures regarding the IT systems incorporated to the healthcare organization's financial reports

V. Conclusion

Today's healthcare services organizations are complex adaptive systems—thus the title of this text as *Adaptive HMIS*. Both these organizations and their systems are characterized by apparently complex behaviors. However, they do have the ability to adapt to rapidly changing environments. The key challenge to those of us seeking to integrate diversified technologies to improve today's complex healthcare services organizations is thus to understand the workings of a complex system and to create a spontaneously adaptive platform for employees to work together. Such a platform must be geared toward greater efficiencies, lowering costs, improving workers' morale, improving quality of patient care, eliminating unnecessary medical errors, and allowing greater interdisciplinary collaboration in implementing needed technologies to ease the administrative as well as clinical workloads of both management and employees.

The healthcare services industry has been evolving from a localized standpoint to a more consolidated and commercial enterprise. Therefore, the demand for better HMIS, additional coordination, and interoperable systems is increasing dramatically. Usable, timely, and cost-efficient HMIS contribute to the quality of care by reducing human errors or minimizing the effect of those that still occur. Overall, major cultural change, financial investment, and logistical planning will be required for future HMIS implementations. It is vital to integrate the systems into the workflow rather than being a stand-alone capability that requires a break from the process. The technology needs to be placed into the existing system. The competitive nature of the medical marketplace and inhibitors should be also taken into account to maximize the benefit coming from HMIS innovation diffusion.

Notes

1. N. Vewrsel, "MedeFile Mounts Media Blitz to Push Its PHR," *Digital Healthcare and Productivity*, June 24, 2008.
2. O. R. L. Sheng and P. J.-H. Hu, "Organizational Management of Telemedicine Technology: Conquering Time and Space Boundaries," *IEEE Transactions on Engineering Management* 46 (1999): 265.
3. Y. Y. Kwankam, "Health Care Technology Policy Framework," *WHO Regional Regional Publications*, Series 24: Health Care Technology Management, Eastern Mediterranean 2001.
4. E. Geisler and O. Heller, *Managing Technology in Healthcare* (Norwell, MA: Kluwer Academic Publishers, 1996).
5. Ibid.
6. "The OECD Health Project: Health Technology and Decision Making" (Organization for Economic Cooperation and Development, 2005).
7. N. M. Lorenzi, R. T. Riley, A. J. C. Blyth, G. Southon, and B. J. Dixon, "Antecedents of the People and Organizational Aspects of Medical Informatics: Review of the Literature," *Journal of the American Medical Information Association* 4 (1997): 79–93.
8. J. Tan, *E-Health Care Information Systems* (San Francisco: Jossey-Bass, 2005).
9. A. G. Bower, "The Diffusion and Value of Healthcare Information Technology," *Rand Health*, 2005.
10. I. S. Kohane, "Synosis: Computer-Based Medical Records," Yearbook of Medical Informatics (1998) Health Infomatics and the Internet. IMIA, pp. 227–229.
11. S. Chau and P. Turner, "Utilization of Mobile Handheld Devices for Care Management at an Australian Aged Care Facility," *Electronic Commerce Research & Applications* 5 (2006): 305–312.
12. Ibid.
13. J. McCormick, "Wireless Hospitals: New Wave in Healthcare Technology," *Health Management Technology* 20 (1999): 12–13.
14. K. Zheng, R. Padman, M. P. Johnson, and H. S. Diamond, "Understanding Technology Adoption in Clinical Care: Clinician Adoption Behaviour of a Point-of-Care Reminder System," *International Journal of Medical Informatics* 74 (2005): 535–543.
15. H. J. Wong and M. W. Legnini, "The Diffusion of Decision Support Systems in Healthcare: Are We There Yet?" *Journal of Healthcare Management* 45 (2000): 240.
16. J. G. Anderson, "Computer-Based Patient Records and Changing Physicians' Practice Patterns," *Topics in Health Information Management* 15 (1994): 10–23.
17. Sheng and Hu (1999).
18. Zheng et al. (2005).
19. J. Cowan and D. Berkowitz, "Technology Assessment at Work: Part I—Principles and a Case Study," *Physician Executive* 22 (1996): 5–9.
20. S. N. Davidson, "Technological Cancer: Its Causes and Treatment," *Health Care Forum Journal* (March–April 1995): 52–58.
21. A. L. Greer, "The State of the Art versus the State of the Science: The Diffusion of New Medical Technologies into Practice," *International Journal of Technology Assessment in Health Care* 4 (1988): 5–26.

22. A. F. Dowling Jr., "Do Hospital Staff Interfere with Computer System Implementations?" *Health Care Management* 5 (1987): 23–32.

23. Geisler and Heller (1996).

24. D. A. Powner, "Health and Human Services' Estimate of Health Care Cost Savings Resulting from the Use of Information Technology: GAO-05-309R," *GAO Reports* (Washington, DC: U.S. Government Accountability Office, 2005): 1.

25. D. Dixon, "The Behavioral Side of Information Technology," *International Journal of Medical Informatics* 56 (1999): 117–123.

26. Powner (2005).

27. J. G. Carroll, "Crossing the Quality Chasm: A New Health System for the 21st Century," *Quality Management in Health Care* 10 (Summer 2002): 60.

28. E. G. Poon, D. Blumenthal, T. Jaggi, M. M. Honour, D. W. Bates, and R. Kaushal, "Overcoming Barriers to Adopting and Implementing Computerized Physician Order Entry Systems in U.S. Hospitals," *Health Affairs* 23 (2004): 184–190.

29. J. P. Glaser, *The Strategic Application of Information Technology in Health Care Organizations*, 2nd ed. (New York: John Wiley & Sons, 2002).

30. T. Shortliffe, "Strategic Action in Health Information Technology: Why the Obvious Has Taken So Long," *Health Affairs* 24 (2005): 1222–1233.

31. J. Tan, J. Wen, and N. Awad, "Health Care and Services Delivery Systems as Complex Adaptive Systems," *Communications of the ACM* 48, no. 5 (2005): 36–44.

32. R. L. Ackoff, "Towards a System of Systems Concepts," *Management Science* 17 (1971): 661–671.

33. R. Gillies et al., "Conceptualizing and Measuring Integration: Finding from the Health Systems Integration Study," *Hospital & Health Services Administration* 38, no. 4 (Winter 1993): 467–490.

34. Tan et al. (2005).

35. Ibid.

36. A. W. Kushniruk, "Analysis of Complex Decision-Making Processes in Health Care: Cognitive Approaches to Health Informatics," *Journal of Biomedical Informatics* 34 (2001): 365–376.

37. "Hospital IT Use Growing Strong," *Trustee* 60 (2007): 4.

38. "EMR Top Hospital IT Priority, Survey Finds," *AHA News* 41 (2005): 6.

39. Ash, J. S. et al., "Physician Order Entry in U.S. Hospitals," *AMIA Annual Symposium* (1998): 235–239.

40. D. L. Dixon, "Other Barriers to Clinical IT," *H&HN: Hospitals & Health Networks* 78, Health Forum (2004): 12–14.

41. L. Alpay, "Empowering Nurses with Information Technology: The Challenge of Delivering Adequate Training." In E. Geisler, K. Krabbendam, R. Schuring (eds.) *Technology, Health Care, and Management in the Hospital of the Future* (Westport, CT: Praeger Publishers, 2003).

42. J. Keen and R. Malby, "Nursing Power and Practice in the United Kingdom National Health Service," *Journal of Advanced Nursing* 17 (1992): 863–870.

43. S. Carlile and A. Sefton, "Healthcare and the Information Age: Implications for Medical Education," *Medical Journal of Australia* 168 (1998): 340–343.

44. Anderson (1994).

45. F. D. Davis, "Perceived Usefulness, Perceived Ease of Use, and User Acceptance of Information Technology," *MIS Quarterly* (September 1989): 318–340.

46. D. R. Dixon and B. J. Dixon, "Adoption of Information Technology Enabled Innovations by Primary Care Physicians," *SCAMC* 18 (1994): 631–634.

47. Wong and Legnini (2000).

48. Poon et al. (2004).

49. Glaser (2002).
50. D. L. Paul, "Assessing Technological Barriers to Telemedicine: Technology-Management Implications," *IEEE Transactions on Engineering Management* 46 (August 1999): 279–288.
51. Shortliffe (2005).
52. Bower (2005).
53. Alpay (2003).
54. Tan (2005).
55. Glaser (2002).
56. Anderson (1994).
57. Poon et al. (2004).
58. Tan et al. (2005).
59. Dixon (2004).
60. Tan (2005).
61. Anderson (1994).
62. Glaser (2002).
63. Glaser (2002).

Chapter Questions

1. Discuss the healthcare services delivery models represented in Figures 14.1 and 14.2. Search the literature and the Web to identify the changes represented in Figure 14.2.
2. Discuss several barriers discussed in the chapter, and identify possible solutions.
3. Refer to the technologies discussed in the chapter, and search the Web and technical literature to identify current trends.
4. Identify other successful or unsuccessful innovations that diffused in healthcare services organizations in the past. What were the common characteristics?
5. Refer to other service organizations, and discuss differences between them and those in the healthcare sector with respect to the diffusion of innovations.
6. Design a small-scale field study before you visit a doctor next time, and ask about the technologies listed in the chapter. Compare your findings with what has been reported in the chapter.

Health Management Information Systems Practices and Cases

Emergency Medical Transportation Resource Deployment

Homer H. Schmitz

Editor's Note: Case 1 uses "AA" as a pseudonym for the company being discussed. It illustrates the planning, design, and use of a computerized dispatch system to enhance the efficiency and productivity of an emergency medical transportation (EMT) provider in terms of resource deployment for nonemergency response. According to Professor Schmitz, any vehicle originally assigned for nonemergency use may suddenly be diverted for emergency use, which makes nonemergency response a very important resource optimization challenge faced by AA, which was, at the time the case was written, a not-for-profit EMT company operating in the greater St. Louis, Missouri, metropolitan area. This case not only allows students to ponder how the strategic planning process actually works in an organizational setting, but also teaches them how to involve key stakeholders in strategic brainstorming and the search for alternative solutions. It also describes how to measure the system performance to better guide a solution design. Essentially, the AA case illustrates the cycle of real-world problem finding and problem solving in the context of HMIS applications in a resource allocation and assignment problem context. Beyond this, Schmitz notes that the resultant HMIS can provide a more general insight to solving other potential problems existing in other parts of the AA system.

I. Introduction

As the emergency medical transportation community evolves, it faces many of the same reimbursement difficulties that faced other segments of the healthcare delivery system as they encountered changes in such system. For example, when looking at the evolution of reimbursement in other healthcare delivery sectors such as hospitals and physician practices, there is a progression from billed charges to other, more restrictive, reimbursement mechanisms, usually culminating in some form of *capitation*[1]—a process by which economic risk is systematically shifted from the reimbursement entity to the healthcare provider. Simultaneously, the total reimbursement to the provider is reduced. This change in the reimbursement mechanism is currently under way in emergency medical transportation and is being experienced from both the government and the private sector. As reimbursement becomes more restrictive, paying less per unit of service, as well as paying less by shifting economic risk for the volume of services provided, the result is a need for the emergency medical transportation provider to increase productivity or to become more efficient in its operations in order to maintain profitability and financial viability.

Emergency medical transportation systems have taken various approaches to increase efficiency in their operations. Because resource utilization represents the single largest expense in the budget of an emergency medical system, strategies to control this utilization have become a primary target for improving efficiency. Resource utilization includes the vehicles, their maintenance, and the crews to operate the vehicles. The primary focus of these efforts is to deploy the resources so that they can deliver the most timely and highest quality services possible and to appropriately prioritize the allocation of those resources when there is excess demand. This case provides a study of the development of a computerized dispatch system that optimizes the use of the resources based on certain predefined parameters.

At the time of writing this case, AA is a nonprofit company operating in the greater St. Louis, Missouri, metropolitan area, including transportation activities in both Missouri and Illinois. The services offered include basic life support (BLS) and advanced life support (ALS) ambulance transportation and van, paralift, and stretcher van transports. BLS and ALS ambulances transport all patients who may require some level of medical care before or during transport. The vans and paralift vehicles may not transport any person who might reasonably be expected to require such care. Vans and paralifts are operated by a single driver, who does not have the training to monitor a sick or injured person. The company operates a fleet of approximately 85 ambulances, five vans, and six paralift vehicles, and it employs approximately 600 people.

The company's range of business activities includes contracts with municipalities to provide 911 primary response activities, backup services, and contracts with various healthcare organizations to provide a continuum of medical transportation services. In addition, the company receives calls from various healthcare facilities and from the public to provide both emergency and nonemergency medical transportation.

AA must respond to a variety of medical transportation needs in the St. Louis metropolitan area. This discussion focuses exclusively on the nonemergency ambulance service, which includes both BLS and ALS transports. These medical transports can have their origin in a call from a healthcare provider (such as a skilled nursing facility or hospital) for either scheduled or nonscheduled transportation to some other facility for medical services or from a call from the public for either scheduled or nonscheduled transportation.

Given this array of business activities, which can have a large number of combinations for types and priorities relating to transportation requirements, the demand for resources is a complex algorithm with a hierarchy of priorities. It is very difficult to keep track of all variables involved without some tools to assist in the prioritization of resource allocation. Therefore, a computer program was developed to assist in these activities.

The Problem

Given the high volume of business activities and the complex relationship governing the prioritization of the transportation resources, a single dispatcher is unable to efficiently and effectively manage the numerous combinations of resources and requests for service. The factors that must be considered in making the decisions relating to the resource assignments make the problem far too complex for a human being to handle in the tight time constraints required without the assistance of an automated resource allocation system.

Types of Trips

The system that was developed at AA allows for two types of nonemergency trips. To service these trips, there are two levels of ambulance capability available for assignment.

- Code 0 trips are defined as prescheduled trips. They are requests that have been made for nonurgent ambulance service well in advance of the desired pick-up time for the patient. This type of request is usually for an appointment or transport that is planned for a future date and time.
- Code 1 trips are not prescheduled and are requests for non-life-threatening circumstances requiring immediate transportation. An example would be a request to transport a patient from a skilled nursing facility to a hospital for evaluation of an elevated body temperature. In this type of trip, it is presumed that the patient's condition is very stable, and there is an agreed-upon expectation between the ambulance company and the requester of the service that the next available (and appropriate) ambulance will be sent.

Emergency requests are not assigned within the framework of this component of the dispatch system, but when an emergency request is received, it is handled as follows. The computer calculates the nearest available ambulance to an emergency request, and the dispatcher assigns the call immediately. This does, however, have an effect on the nonemergency system in that the vehicle assigned to the emergency request is therefore unavailable for a nonemergency assignment. The system resource allocations might need to be reconfigured subsequent to an emergency call because the available resources have changed.

II. Levels of Ambulance Capability

Basic Life Support Ambulance

This ambulance is a vehicle staffed by two emergency medical technicians (EMTs) who have the training to provide basic care and monitoring while transporting the patient. EMTs receive about four months of training in basic patient care. The training enables the EMT to monitor patients, assess illness and injury, and provide comfort and maintenance while transporting the patient. This type of crew is not able to perform services at an advanced level, such as administration of intravenous fluids, drug therapy, or monitoring electrocardiograms. Typical services performed by this level of ambulance would be moving nonambulatory patients, administration of oxygen, and monitoring vital signs. It should be noted that this ambulance type is not qualified to transport patients who require the higher level of care provided by an advanced life support ambulance.

Advanced Life Support Ambulance

One EMT and one paramedic staff this type of ambulance. Paramedics receive about 18 months of training in advanced patient care. Training includes anatomy and physiology; emergency cardiology; pharmacology; and advanced skills such as intravenous therapy, electrocardiology, and airway management. They can provide a higher level of patient care, including intravenous fluids administration, drug therapy, and electrocardiogram monitoring. It is important to note that in order to optimize resource utilization, this ambulance type may also be called on to perform trips that are basic life support requests.

Although the dispatch of vehicles to transport emergency patients is obviously part of the total system, the focus of this case is on the transport of nonemergency patients and the allocation of resources to serve those patients. The reason is that requests for emergency services are responded to immediately in terms of assignment of the nearest vehicle and crew that are qualified for the requirements of the trip. Because emergency transports take top priority in the system, whenever there is a request for emergency resources, the system calculates the emergency resource requirements and then recalculates the remaining nonemergency allocations. This is done on a real-time basis, so the recalculations are done frequently throughout the course of a day. As outlined in previous paragraphs, nonemergency transportation allows for many more options in the decision algorithm, and therefore it represents the most significant challenge in terms of optimizing resource allocation. Assignments for nonemergency trips are frequently changed when a vehicle that was originally assigned for a nonemergency transport is used as the most appropriate resource for an emergency transport.

III. Factors to Consider in Assigning Resources

As the resource allocation system was developed, one of the first series of decisions to be made focused on determining what service factors were important to successful operation and efficient resource allocation.

- *Pick-up time.* All trips must be assigned a pick-up time so that both the requester of the service and the provider can plan appropriately. In the case of the Code 0 trips, the pick-up time is the agreed-upon time between the caller and the dispatcher. Code 1 trips have a pick-up time defined as the same time that the call was received by the dispatcher.
- *Response time.* To measure success, it is important to determine the extent to which the pick-up time is achieved. Thus, a standard of performance was developed and is measured simply by comparing the arrival time of the ambulance to the scheduled pick-up time for the trip. In the case of the Code 0 trip, the system is deemed to be late if the ambulance arrives even one minute after the pick-up time. In the case of Code 1 trips, the system is late if the ambulance arrives more than 30 minutes after the pick-up time. Remember that the pick-up time for a Code 1 trip is the time of the original call. Thus, the standard

of no more than 30 minutes after the pick-up time actually means that an expectation is established that the ambulance will arrive within 30 minutes of the original call. It should also be noted that a further consideration relating to pick-up expectations is that the customer generally does not like having the ambulance arrive substantially earlier than the prescheduled pick-up time. The system standard is that the ambulance will not arrive more than 10 minutes early.

- *Vehicle drive time and distance.* This factor is very important in optimizing resource allocation. The system attempts to minimize the driving time and distance of any individual vehicle while traveling to a call. Consideration is also given to minimizing "total system drive time," which is based on the sum of all the individual vehicle's drive times and distances. It will be shown later that there might be multiple combinations in which a particular vehicle might have the same minimum drive time to a single call. It was decided that, in this case, the system would evaluate those combinations and select for the system the one that had less total drive time.
- *Crew workload.* This consideration is a very important factor in the system relative to employee morale and efficiency across the entire organization. To promote good morale among the crew, the system is designed to attempt to evenly distribute workload so that an individual crew is not worked disproportionately more than other crews.

System Considerations

The computer-aided dispatch system at AA runs on an IBM AS/400 computer hardware platform. The dispatch system is operated on a dedicated computer. All other business applications run on a second AS/400 so that the dispatch system has full access to all of the available computer resources. Because it must operate 24 hours a day and be extraordinarily reliable, it is supported by an uninterruptible power supply, which is fed by a hospital-grade generator. The system architecture provides a database of trips, vehicles, and ambulance staff. Trip information is taken over the telephone by dispatchers, and requests for service are placed in a queue until the appropriate resource is assigned to the call. Each trip in the queue has a pick-up location, destination, and pick-up time in its electronic database record. Given the request for the trip, the system then optimizes the process by continuously evaluating the pending trips and the available resources. It must resolve the trip requests with the available resources in a timely fashion because on-time performance is one of the most important parameters of the system.

Ambulance resources are tracked in the same system. Each vehicle is designated with a vehicle number, vehicle type (ALS or BLS), the time that the vehicle is scheduled to go off duty, number of trips that the vehicle has run during the shift, and its current status and location. *Vehicle status* refers to the current activity of the ambulance. This could be such things as en route to a call, on the scene of a call, out of service, or posted at a location in anticipation of an assignment. Location is tracked in a sector system, which divides the system's service area into 2.25-mile squares. If a vehicle is moving, its start sector and destination sector are stored to allow calculations that extrapolate its location at any given moment. The system is able to calculate distance and drive time to any given set of pick-up locations that are also assigned to the same sector system.

Assignment of Vehicles to Trips

For any given set of trips when there are available vehicles to assign, there are usually numerous possible combinations of vehicles for the pending trips. As the number of trips and/or vehicles gets higher, the combinations obviously increase accordingly. At some point, this set of combinations of vehicles and trips becomes too complex for a human being to analyze with speed, accuracy, and attention to important factors. Decisions have to be made quickly, and system priorities must be satisfied. Therefore, the computer-aided dispatch system was developed to assist the human dispatchers in their responsibilities. Note, however, that a "computer-aided" dispatch system is being described. Ultimately, human dispatchers make the final decisions on assignments. It is possible that the dispatcher is aware of some change in the system that might affect the recommendation made by the computer-aided dispatch system. Authority is granted to the dispatcher to make manual assignments and to document the reason that the system recommendation was not followed.

After extensive discussions with computer programmers and system design staff, the decision was made to attempt to design a system that replicates the hierarchical decision process that dispatchers attempt to follow in their own thinking process. Decisions and assignments were based on a variety of factors that the dispatcher is forced to prioritize "on the fly." As the number of ambulances and trips increased, this task became much more difficult to manage and required some assistance. Thus, the computer-aided dispatch system was developed.

In designing the AA computer-aided dispatch system, the first step was to establish a set of priorities or system parameters that were ranked from most to least important. These priorities formed the basis for the algorithms that produced the system suggestions for resource allocation. In order of priority, the following parameters were built into the system.

Appropriate Response Times

Of primary importance, and the highest priority, is the customer expectation of appropriate response times. Meeting the agreed-upon appointment time is considered to be a primary expectation that must be met.

The standard for Code 0 trips was set to meet the exact prescheduled pick-up time. The decision was made that the system must have a zero tolerance for substandard performance.

The system standard for Code 1 trips is based primarily on the recognition of customer expectations, which have been established on a historical basis over a period of years. History has demonstrated that if the vehicle arrives within 30 minutes of the appointed time, there is reasonable-level satisfaction on the part of the trip requester. When the actual arrival time is more than 30 minutes after the scheduled arrival, complaints tend to increase.

System Drive Time

System drive time was determined to be next most important among the factors to be considered when allocating resources. This is an important element because increased drive time results in higher costs and reduces the probability for an on-time arrival. In addition, lengthy drive times tend to increase the dissatisfaction of crews.

Work Load Distribution

This element was considered to be important but less so than the previously listed two factors. This condition has little to do with customer satisfaction but plays a significant role in crew satisfaction, which is tied to a sense of fairness based on whether each crew does approximately the same amount of work as others over a period of time.

Assignment of Basic Life Support to Basic Life Support Crews

The final factor that was considered for the resource allocation model was the preference to assign BLS trips to BLS crews. Whenever this can be achieved, it results in a preservation of the more highly qualified ALS resources for those times when there might be a higher demand for emergency resources.

IV. The Information System

The information system was developed using the linear programming language Lindo. This choice was based on its capabilities to manage numerous combinations of system variables and side constraints in a very timely manner. Recall that this system must provide computer-aided advice to the dispatchers in a real-time mode. The system was developed so that the program would look for combinations that met the primary criteria of response times. That is, it would look at the pending trips and the parameters associated with each of the trips and try to match those parameters with the available resources. For example, if a trip requires a pick-up in 20 minutes at a particular location, the system would search for vehicles that could satisfy that requirement. Because all vehicles have a measurable drive time to any location, it is possible to test the total fleet to find all vehicles whose drive time would allow it to meet the anticipated pick-up time. If the system finds multiple sets of optimal solutions, it would move on to the next level of criteria. If multiple vehicles would be able to meet the requested pick-up time, the program must accommodate the probability that there would be multiple combinations with an equally desirable outcome. Initially, it would select from among the combinations of the scenario that had the least single drive time for any single assignment. If there were multiple optimal choices at that second level, it would select the combination that had the least total drive time for the entire set of combinations. If there were still multiple optimal choices, then it would select the combination that assigned the trips to the crew with the least number of completed assignments. If, at this level, there were still multiple optimal choices, the system minimizes the number of mismatches between ALS vehicles and BLS assignments.

System Performance Auditing

In any kind of quality improvement effort, it is critically important to be able to determine the results of the changes. This means that it is necessary to measure selected key indicators that can suggest whether the process is being improved or whether improvement is not forthcoming. These indicators would be measured in the time frame before the system was changed and in the time frame after the system was changed. Improvement or deterioration can then be noted. Various statistical indicators can be used to reach conclusions about the changes.

When the computer-aided dispatch program was developed and installed, it was important to obtain feedback from the dispatchers on whether or not they believed that the system worked properly and provided benefits to the organization. An audit system was developed and made a part of the overall system. That subsystem allowed the dispatcher the opportunity to disagree with the recommendations given by the program. After the dispatcher runs the resource allocation program, the AS/400 mainframe sends a data stream to a network personal computer. The actual algorithms are calculated on the personal computer. The AS/400 data stream contains all pertinent information about all available vehicles and all of the trip data that is required to allocate resources. The information includes the pick-up time of the request, the drive time of the vehicle to the pick-up location, the vehicle type, the time the crew is scheduled to go off duty, and the number of runs already completed by that crew.

As was previously noted, if dispatchers disagree with the configuration of the output relating to the resource assignments that are suggested, they press a function key on their computer terminals and are given an opportunity to write the reason for their disagreement. They may then manually assign a vehicle to a trip using their judgment as to the best allocation of resources. At the moment the function key is pressed, another program is invoked that captures all of the data that was used by computer-aided dispatch resource allocation program. A printed report is produced, which is sent to senior data processing and operations management staff for analysis. The report records a printout of all vehicles and their status at the time of the report, a listing of all pending queued trips, and the calculations made by the program that document how each factor affected the final recommendation. This "disagree process" allows the management staff to refine the program if the dispatcher's reason for disagreement adds additional insight to the problem. At the very least, in those conditions where it is determined that the dispatcher's judgment lacked total insight into the problem, this documentation can provide feedback and education to the dispatcher so that he or she has a better understanding of the system, its logic, and its approach to the solution of the resource allocation problem.

System Performance Improvement

Two primary methods measure the system performance improvement provided by the resource allocation system that was developed: response time to trips and improved efficiencies. Efficiency is measured by the number of crew-hours used for a given trip volume. If the same number of trips can be run with fewer crew-hours, the total system expense is reduced. This can be achieved most easily by reducing the amount of time spent per trip. It was the conclusion of management that this goal would be more easily achieved if trips could be assigned in the most efficient way possible. These were the primary goals of the system design effort. It was the belief of AA management that if vehicles could be assigned to trips more effectively, they would be on time for more trips and that the number of units on duty at any given time could be decreased.

The company measures both factors on a weekly basis. Nonemergency, prescheduled trips are measured against a zero tolerance for lateness and for 90 percent response time reliability. Reliability is measured by calculating the maximum lateness on 90 percent of the trips. These standard measures both showed dramatic improvement after the system was in place for only a few weeks.

Code 1 trips are measured against a predefined system goal of 30 minutes. For this category of trips, the reliability improved from almost 45 minutes 90 percent of the time to just under 30 minutes. This means that 90 percent of the time, a medical transport vehicle arrived on the scene of a nonemergency, non-prescheduled trip in 30 minutes or less.

The Code 0 (prescheduled) trip reliability is measured against the agreed-upon pick-up time. Measurements made in the time frame before the computer-aided dispatch program was put into use show that, on average, the medical transport vehicle arrived to pick up the patient within 25 minutes of the scheduled time 90 percent of the time. After the program was initiated, the average response time reliability improved to no more than 10 minutes late 90 percent of the time.

The company also benefited from increased efficiency in the system. AA measures system efficiency as a ratio of trips to unit hours. Because of the improved response time and resulting decrease in average trip time, the trip-to-unit-hour ratio improved from approximately 0.32 to 0.34, which is approximately a 6 percent improvement. A trip-to-unit-hour ratio of 0.32 suggests that 3.125 unit hours are required per trip (1/0.32). A ratio of 0.34 requires 2.94 unit hours per trip (1/0.34). The cumulative reduction of unit hours per week with an average weekly volume of 1,200 trips is more than 200 hours. In a system the size of Abbott Ambulance, the savings could be as much as $500,000 annually.

Participants in the design, programming, and implementation of the system included representatives from all departments affected by the new program. The information systems department was represented by the management information systems manager, who was also responsible for the design and programming requirements on the AS/400 system. A programmer who was experienced in personal computer programming developed the data links between the AS/400 and the personal computer environment that runs the actual planning program. Management from the operations department was involved in the process to help answer questions about the effect of the program on the crews, including modifications to the employee schedule. Managers from the dispatch department participated to ensure that all of the appropriate considerations were included in the program and to ensure that the employees were properly trained in the use of the system. This was particularly important because it relates to understanding the feedback mechanisms that were built into the system.

Future considerations for programs that follow the same basic decision-making process are currently in the planning and programming stages. The same basic process, using the current system architecture, can be useful in several other areas of the company's operation. This could include systems to assist managers in the design of crew schedules based on an analysis of the historical volume data and programs that would allow the dispatcher the ability to allocate ambulance resources geographically in the service area in anticipation of calls being received.

V. Conclusion

Emergency medical services are in the process of coming under the same kind of reimbursement and budgetary pressures that have been experienced in other parts of the medical care delivery system. As the emergency medical services sector works through these changes, there is no reason to believe that it will not approach the change in much the same way as other healthcare organizations, including the application of management techniques to operational problems, which are designed to provide greater efficiency and effectiveness on the part of the provider.

This case described a computerized approach to assist in a more effective dispatching of vehicles, which results in a more efficient allocation of organizational resources. In this particular instance, it also provides a competitive advantage because it results in an improved product. This improved product is based on more timely and reliable vehicle arrivals when they are requested, resulting in higher customer satisfaction.

Because the core system with its resource database has been successfully installed, it is expected that the system will experience additional enhancements, resulting in the potential to gain even more operational efficiencies for the organization.

A properly designed information system provides the opportunity to serve the entire organization. Broadly speaking, the function of an information system is to increase the knowledge or reduce the uncertainty of the decision maker about some future state or event. This applies to all of the functions of management, not just the one for which the information system was designed.

This system was designed to increase the efficiency and effectiveness of the operations of AA. The system's function is to increase the knowledge or reduce the uncertainty of the dispatcher about the optimum allocation of the organization's resources. However, this does not mean that the information accumulated by the system should be limited to operational uses. Given the availability of the information within the system, other parts of the organization can contemplate uses for the information. When this interdepartmental information use can be achieved, it is the mark of a well-designed information system and usually results in a synergistic effect on all parts of the organization.

Note

1. C. Campbell, H. Schmitz, and L. Waller, *Financial Management in a Managed Care Environment* (Albany, NY: Delmar Publishers, 1998).

Case Study Questions

1. When changes are made to a process, it is necessary to measure the results of the change. Statistical inference techniques are a way to determine with more precision whether the changes are meaningful. Please discuss what tests might be used under these conditions and why they are used.

2. Do you believe that it is important to provide the "disagree process" for the dispatchers so that they can change the computer-aided resource allocation suggestion? Why or why not?
3. Certain measures of efficiency improved for AA. Do you believe that the conclusions drawn are valid? Why or why not?
4. Given the successful installation of the system, with its resultant database, what enhancements would you suggest for the current system?

The Clinical Reminder System

Kai Zheng

Editor's Note: The Clinical Reminder System (CRS) represents an advanced form of healthcare management information systems (HMIS); specifically, it is a clinical decision support system geared toward supporting clinical-based decisions rather than administrative decisions. Clinical decision support systems (CDSS) are useful in aiding clinicians with their cognitive thinking and complex reasoning processes through the applications of "clinical data banks and algorithms, analytic or pathophysiologic models, clinical decision theoretical models, statistical patterns recognition methods, symbolic reasoning, and clinical expert knowledge bases. . . ."[1,p.220] In relation to the topics covered in this text, CRS extends the discussion of patient-centric management systems (Chapter 6) and illustrates the need to support clinicians in making the right decision—or, specifically, the decision that would result in better quality care or one that would result in a richer and better quality of life—for the patients. More generally, CRS augments HMIS fundamental thinking (Part I); illustrates specific aspects of HMIS applications and technological functionalities (Part II); calls for a clinician-oriented approach to HMIS planning and management (Part III); and entails new perspectives in HMIS governance, policies, and globalization (Part IV).

I. Introduction

With great potential to minimize practice variation and improve patient care, clinical decision support methodologies and applications have begun to surface throughout the healthcare industry.[2] They form a cornerstone of the health informatics field by applying data-driven approaches to improve the management and utility of patient information, clinical knowledge, population data, and other information relevant to patient care and community health.[3] As defined by Wyatt and Spiegelhalter,[4] *clinical decision support systems (CDSS)* are "active knowledge systems which use two or more items of patient data to generate case-specific advice."

Over the past several years, researchers in the H. John Heinz III School of Public Policy and Management at Carnegie Mellon University (CMU) and practitioners from the Western Pennsylvania Hospital (WPH) have worked together to create software and a model to enhance internal medicine residency training. The Clinical Reminder System (CRS) is the result of this joint effort. Essentially, CRS is a CDSS capable of managing work flow and documentation as well as generating guideline-based reminders at the point of care. Since February 2002, CRS has been deployed in the Medical Ambulatory Care Clinic (MACC, 2002–2003) and the West Penn Medical Associates (WPMA, 2003–present) at WPH. The clinic staff use CRS for managing appointments, for patient check-in and check-out, and for recording vital signs; the residents and attending physicians use the system for documenting observations, prescribing medication and laboratory test orders, and generating reminders to aid in their decision making during patient encounters. The reminders generated by CRS usually take the form of recommended action to have certain tests performed, to receive vaccinations, or to discuss the pros and cons of alternative treatments. Interaction with the system is provided via desktop PCs installed in every examination room at MACC and WPMA.

The first production version of CRS, version 2, was built in 2001 in the client–server architecture prevalent at the time. Figure C2.1 shows the client-user interface programmed in Microsoft Visual Basic. The capstone version of CRS, version 3, is a Web-enabled application programmed in Microsoft C#.Net® and supported by Oracle 10g® relational database. Figure C2.2 shows its main workspace. A live demonstration of CRS v3 is also available at

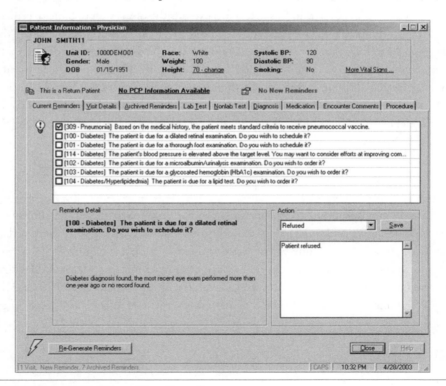

FIGURE C2.1   CRS Client-User Interface.

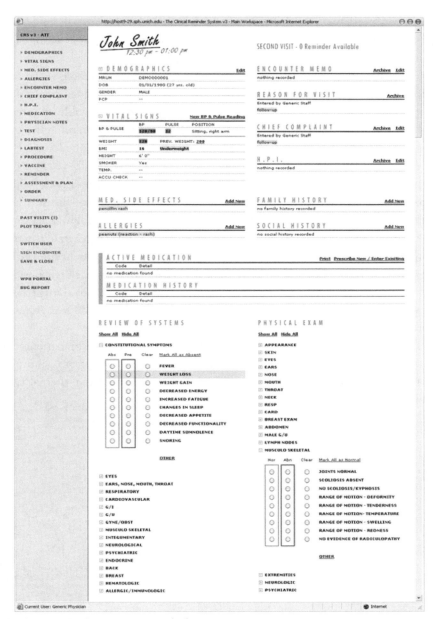

FIGURE C2.2   CRS v3 Main Workplace.

http://crs.heinz.cmu.edu. This version has been implemented and used in day-to-day routine practice in WPMA since August 2005.

CRS is a special type of CDSS—an evidence adaptive decision support system—that provides decision aids with a knowledge base constructed from, and continually adapting to, new research and practice-based evidence, or *evidence-based medicine*.[5] The research team first designed a guideline engineering model that enables structured acquisition and automated execution of evidence-based guidelines. This model, built on several existing guideline ontologies (e.g., Guideline Interchange Format), provides the capability for constructing and executing comprehensive evidence-based clinical guidelines within CRS.[6] CRS also uses this model to visualize and manage implemented guidelines. Figure C2.3 shows a sample visual representation yielded by this model. These visual representations—with embedded medical decision-making logics—are stored in plain text XML files. They are directly editable by care providers using prevalent diagramming software such as Microsoft Visio® and OmniGraffle®. These visual diagrams can be further validated and compiled into assemblies to be loaded into CRS's knowledge database.

At this time, CRS supports management of four chronic health conditions—asthma, diabetes, hypertension, and hyperlipidemia—and five preventive care areas—breast cancer, cervical cancer, influenza, pneumonia, and steroid-induced osteoporosis. Table C2.1 summarizes several key clinical guidelines that have been implemented in CRS. To generate patient-specific decision support reminders, CRS stores and manages comprehensive patient information (e.g., patient descriptors, symptoms, and orders). Standard vocabularies are used whenever possible: ICD-9-CM for diagnoses, CPT® 4 for procedural treatments, and National Drug Code (NDC) for medication prescriptions are currently supported. The U.S. Food and Drug Administration (FDA) periodically updates the NDC following each release.

CRS also stores or retrieves, mostly in real time, a wide variety of patient data from many other hospital information systems, including demographics (from a hospital ADT [Admission-Discharge-Transfer] system), laboratory test results (from the internal laboratories

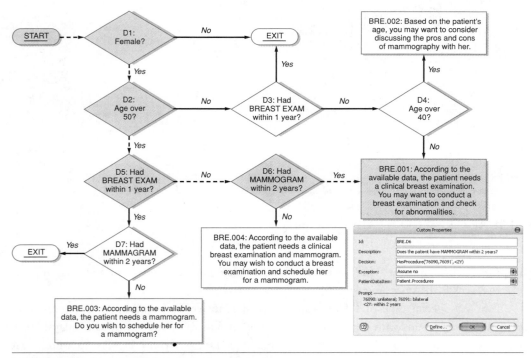

FIGURE C2.3   Model Logic & Sample.

Table C2.1   Selected Guideline Implementations

Area	Issuing Agency	Year
Influenza vaccine	Centers for Disease Control and Prevention (CDC)	2003
Pneumococcal vaccine	CDC	1997
Cervical cancer	American College of Obstetricians and Gynecologists	2003
Breast cancer	U.S. Preventive Services Task Force	2002
Diabetes	American Diabetes Association	2006
Hypertension	National Heart, Lung, and Blood Institute (NHLBI)	2003

Source: Author created.

at WPH), disease diagnoses (from an electronic claims-processing system), and vital signs recorded during medical staff encounters. Over time, CRS has evolved into a "lite" electronic health records (EHR) system, providing necessary functionalities for managing clinical work flow and recording patient health conditions.

II. Acceptance and Adoption of the CRS by Clinician Users

While CDSS provide considerable potential to improve patient care and reduce practice variation, many implementations failed due to unforeseen costs, unfulfilled promises, and disillusionment.[7] Glowing predictions about the all-encompassing and beneficial role of decision support systems in medicine have appeared with increasing frequency in the scientific literature since the 1970s—this optimistic vision however has not yet been realized almost 25 years later.[8]

As noted in Kawamoto et al.,[9] a key feature critical to enabling effective clinical decision support is the *automatic* provision of the support as *part of clinician work flow.* They urge that given its close correlation to successful outcomes ($p < 0.00001$), automated support as part of work-flow is a prerequisite that must be present if at all possible. CRS has been carefully designed and is constantly modified to meet this prerequisite. Nonetheless, providing automated reminders in an ambulatory setting—at the point of care and during busy office hours—is a true challenge. It requires enormous interactions between the users and the system. It also requires a considerable amount of information flow in real time, in addition to a highly efficient collaboration among all involved parties. In the residency-training practice where CRS is currently deployed, it needs additional correspondence, in a timely fashion, between residents and their attending physicians. Moreover, the *point-of-care* provisioning of clinical reminders, an integral feature of CRS, was often found to interrupt the clinic's work flow. For example, the management of patients in the clinic demanded that vital signs be present in the system before physicians start a patient encounter session. This requirement is logically correct, medically appropriate, and should be used to provide fully informed and safe patient care practice. However, such a requirement could present a conflict to many practical concerns associated with the sequencing and scheduling of different caregivers' tasks, with the result that vital signs were often missing from the patient's electronic records during the encounter with a clinician.

A review of evidence from the management information systems (MIS) literature further escalates these concerns. It has been shown that user resistance to end-user systems is a widespread problem.[10] It is also well recognized that end-users are often unwilling to use available systems that, if used, could generate significant performance gains—even if the systems have been optimized as much as technically possible.[11] In the scenarios where use of an information technology (IT) system is mandated, inadequate levels of individual acceptance can diminish its long-term value.[12] At extremes, it may lead to severe consequences such as fierce tension between users and their managers.[13]

Informed by the literature and motivated by shared frustrations between researchers and users of the CRS, the research team has engaged in using innovative research methods to explore the causes of this user resistance, to address them appropriately, and to assess the quality impact of the CRS on clinical performance and patient outcomes measures.

III. Results of User and Usability Studies

A series of research studies was conducted to examine the issues related to technology acceptance and adoption by clinician users. The methodologies applied and the results found are described here.

Quantitative usage analyses were conducted first to assess utilization rates of the CRS. Main variables reconstructed from the computer-recorded usage data were measured by the "percentage of patient encounters in which the system was used to generate clinician directed reminders." By this definition, a valid use must involve an effort to generate clinical reminders (none triggered possible), excluding the usage for the purpose of documentation or administrative use alone. The usage data were analyzed using a novel developmental trajectory analysis (DTA) model, a semi-parametric statistical method that identified three distinct groups of clinician users with specific usage behavior and profiles: (1) "light" users (41.46 percent of all users), who used the CRS steadily over time in about 35 percent of their patient encounters; (2) "moderate" users (36.59 percent), whose initial use rate was the highest (70 percent), but this rate declined steadily to a level comparable with that of the "light" users; and (3) "heavy" users (21.95 percent), whose use rate, initially moderate (50 percent), increased constantly to nearly 100 percent at the end of a 10-month study period. Compliance with the reminders also varied across usage groups: heavy users tended to respond more favorably to the presented reminders, while light users skipped most often. This clustering is also related to user characteristics—specifically, the level of actual usage correlated with gender, citizenship (domestic versus international), and computer use and computer optimism. In addition to the user clustering, this study also found that clinicians' usage patterns might take a long time to mature. The stable, saturated usage levels in this study were reached 10 months after the initial implementation.[14]

In parallel to the usage analyses, periodical *user satisfaction surveys* were administered to collect quantitative user feedback. The CRS was rated high on its interface items, such as "easy to find information," "easy to learn," and "simple to use." However, it received very poor ranking on the system items such as "effective in helping me complete my work" and "being able to complete my work quickly."[15]

Following the quantitative approaches, *qualitative methods* were used to help explain the observed usage behavior. Sources of the qualitative data included semi-structured interviews, open-ended questions (provided as inserts in the user satisfaction questionnaire), online bug reports, and computer-recorded clinical notes (e.g., comments attached to a reminder response). Six negative themes were developed, revealing the causes of some of the known deficiencies: *iterative advisories* ("the same reminder was generated time and time again"), *struggles in data entry* ("it is too difficult and takes too long to enter data"), *detrimental to efficiency* ("slowed down my work"), *solicitation for one single system* ("we should have only one system to access all information needed"), *disrupted physician–patient communication* ("my patient felt upset when I used my computer"), and *lack of guidance in the application work flow* ("I don't know where to start").[16]

The last theme—lacks guidance in the application work flow—motivated a follow-up study on *software user interface optimization*. In this study, the CRS software was modified to capture additional research data on interface usage patterns (e.g., mouse clicks to collapse/expand a tree view). Sequential pattern analysis and a first-order Markov chain model were then used to discover sequential patterns in the CRS interface usage. Such sequences, or click-streams, often reflect clinicians' navigational pathways in their everyday interaction with the system. Data analysis showed that clinician users of the CRS demonstrated consistent navigational patterns.[17,18] These patterns, such as recurring, consecutive feature access, have been used to reengineer the CRS user interface so that the within-application work flow is better aligned with the clinicians' mental model of medical decision making.

IV. Conclusion

While clinical decision support systems have great potential to improve clinical performance and patient outcomes, poor user acceptance may impede their widespread adoption and effective use. Future research for improving the software usability and workflow integration of such systems is in great need, in addition to the development of better implementation and incentive strategies.

Notes

1. J. Tan with S. Sheps, *Health Decision Support Systems* (Gaithersburg, MD: Aspen Publishers, 1998).
2. D. C. Classen, "Clinical Decision Support Systems to Improve Clinical Practice and Quality of Care," *Journal of the American Medical Informatics Association* 280, no. 15 (1998): 1360–1361.
3. E. Coiera *The Guide to Health Informatics* (London: Arnold, 2003).
4. J. Wyatt and D. Spiegelhalter, "Field Trials of Medical Decision-Aids: Potential Problems and Solutions," *Proceedings of the Annual Symposium on Computer Applications in Medical Care* 1 (1991): 3–7.
5. I. Sim, P. Gorman, R. A. Greenes, R. B. Haynes, B. Kaplan, H. Lehmann, et al., "Clinical Decision Support Systems for the Practice of Evidence-Based Medicine," *Journal of the American Medical Informatics Association* 8 (2001): 527–534.
6. K. Zheng, "Design, Implementation, User Acceptance and Evaluation of a Clinical Decision Support System for Evidence-Based Practice," Unpublished doctoral dissertation, Carnegie Mellon University, Pittsburgh, PA (2006).

7. J. G. Anderson, C. E. Aydin, and S. J. Jay, *Evaluating Health Care Information Systems* (Thousand Oaks, CA: Sage Publications, 1994).

8. H. J. Wong, M. W. Legnini, and H. H. Whitmore, "Diffusion of Decision Support Systems in Healthcare: Are We There Yet? *Journal of Healthcare Management* 45, no. 4 (2000): 240–249.

9. K. Kawamoto, C. A. Houlihan, E. A. Balas, and D. F. Lobach, "Improving Clinical Practice Using Clinical Decision Support Systems: A Systematic Review of Trials to Identify Features Critical to Success," *British Medical Journal* 330, no. 7494 (2005): 740–741.

10. F. D. Davis, "Perceived Usefulness, Perceived Ease of Use, and User Acceptance of Information Technology," *MIS Quarterly* 13 (1989): 319–342.

11. R. S. Nickerson, "Why Interactive Computer Systems Are Sometimes Not Used by People Who Might Benefit from Them," *International Journal of Human-Computer Studies* 51 (1999): 307–321.

12. R. Agarwal and J. Prasad, "The Role of Innovation Characteristics and Perceived Voluntariness in the Acceptance of Information Technologies," *Decision Sciences* 28 (1997): 557–582.

13. T. A. Massaro, "Introducing Physician Order Entry at a Major Academic Medical Center: I. Impact on Organizational Couture and Behavior," *Academic Medicine* 68 (1993): 20–25.

14. K. Zheng, R. Padman, M. P. Johnson, J. B. Engberg, and H. S. Diamond, "An Adoption Study of a Clinical Reminder System in Ambulatory Care Using a Developmental Trajectory Approach," *Medinfo* 11, no. 2 (2004): 1115–1119.

15. K. Zheng, R. Padman, M. P. Johnson, and H. S. Diamond, "Understanding Technology Adoption in Clinical Care: Clinician Adoption Behavior of a Point-of-Care Reminder System," *International Journal of Medical Informatics* 74, no. 7–8 (2005): 535–543.

16. K. Zheng, R. Padman, and M. P. Johnson, "User Interface Optimization for an Electronic Medical Record System," *Medinfo* 12, no. 2 (2007): 1058–1062.

17. K. Zheng, R. Padman, M. P. Johnson, and H. S. Diamond, "Evaluation of Healthcare IT Applications: The User Acceptance Perspective," *Studies in Computational Intelligence* 65 (2007): 49–78.

18. K. Zheng, R. Padman, M. P. Johnson, and H. S. Diamond, "An Interface-Driven Analysis of User Behavior of an Electronic Health Records System," *Journal of the American Medical Informatics Association* 16, no. 2 (2009): 228–237.

Case Study Questions

1. What are the major components of a clinical decision support system?

2. What is evidence-based medicine, and how can computerized systems be used to support evidence-based medicine practice?

3. Clinical documentation (such as patient notes) continues to exist primarily in a free-text, narrative format in computerized systems. Discuss the pros and cons of free-text documentation. Discuss its pros and cons in the context of providing clinicians with decision support using computerized algorithms.

4. How did the Clinical Reminder System described in the case study evolve over time into a lightweight electronic health records system?

5. Why has clinicians' adoption and acceptance of CRS become a big issue? Describe the major approaches used in the case study for investigating user adoption and acceptance issues. What are the findings?

6. Based on what is learned from designing and implementing CRS, if you are leading a project team to design a CDSS, what would you do to ensure the system will be accepted by targeted end-users?

Integrating Electronic Medical Records and Disease Management at Dryden Family Medicine[1]

Liam O'Neill and William Klepack

Editor's Note: In this case study, the authors unveil the planning, development, and overall impact of electronic medical records (EMR) on Dryden Family Medicine (DFM). DFM is a rural family practice located in Dryden, New York. Just as with any major healthcare management information systems (HMIS) deployment, the installation of DFM's EMR must be gently managed so as to significantly benefit the organization. As reported, DFM's EMR was implemented with the full conversion to the new system consummated in three phases. The success of this implementation effort was apparent even at an early stage, with impressive efficiency gains achieved in billing, prescription ordering, and other routine processes; with quality guidelines and protocols developed to improve patient care in preventive medicine and disease management; and with increased job satisfaction for nurses, physicians, administrators, and front-desk staff. Owing to enhanced billing documentation following the EMR implementation, practice revenues also increased significantly. For students, then, this case brings together the many practical lessons that can be learned from executing the systems development process, including vendor selection, overcoming the hidden implementation obstacles, understanding the data standards and regulatory policies pertaining to health records management, and documenting the HMIS benefits gained within a rural family practice setting—a setting that is somewhat different from the usual large-scale healthcare services organizational setting, where resource limitation and IT expertise are an even greater challenge.

I. Introduction

For smaller group practices, electronic medical records (EMR) adoption is a huge undertaking that poses significant risks. Patient information constitutes one of the practice's main assets, and patient records must be designed to last for decades. Smaller clinics have added constraints, such as a lack of in-house information technology (IT) support staff and limited IT budgets. Given these obstacles, how can the pitfalls be avoided and the risks minimized? How can progress be measured? How can EMR bring about organizational change while enhancing the core mission of delivering quality care? In this case study, we address these questions from the perspective of one rural family practice.

Our emphasis here is not on financial or other outcome measures in order to describe a "success story" at one organization. Rather our focus is on the process—because it is the *process* of systems development that has been largely overlooked and underestimated. Whereas the "whys?" of EMR have been addressed ad infinitum, it is the "how?" questions that are still poorly understood. An emphasis on the EMR journey (not the destination) is one most likely to resonate with other clinics that are currently struggling with these same issues. In the next section, we provide background on Dryden Family Medicine and describe the limitations of the paper medical records. Section III outlines the vendor selection process, and Section IV describes the stages of EMR implementation. In Section V, we outline the impact of the new system on physicians, nurses, and front-desk staff, and Sections VI and VII describe the financial impact of EMR.

II. Background

Dryden Family Medicine (DFM) is a four-physician family practice located in Dryden, New York. John Ferger, MD, who had just returned from a three-year sojourn with the Public Health Service in Alaska, founded the practice in 1955. Dr. Ferger was an old-fashioned, "country doctor" who still made occasional house calls. He founded the practice to provide family-centered care in a setting that emphasized "kindness, accessibility, understanding, and compassion." By 2004, DFM had grown significantly to encompass a patient panel of more than 7,000 and provided more than 12,000 patient visits annually. Its service area includes the rural towns of Dryden and Ithaca and surrounding areas, and its patients range from farmers and retirees to faculty and students from nearby colleges, including Cornell University and Ithaca College. The practice had grown over the years from a sparse, 900-square-foot office to its current 5,000-square-foot facility that includes imaging and pathology. By 2003, the clinical staff consisted of four physicians, one nurse practitioner, a part-time nutritionist, and a psychologist.

When the practice first opened in 1955, all of the information for a patient visit could be stored on a single 4×6 index card. A decade later, up to three office visits could be recorded on one standard-size sheet of paper. Since then, the size of the paper chart has grown steadily, and in the last decade, the rate of growth has been almost exponential. In the 1980s, reports from specialists grew to include test results, images, and progress notes. By the 1990s, Medicare requirements had expanded the size of the medical record to one, two-sided page for each visit, plus added pages for prescriptions and outside consultations.

Many other factors have contributed to the expansion of the paper medical record. Due to changing demographics, patients tend to be older and have more chronic health problems. For example, hyperlipidemia, the elevation of blood lipids, is now more prevalent due to changes in lifestyle and treatment thresholds.[2] Other factors include Medicare and other third-party billing regulations and an adversarial legal environment that has increased documentation require- ments. For a patient with multiple problems requiring frequent hospitalizations, the paper chart could grow to an inch-and-a-half thick within only one or two years.

As the complexity of medicine and the number of prescription drugs available have in- creased, the paper record has been unable to keep pace with the changes. Neither has paper- based, intra-office messaging been able to meet the need for accurate and timely information.

Demands on the paper charts became such that they needed to be in more than one place at one time. Requests from patients, phone calls from pharmacies, images from specialists, test re- sults from the laboratory, and inquiries from third-party payors all required that multiple staff members have access to the chart. In addition, all of these communiqués had to be integrated into the paper record. Charts became thicker, access became more difficult, and greater amounts of time were needed to answer specific data queries. Routing slips were unsuccessful in keeping track of the charts within the office and in making sure that they did not get stopped at one sta- tion. Whenever a chart was lost or misplaced, a time-consuming search process would ensue.

All these forces served to move the practice away from paper records and toward EMR.

III. The Vendor Selection Process

In early 2002, a steering committee was formed to direct the transition to EMR. This was com- posed of one physician, the office manager, the nursing supervisor, and the front-desk supervi- sor. Whereas the practice had been using an electronic billing and scheduling system for years, the conversion to EMR was viewed as a much more significant and greater challenge, having a scope of impact more profound than any billing system. The wrong vendor could destroy the continuity of the patient's medical record, incur significant additional costs, and disrupt patient care and staff functions. Yet the risks were not only financial: how would their jobs change for the nurses and front-desk staff? Would their patients adjust to having a laptop in the exam room? In spite of the risks, they decided that the "status quo" of paper charts was untenable. Staying with the current system would only postpone an inevitable transition.

The practice had no IT support person on staff and had a limited budget for outside con- sultants; hence it decided to develop an "internal consultant" who could answer the day-to-day IT questions. The office manager grew into this role as she took the lead in educating the other staff members. The committee took a conservative approach to the development process. It ruled out a custom-built system as being too expensive and risky. Instead it preferred an estab- lished product that had been proven to work well in similar settings. Compatibility with the ex- isting billing and scheduling systems was highly desirable because the practice did not want to have to modify its existing systems, if possible. Compatibility, however, was not essential if the system was superior in other respects. The chosen system should also be "future proof," that is, able to adapt to inevitable changes in medical practice, technology, standards, and regulations.

Information sources on EMR vendors included trade journals, product reviews on websites (e.g., www.aafp.org), and consultations with colleagues at other family practices. In October 2002, one physician attended the annual conference of the American Academy of Family Physicians (AAFP), and the conference provided useful information on EMR vendors that included several software demonstrations. He also attended a demonstration at a local hospital that was being proposed to provide a unified system encompassing both hospital and outpatient data.

Among the different vendors, the committee was most familiar with Medent from Community Computer Services Inc. The practice had been using Medent's practice management (billing) software for years and was satisfied with its record of service and support. Medent had also been adopted by several other group practices in the area. The committee invited Medent and two other vendors for an on-site demonstration.

EMR Vendors Selection Criteria

After ranking each of the vendors based on the criteria below, the committee chose Medent. The rankings were based on the following:

Service, support, and system reliability. The vendor should be responsive to questions, provide adequate training, and be immediately available when needed in order to minimize downtime.

Product maturity. Software should be fully developed and implemented in similar settings.

Financial stability of vendor. Vendor must have a sufficient customer base and management expertise to ensure its long-term viability.

Ease-of-use. Information should be easily accessible and fully integrated without requiring excessive navigation of multiple windows.

Security. The system should have built-in safeguards to protect the privacy and confidentiality of patient information.

Regional familiarity/organizational culture. The vendor should be familiar with New York State regulations and able to readily adapt to regulatory changes.

Cost. Costs should be within reasonable limits, but this was a secondary factor. A reliable system was viewed to be far less costly in the long run.

Other vendors were rejected due to immature systems, lack of primary care experience, and uncertain financial futures. Medent was a mature company, which had evolved over more than 25 years as an electronic office system. It had gradually expanded its system modules from billing to appointments to EMR, progressively enhancing its patient management and documentation capacity. Although its clinical quality assurance features were just coming online, the committee had the sense that the company was fully committed to maturing them. Having one vendor for hardware, software, and networking was also a significant advantage because it meant that one phone call would guarantee that a problem would be dealt with efficiently with no "passing of the buck." As part of the terms of the contract, Medent also agreed to provide 50 hours of training.

Technological Specifications

Hardware components included seven notebook computers, seven desktop computers, and a new server with redundant hard drives. Data were transmitted via a wireless network. The system had several features to enhance security and reliability. Audit trails recorded all accesses made to medical records. All data was stored on the server, and no patient data was stored on the notebooks. Remote access to the server could be obtained through a virtual private network (VPN), which meant that all data were encrypted before transmission over the network. The server used the LINUX operating system because it was viewed as more reliable than alternatives.

IV. Stages of EMR Implementation

The timeline for the phased conversion and the stages of EMR implementation are shown in Table C3.1 and Figure C3.1.

In the initial phase, the new system was used mostly for day-to-day operations, such as billing, internal communication, generating prescriptions, and sending letters to patients. The electronic billing function had to work correctly the first time, because the practice could not

---

Table C3.1   Timeline for Phased Conversion to EMR

July 2003 Began using system for internal e-mail and messaging; outside documents received by electronic fax are entered into system. Outside billing firm has access to internal server; all billing is handled online and with real-time access to EMR.

August 2003 Prescriptions generated electronically and faxed to pharmacies.

September 2003 Two physicians begin using the "Progress Notes" feature of EMR for patient progress notes.

October 2003 Physicians can access EMR from home via secure Internet connection (VPN).

November 2003 Staff begins to scan all new paper documents.

December 2003 Staff uses EMR to create patient task lists.

January 2004 All physicians have switched from paper to EMR for patient progress notes; use of paper is reduced or eliminated. Customized templates are designed to create shortcuts based on keywords. Ordering of lab tests begins with some results entered directly into patient records.

February 2004–July 2004 ICD-9-CM coding issues become of primary importance. Customized templates created to reduce potential information loss. Part-time staff hired to input past data on family and social history.

May 2004 Correlation of prescriptions with laboratory values used to produce graphs of test results over time, as in Figure C3.1.

September 2004 Electronic ordering of imaging begins. Digital images are sent via network and added to EMR.

December 2004 All new referrals generated through the system.

February 10, 2005 John Ferger, MD, the clinic's founder, unexpectedly dies; his patients are notified by letters generated by the system.

March 2005 Patient education literature is scanned into the system and linked to EMR.

April 7, 2005 Pain-killer Bextra is taken off the market; patient letters are generated by the system and mailed the same day.

July 2005–Present Health maintenance formulas further developed, resulting in improved disease management and quality of care.

February 2006 Practice adds two new physicians to meet growing demand; paper records are moved into storage.

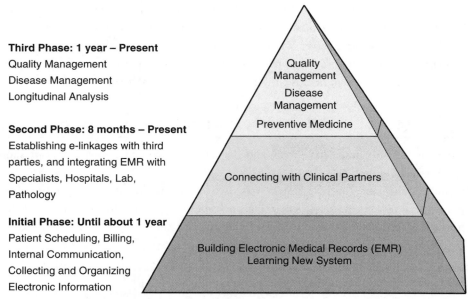

Third Phase: 1 year – Present
Quality Management
Disease Management
Longitudinal Analysis

Second Phase: 8 months – Present
Establishing e-linkages with third
parties, and integrating EMR with
Specialists, Hospitals, Lab,
Pathology

Initial Phase: Until about 1 year
Patient Scheduling, Billing,
Internal Communication,
Collecting and Organizing
Electronic Information

Quality
Management
Disease
Management
Preventive Medicine

Connecting with Clinical Partners

Building Electronic Medical Records (EMR)
Learning New System

FIGURE C3.1   EMR Implementation Stages.

afford disruptions in its revenue stream. As part of the billing system, the practice had developed a database of patient demographic information. This billing database was easily integrated into the new system, saving considerable staff time. The EMR system gave the off-site billing company access to detailed, real-time information from the patients' records, allowing the billing service to maintain a "virtual presence" in the office. Significant efficiency gains were achieved from a drop-off in phone calls and the transfer of paper forms to and from the billing service. There was also less chance of a rejected claim due to missing or incomplete information. Given access to real-time claims data, the office manager could generate custom reports without having to contact the billing service.

The software vendor provided training to the members of the steering committee, who then trained members of their respective groups. By January, all physicians had made the switch from paper to electronic progress notes. Physicians could access the new system from home through a secure, VPN connection. This gave them added flexibility in their work schedules and greatly enhanced their after-hours care of patients.

Significant efficiency gains were achieved in prescription ordering, letter generation, and internal messaging. The faxing of prescriptions greatly reduced the potential for medication errors due to illegible handwriting or incorrect dosages. Staff time was saved due to reductions in phone calls to and from pharmacies. Most patient letters no longer required dictation and could be generated in about one-tenth the time. Whereas the number of letters to patients increased, the physician and staff time needed for this task went down. Internal e-mail and messaging allowed for more efficient internal communication. Because the volume and detail of messages increased, they did take additional time. Thus, not as much time savings were achieved as might have been expected.

In the second phase, the focus shifted from internal operations to strengthening external linkages with outside entities, such as hospitals, specialists, laboratory, and pathology. The main benefits from this stage were the decreased physician time needed to review external reports, faster turnaround time from third parties, and the ability to access the data from multiple in- and out-of-office locations. Facilitating linkages to diagnostic codes improved billing for ancillary services.

The increase in data available to staff created the possibility of triaging pharmacy refills, laboratory data, imaging studies, and specific disease management issues. New algorithms were created that allowed nurses and front-desk staff to close some items that previously required a physician, such as the dosage adjustment of anticoagulants. Thus, nurses could take on added responsibilities, and physicians could spend less time on routine tasks, such as prescription refills.

Most of the electronic linkages with out-of-office entities were at the level of faxing documents. These were stored as image files; therefore, a great deal of processing and staff training was required in order to integrate these into the system.

The third stage of EMR implementation began after about a year and remains an ongoing project. In this stage, the practice set more ambitious targets for enhanced quality management, disease management, practice management, and preventive medicine. Customized templates and algorithms were developed to allow complex tasks and decisions to become routine. For example, nursing protocols are being considered that would enable nurses to handle preventive medicine, such as by ordering a lipid panel for patients with high cholesterol.

The EMR design also allowed for the graphing of lab results over time. For example, physicians could easily graph the impact of two statin drugs (e.g., Lipitor and Zocor) on blood cholesterol over time. By pooling data from multiple practices with EMR, it would be possible to measure the effectiveness of each drug for hundreds or thousands of patients in actual clinical practice as opposed to randomized clinical trials. This represents a significant opportunity for further research on drug effectiveness for chronic diseases, such as high cholesterol and diabetes. Longitudinal graphs of test results can also enhance patient education and self-care, for example, by showing the impact of weight gain on blood pressure.

The ability of EMR to better manage the health of populations was demonstrated in April 2005, when the Food and Drug Administration (FDA) pulled the painkiller, Bextra, due to safety concerns. Within minutes, the EMR system identified every patient taking Bextra. By the end of the day, each had been sent a letter with news of the drug recall. In January 2008, questions were raised over the safety of Vytorin, a cholesterol medication, in heart patients. For patients taking this medication, a reminder was generated to discuss these safety concerns during the next office visit.

Disease management aims to help patients improve their self-care for chronic conditions, while screening patients periodically to ensure that they are meeting their goals.[3] DFM began to develop disease management programs for patients with diabetes, high cholesterol, and hypertension. For patients with hypertension, monthly reports could be generated to answer the following questions:

- Which patients are not taking medication?
- Are they meeting their blood pressure targets?
- Did they receive educational materials?

By collecting periodic data on specific diseases, the practice also laid the foundation for meeting future "pay-for-performance" criteria that have recently gained popularity among both federal and private insurers. These programs establish bonus (incentive) payments for meeting certain quality targets, such as "95 percent of all immunizations provided on schedule."

V. Impact on Job Responsibilities

The EMR system resulted in changes in the job descriptions and responsibilities of all members of the practice. These changes were a test of the staff's flexibility in absorbing the shifts in their roles and the tasks they needed to assume. This flexibility was a key success factor in EMR implementation.

The biggest change for physicians was the need to assign diagnosis codes based on the ICD-9-CM (International Classification of Diseases, 9th Revision, Clinical Modification). The staff had previously done most coding with assistance from physicians. Because the new system was diagnosis-driven, it would not work, even at the simplest level, without first assigning an ICD-9-CM code. Coding issues became a significant source of frustration, as physicians realized how much information was lost through category coding.[4] This reflects some of the limitations of the ICD-9-CM system, which was not designed specifically for use in family practice.[5] Physicians had to learn a new "language," such as the keywords that would lead to the appropriate diagnostic categories. One older physician initially worked around the coding problem by writing down the diagnosis and relying on front-office staff to assign the appropriate ICD-9-CM code later.

Physicians often require a clear and concise description of the patient's diagnosis, and ICD-9-CM categories are not detailed enough for this purpose. To overcome this limitation, the physicians would often customize the ICD-9-CM labels within the EMR system. A patient with aortic stenosis, for example, would be classified as "ICD-9-CM 396: Diseases of Mitral and Aortic Valves." Yet this is not specific enough for daily use, as it contains no information on disease severity. Hence, the physicians would customize the label to read: "Aortic stenosis, moderate; ejection fraction X%; valve gradient Y%."

In addition to coding issues, physicians needed some practice in preserving attentiveness and eye contact with the patient while simultaneously working with their notebooks. It also took several months for physicians to feel more facile with the design features of the new system, as well as its more advanced functions.

The new system enabled the physicians to spend less time on routine tasks, such as dictation, phone calls to patients, billing, and pharmacy. They were also freed from some of the burden of making routine decisions, because nurses and front-desk staff had access to better information, which allowed them to make higher-level decisions.

The office manager played a key role in EMR implementation, as her job responsibilities expanded significantly. As the practice's "internal consultant," she educated the staff on using the new system while providing IT support and system troubleshooting. In addition, she became the liaison with outside entities and helped establish and strengthen electronic linkages. She also worked with Medent's support staff to devise new methods and procedures to optimize EMR utilization.

Employee satisfaction among nurses appeared to improve as the new system enhanced their effectiveness and often made their jobs easier. Nurses were freed from some routine tasks that did not directly add value to patient care, such as pulling patient charts and locating lost charts (Table C3.2). They also spent less time on prescriptions and lab and image orders. Protocols and procedures were developed over time that allowed the nurses to take on more complex tasks that previously required a physician. For example, nurses could identify high-risk patients needing pneumovax, a pneumonia vaccine. They could also order a glysosated hemoglobin (HGbA1c) test for a diabetic patient or a lipid panel for patients with high cholesterol. The nurses also found it much easier to check on patient follow-through with respect to referrals, diagnostic imaging, and laboratory tests.

The EMR system gave the front-desk staff access to more accurate and reliable information quickly. In turn, this allowed them to take on more challenging tasks. They could quickly answer routine inquiries from patients or pharmacies that previously required a physician, nurse, or the office manager. They could answer patient questions regarding waiting time, because the patient's arrival time and the physician's status regarding his or her list of patient appointments was captured in the system. However, time spent on some routine tasks increased, such as scanning, labeling, and routing documents.

VI. Financial Impact

Average monthly revenues increased by 11 percent in the first year following EMR implementation and 20 percent in the second year, compared with the baseline year. The *charge-capture ratio* is defined as total revenues as a percentage of total charges. Over the two-year period, this ratio increased from 65 to 70 percent. There were fewer rejected claims and unreimbursed services after EMR implementation, most likely due to improved documentation and accuracy in billing. The average patient volume per physician did not change measurably over this period. Hence, revenue gains were not attributable to increased patient volume or shorter patient visits.

Billing codes for family practice are primarily based on Current Procedural Terminology (CPT) evaluation and management (E&M) codes. E&M codes reflect the physician's level of service for a given patient visit and are based on such factors as the severity of the problem, the complexity of the medical decision, and the duration of the examination. More than 90 percent of the practice's total billed codes were accounted for by only three M codes: 99213, 99214, and 99215. These codes are defined as office visits for established patients for various levels of service. The EMR system could be expected to improve coding accuracy due to better documentation and coding decision support.

On the cost side, salary costs did not change measurably, because no reduction in staffing materialized. However, the practice did require an additional part-time staffer to scan and label paper documents.

Table C3.2   Impact of EMR on Time Allocation for Various Tasks

	Spent More Time		Spent Less Time	
Physicians				
Coding	Primary ICD-9-CM diagnosis		Information management (internal)	Retrieving data Documentation Dictation
Technical	Computer troubleshooting			
Clinical	Seeing patients		Information management (external)	Prescriptions Letters to patients Image ordering Phone calls to patients Billing-related
Nurses				
Clinical	Seeing patients Disease management		Information management (internal)	Pulling charts Filing records Looking for charts Intra-office communication
Technical	Computer troubleshooting			
			Information management (external)	Referrals Prescriptions Lab orders and image orders Letters to patients
Staff and Front Desk				
Information management (internal)	Scanning and faxing documents		Information management (internal)	Pulling charts Filing records Looking for charts Intra-office communication
Information management (external)	Patient referrals			
			Information management (external)	Prescriptions Lab orders and image orders Letters to patients
			Coding	Primary ICD-9-CM diagnosis
Office Manager				
Technical	In-house IT support		Information management (internal)	Retrieving data
Information management (internal)	Management reports			
			Information management (external)	Investigating billing-related issues

VII. Cost–Benefit Analysis and EMR

Cost–benefit analysis (CBA) has frequently been used as a tool to decide whether to invest in EMR.[6] Thus, it is important to understand both the strengths and limitations of this approach, insofar as it relates to this case study.

CBA can assist in planning and budgeting by focusing on the likely financial impact of the EMR investment. This will lead to an emphasis on *medical management*, that is, the billing function, because this is typically where the largest financial gains can be realized. That said, CBA could not adequately capture the benefits of improved quality, employee satisfaction, and patient satisfaction because these are intangible assets and are difficult to quantify in economic terms. The long-term benefits of EMR—such as prevention, fewer hospitalizations, and a lower disease burden—tend to accrue to other stakeholders, such as patients and society. In addition, the standard CBA tends to underestimate the cost of doing nothing. That is, it does not sufficiently emphasize the opportunity cost of retaining paper records in the midst of a rapidly changing and complex medical environment. At its worst, CBA can become a justification for passivity and inaction, leading to "paralysis by analysis." CBA also does not generally account for regulatory and reimbursement changes (e.g., pay-for-performance) that encourage or even mandate EMR adoption.

VIII. Conclusion

Lessons Learned

Three years after making the switch to EMR, the practice was quite satisfied with the new system. With improved access to information, the staff could answer more questions from patients and pharmacies. Patients enjoyed receiving more mail and reminders from their family physician. While the EMR had a positive financial impact, its main benefit was supporting the core mission of providing quality care. By using the EMR system's more advanced features, the practice could better manage the health of its patients through enhanced disease management. The EMR system also paved the way for the future adoption of "pay-for-performance" criteria.

The practice has so far encountered few problems with system reliability or data security. Much has been made of the federally mandated Health Information Portability and Accountability Act (HIPAA) requirements to ensure the confidentiality of patient health information. Because New York State already had tight regulations on health data privacy, the practice already had data safeguards in place that ensured compliance with the new HIPAA law.

Much of the literature to date has focused on the EMR adoption in hospitals and integrated health networks.[7] Yet 26 percent of all family practice physicians work in solo or two-physician group practices (see www.aafp.org). Despite the great promise of this technology, EMR adoption rates remain relatively low, especially in smaller group practices.[8] A 2007 study by the CDC found that only 12.4 percent of office-based physicians nationwide reported using comprehensive EMR.[9]

In retrospect, the key success factors and lessons learned were as follows:

- *Prior relationship with software vendor.* The billing system was in place prior to EMR implementation. This greatly facilitated a smooth transition.
- *Increased autonomy of staff.* The new system allowed nurses and front-desk staff to take on added responsibilities. To realize the full benefits of the new system, greater staff autonomy and flexibility were needed.
- *Need for in-house IT support.* The office manager played a key role in the transition by providing training and in-house IT support.
- *Importance of coding issues.* The physicians were initially surprised with the time required to assign ICD-9-CM codes. With practice, the time needed for this task decreased.

While some initial successes were achieved soon after implementation, it took a year or more to realize the EMR system's full potential. Part of the project's success was due to its incremental approach that served to minimize the downside risk. The higher-level functions of the EMR could not be achieved without a solid foundation in terms of phases one and two, as shown in Figure C3.1. Thus the goal of EMR adoption came to be seen as a journey, not a destination. Whereas the EMR was initially viewed as a better way of storing patient records, it is now seen as a more efficient and effective way to practice medicine.

An Update: Two Years On

In the past two years, the pace of technological and system change has only accelerated, and the EMR system has evolved with these changes. Disease management functions have been expanded to provide reminders for hemoglobin A1c testing for diabetics and aspirin for heart disease patients. Reminders are also provided for preventive tests and screenings, such as bone density testing, mammograms, pap tests, tetanus boosters, zostavax immunizations (for shingles), pneumococcal vaccines, and colorectal screenings.

In 2008, the Center for Medicaid and Medicare Services (CMS), implemented the Physician Quality Reporting Initiative (PQRI; see www.cms.hhs.gov/PQRI/). The PQRI identified a set of 100 or more primary care quality measures that could be reported through the EMR. An example metric is the "percentage of diabetics with a hemoglobin A1c greater than 9 percent." DFM chose a subset of 30 of these quality metrics to focus and report on. The practice received a bonus payment, equivalent to 1.5 percent of revenues, for meeting the reporting standards during 2007. In the future, CMS will expand the requirements and raise targets in order to qualify for these "incentive" payments (pay-for-performance). Incentive payments such as these can be used to offset some of the ongoing costs of hardware and software maintenance.

In terms of hospital linkages, the practice has created a subroutine that will abstract and fax patient information to nearby hospitals for patients undergoing emergency room and hospital evaluations. Other subroutines have been developed to transfer records to lawyers, worker's compensation claims, and insurance companies. This has saved hours of staff time formerly spent copying and mailing documents.

The outside billing agency maintains real-time contact with the EMR database through a VPN and has continued to do a commendable job. By generating monthly reports, they were able to identify a payor who was out of compliance with the contract terms. An outside consultant was recently hired to review existing contracts and make recommendations for future contract negotiations with third-party payors.

Notes

1. Portions of this chapter were previously published in L. O'Neill and W. Klepack, "Electronic Medical Records for a Rural Family Practice: A Case Study In Systems Development," *Journal of Medical Systems* 31 (2007): 25–33. (Reproduced with permission.)
2. D. Gans, J. Kralewski, T. Hammons, and B. Dowd, "Medical Groups' Adoption of Electronic Health Records and Information Systems," *Health Affairs (Millwood)* 24 (2005): 1323–1333.
3. S. M. Foote, "Population-Based Disease Management under Fee-for-Service Medicare," *Health Affairs (Millwood)* Suppl. Web Exclusives (2003).
4. V. Slee, D. Slee, and J. Schmidt, *The Endangered Medical Record* (St. Paul, MN: Tringa Press, 2000).
5. L I. Iezzoni, *Risk Adjustment for Measuring Healthcare Outcomes* (Chicago: Health Administration Press, 1997).
6. S. J. Wang et al., "A Cost-Benefit Analysis of Electronic Medical Records in Primary Care," *American Journal of Medicine* 114, no. 5 (2003): 397–403.
7. M. J. Coye and J. Kell, "How Hospitals Confront New Technology," *Health Affairs (Millwood)* 25 (2006).
8. Gans et al. (2005).
9. E. S. Hing, C. W. Burt, and D. A. Woodwell, "Electronic Medical Record Use by Office-Based Physicians and Their Practices: United States, 2006," *Advance Data*, no. 393 (2007): 1–7.

Case Study Questions

1. What is pay-for-performance? How could it stimulate or encourage EMR adoption?
2. What are the advantages and limitations of cost–benefit analysis for IT adoption decisions?
3. Suppose the practice had decided not to adopt EMR. What would have been the "cost" of such a decision?
4. What milestones should be achieved, in terms of IT readiness, before a group practice decides to implement EMR?
5. Could there be less of an incentive and different set of challenges for smaller practices to take on HMIS projects such as EMR implementation than large-scale health services organizations, such as a multi-provider health maintenance organization? If so, what are the differences? In terms of the incentives, why or why not?

Delivering Enterprisewide Decision Support through E-Business Applications

Rajiv Kohli and Henry J. Groot

Editor's Note: Decision support systems (DSS), as the name suggests, have to do with providing the information and knowledge to the caregiver and administrative end-users for carrying out important decisions. Apparently, then, DSS are a special type of healthcare management information system (HMIS) contributing to achieving corporate goals and objectives—for healthcare services organizations, this could be patient satisfaction, profitability, and reduced medical errors. DSS concepts, therefore, embody many of the same concepts and thinking needed for achieving successful HMIS implementation. The case reinforces many of the concepts discussed throughout this text: sponsorship, managing change, project management, outsourcing and data standards, security, and privacy issues. It is appropriate, then, for students to see how the HMIS concepts covered in the text can be brought together to achieve a successful implementation for new generations of DSS software within a large-scale healthcare services organizational context.

I. Introduction

This case study presents an implementation of a Web-enabled decision support system (DSS) at Holy Cross Health System (HCHS). HCHS is a national organization with hospitals, called member organizations (MOs), in various markets across the United States. HCHS MOs have more than 4,000 combined beds, employ about 20,000 people, and have a total operating revenue of approximately $1.5 billion. Some MOs have been providing healthcare services for more than 100 years. The MOs provide a range of services, including acute-care hospitals, extended-care facilities, residential facilities for the disabled and older adults, occupational medicine, and community services organizations.

DSS are computer systems designed to help improve the effectiveness and productivity of managers.[1] DSS deliver models that can be used to systematically evaluate policies and alternatives.[2] Conventional hospital information systems help meet the challenge by providing data necessary for policy formation and outcome measurement. However, integrating those systems with DSS can help managers gain insight into the operations, consider alternatives, and develop business strategies.

Operationally, the DSS at HCHS is used for resource allocation decisions, many of which use the costs and time for day-of-stay–level patient data. Such decisions improve the cost efficiency of patient care delivery. For example, an analysis indicated that patient test results from the laboratory to the emergency department were being provided late, causing longer wait times for patients. The redesigned process linked a printer in the emergency department to the laboratory system, where results were printed as soon as the test was completed in the laboratory. At the managerial level, DSS provide information, such as department-level costs and high-cost items (which managers use to contain costs), and look for ways to better integrate services with other departments. For example, using activity-based costing, the registration department manager found that too much time and cost were being incurred in registering patients. Therefore, the manager reengineered the patient registration process by linking the registration system with the medical records system and accessing previously collected patient information. Strategically, the DSS at HCHS is used to make pricing and contracting decisions and merger/acquisitions planning.[3] By modeling a contract using existing costs, HCHS managers decide whether they should enter into a contract or if an existing contract should be renegotiated. There have been instances when a HCHS MO has declined to enter into a contractual arrangement following an expected loss from the modeled contract. DSS data at HCHS have also been used for strategic decisions on discontinuing services or starting new ones.

II. Overview of Decision Support

The HCHS first-generation DSS, which was developed as a flat-file-based case management system, operated from 1983 through 1989. The primary driver for creating the case management system was the federal Medicare diagnosis-related group (DRG)–based prospective payment system (PPS), under which the Health Care Financing Administration (HCFA) would reimburse a predetermined amount for categories of diseases. The PPS meant that HCHS had to better manage its patient care process. The DSS was primarily designed to support patient billing departments at MOs through value-added processes such as cost accounting; high-level expected reimbursement; and patient classification by DRG, services, and markets. At the request of remote users, the reports from the DSS were executed in batch mode and were mailed to the requesting user. The turnaround time was three days for standard reports and one week for ad hoc or customized reports. HCHS first-generation DSS contained only inpatients.

The HCHS second-generation DSS, which operated from 1990 through 1999, was a hierarchical database with indexed files and an improvement over the flat-file, first-generation DSS. It also had user-controlled reporting capabilities available through a wide area network (WAN) linking all HCHS MOs with the corporate office. This was interfaced each night with MO information systems to accept updated patient financial and clinical information. The system processed the data and updated the predefined files each night. The MOs produced reports and performed analyses against these files to support their operational, managerial, and strategic decision making. The DSS resided in a mainframe computer consisting of a hierarchical database with proprietary query tools and value-added applications such as cost accounting, claims management, and "what-if" reimbursement modeling. In addition, it also had an expanded data set that included data from physician offices, home health centers, patient satisfaction, and severity-based clinical models. HCHS second-generation DSS added their patient records, resulting in a tenfold increase in the volume of data. This required efficient report generation and remote printing at users' local printers.

The primary technical drivers for the migration to the second-generation DSS at HCHS were the acquisition of T1 leased lines and a database. The business drivers were the changes in the reimbursement structure such as multiple per diems and payor-defined case rates heralding the age of managed care. HCHS first-generation DSS could not calculate expected reimbursement from some complex managed care contracts.

With such expanded capabilities and an extensive historical database, why should HCHS plan for yet another migration? What limitations was HCHS experiencing with the second-generation DSS? What expectations did HCHS DSS users have? What would HCHS DSS developers like to see in third-generation DSS?

The second-generation DSS, with its hierarchical database, had reached processing limitation, leading to performance issues such as increase in time in executing reports and processing of complex analyses. Further, as HCHS's home-grown applications became complex, the maintenance costs began to rise. At the same time, it was getting harder for HCHS to retain technical personnel who were developing skills in more advanced technologies such as online analytical processing (OLAP) and relational OLAP. The DSS user exposure to the Internet and its ease of access were raising expectations of how the DSS should provide data. The Internet browser, with its minimum training requirements, has become the standard of a computer user interface, thereby adding to the urgency to migrate to the third-generation DSS.

The technology of the second generation had also reached the upgrade and maintenance zenith. Similarly, the software choices with the operating system had their limitations. In addition, the users had matured in their expectations of data access and presentation. They expected advanced data manipulation capability through which they could change the data displays according to their analytical preferences. Table C4.1 shows HCHS migration from the second-generation DSS (legacy systems) to the third-generation data warehouse DSS.

Table C4.1 Characteristics of the Three Generations of Decision Support Systems

Characteristics	First Generation	Second Generation	Third Generation
Period	1983–1989	1990–1999	2000–Present
Technology	Flat-file reporting on mainframe	Hierarchical database with indexed files on mainframe	Relational database; Web enabled
Applications	Case management	Activity-based costing; contract modeling; severity readjustment; patient satisfaction	Physician profiling system; online reporting; activity-based costing; contract modeling; severity adjustment; patient satisfaction
Connectivity	None, single site	User access through WAN	User access through WAN and intranet
Strengths	Support standard costing; patient classification into services, diagnosis-related groups, and markets	User access and control; accurate costing; support for managed care; integrated modules	Greater user access and control; user-friendly graphical interface; efficient reporting; greater portability of data through Web-enabled tools; improved security
Limitations	Remote reporting; delay in user data access; inpatients only	Character based; poor user interface; time-consuming to execute reports	None

III. Implementation

As is the case with most technology-based projects, implementation is the key to the success of DSS and is largely dependent on how well the managerial and implementation issues are managed. These issues include soliciting continued high-level sponsorship of the project, managing change, demonstrating quick successes through rapid application development, considering outsourcing as an alternative, integrating existing tools, maintaining data standards, and coordinating project management.

Sponsorship

Generally speaking, the sponsorship of a project should come from the information systems (IS) and the business leadership. We often find that the sponsorship in technology-oriented projects comes from only IS senior management. While IS sponsorship is required, the sponsorship from the business users is equally important. The literature on information technology (IT) implementation suggests that user sponsorship is a proxy for anticipated usage of the system and a determinant of system success.[4] On the other hand, when the user sponsorship is absent or not solicited, the users perceive that the technology is being implemented without proper understanding of the business requirements.

At HCHS, prior to proposing the transition to the third generation, it is ascertained that the information steering committee and the chief information officer (CIO) sponsored the project so that necessary resources could be obtained. Following the sponsorship, the success of the DSS depended on the actual usage. The DSS, by nature, supports a number of decision makers, most of who have to be motivated to use the data for improved decision making. Therefore, the extent to which the DSS can support business decision making is limited only by user creativity. Although this is a favorable situation for any IS, the undefined set of users leads to a fragmented clientele base. We find our user base spread across clinical, financial, and operations departments and various levels of HCHS MOs. Hence, the unclear business domain made it difficult to get HCHS users involved in the development of a third-generation DSS.

HCHS solicited sponsorship and support from diverse users through a DSS users' group (UG). The DSS UG was created at HCHS to bring together users from various application areas across the MOs to share their use of DSS data in evolving business decision-making situations. Monthly conference calls were conducted, inviting DSS users, and annual meetings were arranged to provide the developers with an opportunity to demonstrate the DSS enhancements. The HCHS DSS UG also served as a forum for feedback from users and built much-needed sponsorship.

Managing Change

The management of change is a critical factor in making any significant change, particularly one that affects the nature of work. Change management also requires cultivating and managing realistic expectations of all parties involved. One such change in healthcare services also affecting HCHS has been the shifting economics of hospital services. Constriction of revenue resulting from managed care is driving the scarcity of capital for investment into IT. This change requires that HCHS investment be made in technologies or systems that will be used effectively. Such a change requires a shift in the thinking of the users, who in the past may have supported investment in IS/IT just because it is "nice to have."

Change management also requires prioritizing projects that require allocation of human and financial resources. Therefore, users of the DSS have to follow a methodology to prioritize those projects that are critical to the business functions. Such prioritization can lead to delaying or limiting the scope of existing projects. HCHS subscribes to a managing organizational change (MOC) methodology to support any major change in business practice resulting from the process redesign or IS implementation. The MOC methodology prescribes assigning a trained internal consultant to the project team to work with the sponsor and the change agent. The MOC consultant assesses the capacity of change among the team members and guides the change process to its successful conclusion.

Rapid Application Development

The rapid pace of change in businesses, especially healthcare services delivery, requires quick actions in response to market conditions. In the same vein, when the response requires developing an IS, the traditional systems, analysis, and design methodologies are not suitable because of the time involved in implementing an IS. HCHS business situations require quick development of the next-generation DSS, even if it is not the complete system with all its features.

The IS literature provides examples of rapid applications development (RAD) and another similar approach involving the users called joint application development (JAD) as substitutes for the complete systems analysis and design. HCHS applied RAD and JAD approaches to develop the third-generation DSS. The consultants and developers of previous DSS worked closely to build a data model in a relational database. Once the data model was finalized and a prototype DSS developed, key users were invited to test the DSS and provide input. Under RAD at HCHS, projects and deliverables have been planned in 90-day increments. HCHS has found such an approach to be cost-effective and one that meets user expectations.

Outsourcing

RAD is of increasing importance because of increasing pressures on the IS department from outsourcing application vendors. Outsourcing is an increasingly popular option for organizations that prefer to strengthen their core competencies yet find it difficult to invest resources in the development of IS. Outsourcing vendors, on the other hand, can invest large amounts of resources that can then be spread over a greater number of customers. Therefore, vendor-provided application software can be a viable alternative to internally developed applications.

HCHS considered outsourcing the DSS development as a viable option. In partnership with a leading vendor, HCHS cooperated to develop the next-generation DSS. Prior to adopting the DSS as a health system standard, HCHS chose one of its hospitals as a pilot site. The vendor-developed DSS consisted of advanced data manipulation tools and a member-centered data model to accommodate the managed care driven market. However, after two years of partnership to develop the next-generation DSS, there is still no corporatewide DSS that can be implemented. Therefore, HCHS decided to develop in-house the third-generation DSS.

Integrating Existing Tools

To the extent possible, HCHS is integrating the third-generation DSS with the previous generation's tools. In the software industry, this is referred to as backward compatibility. There is a significant investment in development, training, and support for these tools that, if abandoned, can lead to business disruption. This is particularly the case for reports created in the previous-generation DSS that are executed periodically for mandatory reporting or business decision making. Although the need for backward compatibility may appear to contradict with the earlier change management discussion, it is an attempt to manage risk of business disruption—even if it implies that some data manipulation tools will be less than optimum. Further, the HCHS OLAP, which runs the multidimensional managerial reporting or MR Cube (Figure C4.1), will benefit from the third-generation DSS by producing synergistic business value for users of both systems.

Data Standards Migration

Maintaining data standards implies that the meaning of a data field is consistent among applications and across various hospitals. For instance, an admit date can mean different things under different conditions. It can mean the date when the patient registered for a procedure, the date when a patient was admitted for observation, or a date when the patient was admitted as

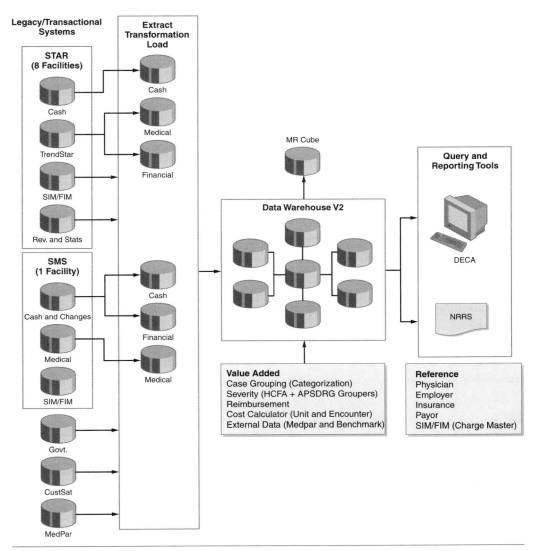

FIGURE C4.1   HCHS Online Analytic Processing.

an inpatient following an observation period. Any of these explanations of admit date would be acceptable as long as they are consistently applied across the organization and users understand the accepted definition. If the definition of admit date is not predefined and acted on, it could vary the length of stay for patients and therefore lead to inaccurate financial and clinical outcomes.

Adherence to data standards is critical in using preexisting reports, in applications such as cost accounting and reimbursement modeling, and in benchmarking quality of care outcomes across the hospitals of HCHS. Data standards have been a challenge for HCHS from the first generation of the DSS. Migration to the third-generation DSS is both an opportunity and a challenge to revisit and assert data standards.

Project Management

Among all the implementation issues, project management is perhaps the most decisive determinant of project success. It is the glue that holds together all the previously discussed issues. Past studies have indicated that most IS projects fail because of lack of control and a weak project plan. KPMG conducted a study of more than 100 projects deemed to have failed and found that two-thirds exceeded their schedules by more than 30 percent.[5]

HCHS manages the DSS and other projects using automated project management software. The use of project management software yields benefits beyond managing the project at hand. It is an effective tool to structure the project, plan for resources, and communicate responsibilities to the participants. It also serves as a means for justifying the resource consumption for the project.

The steps in the project plan and the estimated time frames are key guideposts for, and assets of, a project. Organizations spend significant amounts of money to purchase this "knowledge" from consulting companies so that they can avoid the pitfalls of missing some steps or scheduling unrealistic time frames. HCHS purchased the services of a consulting company to plan and implement the third-generation DSS. HCHS created a baseline project plan that was compared with the actual time and resource at the end of the project. Any deviations from the baseline plan will be studied to effectively manage resources and to improve future project plans.

IV. Challenges and Barriers to Implementation

Each healthcare management information systems (HMIS) implementation is a learning experience and an opportunity to perform better in the future. There are usually a few barriers that impede the smooth HMIS implementation, and some issues remain unresolved challenges. In such situations, it is useful to understand and manage the challenges rather than attempt to resolve all of them. During the implementation of the third-generation DSS, HCHS has recognized the following challenges that it continues to manage.

Valuing the Utility of the DSS Resource

In the last decade, the healthcare business has seen significant changes in transitioning from a socialist welfare model to a free market model. Under the socialist welfare model, healthcare providers were reimbursed for any type of service provided for a sick person with little or no emphasis on efficiency or quality outcomes. The free market approach holds healthcare providers accountable for the efficiency of operations, quality of clinical outcomes, and patient satisfaction. To this extent, the healthcare providers also share in the risk of cost overruns with the payors. Traditionally, employers or insurers have taken on this risk.

Given such a fundamental shift in the business, compounded by an aging population and accelerating growth in IS/IT, generating information for control and decision making has become indispensable. However, the management approach of many healthcare decision makers has not kept pace with the changing business. They see little value in data analysis to establish norms, benchmark their operations against others' outcomes, or examine productivity.

HCHS is responding to this challenge by educating current and potential users of DSS data through presentations at various clinical and financial meetings and demonstrating to them the value a DSS can bring to decision making. It is equally important to educate the physicians within hospitals who may not necessarily use the DSS but who have a significant effect on the outcomes stored in a DSS. The director of the DSS and internal DSS consultants regularly meet with physicians and administrative decision makers to demonstrate, with examples drawn from their data, how they can influence clinical, financial, and quality outcomes.

Another approach being practiced is to develop "hybrid" managers. Hybrid managers are from clinical or financial departments of an MO who are trained in DSS use. These managers then work with their peers and demonstrate the strategic use of the data through practice. We hope that the hybrid managers will act as emissaries for the DSS as a corporate resource.

Understanding the Data

The DSS, like other IS, is a tool that is effective only when the business context is well understood. HCHS found that one of the most challenging aspects of the DSS implementation has been and continues to be the business understanding, or lack thereof, of the data within the DSS. The data in the DSS are highly specialized and sometimes complex. A DSS user has to invest in understanding the meaning of the DSS fields and the values that these fields can assume.

Further, there are calculated fields within the DSS that result from manipulating other fields. For example, the variable cost of a chargeable item is calculated using the field's departmental expenses from the general ledger, total units of the item consumed from the order entry system, and relative value units from the cost information system. The decision maker using DSS data should understand the relationships in this calculation. For instance, a chargeable item that costs $20 in one week can cost $20.50 in the next week. This can occur in the first week of a new quarter in which the departmental expenses have increased or the units of output have decreased, or both. The change in the per-unit cost affects departmental productivity, profitability, and perhaps budgeting. Similarly, the users have to understand that traditional statistical analysis is often not appropriate for ordinal data values. For example, arithmetic mean is not appropriate for the values in the "Zip code" field.

DSS analysts manage this challenge by educating users on the intricacies of calculations and the periodicity of data through a number of ways, such as one-on-one training for new users, periodic refresher courses at each of the hospitals, and training classes at the annual DSS UG conferences.

Evolving Role of Decision Support Services

With the changing user expectations and the market dynamics, the role of the DSS has been evolving into a provider of applications, called an application service provider, in addition to a provider of data for decision support. The user expectations from the DSS have grown significantly from the time when it was a database for storing patient billing information to the present, where it is considered as a strategic business system. The DSS assists in policy formulation and validation, contract evaluations, business process redesign initiatives, and cost control. As the data complexity has increased, the technology and the tools for analytical support have also grown. The user expectations of the DSS have evolved, and users expect the DSS to be accessible from remote locations at all times. These expectations have augmented the responsibility of the DSS service provider to be service oriented and technically astute. This is a challenge when HCHS made a policy decision to focus on its core competencies and stay out of the software development business.

DSS managers perceive their responsibility of generating knowledge and the DSS servicing as a corporate resource for decision makers at all levels of the HCHS and the MOs. To this effect, the DSS service provider has equipped itself with the technology and skills required to accomplish its responsibilities with a customer service orientation.

Measuring Return on Investment

In the era of cost cutting and improving efficiency, IS departments have to justify the investment in IT. The issue of IT payoff has been debated for decades in studies that have reported mixed results. The lack of conclusive evidence of payoff has been termed the *information technology paradox*.[6]

Although in some instances IT investment is a competitive necessity and can be technically complex and intangible in nature, the senior management still expects justification of the investment. The DSS has faced similar responsibilities to justify its continued investment. Although intuitively the role of the DSS is crucial to the competitiveness of HCHS, the DSS has regularly sought feedback from the users on how they use the DSS. The feedback from decision makers helps provide the justification for the value of the DSS. More recently, there have been efforts to examine the payoff from the DSS quantitatively by analyzing three years of monthly actual DSS usage data at each of the hospitals. The results indicate that the DSS does lead to an improvement in organizational efficiency and quality, particularly when combined with organizational business process redesign initiatives.[7] Other studies using DSS data in clinical settings have indicated that using DSS data can help improve clinical care by predicting adverse outcomes[8] and that after adjusting for severity, there were no significant differences between the cost and efficiency of primary care physicians and medical subspecialists.[9]

Data Security and Privacy

Although the most sensitive patient-related information resides at the hospitals, the DSS also contains patient-related and competitive information, the confidentiality of which is of paramount importance. Security checks and validations begin from the site of the user. The HCHS commitment to maintaining security and privacy of patient and physician information is driven by the Catholic tradition of maintaining the "dignity of the person" also reflected in its mission statement. In addition, the Health Insurance Portability and Accountability Act of 1996 (HIPAA) requires that healthcare services organizations protect the privacy of patient information.

In electronic transfers of data, HCHS uses packet switching through public networks in which the data are encrypted twice: once prior to leaving the hospital and again by the telecommunications provider through the frame relay. Further, HCHS ensures security within its systems as well as the databases. As indicated in Figure C4.2, first-level security is enforced when a user accesses the password-protected local area network (LAN). In some cases, the users have to use a workstation at a predefined location in addition to the password to access the LAN. Next, the user workstation has to be authorized to communicate through the WAN.

The second-level security is enforced at the corporate office through a firewall. Only authorized users are allowed to go through the firewall. Once the user request to access an application is passed

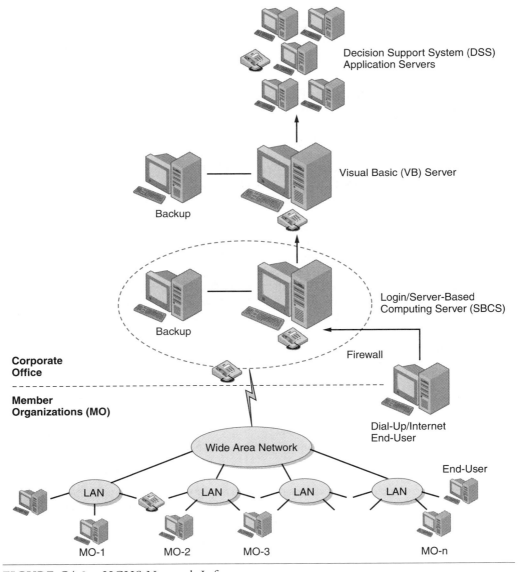

FIGURE C4.2   HCHS Network Infrastructure.

through the firewall, the login server verifies the user name and password. Following this verification, the user's authorization for applications is checked to verify whether the user is a valid DSS user and, if so, which modules are authorized for the user. Once within the DSS application, the security extends to the database level (such as read only, read and write, calculate) and to the field level (such as the department and accounts that can be accessed). For instance, the manager of the pathology laboratory should be able to look at the costs of the pathology laboratory department and at the salaries of those individuals who directly report to him or her. Within the DSS, the patient lookup is by the medical record number as opposed to the patient name. Each database and network access is recorded in a log file that is periodically reviewed by network management personnel. Any questionable access is reported to the department manager for follow-up action.

Notes

1. P. Keen, "Value Analysis: Justifying Decision Support Systems," *MIS Quarterly* 5, no. 1 (1981): 1–15.
2. G. Forgionne and R. Kohli, "HMSS: A Management Support System for Concurrent Hospital Decision Making," *Decision Support Systems* 16, no. 3 (1996): 209–229.
3. R. Kohli, J. K. H. Tan, D. Ziege, F. Piontek, and H. Groot, "Integrating Cost Information with Healthcare Decision Support Systems," *Topics in Healthcare Information Management* 20, no.1 (1999): 80–95.
4. F. Davis, "Perceived Usefulness, Perceived Ease of Use, and User Acceptance of Information Technology," *MIS Quarterly* 13, no. 3 (1989): 319–340.
5. KPMG, Canada, "What Went Wrong? Unsuccessful Information Technology Projects" (1995), http://audit.kpmg.ca/vl/surveys/it_wrong.htm.
6. E. Brynjolfsson, "The Productivity Paradox of Information Technology," *Communications of the ACM* 35 (December 1993): 66–77.
7. S. Devaraj and R. Kohli, "Information Technology Payoff in the Healthcare Industry: A Longitudinal Study," *Journal of Management Information Systems* 16, no. 4 (2000): 41–67.
8. E. Zarling, F. Piontek, and R. Kohli, "The Utility of Hospital Administrative Data for Generating a Screening Program to Predict Adverse Outcomes," *American Journal of Medical Quality* 14, no. 6 (1999): 242–247.
9. E. Zarling, F. Piontek, R. Kohli, and J. Carrier, "The Cost and Efficiency of Hospital Care Provided by Primary Care Physicians and Medical Subspecialists," *American Journal of Medical Quality* 14, no. 5 (1999): 197–201.

Case Study Questions

1. What can HCHS do to anticipate market changes and stay ahead of the business needs?
2. How can HCHS impart training to users on the analytical and proper utilization of the data?
3. Prepare an implementation plan for the next generation of the DSS application. Who would you involve in such a project team, and what expertise should they bring?
4. How would you go about measuring the return on investment for the investment in the DSS?
5. How do you respond to the growing demand for a "true" enterprise model in the very non-integrated reality of healthcare information technology?

Mapping the Road to the Fountain of Youth

Joshia Tan

Editor's Note: Ever since the first couple, Adam and Eve, was instilled with the gift of life, the human race has never ceased dreaming of living forever—each new medical discovery, whether it is an outgrowth of traditional Chinese herbs or Western prescriptions, is a testament to humankind's desire and strive to stay youthful. How, then, can healthcare management information systems (HMIS) contribute to the achievement of this universal desire, even though it is hidden among generations upon generations of policy makers, scientists, administrators, caregivers, and laypersons alike? The solution clearly lies within medicine's promise of an unprecedented convenience, allowing the medicine to be administered anywhere and anytime to aging patients—a solution that fulfills the promise of continuously rejuvenating live human growth tissues. Life, in and of itself, is therefore the future of HMIS. It is the need for life—or, specifically, the respect for a richer and better quality of life—that has spurred new investments into advancing medical sciences and HMIS technologies and applications. It is appropriate, then, to close this text with a case on how HMIS can aid us in our long-drawn journey toward "the fountain of youth."

I. Introduction

Life has one promise: aging is a road that never ends. So until the fountain of youth is excavated, we must be thankful that health care will never stop improving, either. What sort of improvements, then, will have materialized by the time frailty and wrinkles become your personal realities? Convenience, perhaps, so the much-needed healthcare treatments can be primarily performed from your home? Or could it be relief—for you, the caring grandparent—because your grandchildren will never have to suffer through the numerous stages of a precarious disease? Peace of mind could also arise from ready-and-waiting emergency health care, or even from the knowledge of how to optimally develop your lifestyle for health's sake. Whatever you dream about—but especially if your dreams entertain the manifestation of *all* the aforementioned—there is a feasible solution.

II. Home-Based First-Aid System Technology

Imagine a fully automated home-based healthcare system that has more capabilities and functions than a hired personal aide or caretaker. In essence, a healthcare management information system[1] (HMIS) that, on a 24/7 basis, intelligently monitors and maintains an aging person's healthy lifestyle and well-being from the comfort of his or her home. The architectural components of such a home-based first-aid system technology, H-FAST, as we will name it, would simply consist of a few updated appliances, as well as a single new appliance—connecting them internally within the home, as well as externally outside the home. Figure C5.1 depicts a schematic of the architectural setup for a first-version HMIS prototype, H-FAST.

As shown in Figure C5.1, the center of all the updated appliances connecting H-FAST would be a new device—an automated system, complete with video communication capabilities, that serves as H-FAST's central hub. This central hub is constantly linked to the Internet and provides the intelligent monitoring that is needed on a minute-by-minute basis.

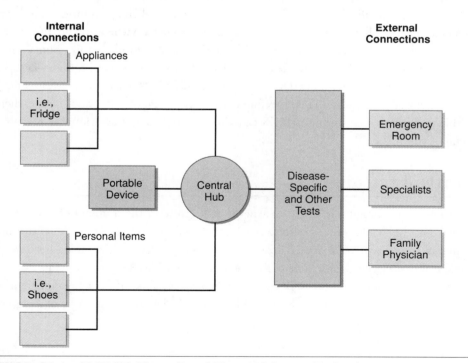

FIGURE C5.1   H-FAST: Home-Based First-Aid System Technology.

Technically speaking, this H-FAST device could be simply a powerful preprogrammed computer hardware-software-interface design with various innovative attachments, which can be gradually added or deleted as the user's needs change with time. Although H-FAST would be made readily available to all consumers in the near future, the technology is especially targeted on at-risk patients, that is, those consumers whose health is deemed to be in jeopardy of sudden, unpredictable, and possibly fatal downturns. It is these patients who will benefit the most from H-FAST, because the device's customized attachments will allow for an unparalleled personalization of care.

H-FAST Basic Functions

Each morning, or however often the at-risk patient's physicians deem necessary, these users will have to submit themselves to prescribed tests, which are also decided by his or her doctors and/or specialists. These specialists, in turn, may be referred within the patient's care provider subscription network, following intensive data analysis from the system. Let us analyze the case of one such would-be patient, Remy Louis Martin XIII. Remy has a family history of Type I diabetes and a body composition very susceptible to heart attacks. Thus, in order to properly test his blood sugar level and artery fluidity, H-FAST would first need the proper disease-specific attachments to be appended and installed. His diabetes specialist, Dr. Moët, then decides that Remy should be administered the blood sugar level test once every three days, while his cardiologist, Dr. Chandon, recommends that Remy be given the artery fluidity test every morning. The H-FAST is accordingly programmed for such a schedule, with the test results transmitted automatically to Remy's physician, Dr. Krug, on a daily basis. Dr. Krug, married with two children and therefore extremely busy, opts to have his patient's test results upload automatically to his Internet-enabled personal data assistant (PDA). Then one morning, H-FAST's tests reveal Remy's blood sugar level to have risen significantly, even though Remy cannot conjure a probable cause and everything else appears normal. Aside from alerting Dr. Krug, the system would also contact Dr. Moët via the Internet. Just as with Dr. Krug's PDA, an alert would register itself onto Dr. Moët's computer, allowing her to act according to the urgency of the situation—this may include scheduling an appointment, consulting Remy over the system, or even redirecting Remy to the nearest emergency room. In essence, peculiarities or calls for concern, as deemed by the tests, would trigger the system into sending an online request to the appropriate healthcare services center (be it the family doctor, specialist, or even the emergency room) so the situation can be handled personally and appropriately.

If time and physical inspection are deemed critical to the particular case, as would be the case with emergencies, a report would be sent to the nearest emergency center, and the video system would initiate. This would allow the emergency room doctors a better idea of the condition's severity, as well as the best way of handling the patient once he or she arrives at the hospital. Let us reconsider Remy's case, for example, and say that it happens to be weekend; Dr. Krug is off to meet some old college buddies in New York, while Dr. Moët is out on a date. Because Drs. Krug and Moët are part of the vast majority of physicians who do not hold office hours on weekends, a request for an ambulance would also be dispatched, sending Remy to the nearest emergency room for the most efficient care possible. This would prevent numerous fatalities—especially from patients who, like Remy, may be fully unaware of their life-threatening symptoms. Because the system only requests an ambulance when necessary, H-FAST would also reduce the wait time in emergency rooms by averting many overly concerned nonemergency patients from being misdirected to the emergency section.

Should the test reveal non-life-threatening symptoms related to the patient's disease, H-FAST would still immediately send a detailed report to the appropriate specialist—in Remy's case, symptoms related to the possible development of diabetes would trigger the sending of a report to Dr. Moët, while symptoms related to the increased possibility of a heart attack would trigger the sending of a report to Dr. Chandon. The specialist can then decide whether to schedule an appointment or simply advise the patient via the video chatting system. For these specialists, the report could also potentially highlight those cases of greater urgency. In other words, H-FAST would differentiate, for the specialist, cases where the patient only has mild, nonurgent symptoms from those where the patient seems poised for a potentially fatal descent throughout the day. For a case of the latter, the patient would be immediately directed to the closest hospital, advised to use the system with greater frequency, or have an appointment scheduled with his or her specialist—or any combination of the aforementioned. If an immediate visit to the hospital is necessary and arrangement for transportation is an issue, a dispatch for an ambulance can also be issued to the address of the patient (which would have been preprogrammed into the system).

H-FAST Advance Functions

Although H-FAST should be programmable to seek out specified peculiarities, it should also be designed to perform a quick routine checkup of common but potentially harmful abnormalities. By doing so, the patient can be alerted of any symptoms that point to colds and other minor illnesses. For example, while using H-FAST, Remy is alerted that a common flu virus has just infected him. Armed with this information, he can then decide between over-the-counter prescriptions and/or schedule an appointment to receive treatment from his family doctor. It would be advantageous for him to deal with the problem as soon as the first signs are detected, because this would allow for the speediest—and most economical—recovery. Moreover, H-FAST could also act as a guardian angel for elderly patients. For example, H-FAST could be paired with a pocket-sized mobile unit for frail elderly individuals; this unit would contain a force sensor and, using the main system as a liaison, automatically send a request for an ambulance once a significant force is detected to have impacted the unit, as would occur in the case of a fall. H-FAST should also have the capability to detect peculiarities not related to the targeted disease and subsequently report it to the family physician for further inspection. Indeed, H-FAST would not only aid the recovery of patients with precarious illnesses, but also allow doctors to treat new cases of deadly diseases in their earliest stages, thus reducing both healthcare costs and the mortality rate.

As mentioned earlier, the core system embedded in H-FAST is a central hub that also establishes internal connections, meaning it would link out to the various updated appliances throughout the house—such as an updated refrigerator. Using the up-and-coming RFID (radio frequency identification) technology, a new H-FAST automated refrigerator could constantly manage both the inventory on its own shelves as well as that of the pantries. Then, by monitoring the removal and restocking of food from the shelves, the refrigerator can send data about the patient's nutrition intake back to the central hub. From there, the central hub could analyze data about the patient's health and compare the patient's ideal and actual diet. Recommendations on amending diet and nutrition, so as to promote a healthier lifestyle, could then be provided at the patient's request.

Numerous other devices can also be connected or disconnected in much the same manner, although such connections or disconnections are by no means limited to household appliances. Take, for instance, Remy's shoes, which have a simple chip embedded into each pair. With this connection, the central hub can then record the number of steps he has taken in a day. With this data, H-FAST can provide Remy, as well as his physicians, a good idea of how his daily walking habits should be adjusted for optimum health. Or, for a more accurate picture of Remy's true daily exercise, he could also wear a watch or bracelet to track his heart rate as it fluctuates throughout the day. Then, using a similar process as found in the shoes, H-FAST can analyze Remy's heart rate pattern for the day and, consequently, offer a reliable picture of how to most advantageously adjust his frequency and duration of exercise.

III. H-FAST Potential Impacts on the Healthcare Services Delivery System

With these new updated appliances and the central hub (as seen in Figure C5.1) implemented in the majority of homes, the healthcare industry will see a revolution in its reliability and benefit to society. Already we are witnessing a redesign of the manner in which healthcare specialists handle patient data, as much of this textbook has proven. As such, by extending our capitalization of the increasingly rapid Internet connections and new age of digitalization to a much further extent, home-based health care will soon become a reality—and along with it, countless benefits.

Indeed, home-based healthcare systems such as H-FAST will allow physicians and practitioners to treat a greater volume of patients, because the patients will be directed to the correct facility. Furthermore, and also because of correct referrals, waiting rooms will be significantly less crowded. In fact, the vast majority of waiting will be eliminated for patients, as our examination of the emergency room improvements confirmed, but this also holds true for the family doctor's office and the specialist's. Because the video capabilities will eliminate most physical visits and because, as mentioned, the various patients will be arranged by urgency, the patient does not have to waste time waiting. This, in turn, will bear a significant impact on societal productivity and the economy. For instance, if H-FAST has detected an artery peculiarity and therefore deems it necessary that Dr. Chandon be informed, Remy does not need to wait around for Dr. Chandon to finally admit him. Instead, he can continue his day without interruption until Dr. Chandon has finished dealing with the more urgent cases, at which point Dr. Chandon can contact Remy through H-FAST and provide the proper consultation. Recall that a visit to the family doctor or specialist can easily be a virtual visit, whether it is through the aid of VoIP (voice-over Internet protocol) technology, because the central hub is always connected to the Internet, or via the video chat. Therefore, instead of sitting in uncomfortable chairs reading magazines, Remy can continue with his productive daily routines until the system rings.

Nevertheless, the benefits of home-based healthcare systems are not merely restricted to increases in efficiency: costs will also be minimized, while the average life expectancy will be maximized. Eliminating wait time translates to fewer costs, as does referring patients to the correct facility. In addition, treating future cases of deadly diseases from their earliest stages—as the system promotes—will further cut expenditures. The expense reductions will materialize on the patient's side as well; whatever the central hub may cost should be more than offset by the eliminated transportation costs and waiting time, not to mention the potential to save the patient's life. In fact, any healthcare insurance company should be more than willing to foot the bill for such a device, especially if recommended by the patient's physicians, because it draws such cost-saving and health-optimizing benefits. These benefits—such as alerts of potentially fatal symptoms and recommendations on how to gain optimum health through changes in the patient's diet and exercise—will, in all likelihood, elongate and strengthen the patient's life span. After all, the main goal of the healthcare industry is to promote and help build long, healthy lives, is it not?

IV. Conclusion

The technological devices and services needed for H-FAST—disease-specific tests, RFID, VoIP, video chatting, portable force sensors, quick Internet connections, step counters, heart rate trackers—have already been developed. All we need now is for this HMIS technology to become economically viable and to be widely accepted by the public and physicians alike. Those qualities, I would like to believe, will materialize in the near future—both paving the way for affordable and efficient home-based healthcare services delivery and allowing us to drive slower along life's one promised road. The scenery is just too beautiful to miss.

Note

1. J. Tan, *Health Management Information Systems: Methods & Applications*, 2nd ed. (Gaithersburg, MD: Aspen Publishers, 2001).

Case Study Questions

1. What sort of advantages would an elderly person draw from H-FAST? A nonelderly person?
2. a. Who would benefit most from H-FAST? Why?
   b. Who should this system be recommended for? Why?
3. a. Design another possible internal connection for this central hub (e.g., to the ventilation system), and explain how it will be advantageous to the patient's health.
   b. Design another possible external connection for this central hub (e.g., to the dentist), and explain how it will be advantageous to the patient's health.
4. What is another up-and-coming technology that could be applied to H-FAST?
5. Name another economical sector (i.e., outside of health care) that could benefit from such a system. Briefly explain how it will improve the chosen industry.

Index